Personality Disorders:
Clinical and Social
Perspectives

JAN DERKSEN

Personality Disorders: Clinical and Social Perspectives

Assessment and Treatment based on DSM-IV and ICD-10

With a Foreword by
Theodore Millon

JOHN WILEY & SONS
Chichester·New York·Brisbane·Toronto·Singapore

Other Wiley Editorial Offices

John Wiley & Sons, Inc., 605 Third Avenue,
New York, NY 10158-0012, USA

Jacaranda Wiley Ltd, 33 Park Road, Milton,
Queensland 4064, Australia

John Wiley & Sons (Canada) Ltd, 22 Worcester Road,
Rexdale, Ontario M9W 1L1, Canada

John Wiley & Sons (SEA) Pte Ltd., 37 Jalan Pemimpin #05-04,
Block B, Union Industrial Building, Singapore 2057

Library of Congress Cataloging-in-Publication Data

Derksen, Jan, *1953*–
    [Handboek persoonlijkheidsstoornissen. English]
    Personality disorders : clinical and social perspectives :
assessment and treatment based on DSM IV and ICD 10 / Jan Derksen.
        p.   cm.
    Includes bibliographical references and index.
    ISBN 0-471-94389-4 (cased) — ISBN 0-471-95549-3 (paper)
    1. Personality disorders. I. Title.
    [DNLM: 1. Personality Disorders. WM 190 D433h 1995a]
    RC554.D4713   1995
    616.85'8—dc20
    DNLM/DLC
    for Library of Congress   94–40652
                                                                         CIP

British Library Cataloguing in Publication Data

A catalogue record for this book is available from the British Library

ISBN 0-471-94389-4 (cased)
ISBN 0-471-95549-3 (paper)

Typeset in 10/12pt Palatino by MHL Typesetting Ltd, Coventry
Printed and bound in Great Britain by Bookcraft (Bath) Ltd

CONTENTS

ABOUT THE AUTHOR

Jan Derksen   *University of Nijmegen, Twaalf Apostelweg 2, NL-6523 LW Nijmegen, The Netherlands.*

Jan Derksen, PhD, is Assistant Professor of Clinical Psychology in the Department of Clinical Psychology and Personality at the University of Nijmegen, The Netherlands, where he teaches assessment and psychodynamics. He is also the director of a primary health care centre and a company publishing psychological tests. His research over the last ten years has concentrated on personality disorders, and he has developed Dutch versions of several instruments for the assessment of, for example, borderline personality disorder. His recent research has been in the Dutch MMPI-2 and the MCMI-III. Jan Derksen has written and/or edited 16 books and published over 100 articles in national and international journals and books.

FOREWORD

The splendidly astute and discriminating clinical portrayals by Freud, Abraham, Kretschmer, Reich, and Schneider earlier this century stirred our curiosities and inspired us to further our desire to understand "character and personality". Unfortunately, in the 1960s, 1970s and 1980s, these characterizations became outdated curiosities, speculations that many said should be replaced by tightly focused and empirically anchored research constructs. The conceptual models and cogent insights of these early clinical theorists resonated extremely well with our own efforts to penetrate and give order to the mysteries of patients' psychic worlds, but they were now out of vogue, so to speak. No longer was personality or its disorders to be seen as an integrated and dynamic internal system of human functioning. The pendulum swung toward empiricism and positivism: only "observable" facts were in the ascendancy. The complex configuration of personality was segmented into its ostensive constituents, disassembled and arranged in one set of component parts or another.

As Allen Frances and I wrote in the preface to the inaugural issue of the *Journal of Personality Disorders,* a change in the status of personality disorders began to brew in the 1970s and 1980s. Slow though this awakening may have been, there were signs of emerging new ideas and challenges that gave promise of reviving the lustre of an earlier period. Especially promising was the observation that the essential element that gave substance to "personality" as a construct — the fact that people exhibit distinctive and abiding characteristics — reemerged. This durability attests, at the very least, to its intuitive consonance with authentic observation, a viability all the more noteworthy when one considers the spirited, if misguided, efforts to undo it. This renaissance is particularly impressive when one considers the vast number of recently popular constructs that have faded to a status consonant with their trivial character, or have succumbed, under the weight of their scientific inefficacy, to scholarly and clinical boredom.

Personality study has weathered its mettlesome assaults and seems to be undergoing a wide-ranging resurgence. Notable here are the widely acclaimed formulations of contemporary analytic theorists, particularly Otto Kernberg and Heinz Kohut. No less significant in this realm are theoretical ideas posited by a reactivated interpersonal school led by theorists such as Lorna Benjamin and Donald Kiesler. Of special note also are the recent "ecumenical" formulations of biologically-oriented theorists such as Larry Siever and Robert Cloninger. Shedding earlier dogmatists are theorists who have "reconnected" pyschopathologic syndromes to personality, asserting not only an intrinsic coherence between them, but proclaiming that generalities do exist among these psychic expressions; notable here is the work of Aaron Beck and Sidney Blatt. The burgeoning interest in syndromes such as the borderline personality disorder has been richly informed by the work of John Gunderson and Michael Stone. Erstwhile adversaries are beginning to "discover the merits of a psychoanalytic—cognitive—interpersonal—biological synthesis" of psychological functions, as well as to promulgate the efficacy of integrated and "multidimensional" approaches to the treatment of personality disorders.

The revival of personality disorders as central to the clinical enterprise arises from other significant sources and considerations. Most mental health practitioners now employ their professional skills in out-patient rather than in-patient settings. The majority of patients are no longer severely disturbed psychotics, though much work is still to be done with this population, but are ambulatory individuals seen in office settings or community clinics. In these new settings we see patients who report personal stressors, social inadequacies, or interpersonal conflicts, typically represented in symptoms such as anxiety, depression or alcoholism. What we are learning is that these symptoms signify the outcroppings of longstanding and deeply ingrained patterns of maladaptive behaving, feeling, thinking, and relating: in other words, their basic "personality style or disorder".

It is not only the changing patient population of clinical practice, then, or the emergence of attractively new personologic theories from refurbished analytic, interpersonal or biological perspectives that signifies the growing prominence of the personality construct. The special status assigned to the personality syndromes in the American DSM-III in 1980 was both a reflection of these changes and instrumental in their further promotion. With the advent of this official classification, personality disorders not only gained a place of consequence among syndromal categories, but became central to its multiaxial schema. The logic for assigning personality its own axis became more than a matter of differentiating syndromes of a more acute and dramatic form from those of a longstanding and prosaic character. More relevant to this partitioning decision was the assertion that personality can serve usefully as a dynamic substrate from which clinicians can better grasp the significance and meaning of their patients' transient and florid disorders. In the *DSM-III* then, personality disorders not only attained a nosological status for prominence in their own right, but were assigned a contextual role that made them fundamental to the understanding and interpretation of other psychopathologies.

Promising new theories, the special role assigned to these disorders in the multiaxial system of the *DSM-III* and *DSM-IV*, as well as the recently published *ICD-10*, all point to the growing clinical importance of personality disorder syndromes. The organization of the International Society for the study of Personality Disorders in 1988, the initial publication of the *Journal of Personality Disorders* in 1987, the co-sponsorship of several International Congresses on Personality Disorders by the Society and the World Psychiatric Association, and the introduction of European Congresses for the study of personality disorders, as well as the establishment of several institutes for personality study on the Continent and in the Americas, have also added to the growing status and crosscultural importance of personality as a clinical science.

Ours is a time of rapid clinical and scientific advances, a time that seems propitious for establishing new settings and producing manu-scripts designed to promulgate these important ideas and syntheses of the personality disorders. The intersection between the study of "psychopathology" and the study of "personality" is clearly one of these spheres of significant intellectual activity and clinical responsibility.

It is to the credit of Professor Jan Derksen that he has seen his way clear to write this impressive work on the personality disorders. The field has grown in the past two decades to immense proportions. Professor Derksen is to be commended for having organized and highlighted its major issues and clinical elements in a most intelligent and highly communicative way. Knowing through my own work how difficult it is to encompass so broad-ranging and ever-expanding a field, I am especially grateful for the balance among diverse viewpoints that the author has given, and for the skill with which he has executed the task of representing alternative models. Using a brilliant and illuminating format to begin this work, Professor Derksen attempts to look at the subject of personality disorders from two contrasting vantage points. He separates the phenomenological reality of cases as they are "actually" experienced by patients seeking help from the approach of theorist-scholars who seek to transcend the particulars of a clinical phenomenon by placing it within a formal system of organized understanding. In this regard, Derksen demonstrates courage and insight when directly confronting numerous philosophical issues that cannot be overlooked when seeking to understand the foundations of the subject. Likewise, he tackles controversial matters in a clear and illuminating manner. Notable also is Professor Derksen's willingness to speculate on a series of directions which he anticipates the field will take.

Balancing his rich coverage of the philosophical, theoretical and scientific modes of analysis is Dr Derksen's extensive use of informative case materials. Of special value, especially to the student, is his detailed presentation of the diagnostic-assessment process, and his instructive recommendations concerning therapeutic "starting points" and "tips" for treatment.

As a European pioneer in personality studies, Professor Derksen has produced a landmark work, applying his wealth of knowledge and experience to creating a well written, highly lucid and thought-provoking book. It joins few others as primary references in the field, enormously valuable for mature clinicians of all theoretical persuasions and, owing to its clear presentation and straightforward manner, eminently useful to students as well.

THEODORE MILLON
September 1994

PREFACE

In my work in primary health care, patients have repeatedly asked for help without presenting any concrete symptoms. Some of these questions could be dealt with in a short period of time. Other requests for help appeared to refer to deep-seated personality patterns which were difficult to change in the context of time-limited work in primary health care. My interest in these personality disorders therefore started in clinical practice and time became available after finishing my doctoral dissertation in 1983.

Because of my interest in psychodynamic theory, I started to study the borderline personality disorder. I contacted Dr Otto Kernberg and did work on his structural interview and also on the Diagnostic Interview for Borderlines of John Gunderson and his co-workers. Gradually the scope expanded to the other DSM Axis II disorders. My combined work — psychotherapy in my private practice, teaching students in clinical psychology and doing research as a member of the staff of the Department of Clinical Psychology and Personality at the University of Nijmegen — gave me the opportunity to bring practice, research and teaching together.

In the summer of 1990 I conducted a workshop on diagnosing borderline patients for Japanese colleagues in Kyoto. In a conversation with Michael Coombs of Wiley the idea of this book was born. In the genesis of a book many influences can be recognized. Over the last couple of years I have had the chance to lecture about personality disorders for many different groups of colleagues. This gave me lots of inspiration and stimulated me to go on studying.

Some colleagues especially helped me with their feedback: Harrie Kempen, Ankie Klein Herenbrink and Wim Snellen. I used their suggestions with great pleasure. The clinical material of this book could be gathered because I could count on my co-workers in the psychotherapeutic practice in Bemmel and the Psychological Expertise

Office in Nijmegen. I am particularly grateful to the patients who shared their problems with me.

For the translation of this book I have had the help of my former English travelling companion Robert Boas. He gave me many good suggestions. Annelies Roverts was always willing to check and double check the manuscript. The staff of Wiley in England had lots of patience with me and assisted me in nearly everything.

Permission to reproduce the following copyrighted materials is gratefully acknowledged: Quotations from DSM-IV are reproduced by permission of the American Psychiatric Association from *Diagnostic and Statistical Manual of Mental Disorders*, Fourth Edition, 1994, Washington, DC. Copyright © 1994 American Psychiatric Association. Criteria from ICD-10 are reproduced by permission of the World Health Organization from *The ICD-10 Classification of Mental and Behavioural Disorders: Clinical Descriptions and Diagnostic Guidelines*, 1992, pp. 202–207, Geneva. Copyright © 1992 World Health Organization.

During the years of work in this area my wife and colleague Ankie Klein Herenbrink gave birth to our three daughters: Sophie Anna, Rosa Marie and Charlotte Bennie. Many nights we resembled two breeding chickens preparing their products. Ankie tolerated my sitting in my office and working late at night. She also stimulated me and gave me the feeling I was proceeding in the right direction.

PART 1

A Personality Disorder: Fact or Fiction?

CHAPTER 1.1　Symptom disorder versus personality disorder

INTRODUCTION

Personality disorders receive a great deal of attention from both clinicians and researchers. For clinicians, this is nothing new. So far, contributions to the development of theories on personality disorders on the basis of clinical practice surpass those made by researchers. This book focuses on actual findings from clinical practice and empirical research on personality disorders. The state of affairs is not only described, but critically evaluated. It has been assumed that it is advisable to make a distinction between personality disorders and symptoms, despite the many remarks and criticisms that can and will be made. This distinction stimulates research and accentuates the observations of diagnosticians and therapists.

Part 1 develops as follows. The first chapter begins with an analysis of the request for help, which is, after all, the catalyst for the entire health care process. The clinician's working method is largely influenced by the patient's request for help, since these requests vary. In many cases, they elicit psychotherapy, which has a wide variety of starting points, strategies, methods and techniques. Following the request for help, the uncovering psychotherapy is analysed further, as it is directed particularly towards influencing the personality of the patient seeking help. The act of requesting help and treatment has thus directly and indirectly led to an attempt to classify and diagnose disorders. The first chapter ends with an examination of this attempt at classification and touches on some of the central problems involved.

The second chapter does not start with the issue of suffering, but with an analysis of the concepts with which clinicians and researchers try to bring order to this subject. Here the central problems that underlie the scientific analysis of the subject matter are discussed.

In the remaining parts of the book, the elements of the first two chapters are developed further. Concrete examples of personality disorders, illustrated with cases, are described in Part 2. Theoretical approaches are discussed in Part 3. The psychodynamic approach is treated most extensively, primarily because the theme of the personality disorder has received the widest consideration in this clinical and theoretical tradition, and also because of the author's familiarity with this way of thinking and working.

In Part 4 clinicians will find a set of instructions for the diagnosis and treatment of personality disorders. These recommendations are based on an eclectic attempt to systematize clinical experience, and they still need to be subjected to empirical research. Part 5 adds to this. These days, it is assumed that sociocultural and economic backgrounds contribute to personality problems. In particular, ideas are introduced and hypotheses formed in this part. Part 6 concludes with a look at the future, with recommendations for classification, research, development of theories, diagnostics and treatment.

THE REQUEST FOR HELP

Various distinctions can be made between the questions with which patients appeal to therapists in both out-patient and clinical mental health care facilities. There is a category of patients who request help very concretely with a complaint: 'I don't dare drive over the bridge in my car'; 'Before I go to bed, I always have to check several times whether the gas taps are turned off, even if I can see it's all right by looking at the position of the black arrow.' They are usually satisfied with the help as soon as they have been freed of their fears and compulsive actions. Another category of patients formulate their problem in such a way that their entire behavioural repertoire becomes clear almost immediately: 'I lack self-confidence, I don't dare to make contacts, and I'm afraid of being promoted', or 'I doubt and worry about everything'; 'I haven't been able to make a decision about anything for as long as I can remember.' Still others complain about a characteristic of their mood: 'I feel unhappy and don't achieve anything'; 'I get aggressive too quickly.' In general, people ask for help with these types of complaints only when difficulties arise in more than one situation and/or interpersonal relationship.

Problems in a person's functioning are not necessarily connected with a disturbed personality, but can refer to a mental conflict experienced consciously or otherwise. For example, this may mean that a person involuntarily remains silent at times when aggression is felt. This can be traced back to an experiential process during the course of the person's life, when it was not possible to use aggression productively. We usually speak of a personality disorder only when a person's entire functioning is marked by certain extreme characteristics. These characteristics survive the various situations which people encounter and are moreover so obstinate, rigid, inflexible and poorly adjusted to social contexts that functioning is affected. Furthermore, pressure caused by suffering may lead to treatment being sought. This suffering does not by any means exist in all cases, nor do patients themselves necessarily make a connection between the effect on their functioning and what psycho-diagnosticians call their personality disorder. Significant others, however, usually do make this connection.

Many people do not suffer directly from their personality disorder. In such cases, they do not spontaneously seek help from a clinical psychologist or psychiatrist. However, they do frequently demonstrate vague complaints to their general practitioner, company doctor, boss or other key figure, such as repeated failure in work, recurrent relationship problems or other adjustment difficulties. Individuals with a personality disorder are often difficult people to deal with for immediate family members and next of kin, employers and therapists (Vaillant, 1987). They see the world, rather than themselves, as being out of line. As a result, they are misunderstood, which stimulates their disorder. Potentially, the study of personality disorders can contribute significantly to public mental health and social welfare. After all, personality disorders are most often at the root of problems that trouble us: violent crimes and other offences, abuse of and dependence on a great number of substances, suicide, relationship and family problems. Darrel Regier, research manager of the American National Institute of Mental Health, believes that once we understand the etiology of and have successful treatments for "just" two types of personality disorders — the borderline and antisocial personality disorders — we will not be able even to begin to express the potential advantages in financial terms for these individuals and society as a whole (Regier, 1993).

In the more positive cases, people question themselves when they enter situations where more demands are placed on intimacy or where more differentiated and flexible adjustments are necessary. The feedback they receive about their behaviour can be crucial in their decision whether to call in professional help. In out-patient practice, patients with a personality disorder frequently appear in connection with a request for help for couple or family problems. In the clinical sector, it is often a matter of severe symptom disorders combined with extensive personality pathology, in which case the symptoms form the basis for the request for help. In the judicial sphere, patients' personality disorders usually form the background for the offences committed. Psychiatric and psychological research and treatment are often considered only when symptom and syndrome disorders also play a role. We must bear in mind that a large percentage of drug addicts are afflicted with personality disorders, as is evident from research data (Derksen & Hendriks, 1991).

The considerable amount of attention paid to personality disorders is particularly stimulated by the increased popularity of the DSM-III classification systems (American Psychiatric Association, 1980). In 1980, personality disorders were placed on a separate axis, which further increased interest in them. This stimulus should not be confused with the actual causes for interest, however. These causes lie in clinical practice, where interest is sustained and popularity nourished. This is definitely related to variations in requests for help. These variations do not mean that complaints for which help was requested a hundred years ago do not occur today. On the contrary: just as a viral disease does not cease to exist as soon as a suitable vaccination has been found, nor have conversion disorders from the end of the last century disappeared. Other types of requests for help have been added, however.

In Western societies, psychotherapy and psychological treatment have become an integral part of health care. Requests for psychological help have increased. Many clinical psychologists and psychiatrists currently treat out-patients who ask for help with a wide range of problems: fear, stress, depression, excessive aggression, interpersonal and marital problems, and addiction. In our culture, the duration of psychological help must be as brief as possible, within the bounds of feasibility. People are under pressure to recover their psychological balance, to resume work, to continue relationships and to function at their highest attainable level.

People's egos are put to the test in our society and subjected to numerous complex demands. Transfer situations are a good example of what people are confronted with. How often do we go from one type of school to another? How often do we take courses to add the latest theories and techniques to our knowledge? Anyone wanting a career will frequently change employers. Anyone wanting to stay in the race will experience the necessity of refreshing his or her knowledge every few months. The demands placed on mental flexibility are enormous.

The different types of behaviour we are supposed to display have also increased. Many people need psychological help to adapt to the requirements of the social environment. As soon as the energy necessary for this increases, people become more vulnerable; then the smallest dysfunction at the level of the ego can more easily become obvious. The need for psychological help for people not immediately showing symptoms or syndromes, but having personality styles unadjusted to their circumstances, can be understood if these developments are considered.

Society places demands on its members and the individual members place certain demands on themselves. For one category of people, this means that they will request help for their lack of independence, for instance, since their job or relationship demands it and they want to meet this demand. In extreme cases, we call this dependent personality disorder. The many merger processes in which the business community is involved, and the rapid changes in company cultures, are difficult for precise, perfectionistic, orderly and control-deficient employees to handle. In stable organizations these employees contributed their share, everyone could always count on them, quality was more important than quantity, and if an employee forgot the rules he or she could come to the perfectionistic worker at any time. Now such employees run the risk of being diagnosed as having an obsessive-compulsive personality disorder and being made compulsorily redundant under the terms of the merger. After all, they could not keep pace with the changes.

These examples are not intended to emphasize one-sidedly that society produces psychic disorders. Personality variables are crucial wherever demands are placed on individual behaviour by the social context. It becomes clear how the individual "has been made" and thus what has gone wrong in an earlier phase as a consequence of social relationships.

This type of request for help has increased in the last 30 years. In the psychodynamic school, the kinds of complaint people exhibit have not unjustly been named narcissistic and borderline disorders; in other words, disorders in which the self is the centre of attention. In our individualistic culture, the person as well as the context places demands on the self. Social aspects will be discussed more extensively in Part 5.

In addition to the fact that increased attention to personality disorders is supported by clinical practice, it is also true in this practice that arguments can be made for the artificial character of the separation between symptom, syndrome and personality. With psychotherapeutic treatment, we cannot draw a clear line between the progress of a symptom disorder and a personality disorder. For instance, psycho-therapy of an Axis I disorder cannot be directed solely towards a psychic conflict, an emotional experience that has not been dealt with; any more than the psychotherapeutic treatment of a personality disorder can be directed solely towards certain patterns acquired in early childhood through identification or traumatization.

PSYCHOTHERAPY

Psychotherapists oriented towards exploratory psychotherapy always attune their treatment much more to the personality of the patient than to a certain symptom. Within that personality, they identify patterns which usually cannot be observed immediately, but which are held responsible for behavioural problems and towards which they direct their treatment. In the course of an exploratory psychotherapeutic process, a great deal of insight is obtained into the history of perceptions and experiences of individual patients. In this context, the concept of a personality disorder becomes vague for many psychotherapists.

In patients both with and without a descriptive classification personality disorder, patterns are involved that are influenced by psychotherapy. These patterns very often relate to one of the following themes: the true self versus the false, unreal self; trust versus mistrust in others and in the world; autonomy versus dependency aspirations; feelings of superiority or inferiority; inhibition versus expression of aggressive and sexual feelings. Two factors can be at the root of these patterns: mental conflicts and psychic structures.

In the first place, highly individual experiences, events and perceptions of events can cause psychic conflicts. A conflict always concerns an interplay of forces: a feeling, wish, behaviour or thought pattern is pushed aside in favour of another aspiration. This puts the psychic system under stress, which is the case to an even greater extent if the suppressed quality is strongly affective.

In the second place, structures underlie these patterns. These structures form a foundation and cannot be usefully divided into other mental qualities. We have to make do with this; we can relate to it and we can let our behaviour be influenced more or less by these structures, provided that we know them well. In this respect, we also come closest to biological influences.

There is a great possibility of the psychotherapeutic endeavour succeeding with a psychic conflict. Through insight and working through problems, a rearrangement of aspirations can take place in which, often very gradually, patterns change accordingly. The disturbed personality as well as the balanced personality changes as a result of psychotherapy. In this psychotherapeutic framework, it is difficult and dangerous to make the type of statement that might be expected, such as that this process of change runs into more difficulties in the case of personality disorders. Perhaps we can say, however, that more patterns need to be changed. Difficulties with the process of change also depend on many other factors, such as suffering. In the course of psychotherapy with patients with a personality disorder, the amount of suffering can increase more than in people without such a descriptive classification.

Much of the psychodiagnostic efficacy of psychotherapeutic experience is founded on drawing conclusions about personality traits on the basis of very limited observations of a behavioural aspect. Clinicians consider the ways patients make contact with them as a structural fact. What patients do or say here and now, probably for a large part unconsciously, is used to acquire an understanding of their behaviour in relation to significant people elsewhere. Much of the effectiveness of experienced diagnosticians and therapists is related to this. The psychotherapeutic influence on the entire person dominates the orientation with respect to symptoms. It is presupposed that the reduction of symptoms will be a consequence of the influencing of the personality as a whole.

In every uncovering psychotherapy where a symptom is the reason for seeking help and the personality is largely balanced and thus does not meet one of the DSM or ICD categories, the deeper-lying personality patterns are extensively discussed. These can be less rigid, less strong and less important in a descriptive way than in someone with an evident personality disorder.

Practitioners may be interested in personality disorders for two reasons. In the first place, partly owing to profound developments in the behaviour therapy tradition, there are treatment techniques that are oriented towards the person and towards the complaint. Because of this, the formulation of indications for treatment has become relevant. A second reason is that patients with a personality disorder in addition to a symptom or syndrome profit significantly less from a short-term symptom-oriented treatment than patients without a personality disorder. "From this perspective, personality disorders may be a previously unrecognized source of variance in the outcome of studies on the treatment of anxiety, compulsions, phobia, and other clinical problems," according to Turner (1987, pp. 136—7). Turner provides some empirical support for this hypothesis in a population of only 13 patients with social phobia. In broad clinical circles, it is accepted that treatment of a symptom disorder causes more problems if a personality disorder is also present. As far as this is concerned, the interest in Axis II disorders is based on clinical need. The pressure to diminish many psychic complaints in a short period evokes the need to differentiate between when this is feasible and when it is not. In Part 4, psychodiagnostics and treatment are dealt with in depth.

The interest in personality disorders derives from the fact that they are now discovered and rediscovered behind all types of complaints. This is not strange, however, if one realizes that, clinically speaking, complaint and person can never be seen as isolated from each other. With symptoms and syndromes that are somewhat vague in character, this temptation is especially prominent. Myalgic encephalomyelitis (ME), also called chronic fatigue syndrome, is a recent example. Patients with ME could qualify for a personality disorder diagnosis.

Researchers and clinicians, ranging from psychoanalysts to behaviour therapists, have recently agreed to a remarkable degree that, particularly where a symptom which is difficult to treat is concerned, it is a matter of a disorder of the whole person. The renewed interest in personality disorders is noticeable in the various orientations. In the preface to the first issue of the *Journal of Personality Disorders*, editors Theodore Millon and Allen Frances write:

> A renaissance in the study of personality disorders was brewing through the 1970s. Slow though this reawakening may have been, there were signs of emerging new ideas and challenges that gave promise of reviving the lustre this field of inquiry exhibited in the '40s and '50s. By virtue of time, reflection and, not the least, a growing disenchantment with available alternatives, the place of personality disorders as a syndrome began to regain its formerly solid footing this past decade. (1987, p. 1)

Researchers and clinicians within the framework of learning theories remained uninterested in personality disorders for a long time; behaviour was analysed as a response to a stimulus that came mainly from the environment. The assumption that behaviour is situation specific has always had a predominant influence. Behavioural therapeutic treatment was chiefly directed towards concrete complaints. If symptoms diminished, the person was left alone. Here also, the climate seems to be changing: the personality as the organizing principle behind behavioural patterns appears to be receiving increasing attention. Of course, it is a fact that this by no means applies to all representatives of these disciplines. This development offered little that was new to the psychoanalysts among the psychotherapists. They had always accentuated the personality factor, but their concepts inspired few empirical researchers. In Part 3, the most important theoretical and therapeutical approaches are discussed.

The concepts with regard to personality disorders outlined in the DSM-IV (American Psychiatric Association, 1994) and ICD-10 (World Health Organisation, 1992), which are for the most part descriptively designed, do have the advantage of a solid base in empirical research. The DSM classification system in particular fits in better with research practice than with clinical practice, but has nevertheless become very influential in the latter.

CLASSIFICATION

After World War II, descriptive psychopathology was unpopular in American, not to mention in European, psychiatry. Dimensional approaches to personality predominated and a psychodynamic orientation formed the basis of mainstream thought. This received a great deal of criticism including that of Szasz and antipsychiatry. Researchers doubted the reliability and validity of diagnoses, others pointed to the negative consequence of labelling, while psychologists and statisticians posited multivariate techniques (Klerman, 1986). In reaction to that, a group of neo-Kraepelians appeared, interested in biological—genetic explanations of psychic disorders with an emphasis on a categorial diagnostic approach. They had a significant impact on the research and conceptual background of the DSM-III (American Psychiatric Association, 1980).

In US psychiatry, the DSM-III is seen as a new paradigm corresponding to that of Kuhn (1972). Combined with this are fundamental medical concepts of individual disorders; an empirical attitude in relation to etiology or pathogenesis of individual disorders; a psychometric and quantitative approach in psychopathology; operational criteria to simplify reliability and validity. Descriptive optics have been employed, not deduction of causation, as well as an attempt to work in an atheoretical manner in order not to set the various currents in the field of psychopathology against each other in advance. Incorporation of the severity of the disorder, its cause, treatment choices and treatment responses has not succeeded in this classification system. These clinically relevant points of view have been the subject of discussion in the DSM task force, but not a single category survived. There is a lack of universal applicability. The use of operational criteria and the multiaxial system has had a great impact on clinical practices in the US, and the reliability of psychiatric diagnoses has increased owing to the operationality of the system.

Since publication of the DSM-III in 1980, research in psychopathology has started to accelerate. Self-rating questionnaires and semi-structured interviews have been developed for specific DSM-III categories. Research on personality disorders has received a strong boost, brought about by the separation of Axis II from Axis I. A number of psychoanalysts (Cooper, Chodoff, Frances) have started contributing to Axis II. During the development of the DSM-III, an attempt was made to design a separate axis for psychoanalytic defence mechanisms and ego functions, but this failed as it was not supported by the American Psychoanalytical Association. At present, the interest of analysts in such an axis seems to have increased, and it is conceivable that it will appear in the future.

The five axes in the DSM-IV are:

- Axis I: Clinical Disorders and Other Conditions that may be a Focus of Clinical Attention
- Axis II: Personality Disorders and Mental Retardation
- Axis III: General Medical Conditions
- Axis IV: Psychosocial and Environmental Problems
- Axis V: Global Assessment of Functioning

Personality disorders are grouped into three clusters. The first is called Cluster A and encompasses the paranoid, schizoid and schizotypal personality disorders. People with these disorders appear odd and eccentric. Cluster B includes the antisocial, borderline, histrionic and narcissistic personality disorders. People with these disorders appear dramatic, emotional and impulsive. Cluster C contains the avoidant, dependent and obsessive-compulsive personality disorders. People with these disorders often appear anxious and fearful. Furthermore, there is a remaining category that can be used for different specific personality disorders or a mixed clinical picture. In Part 2, these personality disorders will be described in detail and accompanied by case studies.

The first three axes are typological, making use of categories, while the last two are dimensions. With these five axes, an attempt was made to answer objections of clinicians who, after all, treat people rather than illnesses. Clinical practice is complex, environmental variables must be involved and personality is considered as relevant.

The greatly increased interest in personality disorders leads one to expect them to have received a place in the DSM-III for the first time. However, this is not the case. In the DSM-I, published in 1952, 27 personality disorders were already recorded. The definition of this type of disorder at the time was as follows:

> developmental deficiencies or pathological traits in the personality structure, with minimal subjective anxiety and little or no suffering. In most cases, the disorder is characterized by a life-long pattern of action or behaviour, instead of a mental or emotional symptomatology.

In 1968, with the publication of the DSM-II, 12 personality disorders were still recorded. In the DSM-I, as well as in the DSM-II, these disorders were described only in general, often very vague terms. The DSM-III of 1980 and the revised version, the DSM-III-R of 1987, are for the first time characterized by rather clear criteria, specific symptoms and behaviours and operational variables.

Empirical research into Axis II personality disorders only began after the DSM-III was published. The division was made on the basis of consensus. This also had rather ludicrous consequences, according to Chris Perry (1990), one of its authors. One example concerns the dependent personality. This appeared in the DSM-I in the passive-aggressive section, was not included in the DSM-II, but reappeared in the DSM-III and remained in the DSM-III-R, although with entirely different criteria than in the DSM-III. A quiz panel might be asked: will the real dependent person please stand up? As a second example, the compulsive personality was included in the DSM-I. This became obsessive-compulsive in the DSM-II, was called compulsive again in the DSM-III and obsessive-compulsive once more in the DSM-III-R. This cyclic renaming reflects in any case the doing and undoing characteristic of people with this disorder. The temporary character of the categories is obvious.

One of the biggest problems of Axis II disorders is not the considerable overlap with Axis I disorders, but overlaps within Axis II itself. The average number of diagnoses of personality disorders per patient, as reported in research by Zanarini et al. (1987), is 2.8. Widiger et al. (1986) specified 3.75. In research by Skodol et al. (1988) the average number was 4.6, while some patients showed as many as 7 or even more personality disorders. According to Morey (1988), prevalence and overlap are more pronounced in the DSM-III-R than in the DSM-III. In other words, the criteria for the diagnosis of personality disorders from the DSM-III-R do not result in the diagnosis of a well-defined personality disorder. This problem has been a significant factor in changes for the DSM-IV. This is not to say, however, that the problem is now solved.

We can observe a curious contradiction in the developments briefly sketched above. With the psychodynamic approach in psychiatry fading more into the background, the descriptive, empirical approach has gained ground. In the latter, a great deal of attention is paid to innate neurobiological determinants of behaviour. It seems as if this is contradictory to the psychodynamic approach, while in the psychoanalytic tradition the role of biological conditions was already firmly embedded with Freud. It is also unjustly suggested that both approaches totally or partly exclude each other. While the dominant approach of the DSM is descriptive, a separate axis with personality disorders has been created that is considerably abstract and theoretical in character. The psychodynamic orientation appears to have been reintroduced through a back door. This occurs, however, with far from consistent frequency.

The majority of the criteria that form the foundation for the DSM personality disorders relate to interpersonal behaviour. This conclusion has been reached by classifying all criteria from the Options Book for the DSM-IV under the following categories: relational style, behaviour, cognition, mood, affect and outward presentation. On the basis of this division, descriptive expression was found to appear particularly in the relational style of the personality. Of the 101 criteria from the Options Book for the DSM-IV, well over 60% fall under the relational style section, in the classification of the criteria applied here. Second place is taken by criteria that relate to behavioural phenomena, with mood and affect coming next, followed by cognitive style and, finally, outward presentation.

The changes that have been implemented do not deviate structurally or essentially from the descriptions in the DSM-III-R and DSM-III. An attempt has been made to avoid the overlap between personality disorders by accentuating or omitting criteria. In the ICD, basically the same has happened. In view of the scoring of the criteria in the various categories described above, it can be observed that a slight shift of direction has taken place in the DSM-IV towards behavioural phenomena, compared to the DSM-III-R. Relational aspects remain prominent, but here and there more emphasis has been placed on their character.

For example, with the schizoid personality, detachment rather than indifference is more central. Also in the case of the paranoid, we see concepts more connected to intrapsychic qualities. The social anxiety of the schizotypal person is associated less with the presence of strangers, and is now also connected with that of acquaintances. Identity problems of the borderline personality are now connected with self-image and a feeling of self, and less with interaction with the environment. The great need for care is emphasized in the dependent personality and therefore more is said about motives. Stubbornness has returned to the obsessive-compulsive personality category and, with it, one of the most important characteristics of the classical, Freudian concept. About the best division of criteria is found in the schizotypal personality, the obsessive-compulsive personality, borderline and antisocial personality disorders. Particularly borderline, antisocial and obsessive-compulsive people have the most solid foundation, certainly in a clinical sense, although empirically as well.

It would have been better to allow the various sections in which personality can be conceptualized (such as affect, mood, cognition, outward presentation) to return to the formulation of the criteria. An even better alternative, perhaps, would be to limit criteria to interpersonal style and to cease speaking of personality disorders. This latter is very theoretical and consequently incompatible with the entire DSM enterprise. Axis II becomes the axis of disturbances in interpersonal relationships. With this, we enter a much more descriptive field. A great many conceptual problems are avoided with such an interpretation and many other aspects of personality can remain legitimately underexposed. A patient with a DSM personality disorder diagnosis has disrupted interpersonal relationships, so the disorder is in the relationships. Because of these disturbed relationships, the individual retains a psychological balance. In a number of cases, one can conclude on the basis of the criteria that these people avoid negative feelings in this way, such as anxiety (in the avoidant and dependent personalities), and gloominess (in the narcissistic and histrionic personalities). Others take advantage of their colleagues (antisocial and narcissistic personalities). In Part 6, a new proposal for structuring and conceptualizing the DSM axis is made in this regard.

AXIS I AND AXIS II

How solid are the arguments frequently used in the professional literature in favour of distinguishing between symptom and personality disorders? We can wonder with Hirschfeld (1993) whether a personality disorder actually differs significantly from an Axis I or symptom disorder. Below, several arguments generally brought forward in this context are examined.

1. A personality disorder is seen as a long-lasting pattern, enduring from adolescence onwards and accordingly independent of any definite social context.

   In the psychoanalytic approach, although also from learning theory and cognitive points of view, childhood is considered an important starting point. There are, however, symptom and syndrome disorders that start later and also continue for a long time. A few examples are certain mood disorders, schizophrenia, eating disorders, impulse control disorders, dissociative disorders such as multiple personalities, and certain psychosexual disorders.

   Furthermore, the descriptive sides of personality disorders can remain concealed for long periods by superficial adjustments. For example, a dependent personality can be concealed by adequate adjustments in an intimate relationship with an independent and caring partner; a narcissistic disorder may hardly be noticed if the person in question has reached a position in society that allows this type of behaviour or even requires it, an army general for instance.

2. Unlike most symptom disorders, personality disorders are usually described as ego-syntonic.

   This is not always true, however. Many borderline patients suffer from their behavioural patterns and actively seek help. The behavioural patterns of dependent and avoidant personalities can cause these people a great deal of inconvenience in their activities in society, which prompts them to seek intensive help. In what respect does this differ from a bridge phobia, for which someone seeks help only when a bridge has to be crossed with a certain regularity?

3. Personality disorders are much more difficult to treat than symptom disorders. The latter are often more transient and in some cases disappear by themselves.

   Many symptom disorders are very obstinate. We do not have to think exclusively of those falling under psychosis, but can consider eating disorders and dissociative disorders as well. On the other hand, certain aspects of some personality disorders can be influenced very effectively. Adaptation to the social environment can be improved by giving the person insight into his or her (im)possibilities. In certain cases, a single interpretation of underlying behavioural patterns can have an extensive and enduring influence on the personality. Incidentally, many clinicians and researchers assume that personality disorders diminish with age.

4. Personality disorders are more fundamental and relate to the entire person, and consequently to cognitive, emotional and behavioural aspects.

This applies to some symptom disorders as well, however. Once again, think of schizophrenia. Furthermore, in the course of exploratory treatment we can trace the primary basis of many symptom disorders back to early childhood. In doing so, we end up in the same period in which the foundations were laid for the personality. To top that, the development of an anxiety disorder in childhood could very well be a highly decisive factor in the development of something like an avoidant personality disorder. This can apply to dependent and borderline disorders as well. A certain condition can result in a trait, as long as this condition appears at a suitable moment and in an intensive manner.

The relationship between symptoms and personality (disorder) today is, theoretically, no better resolved than in the days of Freud. Empirically, the Axis II personality disorders accompany symptoms and/or syndromes to a great extent. Klein (1993) summarizes a number of reasons why this co-existence can be legitimate. In cases of "predisposition" or "vulnerability", one condition, for instance a personality disorder, is a precursor or risk factor for another disorder. In cases of a "complication", the personality disorder is a remaining phenomenon of a more acute disorder. In cases of "co-morbidity", independently caused disorders are present simultaneously. From this point of view, other cases of co-morbidity would be more of a problem and perhaps particularly indicate a measurement error. It is difficult to keep defending the independence of a symptom and a personality disorder as in the past, reasoning on the basis of psychotherapeutic experience. Theoretically, it is conceivable that this is understood as co-morbidity, but this simplifies the complex clinical reality to too great an extent.

A discussion has taken place in relation to various personality disorders in which it has been claimed, for instance by Akiskal (1981), that borderline disorder is a subclinical variant of an affective disorder. In other words, a symptom or syndrome disorder produces an Axis II personality disorder, and it is assumed that it will disappear again when the symptom disorder has ceased to exist. We can also consider this in relation to panic disorder on Axis I and an avoidant or dependent personality disorder on Axis II. So far, no really convincing evidence has been given for this.

In spite of all the doubts formulated above, the view espoused in this book is that making a distinction between a symptom disorder with and without a personality disorder and a personality disorder with and without a symptom (or syndrome) disorder is clinically relevant. The large groups (symptoms versus personality disorders) will not be distinguished so easily in this descriptive way. The psychic structuring of a schizotypal personality disorder with psychotic breakthroughs is entirely different from − perhaps even completely incomparable to − a dependent personality disorder with a structurally well-developed ego. Considering psychodiagnostics and treatment, the descriptive labels for symptoms as well as personality disorders are totally insufficient.

Psychological diagnosis, as described in Chapter 4.1, is necessary to establish an adequate indication for intervention. The exact relationship between the relative contributions of symptoms and personality traits to the pathology can only be understood in the form of hypotheses after the psychodiagnostic process for each individual has taken place separately.

CHAPTER 1.2   Conceptual problems

PERSONALITY

A well-considered use of the term "personality disorder" requires an adequate understanding of two concepts: personality and disorder. Gordon Allport noted (1937) that: "Personality is one of the most abstract words in our language, and like an abstract word suffering from excessive use, its connotative significance is very broad, its denotative significance negligible. Scarcely any word is more versatile." Personality and personality traits are described in various ways in the literature on personality disorders, and these are discussed below.

On the concept of personality, Millon states the following:

> Personality is seen today as a complex pattern of deeply embedded psychological characteristics that are largely unconscious, cannot be eradicated easily, and express themselves automatically in almost every facet of functioning. Intrinsic and pervasive, these traits emerge from a complicated matrix of biological dispositions and experiential learnings and now comprise the individual's distinctive pattern of perceiving, feeling, thinking, and coping. (1981, p. 8)

Personality traits are defined by McCrae & Costa as: "Dimensions of individual differences in tendencies to show consistent patterns of thoughts, feelings, and actions." (1990, p. 23)

In the DSM, a definition of personality traits is given as well:

> Personality traits are enduring patterns of perceiving, relating to, and thinking about the environment and oneself, that are exhibited in a wide range of social and personal contexts. Only when personality traits are inflexible and maladaptive and cause significant functional impairment or subjective distress do they constitute Personality Disorders. (American Psychiatic Association, 1994, p. 630)

The term "personality" is of more recent date than the concept of character and is particularly influenced by personality psychology.

Where theoretical descriptions are concerned, personality disorders particularly rely on psychoanalytic and psychiatric sources. We cannot avoid a brief examination of their origin.

A newborn baby arrives with a temperament which corresponds to a certain activity level, a tolerance for feelings, a certain measure of vitality and an extrovert versus an introvert disposition. This temperament is based on biological and genetic relationships. With this temperament, the baby also shapes his or her environment. In certain types of environment, the opportunity for temperament to have an effect on the social environment is many times greater than in others.

The following contrast can be considered as an example. Two highly educated parents, aged about 30 and who had to wait three years for their first child, are both very involved with the infant and have prepared for their first-born as completely as possible. They spend all their free time with their child. They constitute an entirely different social environment for the child than does a family from a lower social class where a sixth child unexpectedly appears and takes his or her place in the family. Thus the extent to which temperament can establish a position is connected with environmental variables.

A complex interaction between temperament and social environment leads to the development of what we can call character, by which we mean the first modelling of this compromise. The structuring of character takes place from birth onwards. We must realize, however, that there is also interaction before birth, in which the temperament has to deal with the physical condition of the mother's internal organs. For instance, one woman's stomach puts greater pressure on the uterus wall than another's, which limits the foetus' freedom of movement. All kinds of physical aspects of a pregnant woman, such as blood pressure, contribute to the condition of the foetus. Furthermore, the manner in which the mother behaves also plays a part in this process. A pregnant woman who rests a great deal and gives the foetus a chance to move sets the stage for interactions that differ from the opportunities provided by an expectant mother who moves about for ten hours a day due to the work she performs until shortly before childbirth. "Nature" never exists without "nurture", and there are no heads without tails. Character is the more stable design of the adjustment which the child makes to its environment, given its potential drive and affect.

Character is only character when it is more "trait" than "state". We cannot see character as a bridge crossing the gap between temperament and social environment, a comparison often made in the professional literature. Temperament and social environment are already too much involved for that to be the case. Zuckerman (1991) distinguishes two ways to define a trait. In his first definition, traits are systems or dispositions in people which predispose them to observe situations in a certain way and to react in a consistent manner in all kinds of circumstances. In the second place, traits are seen as an addition of the frequency and intensity of reactions to situations from the past. States are the affects, impulses and physiology observed by the person him- or herself for a brief period, which varies from a particular moment to as long as a day. Research in this context indicates that as soon as the length of time exceeds a day, it is more a trait than a state.

The character of a child is formed in the first five years of life. Personality is the ego's representation of character. This ego is formed in the course of upbringing, schooling and experience. Personality completes the raw core which we have termed character. In the development of personality, imitation, identification and learning processes play a large role. The person is further shaped by important people in his or her environment to whom the child, the adolescent and also the adult feel attracted, and by experiences gained throughout life. This more socialized form of character takes more definite shape after adolescence. The building blocks of the personality consist of a kind of cocktail in which biological, physiological and genetic influences are combined with temperament, upbringing and experience.

If the DSM definition is observed critically, one immediately notices that it contains a high degree of abstraction. What is meant by a stable pattern? What part is played by and what is the influence of circumstances? Do changing circumstances not also elicit changing behaviour patterns? A sharp definition of personality and behaviour as the result of the interaction between person and environment is missing. The concept of disorder recurs as soon as traits are supposed to be inflexible and maladjusted and lead to significant functional limitations or personal problems.

When personality traits are inflexible and maladjusted, this is largely related to a concrete, existing subculture and to general norms and values. A well-adjusted employee in Japan has an obsessive-compulsive personality disorder in the eyes of an Anglo-Saxon. Normally functioning women in many Muslim countries have avoidant personality disorders when viewed by a DSM and ICD diagnostician. If they did not behave as they do in that specific culture, they would be considered maladjusted and probably inflexible as well. A paranoid attitude can mean a necessary adjustment in some subcultures. In this respect, these disorders contain a cultural bias, and this is not only true for cultures entirely different from the Anglo-Saxon and Northern European cultures.

The theme of subjective suffering and important functional limitations can also be interpreted in relation to context. People with highly dependent and avoidant personality traits can flourish in a relationship where their partners provide a great deal of support and dominance. People with a narcissistic personality disorder and equipped with a large amount of talent and intelligence can to a considerable extent prove their grandiosity in their own mind. These people often make important contributions to art, science, politics and economics. It is precisely their achievements that enable them to display maladjusted behaviour. The social environment of these narcissists notices this constantly, holds all sorts of opinions about it, perhaps even suffers from it, but the person in question is sufficiently respected, powerful or prestigious that the environment adjusts itself to the person. To put it briefly, in these respects the descriptions of the concepts fall short. A descriptive view alone is insufficient for an adequate attempt to conceptualize personality disorders.

Another presupposition of inflexibility and maladjustment is that of normality. Normality is implied without making it explicit. Does something like a normal personality exist? Is the personality normal if somebody does not receive an Axis II diagnosis, but is still bothered by psychoneurotic symptoms? Freud has emphasized further that normal and neurotic are not qualitatively distinguishable categories. Nobody is completely normal and nobody is completely neurotic. In other words, nobody has only symptoms and nobody is entirely without symptoms. Freud considered a person ill and in need of psychoanalysis only when symptoms prevented working, loving and playing.

In terms of personality, Freud believed that the ideal harmony is reached when erotic, compulsive and narcissistic tendencies influence the personality equally (Freud, 1931). He did readily admit, however, that this generally does not occur. It would suit the DSM well if, in any case, an attempt were made to describe normality in terms of the personality. Then the user could realize more easily where the designers thought processes originated.

CONCEPTUAL CONFUSION

In order to introduce some structure into the conceptual problems caused by terms such as personality and personality disorder, a brief discussion of the philosophy of science follows.

The philosopher of science van Peursen (1984) describes five levels on which terms can be situated: (1) observation terms, (2) empirical terms, (3) constructed terms ("constructs"), (4) intervening variables, (5) theoretical terms.

1. *Observation terms* are related to immediate observation and are at the bottom of the scale of scientific concepts. An example is "green" or "door". The criteria which a patient must meet in order to receive a diagnosis of personality disorder would ideally be placed under this heading. The descriptive view aims in particular at describing reality.

2. *Empirical terms* summarize a group of observation terms and sustain their direct involvement with the perceptual world. The terms "fish" or "bird" are examples of this.

3. *Constructed terms* indicate something which is not observable as such, but which has to come about by means of observations. An example which van Peursen mentions is "momentary speed". A constructed term is indispensable for scientific analysis but indicates something outside observation; it is between a descriptive and an exploratory term.

4. *Intervening variables* are a little further again from observation. An example is the term "drive". This concerns an invisible link that is assumed between a stimulus and its effect on human behaviour. Hidden characteristics of people also fall under this heading. For instance, this person could (under certain circumstances) commit a sexual murder.

5. *Theoretical terms* can be defined neither directly nor indirectly through observation terms. Theoretical terms are more symbolic, such as force, electron, intelligence.

As previously stated, the criteria which amount to a personality disorder would have to consist of observation terms in particular, in accordance with the tradition of the classification system. A problem in this regard is that one wants to a certain extent to establish personality disorders in observational concepts. Personality disorder is on van Peursen's fifth level, a constructed theoretical term. Something is described with this term that cannot be connected directly or indirectly with observation terms. This is nevertheless attempted by the developers of the DSM and ICD, which are based on empiricism and description. Accordingly, the criteria employed describe the behaviour of people as much as possible. Then a jump is made to the theoretically charged term personality disorder. Personality disorder is situated between a stimulus and the observable behaviour. Theoretically, the term used in this manner does not bring us any further, which is to be expected of a theoretical term. Furthermore, the building blocks that precede it, the empirical terms, the constructed terms and the intervening variables, are missing. In other words, it is rather a large leap from the criteria to the concept of personality disorder.

The categorial classification system may be advisable for certain symptoms, but on the abstraction level of the personality a dimensional approach seems more appropriate. This creates the paradox that the descriptive criteria on the behavioural level can be compatible with a categorial classification, while the conclusion to which they must lead can no longer be defined categorially. Personality traits are, after all, inextricably linked with intensity. If one has dependent traits, *how* dependent one exactly is will be of particular clinical relevance. For an obsessive-compulsive person, being occupied with procedures can be limited to the work situation, a tendency which may be useful there. Conclusions at the level of intervening variables relate to something deeper; they concern dispositions and tendencies.

An adequate concept presupposes a theory and this cannot be replaced by a behavioural description, successful or otherwise. It is better to describe the personality in dimensions or polarities, which has, for instance, been done independently and with an interval of some 70 years by Sigmund Freud (1915) and Theodore Millon (1986): subject−object; pleasure−displeasure; active−passive. Apart from Freud and Millon, these or similar dimensions are utilized by a large number of other theoreticians in the field of the personality, and the various theoretical approaches are discussed in Part 3. From van Peursen's point of view, these dimensions are located at the third level and so are closer to observation terms. To maintain personality disorders within the DSM, the only responsible solution is to divert from and supplement the descriptive, atheoretical character. In a later section of this chapter, categorial versus dimensional classification is examined in more detail.

In the DSM and ICD, not only is the complicated concept of personality used, but also the term "disorder". Only when we know what personality is can we speak of a personality disorder. The personality has structure and therefore depth as well; the DSM approach assumes that the surface and the depth converge. Clinical practice often indicates an entirely different direction.

Given the inconsistency in the use of the concept of personality disorder, the object of the DSM to be descriptive, and the fact that most criteria relate only to interpersonal functioning in any case, what would be more obvious than to delete the term "personality disorder" and replace it with "disturbed relationships"? Diagnostically, Axis II then becomes the axis of interpersonal contact and its disturbances. In Part 6 this idea is discussed in more detail.

ADAPTATION

Human thinking often makes use of polarities, one of which is that of person – environment. In our thinking, the person is placed opposite the environment, which does not reflect the real relationship. The behaviour which someone displays is a function of person *and* environment. The relative contribution of each component differs for each piece of behaviour. A limiting factor in this regard is that behaviour is never determined exclusively by either the environment or the person. The more behaviour becomes a stable factor of significance, the more it will be determined by the personality. And vice versa, if a certain behaviour occurs incidentally, the influence of the situation will be greater.

The interaction between person and environment that results in human behaviour is consequently extremely complex. There are situations which hardly allow behavioural choices. In this context, there are all kinds of emergency situations in which fear plays a big role: for instance, becoming the victim of an armed robbery. In such cases, the temperament is decisive for the behaviour that follows. The social context, shaped by culture and social structure, also varies widely. Working alone, day in and day out, in a remote rice field shapes behaviour in a totally different way than does fulfilling a management function at Euro-Disney. Furthermore, people consciously and unconsciously create their own situations. As has become clear in the course of human history, people have always attempted to control and change their circumstances. Many people do indeed feel good when things in their environment go the way they want. People also choose, often unconsciously, an environment that suits their desires and needs, just as swallows seek another kind of climate in winter, in order to continue living pleasantly. In this way, people not only repeat pleasant combinations of circumstances, they also often repeat their unsolved conflicts and problems.

The influence of the situation on behaviour can be imagined in an extreme case. For example, someone could be very strict and precise at work, while at home he or she may act tolerantly and not bother with precision. Someone's behaviour and personality can seem totally different when sunbathing in the garden with a glass of wine within reach, than when wandering at their wits' end after half a day without water lost in the stifling heat of the desert.

When are we dealing with a trait and when with a state? In other words, what is "state" and what is "trait" in this case and how do we determine that? Is there such a thing as a personality or, as Ryle (1949) suggests, do we only possess a series of behavioural dispositions that are activated depending on internal stimuli (thoughts, memories, feelings, fantasies) or external stimuli? In daily interactions we can describe all our friends and acquaintances in a way that leads to a consensus. Whether the people described would recognize themselves in those descriptions is another matter.

In this process of uniformity, what has been described by Erikson (1971) as the ego process is apparently at work. This is one of the tasks of the ego and consists of an organizing principle by which the individual is maintained as a coherent personality, who in the experience of the self and in the reality of others remains recognizable as one and the same. According to this interpretation, something within us works at keeping things together and holding up the prospect for ourselves as well as other people that there is order in the chaos. We should realize that our description of another person is the result of our perception of the interaction between that person and ourselves. In this description, we are intrinsically involved ourselves; what we describe, we have also conjured up. This complexity is difficult to conceptualize objectively; nevertheless, we attempt to do so daily.

In traditional psychodiagnostics, emphasis is placed on the person who displays the behaviour. The behaviour which accounts for the diagnosis, for instance a complaint, must be suitable for this type of psychodiagnostics. If certain complaints, a problematic behavioural aspect or a negative affect are situational, diagnostics aimed at the person are less suitable. Behavioural diagnostics ("behavioural assessment") in this case clearly differ from traditional diagnostics in that the role of the situation is predominant. Both variants have contributed to solving various problems and both have their limitations. A fear of walking alone in the street that was caused by an assault is totally different in structure in this respect to an agoraphobia that has developed since childhood and has no clear traumatic origin. In the latter type of anxiety, we quickly arrive at the personality, according to the DSM classification, which makes a dependent, insufficiently separated impression on the clinician. It can be easily imagined that symptom-specific treatment aimed at regaining confidence in walking alone in the street will be more effective in the former case than in the latter. In the latter case, the criteria of dependent and avoidant personality disorders are easily recognizable; the symptom approach appears far more difficult in these cases.

Clinically speaking, the adaptation viewpoint is relevant in the diagnosis of personality disorders. This point of view describes the way the adjustment between the person and his or her situation develops. Adjustment, or adaptation, should not only be considered as a passive process; it can also be very active, and the desired environment can even be designed. Psychodynamics are of importance here: a person with a precise, meticulous, exacting and perfectionist psychic make-up can adapt more successfully in a profession such as chemical analysis or accounting than if he or she preferred to become a contractor or be a guide for groups of teenagers in Amsterdam. When an obsessive-compulsive personality becomes an accountant in an orderly and conscientious accounting office and can get along well with the boss, this personality disorder may remain unnoticed. When someone with a dependent personality disorder decides at an ill-considered moment to strike out alone and start a company, it is conceivable that the person will request psychological help after a while. In short, adaptation can be successful to a greater or lesser degree. A breakthrough of something like anxiety complaints may occur, but the patient can also "get stuck in the situation", "be at odds with him or herself", avoid things and consequently get into trouble, and so on.

The adaptation viewpoint is a more decisive factor and more influential in diagnosing personality disorder as such than in diagnosing a symptom neurosis. This immediately puts the problems of personality disorder somewhat in perspective. In comparison with an Axis I disorder, such as panic disorder, the symptomatology determines to a greater extent the actual situation of the person than a strong personality trait. The request for help in clinical practice that relates to personality patterns is much broader than the grouping that fits in one of the DSM or ICD categories. Especially in out-patient clinical practice, many patients request help with such complaints as subassertive behaviour. They want more and better social skills, although they do not completely fit the criteria of one of the personality disorders from the C cluster of the DSM-IV (the dependent, avoidant and obsessive-compulsive personality disorders). Narcissistic patterns are found frequently and often lead to a greater or lesser degree to relationship disorders. The clinician has to deal with narcissistic defence patterns and personality traits much more often than when working with patients who properly fit the criteria for narcissistic personality disorder.

CATEGORY VERSUS DIMENSION

Personality disorder defined according to a categorial model fits in well with Western society's tradition of thinking in polarities. Categories are characterized by well-defined borders and each exhibits a qualitative difference from other categories. Because of its distinct description and essential characteristics, a diagnosis is obviously applicable or inapplicable to a patient (Gunderson, Links & Reich, 1991). What more can a researcher desire? If one wants to do justice to complex clinical practice, a personality disorder (and this applies to many symptom disorders as well) can best be represented by a dimensional con- ceptualization: a certain personality configuration or a specific complaint are present to a greater or lesser degree. The borders are vague, as in nature day gradually turns into night. There is no clear distinction. Because of this, the relationship between normality and pathology, in this context personality disorder versus no personality disorder, becomes clear.

A categorial taxonomy produces clear and simple descriptions, fits in reasonably well with clinical conventions and procedures, but leads to simplicity and stereotypical clinical pictures. A dimensional model is more complex, more difficult to research empirically, but offers more precise information (Widiger, 1991). According to Klein (1993) also, dimensional models are preferable to categorial models. The categorial diagnosis lacks qualitative and quantitative details on positive and negative cases. The possibility of separating patients and borderline cases which do not belong here is lacking.

The proposals that have been made in relation to dimensional models can be grouped into two classes (Klein, 1993): models that consider the personality disorder itself as a core construct (polythetic and proto- typical models); and models that conceptualize the categories in terms of more fundamental dimensions.

Implicitly, the DSM and ICD have a dimensional approach (see also Eysenck, 1987). In many criteria, we read that a certain trait is somewhat or more than somewhat applicable (for instance the schizoid personality disorder in the DSM IV: criterion 4, "Takes pleasure in few, if any, activities"). The idea that traits can also be diagnosed testifies to this as well. In these cases some criteria apply, but not the necessary four or five. In the case of the personality configuration, a strong presence as well as a total absence usually evoke problems in adaptation.

DESCRIPTIVE VERSUS STRUCTURAL APPROACH

In contrast to the emphasis on the descriptive, categorial descriptions of the DSM and ICD are the psychoanalytic and psychodynamic theories in this field. In the latter approach, a theoretical distinction is made between the manifest and the latent level. The relation between manifest and latent is not direct but indirect in nature. A certain behaviour, symptom or personality trait usually has a complicated, indirect relationship with an underlying pattern, motive or conflict. This underlying pattern is unconscious, which is the main issue in treatment. What are the bases of these particularly structural personality descriptions?

Psychoanalytic descriptions of character by analysts "from the very beginning" can also, but certainly not exclusively, be placed under the category of descriptive character descriptions. In fact, various psychoanalytic views are mixed: next to descriptive aspects, structural and particularly genetic aspects are constantly present as well. The descriptive aspects are usually considered to be much less important than the (much less visible) dynamic, genetic and structural aspects. The patterns that become visible in analytic treatment should receive a place in the diagnostics as much as possible.

The existence of drives played an important role in Freud's definition of character: character traits are direct expressions of, reaction formations against or sublimations of drives (Freud, 1908). In all cases, the drive in its original form has maintained its influence. The quality of drive in childhood exercises an important influence on behaviour, although not necessarily directly. This can be recognized in clinical practice from the fact that, in personality disorder, a segment of childish behaviour has continued to influence the person. In fact, the same train of thought is found in a development of inner potential in social relationships. Reich (1928) had a more expressive name for character: the armour of the ego. In 1990, character was described in a psychoanalytic dictionary, edited by the American Psychoanalytic Association, as follows: "The enduring, patterned functioning of an individual" (Moore & Fine, 1990).

Seen through the eyes of others, character is a habitual way of thinking, feeling and acting. Psychodynamically, character is a person's habitual way of dealing with intrapsychic conflicts. Character is composed of an integrated constellation of character traits. These traits by themselves are a mixture of drive derivatives, defence mechanisms and superego components. Character traits are, like neurotic symptoms, forms of compromise. But character traits are more stable than symptoms, better able to overcome fear and are perceived more as ego-syntonic. According to Moore & Fine (1990, pp. 37–8), character traits can be considered as behavioural patterns that develop over time as a result of an attempt to solve an intrapsychic conflict. Character is, seen conceptually, most related to defence style.

The term character is still used more frequently in psychoanalysis than the term personality (Kets de Vries & Perzow, 1991). If the term personality is employed, it refers to a broader application: the observable, usual, ego-syntonic and, under normal circumstances, relatively predictable behavioural pattern. Character and temperament fall under this definition.

The genesis of the personality takes place in the course of the life of an individual and in intensive interaction with the social context. Symptoms can appear at all times in the course of life and they generally become visible much later than personality traits. During their development various "layers" arise, as psychoanalytic theory attempts to demonstrate. In the various layers and in the connection between them (in other words, in the structure), disturbances can also occur that do not fit well into the DSM and ICD categories on a behavioural level. The large overlap found among personality disorders is probably related to this. If a person meets the criteria of a certain disorder, he or she will usually meet the criteria of several other personality disorders as well. Furthermore, we know from clinical practice of patients who do not meet one of the registered personality disorders, but who do have a greatly disturbed personality.

Adjustment to social situations is often such that the deeper disorder does not become visible in a descriptive respect. A commonly occurring example is the borderline personality organization, worked out by Kernberg (1984). The structure of the ego is diagnosed using the psychoanalytic structural interview. This diagnostic does not make primary judgements about the descriptive level. In this way, a personality disorder is also determined that, as the clinical experience has taught us, can meet the descriptive criteria as soon as the person becomes increasingly burdened and decompensates. Reasoning on the basis of the DSM, we are dealing with a "hidden" personality disorder which is not classified. The clinician, however, must certainly keep this in mind.

The structural point of view does not coincide with a more serious personality pathology as often as it is thought to. From a clinical standpoint, the severity is the result of the combined play of several factors: temperament, character, personality and, particularly, adjustment to social context and social support. In this respect, we also count intelligence and introspection as part of personality.

In the clinical situation, it happens quite often that serious personality pathology is found in patients with an impulse control disorder on Axis I, but not of the type that can be arranged according to the prescribed criteria. One may wonder if disorders in impulse control should not be classified under Axis II. The fact that a remainder category exists for this does not render the theoretical foundation appropriate, but rather the reverse.

Furthermore, we find patients in clinical practice who do not sufficiently meet the criteria of one of the DSM or ICD personality disorders, but who are characterized by a great many personality problems. This could be someone with very good cognitive development, judging by the educational background, but a developmental deprivation in an emotional sense.

Example

An example is a 28-year-old mathematician who amuses himself exclusively with computer games. He does not look for a job, has no interest in relationships and is a great problem in the eyes of his parents. He himself experiences few problems. He entertains himself in his way, does consider the future, is not afraid to accept a job or start a relationship, just does not seek them. The criteria for a mood disorder apply no more than those of a DSM personality disorder. A structural test of his ego excludes a borderline and psychotic ego. A test psychological examination does not indicate symptom disorders. Judging by his answers to some personality questionnaires, he is reasonably content, does not worry about his difficulties, and has very low performance motivation without negative fear of failure.

Projective examination by means of the Draw a Person Test and the Rorschach Test indicates an inhibition in emotional development, apart from the cognitive side, we are dealing with a big toddler. His drawings of people are very remarkable: little, immature, dolls without detail. His behaviour tempted the psychological assistant to utter: "He should go back to scouting." Advising psychotherapeutic treatment was useless, owing to the complete lack of motivation. He had no insight into the problematic sides of his behaviour. This insight will possibly start to develop if he takes a job. Without meeting the descriptive personality specifications (except, of course, classification under the remainder group), serious developmental retardation is what we are concerned with here. Expressed more generally, people with inhibited emotional development, indicated in the clinical, more psychodynamic literature as infantile personalities, cannot be placed in the actual classification systems.

Arguing from the standpoint of clinical practice, the classification system of personality disorders will make progress if structural qualities inspired by the psychodynamic orientation are added to the particularly descriptive qualities. Concretely, this means that in structural terms the ego will be diagnosed with the aid of defence mechanisms, identity integration and reality testing. In this manner, these diagnostics fit the categories that are still considered important in clinical practice. Diagnosis of this structural level is then completed with the descriptive assessment, which would preferably consist of dimensions — in other words, of traits that are more or less strong.

INSTRUMENTS

In clinical practice, the personality disorder diagnosis is, as a rule, made using the psychodiagnostic interview. In Part 4 this psychodiagnostic process is discussed at length. In empirical research, what are normally used are questionnaires that are filled in by the patients themselves or semi-structured interviews (Reich, 1987). Identifying a symptom with the aid of a questionnaire or other psychological testing technique is less complicated than identifying a personality disorder in this way. Weissman (1993) and Tyrer (1990) sum up a number of methodological problems in this context:

1. People with a behavioural pattern that is constantly present and seen as problematic in a classification system do not necessarily recognize this themselves when asked about it. Their own "baseline" cannot be used to determine estimations of the degree of abnormality, which does succeed with certain symptoms. During a diagnostic interview, the statements of a significant other about patients with a personality disorder could be more reliable than those made by the patients themselves.

2. Personality traits vary considerably because of the presence of symptom disorders. As a result, every measurement must take the

presence of symptom disorders into account. In periods of absence of symptoms, measurements should take place repeatedly.

3. The determination of personality disorders in an epidemiological study is especially complicated, since large populations are required for this and the necessary interviews demand a great deal of time and a high degree of training for the interviewer. The limited research related to the validity and reliability of self-assessment questionnaires in comparison to assessments by family members and clinicians partially indicates that judgements by people other than the patient are more reliable and valid. In epidemiological studies, certain personality disorders or certain traits of disorders will be systematically underrepresented.

4. Moreover, a constantly present pattern is difficult to identify in a single interview.

5. Because the interest in research into personality disorders is relatively recent, experience in research is still only limited and the instruments that are available are still inadequate. The results obtained with the various instruments are often poorly comparable.

In epidemiological studies so far, approximately 1300 subjects have been studied with six different kinds of instrument (Weissman, 1993). In the normal population, between 10% and 13.5% of the DSM-III Axis II disorders are established. The percentage is low for the paranoid and schizoid (0.4% to 0.9%) and rather variable for the schizotypal (3% to 5.6%). For the histrionic personality, the figure lies between 1.3% and 3%. The narcissistic personality is more uncommon at 0.4%, while the borderline is variable and amounts to 4.6%. The antisocial personality is 2% to 3%. The avoidant personality is rare; the dependent and the obsessive-compulsive are between 4% and 6% with the aid of a questionnaire and between 1.6% and 2.2% with an interview. The passive-aggressive personality is higher in the interview: 1.8% to 3%. With a questionnaire method, it is only 0.4%.

The following instruments have been developed especially for measuring DSM-III personality pathology.

Semi-structured Interviews

Structured Interview for DSM-III Personality Disorders (SIDP) by Pfohl, Stangl & Zimmerman (1982).

International Personality Disorder Examination (IPDE) by Loranger *et al.* (1991).

Structured Clinical Interview for DSM-III-R Personality Disorders (SCID-II) by Spitzer & Williams (1986).

Diagnostic Interview for Personality Disorders (DIPD) by Zanarini *et al.* (1987).

Questionnaires

Personality Disorder Questionnaire (PDQ-R) by Hyler *et al.* (1988).
Millon Clinical Multiaxial Inventory (MCMI-III) by Millon (1987b, 1994).

Using Instruments

In order to conduct research, large groups of patients or normals are often required. A self-completion questionnaire is then the most practical. The PDQ-R is a frequently used example for this purpose; the list can be filled in by patients in about half an hour. The simplicity of this list is remarkable. The criteria for Axis II of the DSM have been almost directly converted into questions. Accordingly, the results show a low correspondence to results obtained by means of semi-structured interviews and an overpathologizing of personality disorders. The list is not really suitable for determining one of the personality disorders, but can still be used as a rough screening instrument for an initial exploration of personality disorders in a large population.

Better results are reported with Millon's MCMI. Millon has based his questionnaire on his theory of personality disorders and accordingly has gained an advantage. Given the complex and abstract subject and the necessity of a theory, this is the instrument of choice for a questionnaire.

Semi-structured interviews are more complex to administer. Conducting research with these takes more time, but the data obtained gains reliability and validity. The advantage of the IPDE is that it can be used to examine both the DSM-III-R and ICD-10 personality disorders. In a large-scale international project, a great deal of experience is acquired by means of the IPDE. If limited changes can render this instrument suitable for the DSM-IV personality disorders, it would be the first choice.

The instruments mentioned above relate to all classified personality disorders and some involve several symptom disorders. In relation to separate measurement of, particularly, the antisocial personality disorder, the borderline personality disorder, the schizotypal personality disorder and the narcissistic personality disorder, a handful of questionnaires, semi-structured and completely structured interviews have appeared. These instruments are indispensable, especially for researching a specific personality disorder. A problem usually is that the demarcation of other personality disorders in the same cluster is difficult.

A good example of a successful instrument is the *Diagnostic Interview for Borderline Patients* (DIB), originally developed by Gunderson and his co-workers (Gunderson & Kolb, 1976; Kolb & Gunderson, 1980; Gunderson, Kolb & Austin, 1981; Gunderson, 1982) and revised by Zanarini, Gunderson & Frankenburg (1989). Much research has been performed on and with this semi-structured interview and the popular borderline personality disorder diagnosis has gained reliability and validity because of it (Green, 1987). For an overview see Derksen (1988a, 1988b, 1989, 1990a).

CONCLUSION

So far, the literature on personality disorders provokes more questions than it is capable of answering. In each aspect of this popular subject matter, we can run into one or more problems. Personality and personality problems belong to a broad area of the daily experience of human interaction. At the same time, from an empirical point of view, this subject is difficult to control. A personality disorder is unique in the following respect: it is clinically factual, empirically fictional and theoretically chaotic.

PART 2

DSM-IV and ICD-10 Personality Disorders

CHAPTER 2.1 The paranoid personality disorder: the drug addict

The father of a 30-year-old male drug addict contacted us to ask for help with his son. He had read a newspaper article on borderline personality disorders and thought it was relevant to his son's case. He hoped to be given better professional help than his son had so far received.

FIRST IMPRESSION

The drug addict attracts initial attention because he does not evoke the stereotypical impression of an addict. He appears well groomed and not particularly ill. He comes across as an intelligent but helpless theorist troubled by his failures in life. In the course of the contact, he expresses himself cautiously, is very alert, emphasizes that he has confidence in the testing and that he wants to co-operate completely. He states this so often that one begins to mistrust his statements. His down mood becomes more apparent in the course of the contact. During the testing, his emotions are under control; there is no friction. He is very co-operative.

SYMPTOMATOLOGY AND PERSONALITY

At this time he is on methadone, but occasionally uses heroin, medication, beer and wine. Furthermore, he smokes a great deal and uses soft drugs once in a while. He reports sleep disturbances and backaches. His appetite is normal. In his activity pattern, a light bipolar disorder appears to be hidden. His down mood seems to stimulate substance abuse. These depressive episodes are also characterized by suicidal thoughts.

During contact, he comes across as very sensitive. He is quick to think that other people are against him and are rejecting him. He complains about the thin walls of his apartment. He is irritated by his neighbour and seems to hear sounds that are not heard immediately by others. Closer examination does not completely clarify if this symptomatology is delusional and ego-syntonic or open to correction and of a passing nature.

BIOGRAPHY

The drug addict is the only child of two caring and well-educated parents. His father seems well integrated and makes a good impression. He is retired and was previously director of an advertising company. The mother suffered from toxaemia in pregnancy and the baby was born a month too early, weighing only 3 lb 1 oz, and he spent six weeks in an incubator. Motor disorders were observed during infancy. He did not stand out in elementary school, he learned quickly and later gained average marks. He went through secondary school with good results and entered a more advanced secondary school, but did not graduate from it. He made an effort to enter music school but was turned down.

During puberty everything he attempted went wrong. The relationship with his girlfriend ended. He was shattered by his rejection by the music school. He avoided mandatory military service, became unemployed and began drinking. Increasingly, he began to increase substance abuse, lived apart from his parents but continued asking them for assistance. For example, he still eats at home every day. He claims never to have come into conflict with the law nor to have obtained money or drugs illegally, although while under the influence of the latter he has become destructive, got into fights and behaved obscenely.

He has been institutionalized six times for treatment for his drug addiction. Each time this failed. He believes that as soon as he cuts down on drugs, his "psychosis" emerges making him quarrelsome and suspicious and the treatment fails. He then escapes and falls back on drugs again. At this time he is not considered bad enough for psychiatric hospitalization and the drug addiction clinics can do little for him.

Socially he is isolated. He has no intimate relationships and no real friends.

PSYCHOLOGICAL TESTING

The following tests were administered: Wechsler Adult Intelligence Scale (WAIS), Minnesota Multiphasic Personality Inventory (MMPI), Dutch Shortend MMPI (NVM), Thematic Apperception Test (TAT), Four Pictures Test, Drawing Test and the Sentence Completion Test (SCT). We must take into consideration that the results might be influenced by the fact that he is on drugs. It is recommended that a new testing session take place as soon as he stops the substance abuse.

On the WAIS, he scores a verbal IQ of 122 and a performance IQ of 98: total IQ = 112. The biggest difference is between *Digit span* (10) and *Picture arrangement* (3): 7 points. His hyperalertness and concentration are confirmed by high scores on *Digit span*, and furthermore suspicion and mistrust can lead to disturbances with *Picture arrangement* (Meyer, 1989). His verbal talent is excellent and in relation to this he is apractical. Furthermore, his insight in social situations seems to remain behind other cognitive capacities. Also, the lowered result on the performance part points toward his depressive symptoms.

On the MMPI, the validity scales are as follows: L = 46, F = 59, K = 42. So the test is trustworthy and validly answered. Often, paranoid patients are so alert that they hide their psychological condition and thus do not produce an elevated *Paranoia* scale on the MMPI. As is to be expected in view of these control scales, the highest score with this patient is on the *Paranoia* scale: 81. *Schizophrenia* and *Psychopathic Deviate* follow at some distance (namely 75 and 74, inclusive K). Both of these relative increases are also known with the paranoid personality and are indicative of poor social adjustment. Elevation on these scales means in the case of the drug user that no overt psychotic characteristics are present. But he is suspicious, gets easily into arguments and is potentially hostile. What stands out the most is a strong sensitivity in interpersonal relationships. Somebody with such a score quickly misinterprets other people's remarks as personal criticism. The defence mechanism projection is often in evidence here; his own latent anger and criticism are attributed to the other person and because of this an irritating type of interaction develops.

On the NVM, his scores are very high on *Negativity* in comparison to normals (high in comparison to psychiatric populations), above average for both norm groups on *Somatization*, very high to high on *Shyness*, very high to high on *Psychopathology* and average to above average on *Extroversion*. The picture that develops from this list is of a vulnerable man without much resistance to stress. He does not noticeably have an antisocial structure, but because he is under great tension he experiences a great deal of uneasiness, feelings of anxiety and a high degree of suffering. This suffering is greater than he can ward off through somatization. Based on his score on *Shyness*, it appears that tension in this man leads to avoidance behaviour. He shows a great deal of consideration towards others and only uses substances when alone in order to reduce tension.

On the Sentence Completion Test, he appears to be a lonely man who suffers through poor social skills and lack of social contact. His critical attitude to other people and his expectation of hostility on their part show up again in this task.

His Four Pictures Test reflects his inner experience in a somewhat poetic manner. The story is of an interaction with someone else, but only describes the inner world of the main character. The latter is incapable of maintaining human contact. His experiences dominate and at a certain moment lead to contact being abruptly broken off, he is alienated from other people and experiences them as a nuisance. His inner world fools him; he is a prisoner of it.

In the various stories he tells during the TAT, he uses a lot of fantasy and describes people with ambivalent feelings who often fail in things they are doing, but also pick up the pieces again. Recurring themes are the quality of the family background and family, making a career by study and work, the use of too much alcohol, threat and unfaithfulness in relationships, loneliness and abandonment.

DSM-IV DIAGNOSIS

Axis I   Substance dependency, serious
Axis II   Paranoid personality
Axis III No diagnosis
Axis IV   3 moderate
Axis V   Current GAF: 35
          Highest GAF past year: 35

DSM-IV AND ICD-10 CRITERIA

In the DSM-IV, the paranoid personality disorder is described as a pervasive distrust and suspicion of others so that their motives are interpreted as malevolent. It begins in early adulthood and presents in a variety of contexts, as indicated by at least four of the following:

1. Suspects, without sufficient basis, that others are exploiting or deceiving him or her.
2. Preoccupied with unjustified doubts about the loyalty or trust-worthiness of friends or associates.
3. Is reluctant to confide in others because of unwarranted fear that the information will be used maliciously against him or her.
4. Reads hidden devaluing or threatening meanings into benign re-marks or events.
5. Persistently bears grudges, i.e. is unforgiving of insults, injuries, or slights.
6. Perceives attacks on his or her character or reputation that are not apparent to others and is quick to react angrily or to counterattack.
7. Recurrent unjustified suspicions regarding fidelity of spouse or sexual partner.

A paranoid personality disorder does not occur exclusively during the course of schizophrenia, a mood disorder with psychotic features or another psychotic disorder, and not owing to the direct effects of a general medical condition. If criteria are met prior to the onset of schizophrenia, add "pre-morbid", e.g. "Paranoid Personality Disorder (pre-morbid)".

Of the following seven criteria of the ICD-10 paranoid personality disorder, at least three criteria must be met to a marked degree:

1. Excessive sensitiveness to setbacks and rebuffs.
2. Tendency to bear grudges persistently, e.g. refusal to forgive insults, injuries, or slights.
3. Suspiciousness and a pervasive tendency to distort experience by misconstruing the neutral or friendly actions of others as hostile or contemptuous.
4. A combative and tenacious sense of personal rights out of keeping with the actual situation.
5. The same formulation as criterion 7 of the DSM.
6. A tendency to experience excessive self-importance, which becomes manifest in a persistent self-referential attitude.
7. Preoccupation with unsubstantiated "conspiratorial" explanations of events around the subject or in world at large.

In relation to the DSM-III-R, in the DSM-IV only some criteria of the paranoid personality disorder have been redefined. The research findings in this area are still limited. During the course of the history of this concept, experts have pointed out the relation to schizophrenia and especially with the "schizophrenia spectrum". The delusional disorder has its place here. Concerning the other personality disorders, the highest rate of overlap is with the schizotypal personality disorder (Bernstein, Useda & Siever, 1993). At the moment there is not enough empirical and genetic evidence to make a decision about a new subdivision. In phenomenological studies serveral types of paranoid personality disorder can be distinguished. Some overlap extensively with schizotypal personality disorder, others primarily with Cluster B personality disorders.

In future it is possible that there will be one group of "psychotic personality disorders" with paranoid, schizoid and schizotypal traits. These patients show a stable pattern of "psychotic-like" traits without actually developing into psychosis. The differential diagnosis between this new group and the delusional disorder will remain a problem. In Chapter 6.1 this subject will be discussed in more detail.

From the genetic perspective roots are shared with the schizophrenia spectrum. From a structural psychodynamic perspective, these patients have a psychotic personality organization, and their psychological balance has been realized in a different way from patients with a psychotic disorder on Axis I. Generally speaking there is more acting-out behaviour, which has to do with the incomplete structure or defective integration of the superego. Also from a structural perspective a differentiation can be made with a group of patients who have comparable traits but which are not so pervasive. Usually a borderline personality organization can be diagnosed here. They can be placed in Cluster B.

The borderline personality disorder of the DSM-IV contains a criterion about paranoid ideation. The suspicion that we encounter in daily life amongst non-patients can be observed in people with a structurally well-developed ego. This suspicion can normally be reduced to a state characteristic of certain circumstances, for instance at work, that causes someone to be a laughing-stock or to be criticized a great deal. As soon as the security of a function or relationship ceases or is threatened, the person may react with suspicion. If the personality is responsible for the suspicion rather than the circumstances, this can usually be related to repressed conflicts in early childhood relationships with one or both parents.

CHAPTER 2.2 The schizoid personality disorder: the librarian

For a year and a half, a 54-year-old librarian has been suffering from joint pains for which no physiological cause has been found. In the last year, he has been absent from work a great deal in connection with his complaints. The development of these difficulties goes hand in hand with a reorganization taking place in the library. A great deal of effort is needed for him to continue his work and the question to the company doctor is whether or not this man is disabled.

FIRST IMPRESSION

The librarian arrives for the psychological examination half an hour early and with a sluggish walk. At first sight, he gives an impression of an immaculately groomed man who makes a great effort to keep his tension well under control. He looks ten years older than his age.

In the contact he is co-operative and correct, although embarrassed at having been sent to a psychologist. He prefers a somatic diagnosis and treatment for his complaints. His incapacity to put feelings and fantasies into words is noticeable. He describes everything in terms of concrete situations and behaviour. He does not take initiatives in the contact, nor does he say anything of his own accord, only when he has been asked. He makes a very introverted and sombre impression. During the examination, no meaningful growth in contact takes place.

SYMPTOMATOLOGY AND PERSONALITY

The development of his complaints shows a progressive course. Some years ago, the aches started in his shoulder and arm. The pain was felt in the muscles as well as in the joints. He was referred for physiotherapy and received painkillers from his physician. After both knees started hurting as well, the librarian consulted various medical specialists, although this did not lead to any result.

His complaints of pain are not constant and are quite vague. The pain changes in intensity and he is most bothered by it in the evening. He experiences the pain primarily in his neck and shoulders.

The librarian is recognized as what can be called a remarkable "psychosomatic personality". His "penser opératoire" or alexithyme traits are obvious: he appears incapable of expressing feelings and fantasies. The secondary gain of his pain complaints and movement disorder appears to consist of the fact that his wish to be at home is granted. Both he and his wife accept his disability, and he prefers being at home with complaints to being at work without them.

His mood is depressive, although he does not qualify for the criteria of a major depression, nor for dysthymia. He makes an avital impression.

Self-reflection and introspection are lacking. The following defence mechanisms are noticeable: suppression of affect, isolation, rationalization and reaction formation.

BIOGRAPHY

The librarian is the eldest of a family of four children. He does not mention childhood neurotic traits and phase and school development went smoothly. His father is described by him as an orderly, rational, distant man who was primarily occupied with bringing up the children. Punishments were not given, and the parents tried from the beginning to appeal to the children's reason. His father was a teacher and had been found unfit for work because of tension complaints. After all sorts of changes in the educational system, his father developed serious neck and shoulder complaints.

At first, it appeared to be a matter of a family burden and the development of the complaints by the librarian seemed to indicate a repetition of his father's complaints. He appears to have identified with his father to a remarkable degree and ascribes the same character traits to his father and himself. He says he did not have much of a bond with his mother. He describes her as emotional, spontaneous and a person who did the fun things first and left the less pleasant things till last.

During his upbringing it was imprinted on the children that negative and aggressive behaviour was unacceptable for children of a teacher. The librarian appears to have taken this personally; he remembers being angry at school once and having thrown someone against a wall. Then he had the scary fantasy that he had murdered this person. Since then he does not remember ever being angry again.

In spite of excellent achievements at school, he left at the age of 14 and went to work in a library. This was among other things based on psychological advice which suggested that he could not get along with his peers. His future spouse, who had also dropped out of school, introduced him to the library. After a year and a half of dating they got married. He says that he does not remember any intense feelings for her and that their sexual life was not very active. The couple do not maintain any social contacts and make family contacts only sporadically. The only guest they have is the wife's mother. He likes this visit because it brings regularity into their lives. They never wanted children, who would disturb the regularity.

The librarian has always worked in the same library, first as an errand boy, later in the ordering department, and finally as head of the placement department. In his work, he considers himself to be very orderly, precise and perfectionistic ("no book is out of place"). He prefers doing routine work ("then at least I see a concrete result"). The problems with his health started at the moment that reorganizations and budget cuts happened in the library. Automation and centralization had to be introduced. Because of this, his contact with other personnel increased. The reorganization forced him into more contact with familiar as well as unfamiliar colleagues, and it seems that too much was therefore asked of him. Talking about the system changes, he uses words such as "blasted" and "darned". When asked if these expressions mean for him that he is angry about what happened, he reacts with confusion and tension.

PSYCHOLOGICAL TESTING

The following tests were administered with the librarian: WAIS, several neuropsychological tests, SCL-90, the Dutch Personality Questionnaire (NPV), GLTS, MMPI and the Four Pictures Test.

On the WAIS he scores a verbal IQ of 128 and a performance IQ of 132, and a total IQ of 133, falling into the category of "very gifted". The neuropsychological examination does not reveal any peculiarities.

On the SCL-90 he scores high on practically every subscale.

On the NPV, he scores high on the subscales *Social inadequacy* and *Rigidity*. He appears here as someone who is very rigid, reserved and unresponsive in social contacts. His self-esteem is low.

On the GLTS he scores very low on *Extroversion*, *Temperament* and *Authoritarianism*. Based on this questionnaire, he appears as someone who has strong self-control, with a virtual lack of impulsivity and hardly capable of experiencing feelings.

On the MMPI he scores 71 on the K scale. His score on the L scale is 40 and on the F scale 50. This indicates that he consciously wants to present himself as normal and his responses further reflect a high defence in regard to psychological weaknesses. In terms of the L scale, one can conclude that the score is not so much due to not being honest, but purely due to lack of insight. He seems to want to maintain control at all costs. People with such a score on the K scale are often very shy, inhibited and hesitant in terms of emotionality and making contact with others. They lack self-insight and understanding. Other notable scores are 80 (including the K correction) on *Hypochondriasis*, 75 on *Depression*, 71 on *Hysteria* and 72 on *Schizophrenia*. Very low scores are obtained on *Psychopathic Deviate* (32) and *Hypomania* (25). The librarian appears as a sombre, somatizing man who is shy and reserved. He is inhibited, overly conventional, maladjusted and has a strong need for approval. He has very little energy, appears avital and possibly depressed. At the same time, he refuses to face the psychological aspect of his problems and somatizes his tensions. The elevation on the *Schizophrenia* scale must be interpreted in the light of feelings of incompetence, inferiority and dissatisfaction. He tends to withdraw into his own little world.

On the Four Pictures Test, he writes the story of a divorced man who becomes lonely and lives in a shabby room with only a bed in it. The sole contacts he still has are with his brother and a landlady who keeps a constant eye on him. He is gloomy and worries a great deal about the adverse consequences of his divorce and the high alimony.

The librarian is a very intelligent man, but also somebody with an extremely limited social life. He has many fears, tensions and inhibitions. He is rigid, overconventional, inflexible, reserved and sombre. Through his psychosomatic complaints, he reacted to his incapacity to start social interaction the moment that this was asked of him. Just like his father he has withdrawn to his home situation and avoids further contact.

DSM-IV DIAGNOSIS

Axis I   Somatoform pain disorder
Axis II   Schizoid personality disorder (primary diagnosis)
          Obsessive-compulsive traits

Axis III Joint pains
Axis IV Psychosocial stressors: reorganizations and cutbacks at work
have overextended the capacity of this man
Seriousness: 3
Axis V Current GAF: 30
Highest GAF past year: 40

DSM-IV AND ICD-10 CRITERIA

In the DSM-IV the schizoid personality is circumscribed as somebody
with a pervasive pattern of detachment from social relationships and a
restricted range of expression of emotions in interpersonal settings. It
begins in early adulthood and is present in a variety of contexts, as
indicated by at least four of the following:

1. Neither desires nor enjoys close relationships, including being part of
   a family.
2. Almost always chooses solitary activities.
3. Little, if any, interest in having sexual experiences with another
   person.
4. Takes pleasure in few, if any, activities.
5. Lacks close friends or confidants other than first-degree relatives.
6. Appears indifferent to the praise or criticism of others.
7. Emotional coldness, detachment, or flattened affect.

These symptoms do not occur exclusively during the course of
schizophrenia, a mood disorder with psychotic features, another psychotic disorder, or a pervasive developmental disorder, and are not due
to the direct effects of a general medical condition.

In the ICD-10 the schizoid personality disorder is described by seven
criteria, of which at least three must be applicable.

Criteria 1, 2, 4, 5 and 6 of the ICD-10 are identical to criteria 4, 7, 6, 3 and
2 of the DSM-IV.

3. Limited capacity to express warm, tender feelings for others as well
   as anger.
7. Excessive preoccupation with fantasy and introspection.

The description of a schizoid pattern goes back to Bleuler who indicated
an inwardly directed tendency, away from the outside world, and an
absence of emotional expressivity. The psychological world of the

schizoid person makes a dull impression because of this, but in the literature a certain kind of sensitivity is also pointed out (Kalus, Bernstein & Siever, 1993). This contradiction still lives on in the different types of schizoid personality that are described on a clinical basis. Empirical research has only been done in a very limited way.

As is evident from the descriptions of these personality disorders, one cannot expect to find this type frequently as a patient in the waiting room. Thus this was one of the problems in describing the schizoid personality in the DSM-III. In order to increase the sensitivity of the three criteria at the time the criteria have been expanded to seven, but even then the extent is limited. In the DSM-IV, the criteria have been sharpened on the basis of meagre research and the pattern of detachment has replaced what was initially called indifference in social relationships. Criterion 4 has been thoroughly revised; it previously concerned difficulties in experiencing and expressing strong emotions.

The demarcation of other Axis II disorders such as this, based on research as well as clinical judgements, is the most difficult concern of the schizotypal personality disorder and of the avoidant person of Cluster C (Kalus, Bernstein & Siever, 1993). The schizoid personality in the DSM description is characterized in particular by so-called "negative symptoms": a great deal is lacking. In schizophrenia these symptoms are always clinically relevant and often appear first as a variation of the "positive symptoms" of a schizophrenic process. In terms of genetics, there is still no evidence available of a connection between schizophrenia and the schizoid personality disorder. In relation to the avoidant personality, it can be theoretically stated that the wish for intimacy is present, which is in contrast to the schizoid person. Empirically, such a difference is often difficult to distinguish.

As is evident from the case above, not only is a somatoform disorder on Axis I present but also a depressive mood, even if the latter cannot be scored. It is my impression that the schizoid personality can be split into two types. The first type looks more like the schizotypal person, and also has more positive symptoms fitting within the psychotic reaction. Psychodynamically seen, the primitive defence mechanisms, the fragmented identity and the weak relationship to reality are present. This type could in the future either be given a place on Axis I, as applies to schizotypal traits, or could be added as an Axis II disorder together with the schizotypal and some paranoid personalities. The second type will show a great deal of overlap with the new description of the depressive personality disorder and, in a clinical respect, the compulsive traits will be noticeable. With this type we can also find obsessions concerning sexuality, masturbation and the like. This looks similar to what can also be diagnosed with many obsessive-compulsive personalities. Where the ego structure is concerned, this latter type fits within the neurotic reach. All forms of psychotherapy can be indicated here. The tendency to turn away from relationships and intimacy is put into words as a wish, but in the course of treatment this position "thaws out". Deep down, the patient discovers his or her need and desire for contact and attachment. This only frees itself when the traumata that took place in the interpersonal atmosphere of the child at a very young age can be worked on.

CHAPTER 2.3　The schizotypal personality disorder: the traffic warden

A 53-year-old traffic warden was sent home from work by his supervisor. The reason was that he could not answer for the consequences of his behaviour in situations over which he had no control. He had previously been told that he could no longer work the street shift. When working on the street, he often panicked and acted unpredictably; he would become aggressive or would suddenly walk away from a situation. His colleagues on the street shift said that they did not want to work with him any longer and thus he was assigned to the office shift, indoors. During his office shift he would knowingly make mistakes, resulting in administrative chaos. Earlier evaluations of his functioning resulted in his projecting a negative image, although for one reason or another he retained a special position in the office. He received special treatment from his supervisor and his mistakes were covered up out of charity or kindness. When the department was reorganized with a view to better management, the longstanding problems of the traffic warden's work became apparent to others and it was decided that it could not continue. He was asked to undergo a psychological examination for his work problems.

FIRST IMPRESSION

The traffic warden is picked up at his home by his supervisor to be taken to the psychological testing. He appears moderately well groomed and looks a little older than he actually is. He has a sturdy build and makes a dominating impression. His psychomotor functioning is normal and no attention or concentration disturbances can be identified. During the examination, he sits in a relaxed way and does not appear anxious about the situation.

What is remarkable is his continuous gaze at the examiner. He makes comments about the examiner's own psychological condition. By doing this, he appears to be trying to arouse feelings of fear and defensive reactions in the psychological examiner. He says that people often tell him that they are afraid of him, and reports seeing things in others that they would rather not know. By commenting on what he sees in his partner in conversation, he controls the conversation.

SYMPTOMATOLOGY AND PERSONALITY

We see a somewhat eccentric man who appears to experience few neurotic conflicts. The traffic warden says that he has no problems and is content with his present life. The only change he would like is to have more money. "I sit all day in my chair, doing nothing. I would prefer to be alone and not have anything to do with anyone else." He reports having no friends. He tries to avoid contact with his wife and children as much as possible. For example, when his family is downstairs watching the television, he is upstairs. When his family is upstairs, he watches television downstairs.

The mood of the traffic warden appears normal, although his affect regulation is inadequate and limited. His experiences appear to be impoverished and bizarre. He talks about very painful situations with indifference.

He says that he is a strong believer in God, with whom he has a personal relationship. By relying on God for strength, he says he is able to take away other people's pain. His proof of this is that he has taken away his father's pain when the latter had both his legs amputated. The traffic warden appears to have disturbances in cognition and magical thinking.

He reports having contact with his daughter who died a few years ago of cancer. He states that he can talk with his deceased daughter in a very real way, especially when he visits her in the cemetery. During their conversations, he reports that she asks him about her son who is living with her husband's parents. For the traffic warden this contact with his daughter seems normal.

Dealing with the death of his daughter is quite difficult, reports the traffic warden. He says that since she died he has had problems at work. When he is abused by someone who has received a parking ticket, he says he cannot handle it and becomes very aggressive. When he is describing these incidents, his use of speech is vague and very abstract. He uses words such as "the force" and when the examiner asks for clarification, he is surprised that the examiner does not understand what he is talking about. The traffic warden's speech is well ordered and coherent and his thinking does not seem associative.

His personality makes a fragmented impression. In his description of himself, there are many contradictions which appear to have a life of their own and not to relate to each other. His experience of reality seems to be black and white, but he denies these contrasts when confronted by the examiner. When explanations are offered for his experiences, he reacts with confusion and strong aggressive feelings. His descriptions of his relationships are also dominated by this splitting mechanism. He experiences people as either completely good or completely bad. He talks of his deceased daughter and her son as "half gods", whereas he views his wife and other two children in a very negative light. He says that he stays at home only for his grandson; otherwise he would like to go off on his own, drifting about and being absolutely free.

The traffic warden appears to have no sense of being ill. He seems to have little capacity for introspection or reflection. He appears to resist looking at his own behaviour and instead is very defensive and aggressive toward others. Meaningful emotional contact or growth does not take place during the examination.

BIOGRAPHY

The traffic warden is the elder of two children. His sister is six years younger. His father was a foreman in road building and died of cancer about 20 years ago. He describes his father as a strict but fair man who used to beat him with a double-folded military belt. His mother, in contrast, he describes as an unjust woman, who favoured his sister over him in every situation. For example, he had to walk to school whereas his sister had a bicycle. Further, he says he has nothing more to say about his parents and does not want to examine them more closely. When asked what the atmosphere was like in his home when he was a child, he says that he always had the feeling of being on the outside, but does not want to discuss it.

He could not offer any information about his mother's pregnancy and delivery of him, nor about his early childhood years. When asked about any traumatic events or neurotic behaviour during his childhood, he says that "they did not talk about those things in those days". As a child he says that he had enough friends.

During the end of elementary school, in the fifth grade, he was held back a year since he did not get along with the teacher. At the age of 15 he went to work for a butcher and at the age of 16 he started at butcher's trade school. He obtained his diploma with little trouble. After completing this training, he maintained fewer and fewer social contacts and became more and more focused on himself. In the interview, he refuses to tell how and where he met his wife. "If you continue like this, I will withdraw all my statements and you will have to figure out your psychological report all by yourself."

After receiving his butcher's diploma, he went to work in the meat industry at the age of 18. He did not like this work and left his job after six months. He wanted steady work instead of constantly switching, so he took a job with a steel construction company with which he stayed for 12 years. He worked himself up to be a foreman. He says he never had problems there and always liked the work. When the company broke up, he started working at a coat company. After about a year there, his father became ill and he had to take the latter's place in a road-building project overseas. When the project was completed, he stayed home for a year and through a temporary work agency obtained a position at the town hall. Some time later he was offered a job as a traffic warden. The traffic warden said he also always liked this work and never had any problems until the death of his daughter. It is since that time that he has found himself no longer able to handle the insults of the public and he reacts aggressively. Furthermore, he says that following a departmental reorganization he has difficulty with the fact that several of the part-time traffic wardens were suddenly promoted, and he was not. In addition, he reports that he is not able to work with his new supervisor.

A conversation with the head of his organization reveals that the traffic warden had functioned very badly from the start. He constantly needed guidance, although his errors were usually swept under the carpet. The former head of the traffic warden's office said that he was never suitable for this type of work. The traffic warden was eventually dismissed and sent home. His colleagues had a party to celebrate his departure, indicating how much he was disliked.

PSYCHOLOGICAL TESTING

The traffic warden's intelligence was measured with the WAIS. His performance on the test reflect a total IQ score of 98 (verbal 102, performance 94), coming within the range of "normal". His cognitive capacities appear to be in accordance with his function as traffic warden. Thus his poor work performance can not be explained by insufficient intellectual capacity. His scores on the subtests *Arithmetic* (6) and *Digit span* (7) indicate an undisturbed attention and concentration capacity. The relatively lower score on the subtest *Digit symbol* (3) is typical of unstable, easily irritated people. The traffic warden does not seem capable of carrying out a simple but monotonous task without showing irritation. The low score on the subtest *Object assembly* (2) is indicative of an apractical aptitude. A negative indication for psychotherapy is concluded.

To examine his psychological complaints and his personality, the following tests were used: MMPI, NPV, GLTS and SCL-90. The highest score obtained on the MMPI was on the F factor: 82. His scores on the L and K factors were 58 and 47 respectively. On the clinical scales, *Paranoia* was the highest: 70. The high F scale score is usually indicative of an atypical and deviant way of answering. A high scorer has a whole variety of unusual characteristics. Furthermore, high scores can be indicative of resistance to the testing. The dejected profile of the traffic warden is likely to confirm this hypothesis.

Notable on the NPV is that the traffic warden scored maximally on all the personality traits except for *Self-esteem*. The highest score (7) on the GLTS is for *Carefreeness*. Often this means that we are dealing with an introverted, closed personality, with whom it is difficult to get into contact. It is remarkable that he hardly worries about his psychic condition and there is absolutely no sense of illness. On the SCL-90, he scores high to very high on *Depression*, *Sensitivity*, *Hostility* and *Sleeping problems*.

The conclusion of the testing is that we are dealing with an eccentric man of average intelligence who appears to view the world with suspicion and who experiences dissatisfaction in relationships with other people. He experiences strong feelings of aggression, irritability, anger and resentment. These negative feelings are projected so that a paranoid-hostile attitude towards others is prominent. Furthermore, he is a man with unusual characteristics and an unusual attitude towards life, a peculiar man who seeks isolation.

DSM-IV DIAGNOSIS

Axis I   No diagnoses on Axis I
Axis II   Schizotypal personality disorder (with psychotic decomposition of short duration)
Axis III   No data

Axis IV   Psychosocial stressors
          The death of his daughter and the disturbed mourning pro-
          cess have lead to the awakening of his latent schizotypal
          personality disturbance that has existed for years
          Severity 5 (extreme)
Axis V   Current GAF: 35
          Highest GAF past year: 40

DSM-IV CRITERIA

The schizotypal personality disorder is, according to the DSM-IV,
characterized by a pervasive pattern of social and interpersonal deficits
marked by acute discomfort with, and reduced capacity for, close
relationships as well as by cognitive or perceptual distortions and
eccentricities of behaviour. It begins in early adulthood and is present in
a variety of contexts, as indicated by at least five of the following:

1. Ideas of reference (excluding delusions of reference).
2. Odd beliefs or magical thinking that influence behaviour and are
   inconsistent with subcultural norms (e.g. superstitiousness, belief in
   clairvoyance, telepathy or "sixth sense", in children and adolescents,
   bizarre fantasies or preoccupations).
3. Unusual perceptual experiences, including bodily illusions.
4. Odd thinking and speech (e.g. vague, circumstantial, metaphorical,
   overelaborate, or stereotyped).
5. Suspiciousness or paranoid ideation.
6. Inappropriate or constricted affect.
7. Behaviour or appearance that is odd, eccentric, or peculiar.
8. Lack of close friends or confidants other than first-degree relatives.
9. Excessive social anxiety that does not diminish with familiarity and
   tends to be associated with paranoid fears rather than negative
   judgements about self.

These symptoms appear not exclusively during the course of schizophrenia, a mood disorder with psychotic features, another psychotic
disorder or a pervasive developmental disorder.

If criteria are met prior to the onset of schizophrenia, add "pre-morbid",
e.g. "schizotypal personality disorder (pre-morbid)".

In the ICD-10 a comparable personality disorder does not exist.

With the schizotypal personality, the accent lies on the peculiar
characteristics and the cognitive—perceptual disturbances. There is only
one criterion for relationships (8). All other criteria appear to point to

symptoms rather than to personality characteristics. So the sum total of symptoms, while stable, present leads to the diagnosis Schizotypal Personality Disorder.

The schizotypal personality disorder is the youngest shoot on the stem of Cluster A. It has a shared history of origin with the borderline personality disorder. In the 1970s one of the ways the borderline concept was used was to point out that psychopathological characteristics were genetically related to the schizophrenia spectrum. Rosenthal and Kety (1968) used the "borderline schizophrenia" concept in this respect. Towards the Axis I disorder schizophrenia as well as towards the Cluster B disturbance borderline personality disorder, the demarcation of the schizotypal personality disorder is a problem. A borderline concept that also offered room for characteristics which look like schizophrenia was considered much too broad.

In part because of this, the schizotypal personality disorder came into existence as an independent category. It has been based in part on a genetic relationship with chronic schizophrenia, but is meant to emphasize chronic psychotic-like phenomena.

Siever, Bernstein & Silverman (1991) gave an overview of the state of affairs, directed toward these demarcation problems of schizophrenia on the one hand and in particular the borderline personality disorder on the other.

In relation to the borderline personality disorder the problem of differentiation appears especially if there are psychotic-like symptoms with the borderline patient. In 50% of cases, according to Zanorini (cited by Siever, Bernstein & Silverman, 1991), overlap has been found. The thought here is that with the borderline patient these psychotic-like symptoms appear in the context of affective symptoms such as depression, aggression or fear. With the schizotypal patient this is more continuous and apart from affective phenomena. The traffic warden shows a serious schizotypal structure. Manifest psychotic break-throughs appear to be present. This type of patient does not easily seek help on their own or through referral. In the case described above, an assessment was done that was not asked for by the patient but rather the patient was referred for diagnosis. We encounter this type of patient in in-patient rather than out-patient units. In our clinical experience over the last 15 years in primary health care, we have come into contact with no more than a handful of schizotypal patients, and often these were comparatively less severe cases.

The different studies express social isolation, strange speech, peculiar behaviour, suspicion and paranoia as central to the disorder. Overlap is also noted with obsessive-compulsive and the avoidant personality disorder. In the first contact of the out-patient with the clinic secretary, a schizotypal patient can make a strongly compulsive impression, elaborating at length, worrying and brooding. The more schizoid characteristics often only manifest themselves when contact has existed for a longer time and there is a basis of confidence present. Here the suspicion that characterizes these patients plays a big role. In contrast with the case of avoidant people, the social fear does not diminish with increasing familiarity with those who evoke fear.

There exists a large overlap with depressive disturbances. Siever, Bernstein & Silverman (1991) state that 51% of patients with a severe depression (major depressive disorder) are also diagnosed with schizotypal personality disorder. In a follow-up study by McGlashan (1983) it was evident that after 15 years, 55% of the schizotypal patients were diagnosed with schizophrenia. From a diagnostic viewpoint, it is important to investigate and to observe that patients who appear schizotypal may actually be in the process of developing a schizophrenic break. Patients for whom schizotypal symptoms are found among relatives are more often diagnosed with chronic schizophrenia. These data seem to indicate that schizotypal symptoms may be present for a long period and ultimately lead to a schizophrenic break. The genetic component appears to be strong here. In other cases, the diagnosis of borderline is likely to be more accurate.

In view of these data, and all the more since symptoms are listed in the DSM criteria, it might be better in future to place the entire clinical picture on Axis I and classify patients under schizophrenia disorder. To date, this proposal is also supported by biological studies and studies on treatment effects.

CHAPTER 2.4   The antisocial personality disorder: the labourer

A 30-year-old man reported for a psychological examination because resuming work after a period of more than six months' sick leave had not been successful. He is employed as a labourer in the packing industry. In connection with treatment for alcohol and gambling addiction, he ended up on sick leave. He quit treatment, however, and his complaints persisted. Gradual work resumption on the basis of work therapy was not successful, however, as appointments regarding the matter were not kept. When present, his functioning is good.

FIRST IMPRESSION

The labourer arrives 25 minutes late for the appointment. He claims to have been held up by a traffic jam. In the contact, he makes a co-operative, friendly impression. He is small in stature and athletically built. He smokes constantly. He does not appear to have a mood disorder or to be bothered by neurotic complaints. His orientation in time, place and person is undisturbed.

SYMPTOMATOLOGY AND PERSONALITY

The two most important problems which the labourer mentions are gambling addiction and alcohol abuse. Gambling occurs at intervals. When he feels good he does not gamble, but as soon as he feels worse he gets "a haze before his eyes" and starts a period of gambling. He does this in casinos and in gambling halls. He continues for the entire night and in the morning is already waiting until he can go to a slot-machine. The gambling addiction became serious five years ago; before that it was present, but to a lesser degree. For the last six months, he has had a contract with a debt mediator to make payments in instalments for his debts. These debts amount at this time to about £6000.

His drinking problem is more constant. He cannot go a day without drinking beer and says he drinks about 2 pints daily. Sometimes he drinks several six-packs as well as all the hard liquor he can obtain. He began drinking alcohol at the age of 15, and had his first accident driving a moped when under the influence of alcohol at the age of 16. He ran over the edge of the road and was in a coma for six weeks, and also had a double leg fracture. Later he was in another accident which he caused and for which he was also found guilty.

Moreover, what is apparent from the examination is that the labourer has memory and concentration problems. There appears to be a great deal he can no longer remember, things which happened long ago as well as recently. For example, he no longer knows what kind of jobs he has had over the last ten years. His concentration is problematic, and as soon as he wants to do something he takes on too much at once. He cannot plan well. His thoughts drift away from what he is doing and because of this he becomes confused.

He does not mention neurotic symptoms that can be classified, in the sense of anxiety disorders, obsessive-compulsive disorders or psychotic symptoms. His mood changes, he has periods when he has the feeling that he can take on the entire world and at other moments feels miserable. These complaints do not meet the criteria for a manic-depressive condition, however. The worst moments trigger his gambling behaviour and alcohol abuse. During moments when he has consumed a great deal of alcohol he would, according to his wife, do crazy things, such as bang his head and hands against the wall. He cannot remember doing this, however.

BIOGRAPHY

He was the fifth child in a family of six children. He has nothing to tell about his childhood. He passed all years in both elementary school and technical high school. In addition to the electro-technical direction he took, he also followed a training in car mechanics.

He describes his family of origin and the atmosphere in his parental home in positive terms. His mother is still particularly important to him. He says he was never hit as a child. His father worked as a labourer on the railway and was constantly active building railways. His father died of cancer when the boy was 15. He remembers little of that period and mourning does not appear to have taken place.

During elementary school he repeatedly played truant. He was badly behaved in other ways but this did not go as far as stealing. During vocational high school there was a similar pattern, but he denies stealing or using drugs.

With the onset of puberty, he developed a strong interest in money and alcohol. From that time on he was away from home a great deal and went to many local fairs and discos. At the time his father died, he was absent from home a great deal and his chief concern was that now he would not get a moped. Shortly afterwards he turned 16 and had his first accident under the influence of alcohol. After his technical education, he became a "jack of all trades and master of none". The jobs he had were as painter, taxi driver and barge captain.

When he was about 17, the labourer became involved in a fight; he pulled out a knife and nearly stabbed his opponent to death. For this he was convicted.

He became acquainted with his wife 11 years ago. Her parents did not approve of him. She had many problems at home; she left and the young couple went to live in a trailer home. They married after they had known each other for five years and in that same year their first child was born. Two years later the second child followed.

The marriage has experienced serious difficulties related to his gambling problems and alcohol abuse. He has had other relationships with women and often visits prostitutes.

In his current work he has to operate a machine. He says he is not able to do this now as a result of his concentration problems. In itself, he likes the work. He prefers to work at one of the branches of the company rather than another where he was employed before his sick leave. He prefers doing shift work, particularly the night shift.

Alcohol and gambling problems are not present with his brothers and sisters, nor did his father and mother have such problems. His mother never remarried, but does have a boyfriend. The condition of her health has deteriorated owing to a cerebral haemorrhage. It appears that the rest of the family has found more equilibrium in life. In this respect, the labourer feels like an outsider. In his wife's family, problems are constant: many fights and divorces. He often becomes annoyed over this and concocts plans to give a thorough beating to one of the family members.

He has had three short hospital admissions for his addictions. Each time he left the programme prematurely, and he dreaded the stay in hospital. He also believes that he can solve his problems on his own, but fails time after time.

PSYCHOLOGICAL TESTING

On the intelligence test with the help of the WAIS, the labourer scores a verbal IQ of 88, a performance IQ of 100 and an average IQ of 92. This puts his intelligence in the area of "low–average", in which verbal abilities score (statistically significantly) lower than logical analytic ones. On this test there are no indications of cognitive deterioration and there is no clear indication of alcohol abuse either. He is observed to have very limited general knowledge, limited verbal ability and a limited conceptual world. Arithmetic skills are remarkably good. No serious memory, concentration or imprinting problems are apparent from the examination. No deviations are evident either from the administration of the Bourdon Wiersma Test or the 15 Words Test.

The MMPI profile shows the following scores: L = 55, F = 59, K = 59. Scale 1 = 62; Scale 2 = 68; Scale 3 = 77; Scale 4 = 80; Scale 5 = 53; Scale 6 = 62; Scale 7 = 61; Scale 8 = 61; Scale 9 = 69; Scale 0 = 65. K correction has been used. The 4–3 code (*Psychopathic Deviate* and *Hysteria*) is, according to Graham (1990), characterized by chronic intense anger. Periodically aggressive breakthroughs occur. People suffering from this blame others for their difficulties and are very sensitive to rejection by others. Outwardly, they can come across as reasonably adjusted socially, but inwardly they are rebels. Marital problems, poor sexual adjustment and promiscuity occur. At certain times they drink a great deal.

His NVM profile is as follows: *Negativism* above average (norm group of psychiatric patients) and high (normals); *Somatization* very high for both norm groups; *Shyness* low and below average; *Psychopathology* average (both groups); *Extraversion* also average. His stress resistance and capacity are normally developed according to this questionnaire. Under too much pressure, he reacts with a strong tendency to somatization and behaviour problems. The build up of his conscience is lacunary, and social anxiety and inhibition are lacking. From time to time he reacts with aggressive breakthroughs.

On the GLTS, he scores very high on two scales: *Sensitivity* and *Temperament*; average for *Authoritarian behaviour* and below average for social *Extraversion*, *Carefreeness* and *Masculinity*.

His story on the Four Pictures Test is short and describes the adventures of a homeless person. It is about a man who really wanted things to be different, but had too many problems at home. He receives shelter as soon as his state of neglect becomes serious and his condition critical. Then he is listened to and fed. He has a better daily schedule and watches tennis. People who used to say nothing to him talk to him again, and he once more belongs to society.

The personality examination presents the picture of an impulsive, stimulus-sensitive person with deficient capacities to control his own impulses sufficiently and constantly. He is always in search of a "kick" or distraction. He has the tendency to manipulate others to meet his needs. He has a self-image that is unrealistic and somewhat coloured by grandiosity. He has a strong tendency to dependent (addictive) behaviour and at the same time he denies his dependency needs. He tends to blame the causes of his problems on others. Projection takes the place of his own feelings of discomfort, there is a chance of unpredictable, cool impulse breakthroughs (acting out). The norms and values of society are ignored by him and the chance of asocial, antisocial and possibly criminal behaviour is great. He presents himself as rebellious towards (supposed) authority figures. Aggression is very close to the surface and it is difficult for him to regulate it as the aggression is also barely covered by anxiety.

DSM-IV DIAGNOSIS

Axis I   Pathological gambling
          Alcohol abuse
          Alcohol dependency
Axis II   Antisocial personality disorder
Axis III No diagnosis
Axis IV   Instable work and home situation
Axis V   Current GAF: 50
          Highest GAF past year: 50

DSM-IV AND ICD-10 CRITERIA

In the DSM-IV, the patient must be at least 18 years old and there must be evidence of a behaviour disorder that started before he or she was 15, if the latter is to be considered for the diagnosis antisocial personality disorder. Furthermore, there must be a constantly present pattern of ignoring and violating the rights of others since the age of 15, such as is evident from at least three of the following criteria:

1. Fails to conform to social norms with respect to lawful behaviour, as indicated by repeatedly performing antisocial acts that are grounds for arrest.
2. Irritability and aggressiveness, as indicated by repeated physical fights or assaults.
3. Consistent irresponsibility, as indicated by repeated failure to sustain consistent work behaviour or honour financial obligations.
4. Impulsivity or failure to plan ahead.
5. Deceitfulness, as indicated by repeated lying, use of aliases, or conning others for personal profit or pleasure.
6. Reckless disregard for safety of self or others.
7. Lack of remorse, as indicated by being indifferent to or rationalizing having hurt, mistreated, or stolen from another.

The occurrence of antisocial behaviour does not take place exclusively during the course of schizophrenia or manic episodes.

In the ICD-10, the dissocial personality disorder is mentioned. The following criteria must be adequately met:

1. Callous unconcern for the feelings of others.
2. Gross and persistent attitude of irresponsibility and disregard for social norms, rules, and obligations.
3. Incapacity to maintain enduring relationships, though having no difficulty in establishing them.
4. Very low tolerance to frustration and a low threshold for discharge of aggression, including violence.
5. Incapacity to experience guilt and to profit from adverse experience, particularly punishment.
6. Marked proneness to blame others, or to offer plausible rationalizations for the behaviour bringing the subject into conflict with society.

Persistent irritability and the presence of behaviour disorder during childhood and adolescence complete the clinical picture but are not required for the diagnosis.

A great deal of criticism has been levelled at the design of the criteria for the antisocial personality disorder. The DSM concept is especially geared towards the criminal who often functions at a low intelligence level. The more developed psychopath, who comes across as apparently adjusted, is not included in this classification and is not identified with it either. In criminal and forensic settings, the antisocial personality disorder of the DSM is overdiagnosed (Widiger & Corbitt, 1993). This leads to the psychologizing of criminal behaviour. Furthermore, the delineation of patients who abuse substances presents a problem. Many patients who are addicted display behaviour that veers rather quickly in the direction of antisocial patterns. Only the "outside" is noticed, however, and too little attention is given to underlying structures, such as the development of the superego, the integration of the superego in the personality, and the distance between the self and ego-ideal, which for antisocial personalities are, clinically speaking, fairly crucial. The former concept of psychopath was specially related to disorders in these psychic structures and did not focus mainly on the behaviour disorders that are so crucial today. However, impulsivity and acting out can be observed in many more personality disorders. Furthermore, the DSM-III-R offered a very extensive, and not a particularly practical, criteria set with all items and subitems for children and adults. All of this, however, does not alter the fact that where empirical research is concerned, support for this DSM concept is much greater than for most other personality disorders.

In the DSM-IV the criteria have been simplified. There are less criteria, they are often more precisely formulated and many examples have been left out.

CHAPTER 2.5 The borderline personality disorder: the bank employee

A 22-year-old male administrative assistant at a large national bank has been ill for the past six months. His complaints are of a psychological nature and thus he sought help at a mental health care institution. He was referred to a clinic specializing in the treatment of, among other disorders, the borderline personality disorder. Because of this referral, the bank requested a thorough psychological examination.

FIRST IMPRESSION

We see a lean young man with sleeked-back, medium-length hair and a pale complexion. His facial features are deeply furrowed and his face shows a lack of vitality and enjoyment of life. Interpersonally, he makes an emotionally detached, helpless impression. He does not appear capable of giving an independent and purposeful form to his life. He seems to struggle pathologically with the question: May I and can I exist? His self-esteem appears low and he communicates the feeling of not having control over his own life.

In his use of language, one notices he avoids using phrases such as "I want" and instead stereotypically replaces them with phrases such as "I must". The language he uses reflects not only fear and doubt but also inadequate autonomy.

Affect regulation of the examinee is disturbed; this is characterized by an inability to integrate more impulsive feelings. Animosity and gloominess seem, in combination with an incapacity for enjoyment, to characterize his world of experience.

It is not possible to establish a balanced emotional contact with him; the contact is disturbed by his impulsive reactions and anger.

SYMPTOMATOLOGY AND PERSONALITY

The bank employee shows an ample range of vague neurotic complaints that consist primarily of free-floating fear and mild multiple phobias. The symptoms are subject to constant fluctuations. The mental capacity and stability of the examinee seem low and he only appears to keep himself going on a daily basis by way of his intelligence, which seems to be good, and his acting-out behaviour. Periodically he has impulsive break-outs in the form of violent fits of anger and antisocial behaviour. In such a state he, for example, abused his 18-year-old girlfriend. He has suicidal tendencies. Also he has a past history of repeated misuse of alcohol. He says that he feels guilty about his antisocial behaviour and would like to make a change.

During the diagnostic interview, one notices the presence of primitive defence mechanisms, such as splitting, idealization and devaluation. He describes himself and other people as "totally good" or "totally bad", without integrating both extremes. The unstable relationships of the bank employee seem to have a similar black—white pattern. Furthermore, we see an inability to be alone and to experience rest and silence. Being alone leads to feelings of anxiety and confusion and is therefore actively avoided. Under stress, his defences become intensified, visible through splitting, his ego functions are then under pressure and his ability to integrate decreases. He is further characterized by a weak sense of reality, although his reality testing is intact. He is not familiar with the experience of having delusions or hallucinations. He worries about his condition, and interpretations that connect the material he produces in the present with his past experiences result in an improvement of his psychological equilibrium at that moment.

BIOGRAPHY

The bank employee has an elder sister with whom he maintains a regular and, according to him, good relationship. His father is in his late fifties and works for the government. He describes his father in rather derogatory terms: as a weak, unsure man who cannot stand up to his mother. According to the bank employee, his father's life as well as the children's were completely run by his mother and nobody in the family had a say. He said he was frequently maltreated by his father on his mother's orders; in the examinee's own words, his father would then use "a wooden walking cane with an iron point". His mother is now in her early fifties and is seen by him as an intelligent, caring, but at the same time dominant and demanding woman, who did not leave room for the input and autonomy of her two children. The atmosphere in the family was, in the experience of the bank employee, very bad; there were many fights and threats of physical violence, such as, "Go to sleep or I will beat your brains in with an axe." He describes himself as a fearful, depressed child who became more sneaky and aggressive every day: "It did not make any difference if I did A or B, you were beaten anyway." Child neurotic traits were frequently present: insomnia, complaints of a phobic nature, fear of the dark, bedwetting and nightmares.

As far as he knows, his mother's pregnancy was normal and the delivery was without complications. The latter took a long time and led to permanent infertility for his mother. In regard to developmental stages, he does not have any information.

He went through kindergarten and elementary school with ease. After elementary school he went to a preparatory school for the sciences, but failed after three years since he could not study at home. He then went to another secondary school from which he graduated. Next he studied economic administration. Eventually he quit because he no longer wanted to study.

He always had enough friends as a child. Since his early adolescence, however, contacts had become more difficult to establish and he did not manage to build up a stable circle of friends. At the age of 17, just before graduating, he went to live on his own after a family fight. His friendships were mostly of short duration and intensely coloured by idealization and devaluation.

In his current situation he finds himself relatively isolated socially. His emotional contacts are limited to his girlfriend who is four years younger and still living with her parents. This relationship is also under a great deal of pressure, especially since he has maltreated her on several occasions and he is not capable of an emotionally equal relationship. He had his first sexual experience with this girlfriend. He does not want or is not able to share further information concerning his sexual development.

His hobbies are soccer, handiwork and going out. He says he smokes, but not too much, and no longer uses alcohol in case this leads to outbursts.

His work history is limited given his young age. Before he was appointed at the bank, he worked for temporary employment agencies as well as in a restaurant. Now he is working as an administrative associate in stocks and he reports functioning well in this position. He is able to handle his work well as regards content and there are no serious conflicts with colleagues. As a result of his psychological problems, he is ill.

PSYCHOLOGICAL TESTING

With the aid of the shortened Groninger Intelligence Test (GIT), we obtain a general IQ of 139, a score thus reflecting a high intelligence. It was observed while taking the test that he had trouble concentrating on a concrete task.

To assess symptoms and personality, the following tests were administered: MMPI, Dutch shortened version of the MMPI (NVM), SCL-90, Performance Motivation Test (PMT), The Guilford-LTP Temperament Survey (GLTS), Rorschach test and the Four Pictures Test.

The L and K scales of the MMPI indicate values of 43 and 40, the F scale is 54. On the MMPI, he shows a two-topped profile: a *Psychopathic deviate* score of 86 and a *Paranoia* score of 82. This type of person, broadly speaking, is described as hostile, not to be trusted, irritable, immature and egocentric. These people usually show an inability to start intimate relationships. They normally exhibit a high degree of social maladjustment and blame others for their own failures. By blaming others, the person is prevented from developing insight into his or her own feelings and behaviour. Such people are very sensitive to real or imagined criticism by others. They avoid feelings of rejection and maintain a certain level of security primarily through manipulation of others. Substance dependency is frequently seen with this type of profile (Groth-Marnat, 1990; Berg, 1983).

Compared to normals, the bank employee's scores on the NVM are very high on *Negativism* and *Psychopathology*. On *Somatization* he scores above average, *Shyness* high and *Extroversion* average. These scores result in the image of a person who is vulnerable to stress and who at this moment is under a great deal of pressure and then becomes quickly aggressive. On the one hand, he regulates the tension through physical complaints and neurotic symptoms; and on the other he has a below-average score on shyness in comparison with the psychiatric population. This may indicate that his internal control mechanisms, his inhibitions dictated by the conscience function, show gaps. Antisocial behaviour can thus be the result.

On the GLTS he scores in the 10th decimal in terms of *Sensitivity*, 9 for *Authoritarian behaviour*, 9 for *Response tendency* and 8 for *Ability to respond*. On the low side are *Extroversion* (2) and *Carefreeness* (1). To conclude, *Masculinity* has a score of 5.

On the PMT, he scores 5 for *Performance motivation*, 9 for negative *Fear of failure* and 3 for positive *Fear of failure*. On the SCL-90, he scores low only on *Agoraphobia*, average on *Depression*, and on the rest of the scales high to very high.

A few notable answers on the Rorschach test are as follows:

- *Card I*: Two birds have another bird in their grip, they pull the victim apart (entire card, in reversed position). A mask of a wolf (entire plate plus white interpretation, reversed position).
- *Card II*: A face with a nose bleed (entire plate). Somebody whose head has just been knocked off (entire plate). A satanic figure (entire plate).
- *Card III*: A piece of the throat with a wound and blood (an unusual detail).
- Furthermore, the masks come back on cards IV, V and X. Then on card VIII he indicates the "insides of somebody" and on card IX "a child that has been born" (whole response).

From the semantic interpretation of this set of Rorschach cards, with the aid of the Comprehensive System developed by John Exner (1986), it appears that the subject has many feelings of tension and anxiety. He is extremely negative and this expresses itself in anger, substantially limiting his ability for social adjustment. His self-image is very negative; often such people feel damaged. Control of feelings is deviant with him: his thinking, decision making and behaviour are influenced to a high degree by his feelings. His way of solving problems is not characterized by inner consideration, but by interaction with the environment. Unlike most people he experiences a strong need for closeness to others. As a consequence, he has problems with initiating and maintaining deep relationships. His image of others appears formed more by his fantasy than by actual experiences. He surfaces from the test as someone who is strongly on guard, suspicious and who has some paranoid characteristics. To conclude, one observes in the Rorschach protocol that the bank employee uses intellectualization as a way of attacking emotional threat and stress. During the initial period of treatment, such a person shows a great deal of denial and avoids the confrontations of the person treating him or her.

The total picture which surfaces from the psychological testing is that of a young man with very high intellectual ability, many neurotic symptoms and a seriously disturbed personality. The feeling that dominates him is anger and he can be characterized as having a negative attitude. Together with a strong suspicion, bordering on paranoia, a disturbed affect regulation and a low resistance to stress, we are dealing with someone who is often a problem for himself and for others. In order to maintain his equilibrium, he uses denial and rationalization and perceives others and reality in a distorted way. When this fails, he reacts with acting-out behaviour. There is also a high degree of suffering and therefore a request for help.

DSM-IV DIAGNOSIS

Axis I   Generalized anxiety disorder
Axis II   Borderline personality disorder
Axis III   Medical factors: lack of data
Axis IV   Psychosocial stressors: profoundly disturbed family relation-
           ships, relationship problems and work problems
Axis V   Current GAF: 35
           Highest GAF past year: 45

DSM-IV AND ICD-10 CRITERIA

In the DSM-IV, the borderline personality disorder is described as a pervasive pattern of instability of interpersonal relationships, self-image, affects and control over impulses. It begins in early adulthood and is present in a variety of contexts, as indicated by at least five of the following:

1. Frantic efforts to avoid real or imagined abandonment (do not include suicidal or self-mutilating behaviour covered in criterion 5).
2. A pattern of unstable and intense interpersonal relationships characterized by alternating between extremes of idealization and devaluation.
3. Identity disturbance: persistent and markedly disturbed, distorted, or unstable self-image or sense of self.

4. Impulsiveness in at least two areas that are potentially self-damaging (e.g. spending, sex, substance abuse, reckless driving, compulsive eating. Do not include suicide or self-mutilating behaviour covered in criterion 5).
5. Recurrent suicidal behaviour, gestures, or threats, or self-mutilating behaviour.
6. Affective instability due to a marked reactivity of mood (e.g. intense episodic dysphoria, irritability, or anxiety usually lasting a few hours and only rarely more than a few days).
7. Chronic feelings of emptiness.
8. Inappropriate, intense anger or lack of control of anger (e.g. frequent displays of temper, constant anger, recurrent physical fights).
9. Transient, stress-related paranoid ideation or severe dissociative symptoms.

ICD-10 CRITERIA

In the ICD-10, two subtypes are described with the emotionally labile personality disorder: the *impulsive* and the *borderline* type. The following five criteria characterize the emotionally labile personality disorder in a general sense:

1. A marked tendency to act unexpectedly and without consideration of the consequences.
2. A marked tendency to quarrelsome behaviour and to conflicts with others, especially when impulsive acts are thwarted or censored.
3. Liability to outbursts of anger or violence, with inability to control the resulting behavioural explosions.
4. Difficulty in maintaining any course of action that offers no immediate reward.
5. Unstable and capricious mood.

For the classification of the impulsive type, at least three of the symptoms mentioned above must be present, one of which is criterion 2. For the classification of the borderline type, at least two of the symptoms mentioned above must be present, and in addition at least one of the following:

6. Disturbances in and uncertainty about self-image, aims, and internal preferences (including sexual).
7. Liability to become involved in intense and unstable relationships, often leading to emotional crises.
8. Excessive efforts to avoid abandonment.

9.   Recurrent threats or acts of self-harm.
10. Chronic feelings of emptiness.

In their overview of empirical research on the borderline personality disorder, Gunderson, Zanarini & Kisiel (1991) state that co-morbidity with other Axis II personality disorders is high. In studies based on the DSM-III-R borderline concept, this is seldom the only Axis II diagnosis. In clinical practice, however, this is often the case. For many clinicians, borderline remains synonymous with serious personality disorder, quite comparable with how this was worked out by early theorists (Stern, 1938; Knight, 1953). The psychoanalytic influence on the borderline concept was crucial, but also from an empirical perspective most research has been in this personality disorder.

There exists a strong overlap with the other Cluster B disorders. This applies especially to the histrionic personality. To a lesser degree, overlap has been found with the masochistic personality and with the avoidant personality. In respect to Cluster A, there is overlap with the schizotypal person. Since the DSM III-R, the overlap with the antisocial personality has been diminished. As far as Axis I is concerned, there is extensive literature that further examines the overlap with mood disorders and more recently with post-traumatic stress disorder. Trauma can lead to several of the criteria, such as unstable identity, self-destructive tendencies, and inability to bear abandonment. In studies on the family background of borderline patients, physical and sexual abuse frequently stand out. Abuse early in life can be an etiological factor of importance and could still obtain a place in the later versions of the DSM. In relation to post-traumatic stress disorder, with the borderline patient a recent source of stress is, in principle, lacking and it is of a decisive nature that a relatively stable personality pattern should be found to allow the borderline diagnosis.

In the DSM-IV, therefore, various criteria have been worked on in order to diminish the overlap with Axis I as well as the Axis II disorders. A new criterion has been added; many studies indicate that cognitive perceptual problems are indicative of borderline patients and therefore criterion 9 has appeared. With this addition, the time-old idea that has survived clinical practice is also met: that of short, reactive psychotic episodes.

CHAPTER 2.6 The histrionic personality disorder: the counter clerk

A 30-year-old counter clerk at a large bank had had trouble working with her colleagues for some time. She was referred for psychological assessment to determine whether she had problems in functioning. If so, the question was whether she could become aware of that and, ultimately, what the possibility was of her changing.

FIRST IMPRESSION

The counter clerk comes across as a well-groomed woman who looks her age. She displays no deviations in terms of time, place and persona. Her consciousness is intact. She seems very preoccupied with the impression she makes on others and makes an effort to look attractive. She seems to exercise a great deal of rational control in what she says and does, exhibiting no real spontaneity. She seems to be continually playing a role. She tries to gain an impression of what is expected of her and models her behaviour accordingly. Affect and mood are highly variable. Her facial expressions change continually and she maintains adequate eye contact. She comes to the session accompanied by her mother.

At the beginning of the assessment, she says that she has come at the request of her employer. She has no opinion about the assessment, but she characterizes herself as innately curious. She says she has not really considered why her employer wants her to be assessed.

When questions are directed more specifically towards her personality and feelings, she grows uncertain and vehement. Her emotions are superficial. At various points, she stands up to go, but does not dare leave.

SYMPTOMATOLOGY AND PERSONALITY

Initially, she says that she does not currently have any symptoms. Later she indicates that she has problems working with others. When asked about the possibility of her having a part in these problems, she becomes childishly angry and accuses the psychologist of trying to start an argument. She later indicates that she often cries, but immediately afterwards plays this down by pointing out that everyone does so. She seems confused when confronted with her behaviour and experiences during the assessment, which results in her saying things such as: "Bah, I want to leave. We are just going to argue. I don't want to talk about private matters."

Only feelings of insufficiency and sensitivity emerge as abnormally intense from the written symptom assessment. Furthermore, no clear clustering is recognizable.

Her personality is remarkable for its highly histrionic traits and underlying extreme uncertainty. She appears completely dependent on others to give form to her life, which she accomplishes through imitation. It seems that she scarcely has her own, autonomous personality. It is noticeable that she uses projection in the interactions; it appears that she wants to start an argument and then blame the other person for it. In addition, she consciously attempts to avoid subjects which she believes will elicit tension. She exhibits passive-aggressive traits that routinely take the form of mild acting-out behaviour. Her personality organization seems to function at borderline level.

BIOGRAPHY

The counter clerk has never been married, lives alone and has no children. She was born in the west of the Netherlands and is the second of four children (two girls and two boys). Her father was a civil servant and her mother a housewife. She maintains weekly contact with both parents. Nothing exceptional is known about the period of pregnancy and parturition.

She describes herself as a busy, restless child, "a quick and agile thinker". According to her, her mother is the boss in the family. She has a Dutch Reformed Church background. She remembers that even in kindergarten she wanted to give the correct answer to questions, but was often not allowed to, which she regrets very much. She was a good student in primary school. She took classical ballet lessons, but her mother made her stop. The family moved when she was 11 years old. Around this time, her father suffered a nervous breakdown. She refuses to elaborate on this.

After moving house, she felt uncertain and tried to win the favour of others. She longed for acceptance, but found it very difficult actually to obtain it. Her mother did not support her, but her father did. In essence, she always felt an outsider in the family. She gives little information about her brothers and sisters.

A few years later, the family moved again to another part of the country, where she was enrolled in junior general secondary education. She did not fail any classes and maintains that she got fantastic grades. She remarks that she was actually supposed to go to a senior general secondary (pre-university) school (on the basis of the National Institute for Educational Measurement test, given when she was 11), but this fell through because that type of education was not available in the town where she lived. She did, however, resume ballet, volleyball and catechism. She was reasonably happy then and also had friends. After receiving her junior general secondary education diploma, she attended the fourth and fifth senior secondary education classes, with good results.

She lacked a clear concept of what she wanted to do with her future and decided to enter nursing. She failed an in-service training programme, however, and felt rejected and deeply disappointed. The Employment Exchange referred her to an opening at a bank, where she applied and was hired for a counter clerk position. After being transferred away and then back, she did not work for about seven months owing to stress, after which she was transferred again. She describes the latter position as "fantastic" and believes that the manager was also satisfied with her performance. She indicates that there was also tension in this situation at first, particularly when working in a team was involved.

For the last two years she has attended regular sessions with a psychiatrist who occasionally gives her medication.

Her parents did not tell her about the facts of life. However, there was no taboo on discussing sexuality. She began to menstruate when she was 14 years old, an event which she had looked forward to. From that time on, she was interested in sex. She asserts that she likes sex and loves men. She had seven short-term relationships with men about ten years ago. Somewhat later she had a relationship with a man who was a few years younger than she was, which lasted about nine months. In retrospect, she thinks of it as a horrible period; her boyfriend at the time was allegedly "perverse" and forced her to participate in activities with which she did not agree. After this, she had two more short relationships with men, the last three years ago which lasted three months. Although she contends that she likes sex, she says that she had "not had any for the last few years". Regarding masturbation, she says: "I'm not into it." She has never lived with a man.

PSYCHOLOGICAL ASSESSMENT

Due to her vehement opposition, full administration of the WAIS was not possible. Eight subtests were administered, on which her effort and co-operation were variable. She scores 110 on the verbal IQ and receives an IQ of 125 on the Raven. Her intelligence seems, at any rate, adequate for her function. As often occurs in histrionic personality disorder, better performance on the action part is to be expected, in view of the difference between the Raven and the verbal portion of the WAIS.

The following tests were administered for symptom and personality assessment: SCL-90, MMPI, NVM, Performance Motivation Test (PMT) and SCT.

She scores mainly below average on the SCL-90. Her scores are high (in relation to the normal population) only on *Inadequacy* and *Sensitivity*.

Her MMPI profile (control scales: L = 50, F = 43, K = 61) shows two peaks (9−4 profile): the *Hypomania* scale is 74 (with K) and the *Psychopathic deviation* scale is 69. *Hysteria* is in third place with a score of 63 and *Paranoia* in fourth place with a score of 61. The *Masculine−Feminine* scale is remarkably low at 25, as is the *Social introversion* scale at 32. This profile is frequently found in histrionic personalities (Meyer, 1989). The 2−3/3−2 and the 3−4/4−3 profiles often occur in this type of personality. In this case, however, this is not applicable owing to the lack of symptomatic suffering. This person minimizes her problems and tries to place herself in a favourable light. Furthermore, she demonstrates exaggerated femininity which, in combination with a heightened *Psychopathic deviation* scale, indicates manipulation, hypersensitivity and underlying antisocial feelings. In combination with a heightened *Hypomania* scale and reduced *Social introversion*, she can be described as sensation seeking, impulsive, pleasure oriented, extroverted and energetic. She uses social techniques in order to manipulate others.

The description above is confirmed by the NVM. She combines an extremely extroverted disposition with a reduced resistance to stress and a tendency to acting-out behaviour as a result of a diminished functioning of conscience. Her personality pattern is highly ego-syntonic. Her energy level is high, there is considerable negative tension and she possesses insufficient neurotic and psychosomatic resistance, so that the negative tension is channelled into acting-out behaviour.

Her *Performance-motivation* on the PMT is very high (10), but is coupled with substantial negative *Fear of failure* (8).

In the Sentence Completion Test (SCT), she sketches a very positive and optimistic picture of herself. She idealizes her past and the here and now in this test. Somewhat greater uncertainty and fear of failure become visible in the second part of the test. She appears to be afraid of relationships failing in the future. Her great preoccupation with her appearance and envy of other women emerge. In an afterword, she wrote that for her this test is "invalid, due to the large number of questions". Half way through she grew tired and still had many items to complete. "That's why the answers are not exactly as they should or could be. The test provides a random picture," she assured the assessor. It seems as if her control of the situation began to lessen a little, so that the doubts and uncertainties she warded off became visible, which was definitely not her intention.

DSM-IV DIAGNOSIS

Axis I   No diagnosis
Axis II   Histrionic personality disorder
Axis III   No diagnosis
Axis IV   Dysfunctional at work, 3
Axis V   Current GAF: 69
            Highest GAF past year: 69

DSM-IV AND ICD-10 CRITERIA

Histrionic personality disorder is characterized in the DSM by a continuous pattern of exaggerated emotionality and attention seeking. It begins in young adulthood and remains a factor in all types of situation, such as is described in the following five criteria:

1. Is uncomfortable in situations in which he or she is not the centre of attention.

2. Interaction with others is often characterized by inappropriate sexually seductive or provocative behaviour.
3. Displays rapidly shifting and shallow expression of emotions.
4. Consistently uses physical appearance to draw attention to him- or herself.
5. Style of speech that is excessively impressionistic and lacking in detail.
6. Self-dramatization, theatricality, and exaggerated expression of emotion.
7. Suggestibility, i.e. easily influenced by others or circumstances.
8. Considers relationships to be more intimate than they actually are.

Histrionic personality disorder is characterized in the ICD-10 by the following criteria, three of which must be satisfied:

1. The same as criterion 6 of the DSM.
2. The same as criterion 7 of the DSM.
3. Shallow and shifting affectivity.
4. Continually seeks tension, others' approval and activities in which he or she is the centre of attention.
5. Inappropriate sexually seductive or provocative behaviour.
6. Immoderately concerned with physical appearance.

Egocentricity, pleasure seeking, constant desire for admiration, lack of consideration for others, feelings that are easily injured and persistent manipulative behaviour complete the clinical picture but are not necessary for the ICD diagnosis.

Histrionic personality disorder is the DSM and ICD version of the hysterical personality or hysterical character that has long existed in the psychoanalytic and psychopathological literature. The hysterical syndrome can even be traced back as far as Hippocrates. Freud developed two forms of this syndrome: conversion hysteria, such as anaesthesia and hysterical paralysis; and anxiety hysteria, which is expressed in numerous phobias. In addition to the area of symptoms, the specificity of hysteria was further sought in the dominance of a certain identification type and certain mechanisms (especially repression) active in the oedipal conflict, occurring primarily in the libidinous area of the phallic and oral phases. These libidinal fixations were supposed to be largely responsible for a patient's hysterical character traits. A distinction was made in later developments between healthier and severer degrees of hysteria ("So-called good hysteric", Zetzel, 1968).

In his description of the empirical state of affairs in preparation of the DSM-IV, Pfohl wrote (1991):

> The criteria for the histrionic personality disorder must be viewed primarily as a good-faith attempt to operationalize a rather polymorphic concept rooted in the descriptive literature and clinical tradition, rather than as a valid diagnosis whose implications are supported by empirical research. (p. 169)

Pfohl added that there is sufficient empirical support for internal consistency and also some external validity. The biggest problem is the overlap with other Cluster B personality disorders, primarily the borderline personality, but also the antisocial and narcissistic personalities (Pfohl, 1991). In the overlap with borderline disorder, we again recognize the seriously hysterical patient from the psychoanalytic literature. This "bad hysteric" functions at a borderline level, instead of, as is also possible, at a neurotic level. With regard to Axis I, it is noticeable that a somatic disorder is frequently diagnosed as well.

One criterion (no. 1) has been omitted and one (no. 8) added to the DSM-IV, in comparison to the DSM-III-R. There has also been some reformulation, aimed at creating more agreement between these criteria and those in the ICD-10.

CHAPTER 2.7

The narcissistic personality disorder: the biology teacher

A 48-year-old biology teacher had worked full time at a high school for 20 years. Three years ago, he underwent a coronary bypass operation following a cardiac arrest. Physically, he has been well since the operation. On the advice of his general practitioner, he reported sick last year since he would otherwise have been at odds with everything and everyone. The psychological examination began with the following questions: Is the examinee, in psychological terms, completely or partially suitable for his function, given the history of his illness? If so, which personality factors should be kept in mind?

FIRST IMPRESSION

The teacher is a normal, well-groomed, corpulent and sturdily built man who looks his age. Orientation in time, place and person is undisturbed. There seem to be no serious formal disturbances in regard to content of thinking or observation. His consciousness is clear. His affect is strongly suppressed and is difficult at first to understand. He shows a somewhat forced positive mood and a (narcissistic) tendency to bring about a certain equivalence in the interaction. He maintains good eye contact and he shows sufficient facial expression. There is no marked growth in contact during the session. The interaction is strongly coloured by rational and rationalizing thought patterns, sometimes in combination with a somewhat indifferent and defensive attitude. The information provided by him is descriptive in character and he shows no noticeable understanding of his own emotional life.

SYMPTOMATOLOGY AND PERSONALITY

He does not mention actual complaints of either a psychological or physical nature. Sometimes he is bothered by tachycardia and he relates this in part to his back problems. On the one hand, the teacher emphasizes the unpredictability of these complaints. On the other hand, he indicates that he has control over them: certain sudden movements bring on the complaints. The complaints do not frighten him; he says that he is "used to it". He adds, "There is, of course, the possibility of early death." Since the bypass operation he has been using about five different medications.

The teacher says that at the moment he feels well mentally. About the problems in the work setting, he emphasizes a lack of support on the part of management and because of this he says he is unable to function well, although he wants to.

From the written complaint examination no single factor is prominent, indicating that his level of psychological functioning is subjectively experienced as normal. The impression is that the complaints are barely recognized either.

An extreme defensiveness caused by anxiety and tension is observable in the teacher's personality. This defensiveness is characterized particularly by rationalizing and intellectualization. Deeper, more primitive defences are covered by those of a more developed kind. He appears to do his best to make a good impression. He appears to experience great difficulty in coming into contact with his emotional world (and that of others) and makes a somewhat alexithyme impression.

The teacher does not smoke and has two alcoholic drinks per day. He mentions no problems concerning his sleeping, appetite ("may be a little too good") and libido. The medication he uses is exclusively for his cardiac state.

BIOGRAPHY

The teacher has been married for 19 years and has two children of his own: a girl of 15 and a boy of 14. His wife has four children by a previous marriage who are all in their twenties now. He says that these children are also considered as his own. He was previously married at the age of 18; this marriage ended after approximately six months.

The biology teacher is the elder of two children. His sister is three years younger. He is not in touch with her: "Our personalities do not agree." He casually mentions, without providing details, that she has on several occasions attempted suicide. His father died of pneumonia in 1970 at the age of 72. He was a lawyer, employed by the government, who had studied theology, economics and English as well as law and had attended music school. His mother died seven years ago after suffering from Alzheimer's disease. She was a geography teacher.

He describes the atmosphere in his home as miserable. There was no room for emotions or the expression of feelings. His parents were simply not available. He does not remember ever being caressed or cuddled. Other people, such as his grandmother, aunt and a housekeeper, took over the parental responsibilities. He says, in this connection, that he created his own work or experience and describes how he often went out on his scooter to explore the city. Until high school he really did not have any friends and was somewhat withdrawn, although not really introverted. The family religion was Catholic, but not in a strict sense. His father beat him and as a child he regarded this as normal.

In elementary school (where his mother was also a teacher) he passed all his courses, but since he was not thought ready for high school he stayed in the seventh grade. He suspects that the school held him back because it did not have enough students. After elementary school he attended high school. He repeated eighth grade since he did not put in enough effort; he often went to parties at that time ("I was in a good environment") and formed part of a group. The "partying", as he describes his free time, caused him to fail exams as well. Asking about his father's opinion of this, he replied: "I was not there as far as my parents were concerned."

For about two years he worked for an electronics company as a commercial-economic employee. Then he was drafted into the army. After about six months he collapsed following a march and was sent home early for an extended leave of absence. Now, looking back, he thinks that all of these things may be connected to the presence of his currently diagnosed cardiac problems. However, the structure and rules of the military appealed to him.

After he had left the army, the teacher returned to his former employer for several months. Then he left the Netherlands to work in England in a hotel for a year doing a little of everything. "Outwardly, I had a good time, inwardly not." He returned to the Netherlands and moved in again with his parents. Through them he obtained a job in administration with a company. During this period, he tried again to obtain his high school diploma by taking evening courses. At first, this was not successful. He changed employers once more while remaining active in the economic administrative field. Now he stayed with the same company for three years. In this last period, he once again made an effort to obtain a high school diploma by attending evening school, this time with positive results.

He had come up with a plan to go to medical school but was rejected in three consecutive years. He then chose to study biology because of his interest in nature. This change from evening to day classes was difficult for him, particularly in the beginning.

After the last year of high school, at the age of 18, the examinee married an old girlfriend. The picture he sketches of this period remains very vague. His wife wanted to return to her mother after six months and he adds: "Maybe I was somewhat too conceited." It is interesting that he has a tendency to skip this period in a more or less chronological review of his story.

When he was in his late twenties, he met his present wife whom he married the same year. He moved in with her, quit studying and found a job as a teacher. Regarding the interrupted study he remarks: "Well, I really only had some practical time left to do." In connection with his work, he obtained several certificates. The couple moved several times after this.

The teacher indicates that his cardiac problems have to be seen quite separately from his work experience at school. He describes the problems in school as directly connected with the work setting and particularly with the headmaster; with other activities there are no problems. The problems arise from the relationship with students, and turn out as they do because he is not supported by the headmaster, as he admits. The headmaster, for example, considers that the presence of many parents at parent—teacher evenings is evidence of his poor functioning. Others would not agree with this conclusion.

His general practitioner has advised him to report sick permanently on the basis of hypertension. He indicates in this connection that irritations accumulate within him. Also, when there are acute problems in the class, he first tries to consider all the points rationally before reacting.

The teacher is not capable of giving a spontaneous, empathic image of his wife and their present relationship. The information he supplies appears full of gaps. Interestingly, also, his own children are not mentioned very often in his story, certainly if compared to the children from his wife's first marriage, who have done well. On enquiry, it appeared that his own children followed a special kind (lower level) of secondary education; this seemed to have to do with fear of failure in the daughter's case. His son may have consciously worked towards placement in special education. All these things are so trivialized by him that it is not possible to form an adequate picture of the problems.

Spontaneous information regarding his heart disease and operation is marginal. However, he admits having cried when he "watched along" during heart catheterization. Here again, in a narcissistic style none the less: "I knew, of course, very well what what I saw on the screen meant."

His picture of his social life is again full of gaps and is dominated by soccer. Once he thought of a career as a professional soccer player and therefore encouraged his son to try this. He says he has been involved as adviser of a soccer club at the soccer school. For the last 20 years the examinee has been active as a referee, but now only once in a while. He gets a kick out of the group and the interactions, clear rules and structure of the game also appeal to him. He says he has a broad range of interests and aims particularly at "taking in knowledge" and professional literature. He also mentions studying Italian. Doing nothing is difficult for him; he strives always to have plans, even for every evening.

The teacher likes walking and prefers doing this alone. He used to walk with some of his students. This came to an end when he heard that he was suspected of homosexual feelings; feelings that he absolutely denies.

When he was about 10 he became conscious of his sexuality and at the age of 13 he had his first sexual contact with a girl. Once a boy from his class "tried something", but the examinee turned him down.

PSYCHOLOGICAL EXAMINATION

On the intelligence test, with the assistance of the WAIS, he scores a verbal IQ of 127, a performance IQ of 132 and a total IQ of 132. His lowest scores are on *Comprehension, Digit span* and *Digit symbol*. The examination of his capacity gives the image of capacities in the area of "gifted". Performance capacities are even higher than verbal, although not statistically significant. Differential interpretation of WAIS subtests indicates a somewhat reproductive intelligence, and the comprehension capacity remains, relatively speaking, a little behind. There are no indications of cognitive deterioration. His IQ on the Raven is 130.

His scores on the SCL-90 are almost all very low in comparison to the norm group of psychiatric patients and below average in comparison to the normal population. On a questionnaire for compulsive behaviour, he obtains a heightened score.

His MMPI profile is a dejected one. L is 62, F is 36 and K is 60. Seven clinical scales are under 40, the others just a little above. The highest score is on scale 9: 50 with K correction.

His NVM can be interpreted also as a socially desirable profile: *Negativism* very low and low, *Somatization* very low for both norm groups, *Shyness* low and below average, *Psychopathology* below average and average, *Extroversion* average and above average. Except for the denial of complaints and tensions, this profile also indicates a deficit in the development of his social inhibitions and conscience function. If tension builds up for him, he is likely to react with acting-out behaviour.

On the Achievement Motivation Test, he scores the maximum for the *Achievement motivation*, very low (1) for negative *Fear of failure* and high (8) for positive *Fear of failure*.

On the Scale of Interpersonal Values, he scores high on *Conformity* and *Leadership*. He scores low on *Altruism* and *Independence*.

On the Sentence Completion Test, problems in his relationship with his father are expressed, of whom he seems to be very critical. He describes himself as a hardworking, amiable, intellectual person who likes to be appreciated for his achievements. His vulnerability shows up too, as well as the importance he attaches to money and success.

We see a narcissistic, somewhat obsessive-compulsive, very intelligent man. From the personality examination he comes across as extremely defensive but socially acceptable during the test examination. More primitive defence mechanisms (although covered by developed defences) make it possible to deny and negate tension, underlying aspirations and feelings of displeasure. He has an alexithyme attitude and finds it difficult to put into words his own feelings or those of others. His emotional world is difficult to penetrate and is masked by rationalizations and denials. Under pressure, he lacks intrapsychic inhibitions. Narcissistic tendencies colour the interaction continuously: the examinee enters, presenting himself as a scientist, he indulges in name dropping and creates an atmosphere of affective contact, but this does not *build up* at all and there is no affective openness.

Psychodynamically, we are presented with an affectively seriously deficient (early) youth environment and a related ambivalent relationship with his parents and in particular with his father. This relationship with his father, of whom he is highly critical, appears to have generalized towards other authority figures. His problem with the school headmaster must be understood in this context. Furthermore, he appears to be seriously frustrated in his passive needs for love and these are handled in a narcissistic way. In terms of the affective component, relationships seem to be surrounded by many problems that are coloured by ambivalence and may have an instrumental character in the underlying Cluster B traits. The teacher has essentially never experienced real, unconditional empathic acceptance, still has a strong need for this, and will also experience great difficulty in offering others a similar warm environment (in a non-material sense). In a way, it appears that the examinee has learned to be satisfied with surrogate relationships and false affectivity.

He has considerable feelings of inadequacy which he denies. Somewhat arrogantly, he demands acceptance by dropping the names of well-known and influential people. He tries in this way to underline his own self-worth and thus to escape negative feelings about himself. An underlying narcissistic attitude seems to be present, particularly in regard to his feeling of inadequacy in the area of intellectual development.

In a sense, he observes the external world somewhat subjectively and thus keeps it as free of tension as possible. The picture he creates of a well-functioning person does not quite fit with reality. If he were more himself, one would suspect that he lacked adequate defence mechanisms to keep impulsivity, vulnerability and feelings of tension under control.

The tendency that is present with the teacher to put aside feelings and irritation and to react later (rationally) appears to be a favourable trait in the light of the cardiac disorder. His need for structure is great. He has difficulty in building up and starting deep affective relationships. The craving for being a leader is strong.

DSM-IV DIAGNOSIS

Axis I   Mental factors that influence the physical condition
Axis II Narcissistic personality disorder
         Obsessive personality traits

Axis III   Status after coronary bypass
Axis IV   Work situation, 3
Axis V   Current GAF: 60
            Highest GAF past year: 60

DSM-IV AND ICD-10 CRITERIA

In the DSM-IV the narcissistic personality disorder is characterized by a pervasive pattern of self-aggrandisement (in fantasy or in behaviour), need for admiration and lack of empathy. It begins in early adulthood and is present in a variety of contexts, as indicated by at least five of the following:

1. Has a grandiose sense of self-importance (e.g. exaggerates achievements and talents, expects to be recognized as superior without commensurate achievements).
2. Is preoccupied with fantasies of unlimited success, power, brilliance, beauty, or ideal love.
3. Believes that he or she is "special" and unique and can only be understood by, or should associate with, other special high-status people (or institutions).
4. Requires excessive admiration.
5. A sense of entitlement, i.e. unreasonable expectations of especially favourable treatment or automatic compliance with his or her expectations.
6. Is interpersonally exploitative, i.e. takes advantage of others to achieve his or her own ends.
7. Lack of empathy: unwilling to recognize or identify with the feelings and needs of others.
8. Is often envious of others or believes that others are envious of him or her.
9. Arrogant, haughty behaviour or attitudes.

The ICD-10 does not recognize any comparable personality disorder.

Narcissistic disorders are widely recognized. Their source is mainly psychodynamic. Most literature on this subject has a theoretical or clinical character and only limited empirical research has been carried out. Although narcissistic disorders occur frequently in clinical practice, according to many clinicians, this does not apply to the diagnosis of the narcissistic personality disorder in the DSM as a single category. This has increased somewhat after the shift from the DSM-III criteria to those of the DSM-III-R (Gunderson, Ronningstam & Smith, 1991). The narcissistic disorders as diagnosed and treated by the clinician consistently deal with self-esteem. This can take two forms: grandiosity and inferiority (see also Chapter 3.1). Furthermore, narcissistic conflicts are certainly not always descriptively present and can be overlooked during a diagnostic examination. The narcissistic personality disorder in the DSM remains limited to a certain group of patients who usually also meet criteria for one or more other personality disorders of Axis II. In short, what the clinician calls a narcissistic personality disorder shows overlap with the DSM category of narcissistic personality disorder, but affects many more patients. At the same time, this category has been taken up in the DSM because it is so common in clinical practice.

With the arrival of the DSM-IV, changes have been brought about with respect to the DSM-III that originate particularly in comments from clinical practice supplemented with the limited existing empirical research. The criterion in which strong reactions to criticism are described has been removed. Demanding attention and fishing for compliments have disappeared as well. These traits showed too much overlap with other personality disorders. Criterion 9, arrogance and haughtiness, is new and easy to recognize in clinical practice. It seems likely that in the future many adjustments will have to be made to the description of this disorder.

CHAPTER 2.8　The avoidant personality disorder: the postal employee

A 32-year-old male postal service employee sought treatment on referral by his general practitioner. He had the feeling that he had collapsed; all his bottled-up emotions had become active. Now he wanted professional help with his problems. He had been on sick leave and was now considering resuming work.

FIRST IMPRESSION

The postal employee is a slenderly built, dark-eyed young man with a youthful appearance. He seems shy, his handshake is weak, and when confronted with others he turns his eyes and body away.

During conversation he formulates his sentences cautiously and reflectively. He speaks in a soft voice. He makes a predominantly gloomy impression, although without vital depressive characteristics. He is tense but becomes more at ease during the conversation. He comes across as very critical of himself and confesses his sins with an exaggeratedly guilty conscience.

He shows feelings of inferiority and gives the impression of being lonely. His word choice is cautious. He does not show intense feelings during the testing and irritation and aggression seem foreign to him. He makes contact but does not really start a relationship.

SYMPTOMATOLOGY AND PERSONALITY

The postal employee complains of being shy. He says he has always been able to cover this up reasonably well but now he has come to breaking point. He has kept pushing away his loneliness and gloomi-ness and he has never been able to relax, but now he cannot keep up this pattern any longer. He ended up on sick leave but now wants to pick up his work again. He says he feels guilty of cheating others. He has been constantly alone and felt lonely but has kept this hidden from others. He never went out: "I always say no to invitations, but I mean yes." Instead, he keeps busy with his hobby: gluing model aeroplanes. He says he is always assessing situations "behind closed doors". In his thoughts he is constantly thinking about how people view him. He does not look them in the face, even while at work behind the counter. He is lonely and he feels the need for contact, but he avoids this out of fear of rejection. He says he does not have any real friends and confidants but would like to have. He strongly desires more contacts, but does not dare to take any steps in that direction. He has turned down a promotion since the new position would mean that he would have to come into more contact with others.

Furthermore, he has a strong fear of going to the dentist. It has been 12 years since he has been for a check-up, even though he is in urgent need of dental work. He says he often puts things off until the problems accumulate and his anxiety level is very high. He appears to make an adequate distinction between his inner and outer world, himself and others.

Every morning he wakes up feeling anxious. He pushes away these gloomy feelings and instead worries about world problems. He admits an incapacity to relax and is inclined to check things in his home extra carefully. He says he has problems with his memory, especially his short-term memory. To conclude, he is bothered by ringing in his ears.

He describes himself as a shy person, lonely and with many suppressed problems. He has difficulty expressing feelings, especially feelings of anger. Furthermore, he thinks that he is very precise and a perfectionist. As soon as an object is even minutely damaged, he throws it away. He rarely asks others for advice as he thinks he can do everything alone.

The defence mechanisms he uses appear to be the following: repression, rationalization, isolation, reaction formation and externalization.

BIOGRAPHY

The postal worker was born the third child in a family of four children. He has a brother five years older and a sister two years older who both live away from home. He himself still lives with his parents, as does his other brother who is five years younger. The pregnancy and childbirth were normal. He developed quickly but infantile eczema began when he was six months old. He then spent a month in hospital. At the age of four he broke off a piece of his hip joint as a result of a fall and spent two months in hospital. During that time his mother was pregnant with his younger brother and he remembers that only his father visited him. At the age of six he had pneumonia twice. He dislikes many foods such as fish, yoghurt, salmon salad and all kinds of stewed dishes. Allergies play a role here.

He recalls few particulars about his upbringing. He finds that his mother is the most important person in his life and describes her as a nervous, decisive, very precise and very enterprising woman. She comes from a large family, has several sisters and maintains many contacts. If she is sad she cries. She grows stronger and stronger, which is especially expressed in her active social life.

During the first two years of elementary school he was rebellious. He got into a lot of mischief, broke windows and started fires. In the fourth grade a teacher "got a hold over him" and from then on things went much better in school and out. He passed all his courses and went on to secondary school. During this time he played the tough guy and was so vain that among other things he never wanted to wear his glasses. When he got a moped the engine was so tuned up after three days that he could ride it at 70 miles per hour. As a result of setting fire to grass on a dike, he came into contact with the police. He had enough friends at this time and although he did not make an effort with them, they sought him out anyway.

After graduating from secondary school, he went to a technical school for two years. Then he stopped studying electronics and went to work at a small installation company. He signed up for four years of military service because he "did not know anything better" and after that he ended up in the postal service.

An important event took place when he was 21 years old. His father bought a new house, the middle one of a block of three. This house did not have a back entry of its own. The neighbours had one but did not allow the family to use it. Problems with the neighbours followed and lasted for 20 years. As a consequence of this he thinks his father became manic-depressive, tried to commit suicide and then set their house on fire. His father was institutionalized and underwent psychiatric treatment. During that time, the examinee's mother and younger brother cried a great deal. He was in the army at the time and remembers feeling that it did not affect him at all. Since that time, however, others have told him that he "has let his head hang low". He thinks that he has undergone a character change.

When the problems intensified he first concluded that it was all because of work and on an impulse quit his job. When he came to his senses, a social worker assisted him in withdrawing his resignation.

The postal employee has never had a steady girlfriend but he says he would like one. In the course of the testing he told the female psychological assistant that he had become terrified of Aids as a result of an article in the newspaper which said that the HIV virus can also spread through vaginal secretion. He admitted having had contact with prostitutes about 30 times through a club. This sexual contact always took place with the use of condoms, but after reading the article he became frightened and does not sleep well at night. Also as a result of this fear of Aids, he has been able to overcome his dental phobia by exchanging one phobia for another, has been able to take the step of making an appointment and has begun treatment. He describes his visits to prostitutes as a general betrayal of his mother. He thus frequently mixes with the "underworld" and has a sense of guilt afterwards.

PSYCHOLOGICAL TESTING

With the aid of the WAIS, a valuation of his intelligence took place. He scores a general IQ of 127, verbal IQ of 121 and performance IQ of 130. The only exceptional score is a 3 in *Digit span*. During this subtest he apologizes because he cannot do it very well, and says: "I work with sounds, I am not very good at this." He also has difficulty with telephone numbers. Besides anxiety, restlessness and concentration problems, there are indications for organic causes perhaps related to his complaints of memory problems. Neuropsychological testing will eventually allow for further clarification.

For the purposes of personality testing, the following tests were administered: MMPI, NVM, Scale for Interpersonal Behavior (SIG), Assertiveness List, Four Pictures Test, SCT and Drawing Test.

The scores on the L, F and K scales of the MMPI are respectively 54, 66 and 40. The rather low K score can indicate a self-critical attitude and possibly also exaggeration of his problems (Graham, 1990). His profile is on the whole raised: the highest score he obtains is on scale 2 (*Depression*) 78; then with the K correction on scale 4 (*Psychopathic deviate*) 76; and on scale 6 (*Paranoia*) also 76. On scale 8 (*Schizophrenia*) 75;

scale 7 (*Psychasthenia*) 74; on scale 1 (*Hypochondriasis*) 73; and scale 0 (*Social introversion*) 71. The total profile evokes the image of somebody who is poorly adjusted to his social surroundings. Depressiveness and apathy are present. His tendency to withdraw from social relationships probably plays a role in his lack of intimate involvement with others. His attitude is cynical and resentful; fear and tension also occur frequently. Possibly he may have alternating periods of impulse breakthroughs, acting-out behaviour with gloominess, and a somewhat schizoid lifestyle. The latter is also connected to his excessive sensitivity and violent reactions to the opinions of others. Because of this he is cautious and finds himself in a constant state of anxiety. He feels alienated, misunderstood and not accepted by others. The elevated score on scale 4 is unexpected in a profile for this personality disorder, but is indicative that he still has energy that is being channelled into anger. The elevated score on scale 8 indicates his actual crisis; he is stuck, he feels rejected and withdraws from social connections (Meyer, 1989).

On the NVM, he scores high to very high on the *Negativity* scale based on norms for a psychiatric group and the general population. On the *Somatization* scale he scores average and high, on *Shyness* high and very high, on *Psychopathology* average and high and on *Extroversion* average. These test results show a man who is permanently under pressure and has many feelings of uneasiness. He comes across as a very shy, socially anxious man who has a great deal of avoidance behaviour and is tight-lipped. He handles stress through avoidance and withdrawal rather than by translating it into physical complaints.

On the Assertiveness List he scores mainly as unassertive.

In his story on the Four Pictures Test, he describes a main character who works very discontentedly in a shipyard. Together with his brother, he lives in a house where both are taken care of by a housekeeper. His younger brother is totally different in character, he does not work but spends his time playing tennis and maintaining contacts with friends, male and female. This brother has received the greater part of an inheritance from an aunt and it appears that the main character has missed out on the inheritance because he used to torment his younger brother constantly. The main character realizes, as he broods in bed, that he is guilty of this tormenting and that because of it he and his brother are far apart. He is obsessed by feelings of loneliness, guilt, anger and dissatisfaction with his existence.

In his Sentence Completion Test, his poor social life returns as well as his wish to bring about change in it. Feelings of guilt are related to his lies and his conceited attitude.

An overall picture emerges from the psychological testing of a man with a very good level of intelligence and with a very maladjusted behaviour pattern based on a personality disorder. He is gloomy and lonely and leads a withdrawn, schizoid existence. He is permanently under pressure and has many feelings of dissatisfaction, fear and stress. He is not capable of initiating and maintaining a meaningful intimate relationship. He desires it, yet avoids all steps in this direction because of fear of, and oversensitivity to, rejection. At intervals it is conceivable that he has impulse breakthroughs, perhaps connected with his visits to prostitutes.

DSM-IV DIAGNOSIS

Axis I   Social phobia
Axis II   Avoidant personality disorder
Axis III   No diagnosis
Axis IV   Slight dissatisfaction with work, poor relationships with family, 2
Axis V   Current GAF: 55, moderate problems in professional functioning and in contacts
            Highest GAF past year: 55

DSM-IV AND ICD-10 CRITERIA

In the DSM-IV, the avoidant personality disorder is described as a constant pattern of social inhibition, feelings of inadequacy and hypersensitivity to negative evaluation. It begins in early adulthood and is present in a variety of contexts, as indicated by at least four of the following:

1. Avoids occupational activities that involve significant interpersonal contact, because of fears of criticism, disapproval, or rejection.
2. Is unwilling to get involved with people unless certain of being liked.
3. Restraint within intimate relationships due to fear of being shamed or ridiculed.
4. Preoccupation with being criticized or rejected in social situations.
5. Inhibited in new interpersonal situations because of feelings of inadequacy.
6. Belief that one is socially inept, personally unappealing, or inferior to others.

7. Is unusually reluctant to take personal risks or to engage in any new activities because they may prove embarrassing.

In the ICD-10, the anxious (avoidant) personality disorder is described by six criteria of which at least three have to apply:

1. Persistent and pervasive feelings of tension and apprehension.
2. Similar to criterion 6 of the DSM.
3. Excessive preoccupation about being criticized or rejected in social situations.
4. Similar to criterion 2 of the DSM.
5. Restrictions in lifestyle because of need to have physical security.
6. Avoidance of social or occupational activities that involve significant interpersonal contact, because of fear of criticism, disapproval, or rejection.

The avoidant personality disorder first appeared in the DSM-III, but one can find similar descriptions earlier in the clinical literature. The terms that are used for it are, among others, phobic personality, anxious personality, detached personality, and the "need–fear" dilemma. As far as the form in which this disorder is moulded in the DSM-III is concerned, an empirical foundation is still lacking, as is a theoretical foundation, according to Millon (1990), even though this does not play a role in the DSM developments. In clinical practice and in rare studies, continuation of this personality disorder in the DSM is supported.

In the DSM-IV, there has been an attempt to reduce the problems of overlap with social phobia on Axis I and the dependent, schizoid and schizotypal personalities on Axis II by changes in criteria. A clinically relevant difference is the fact that the avoidant person desires relationships with people but does not dare to initiate them. In contrast, the dependent person initiates relationships but does not dare to let go of them. This evokes associations about genesis that are confirmed by clinical experience. The dependent person appears to have found too little stimulus in early childhood to start the separation–individuation process. Dependency in the form of a symbiotic bond seems to have been too good and too satisfying. These patients often express the following. "We were always pampered, didn't really have to do anything ourselves, we were always taken care of." With the avoidant person, however, it looks as if the dependency has become disturbed. Traumatic experience evokes avoidance out of fear of going through the same trauma again. For clinical practice, this is an important distinction that obtains a place in the therapeutic relationship.

Many of the DSM and ICD criteria of the dependent person and avoidant person refer to comparable problems, clinically speaking. In the out-patient clinic especially we often see patients with anxiety complaints and perceive in their personality dependent and avoidant traits.

A person suffering from the schizoid personality disorder is indifferent to interpersonal relationships and therefore not anxious like the avoidant person. Nor do schizoid people devalue themselves much. Making this distinction presupposes in many cases a good clinical study of the patients concerned. It does not seem too far-fetched to suppose that with the schizoid patient traumatization has been so intense that the wish for affection and closeness has also been destroyed. This could be the result of more serious traumatization in early childhood.

Avoidant personality characteristics can also be found in patients who function more deeply on a borderline or psychotic organization level. At first they may present themselves as developing a neurosis, but in the course of the treatment or with more intense psychodiagnostics one encounters qualitatively different problems. The diagnostician has to stay on the alert for this.

CHAPTER 2.9   The dependent personality disorder: the cashier

A 23-year-old cashier came for treatment with the following symptoms: hyperventilation, tension complaints in her stomach, fear of being alone, fear of illnesses and a phobia about bridges. She had the impression that the complaints became worse at moments when she felt irritated and could not get rid of this irritation. As a result of her complaints, she had taken four months' sick leave from her job.

FIRST IMPRESSION

The cashier comes across as a normally groomed young woman who makes a shy and anxious impression. Her orientation in time, place and person is undisturbed. Her awareness is clear and there are no serious thought or perception disturbances. Her mood is sombre, she tends to seek support in the contact and she seems lonely. She talks easily and a great deal but her topics of conversation are superficial ones. She seems very sensitive to what takes place in the contact, appearing to be afraid of rejection in particular. She avoids anything that might lead to a conflict in the contact.

SYMPTOMATOLOGY AND PERSONALITY

At the end of the previous year the cashier felt she was becoming ill while at work. She decided to go home and stepped into her car. During the drive, she became short of breath and felt warm. She panicked. Influenza was diagnosed and she stayed at home for a week. The panic returned every time she thought of getting into the car again. The anxiety attacks extended to her home situation, particularly in the evening. At present, she suffers an anxiety attack once or twice a week. Apart from the panic she hyperventilates and she does not dare to be alone. She mentions that she has strong "anticipatory anxiety"; she repeatedly expects to become anxious again and owing to this she feels constantly tense and restless inside. She tries to regulate her breathing through abdominal breathing and she obtains help from a physiotherapist to become more relaxed. She often feels dizzy when getting up. She has difficulty staying in a crowded auditorium; she feels the need to leave. The phobia about bridges varies; one time it is intense, another it is much reduced. She is also afraid of large dogs.

She reports that she does not like the environment at work. Because of the poor work environment, there is a high turnover of personnel. Behind the cash register, she often feels hurried and then becomes obsessed with leaving: "I must get out of here."

She describes herself as a busy, but cheerful type, although she can be quiet as well. She prefers to have people around her all the time and she is constantly looking for company. She asks a great deal of advice from others and especially from her mother. She finds it very difficult to accept criticism and she cannot bear quarrelling. She does not mind being the centre of attention. She used to go out a great deal but now she feels down and does this less. She tries to stand up for herself, even though she finds it difficult. She has a tendency to pass responsibilities on to others and she does not take any initiatives herself.

She smokes a great deal and she uses several homeopathic medicines to calm herself.

BIOGRAPHY

The cashier comes from a family of two daughters, of which she is the younger. She has nothing much to say about the pregnancy and childbirth. She considers she had no child neurotic traits: "I have a caring father and mother," she declares. She describes the environment she grew up in as pleasant, everything was fine and she felt cheerful and happy. As a child, she was always busy doing things, wanted to do everything at once and laughed a great deal.

Her father worked as a bus driver. When he was in his early fifties, he had a nervous breakdown as well as back problems. This lead to his receiving disability pay for medical reasons. From what she says it can be concluded that her father reacted to his disability with depression. He started drinking then and smoked a great deal. He would reproach his wife and daughters a great deal, especially on Sundays. This led to a tense atmosphere at home and the cashier withdrew from her family, went to bed early and worried about the situation. Later, she increasingly sought safety outside the home. She often felt ashamed of her home situation. Her mother had stomach complaints at this time and suffered from gallstones. Her sister did not have any complaints.

The home she grew up in had thin walls. At night, in particular, she could follow the fights which the neighbours were having. She would always feel very frightened that the quarrels would come to blows. As a child she visited these neighbours a great deal and they also fought in her presence. She hated this. Once she could hear a neighbour being thrown down the stairs by her husband. Now when she sees people quarrelling she starts crying. She herself almost never gets into a quarrel.

In the first grade in elementary school, it was already observed that she was too slow and therefore she was placed in special education. She can remember that it was very difficult for her not to be able to see her teacher any more. She attended, for one day only, a special school in a large city. She did not feel at home there and so she was placed in a school in the neighbourhood that was familiar to her. She still played with her girlfriends from the previous elementary school.

She suffers from feelings of inferiority with respect to her special education. She often has the feeling that she cannot keep up with others. In her view, other people can do everything better than she can. After elementary school she attended a special secondary school for administration. During that time, she did not know which direction to choose and so she first chose the domestic side and later worked in stores. She could barely keep up. The practical experience was bothersome and she felt she was treated as an inferior. She was being used for duties that were not part of the work experience: cleaning toilets, doing the dishes and vacuum cleaning. She had the feeling that the boss did not like her and she responded to this by doing her best in an attempt to win his approval.

She worked in various stores and took a course in baking. She kept looking for a permanent job, as most of the jobs she did were temporary. She tries to avoid tension in her work situation by adapting as well as possible. For the past year and a half, she has worked in a supermarket where she has also developed complaints. In this store, she has worked in different departments. She considered working behind the cash register as a challenge, but after some time the pressure of the increasingly long lines of people became too much for her. Because of absence owing to illness, she missed out on the chance to become head of cashiers. Initially, she felt at ease in the group of employees. However, the high turnover rate among personnel eventually caused her to feel like a stranger and outsider. She had trouble adjusting to the group all the more when a colleague got the job she herself had wanted. Criticism of her behaviour by her boss led to her ending up on sick leave.

Sexuality was not discussed in her family and she cannot remember being curious about it. She received sex education in school. At home the risks of sex were pointed out. She has a boyfriend who is five years her junior. She describes him as a gentle young man who also has psychological difficulties; he is quick to say if he does not know something, he cannot make decisions and also cannot bear fighting. After a year of going steady, their relationship took on a sexual dimension as well. A short previous relationship had ended and as a result she was for a time extremely upset. She felt very lonely at that time as well.

PSYCHOLOGICAL TESTING

The intelligence testing, with the use of the WAIS, shows a verbal IQ of 91, performance IQ of 116 and a total IQ of 102. This is an average score with a very big difference between the verbal and performance scores. Her poor school education is playing tricks on her here. Her lowest score is on *Information* and the highest on *Object assembly*.

The MMPI-2 profile does not offer a noticeable difference in comparison to the norm group. The L and K scales are elevated: 55 and 54 respectively. The F scale is 42. The clinical scales are on, or just under, average. Scale 9 is the highest, 56; and scale 6 the lowest, 42. In view of the low F and the relatively elevated L and K scales, we can conclude that she has the tendency to ward off psychological problems. She appears to show some sort of insensitivity, perhaps comparable with what is understood by alexythymia in the area of perception of emotional processes. This is expressed in the form of the defence mechanism of denial.

The NVM profile is as follows. *Negativism* is low in comparison to the general population and very low in comparison to the psychiatric group. *Somatization* is very high and above average; *Shyness* high and average; *Psychopathology* low and very low; and *Extroversion* average and above average. The cashier emerges out of this profile as somebody with a somatization profile: she reacts to stress by developing somatic and psychosomatic complaints. At this moment the pressure on her is low, probably because she is not working. If she were to work, however, and tension were to increase, she would immediately develop an array of complaints. She is poorly adjusted to her social environment, in particular. The relatively low score on *Negativism* and *Psychopathology* can possibly be interpreted as defensiveness and denial as well, compared to what was observed on the MMPI-2.

From examining her social skills with the help of two assertiveness questionnaires, she appears to be particularly afraid of aversive social stimuli. She has great difficulty in accepting potentially critical comments from people in her social environment. She is afraid of rejection, is extremely fearful of conflicts, and always wants to be considered agreeable.

The drawings of people she has made are noteworthy because she does not draw adequate shoulders and a chest. She draws little figures. Her drawings of trees and a house are particularly pleasant and cheerful, with a great deal of context, as well as very child-like and idyllic.

On the Four Pictures Test, a male protagonist is central to her story, and he is "probably lonely and sad". He meets friends, they go out for a day, shopping, eating, drinking and playing tennis. Nobody wants to win because the one who wins has to cook. Once again, eating, drinking and chatting are central. It is a superficial, childish story in which oral themes dominate. The satisfaction that is offered by the companionship of a group and by eating, drinking and talking together takes the place of unpleasant feelings that seem to belong to being alone. In the Sentence Completion Test, the phrases "being nice", "honesty", "nice people" and "doing fun things together" often occur. There is a lack of differentiated emotionality in this material.

The personality testing reveals a verbally low average, practically well-developed, childish and dependent young woman who is bothered by various anxiety complaints, including those related to physical ailments. The adjustment to the social environment is disturbed by her dependent and conflict-avoiding personality traits. She is unable to cope with the demands and problems that an average working situation involves. She escapes into illness and seeks consolation in a protective relationship. She has no insight into her problems and cannot profit from reflecting upon her feelings. Insight is lacking into the manner in which she has contact with others and the problems she has with this. She tends to regard psychological help as a source of support and an opportunity to be dependent and let herself be guided. She has a tendency to avoid her problematic work situation.

DSM-IV DIAGNOSIS

Axis I   Panic disorder with agoraphobia (moderate)
Axis II   Dependent personality disorder
Axis III No diagnosis
Axis IV   Mild; unstable work situation
Axis V   Current GAF: 60
          Highest GAF past year: 70

DSM-IV AND ICD-10 CRITERIA

In the DSM-IV, in order to make the diagnosis dependent personality disorder a person must have a pervasive and excessive need to be taken care of, which leads to submissive and clinging behaviour and fear of separation. This begins in early adulthood and is present in a variety of contexts, as indicated by at least five of the following criteria:

1. Is unable to make everyday decisions without an excessive amount of advice and reassurance from others.
2. Needs others to assume responsibility for major areas of his or her life.
3. Has difficulty expressing disagreement with others because of fear of loss of support or approval. (Note: do not include realistic fears of retribution.)
4. Has difficulty initiating projects or doing things on his or her own (due to a lack of self-confidence in judgement or abilities rather than lack of motivation or energy).
5. Goes to excessive lengths to obtain care and support from others, to the point of volunteering to do things that are unpleasant.
6. Feels uncomfortable or helpless when alone, because of exaggerated fears or being unable to look after himself or herself.
7. Urgently seeks another relationship as a source of care and support when a close relationship ends.
8. Unrealistic preoccupation with fears of being left to take care of himself or herself.

In the ICD-10, the dependent personality disorder is described by six criteria of which at least three must be applicable:

1. Encouraging or allowing others to make most of one's important life decisions.
2. Subordinating of one's own needs to those of others on whom one is dependent, and undue compliance with their wishes.
3. Unwillingness to make even reasonable demands on the people one depends on.
4. Feeling uncomfortable or helpless when alone, because of exaggerated fears or inability to look after oneself.
5. Preoccupation with fears of being abandoned by a person with whom one has a close relationship, of being left to take care of oneself.
6. Limited capacity to make everyday decisions without an excessive amount of advice and reassurance from others.

In comparison with the DSM-III-R, various reformulations have been made of the description of the most important traits of the disorder, as well as the criteria. The strong need for care, which leads to dependent and submissive behaviour, is now placed centrally. One criterion, "easily hurt by criticism or rejection", has been omitted. Conceptual overlap of the DSM-III-R existed in particular with the borderline (fear of desertion, even though the reaction to desertion is different), the avoidant (sensitive to criticism, feeling inadequate, need for reassurance), and the histrionic (need for reassurance and approval) personalities. Empirical research supports this overlap (Hirschfield, Shea & Weise, 1991). The reformulations have the objective of taking this into account. The question remains whether these adjustments of the description and the criteria will decrease the strong overlap with other personality disorders.

In clinical practice, one often finds that patients with a dependent personality disorder ask for help as soon as they have developed anxiety complaints. Dependency on others goes back to the attachment process of parent and child during childhood. This process is settled in the childhood years and the pattern that is formed here repeats itself in later intimate relationships. The separation—individuation process is also supposed to go through an initial phase in the childhood years. In this complex emotional process much can go wrong, conflicts can arise, ambivalent attachment patterns can be formed and insufficient autonomy can be developed. Anxiety leads to the fact that conflicts do not come to light but are instead suppressed. Extreme dependency is one of the ways of avoiding anxiety and covering up emotional problems. The adolescent years offer the person a second chance to give form to the independence, separation and individuation processes. With the dependent personality disorder, we can often observe an inadequate separation from the external parent figures as well as from the internalized images of the parents. Very strikingly the dependent personality has not learned to make productive use of the potential for aggression. Aggression is after all the breeding ground for the energy that makes separation possible, just as love enables us to (or forces us to) be dependent.

The disturbed separation process often expresses itself in a veiled form. When a disturbance of the actual intimate relationship takes place, a patient may develop one of the anxiety disorders as classified in the DSM. In fact, disappointment in the partner presents itself when the latter turns out not to be the source of satisfaction, support and love that one had wished for. Mostly this process is kept from conscious awareness by the person. In this case the attachment difficulties to one or both parental figures in childhood are repeated. A panic disorder or phobia bears witness to a relationship crisis taking place partly unconsciously in the present and the past. The dependency already existed but did not cause many problems since the relationship still seemed to be satisfying. Now that anxiety symptoms appear, the dependency becomes stronger. It was already stimulated by anxiety early on in life; now that the anxiety has none the less reappeared the tendency to dependency is also once again stimulated. Axis I and Axis II go hand in hand here, perhaps more than with other personality disorders from Cluster C.

CHAPTER 2.10 The obsessive-compulsive personality disorder: the social worker

For a period of two years a 40-year-old social worker had been increasingly absent from work owing to illness; this was related to complaints of being overworked. As part of psychological treatment, he had recently reduced his work time to four days a week. Since then, his treatment had ended. A psychological examination had been requested to see if at this time he was functioning at his full potential. The question at hand is what capacities he possesses at this time.

FIRST IMPRESSION

We see a well-groomed man who looks healthy and who looks his age. He makes a modest, submissive impression. Worry seems to dominate his emotional life. The social worker tries to do his best and to make a good impression. He minimizes his problems and his life appears to be in order. During the second testing day he presents a small piece of paper with written notes on it, in which he demonstrates aggression in a very controlled way and with which he tries to justify himself. In addition, he allows the examiner to see how much he is suffering. He says that in the period between the two days of testing he was extremely upset, worrying continuously and feeling guilty. Generally speaking, he adopts a co-operative attitude during the testing and contact grows between the examiner and client.

SYMPTOMATOLOGY AND PERSONALITY

The social worker mentions a series of symptoms: doubt, worry, perfectionism and a preoccupation with rules. He is rigid and persevering in emotional and material matters. When under examination, he tries to do everything as well as possible, making it difficult for him to complete everything.

During the clinical personality assessment we see an emotionally immature man who strengthens his dependent position by manipulative behaviour. He seems to struggle with the theme of "dependency versus independency". He is bothered by the fear of losing the love of his mother and father. Strangely, he consistently leaves decisions to others. He seems to prefer safety and security to independence. In the contact with him, an outspoken subservient attitude is noticeable. All of this, however, results in conflict. He tries painstakingly to make the rules and regulations at work his own and at the same time he resists them.

The social worker experiences a great deal of pressure and dissatisfaction because of his inability to change his compulsive behaviour. Moodiness and depression go hand in hand with feelings of inferiority and insecurity. His sleep is disturbed. He is aware of illness but has no insight into it. His defence mechanisms appear to be centred around repression and denial. In addition, we see the defence mechanism of reaction formation operating, namely where feelings of dependency are concerned. His worries and burdens can be forgotten by his presenting himself as comforter and helper in social contacts.

BIOGRAPHY

The social worker is the oldest in a family of four children. He has a brother and two sisters. Childbirth and pregnancy were normal, as were the stages of development. Child neurotic characteristics took the form of bedwetting. He has experienced the atmosphere at home as good.

His father died twenty years ago from a heart attack and is described by him as a "fellow who wouldn't hurt a fly" and at the same time as an authoritarian figure. His father's wishes were law. He thinks back to his father with a lot of pleasure and misses him. Just at the moment when he, in retrospect, could have built a friendship with his father, the latter died. His father had a high position in the civil service of the local town.

The picture that the examinee sketches of his mother remains remarkably vague. The social worker has continued living with his mother because, according to him, circumstances brought this about. His mother cooks for him and does the household chores. They do a lot of things together, such as shopping for groceries. According to him, his mother adopts a dependent position towards him. For instance, he has to do all the household administration and she does not make any effort to master this. He has had a girlfriend for five years now and his mother experienced this relationship in the beginning as a problem, although at the same time she says she is happy for him.

He cannot remember anything about kindergarten because he had asthma at the time and was thus frequently absent. Every year of elementary school he was moved to the next year's class on probationary terms. In the sixth grade he voluntarily stayed back a year. Next, he attended a special school to repeat two extra years of elementary school. At school he had continuously to push himself in order to keep up with the work tempo. It seems as if he was hindered in his school performance by a certain degree of compulsiveness. Although he had asthma, he says he was treated as normal and not as a problem child. He reports having a "mighty good youth". He was never teased and had a lot of friends. He was popular and entertaining in the company of others as he could imitate many actors.

For many years he put off starting an intimate relationship with a woman. He wanted first to finish his schooling and build a secure future. All his former friends are married and have children. Because he has never wanted to impose himself upon others and quickly feels superfluous, many of his social contacts have faded away. He no longer has close friends, although he does have friends with whom he does sporting activities.

He has had a relationship for five years now with a former friend who is now a widow. The girlfriend is seven years his senior and is described as a real friend: somebody who laughs and cries with you, who helps you, on whom you can count. She takes all the decisions and can do no wrong in his eyes; everything she does is fine with him. His first sexual experience was with his girlfriend and he reports the sexual relationship as satisfying. He did not receive sex education in the past and masturbation is unknown to him.

At this time he says that he can take more distance from his mother. Instead it appears that he has become more dependent on his girlfriend. His girlfriend has two children, a son of 21 and a daughter of 20. He views these children as friends. He has come to accept that he himself will no longer have children of his own.

After finishing school he went to work as a volunteer in a small town. Here he performed all kinds of odd jobs. Later he obtained a steady position at the department of social affairs. Initially, he had no difficulties in adequately performing his duties as he was not yet limited by all kinds of rules. He had no problems interpersonally despite the existence of two opposing camps at work. He managed to sail in between and befriend everyone. During this time he successfully followed various courses and training and changed jobs when an attractive position became available in a neighbouring town. At this time he feels confronted with more and more extensive and complicated rules and regulations, a need for stricter control and an ever-increasing expanding clientele. He misses the support of refresher courses to brush up on the new skills and knowledge necessary for his current function. For the last few years he feels he has barely been able to keep up with his work responsibilities.

The daily schedule of the social worker shows a characteristic and revolving pattern. He gets up at 6.45 a.m. and is at his work at 8.30 a.m. At 12.30 he has lunch at his mother's and he is back at his work by 1 p.m. From 4 p.m. until dinner, he works in his or his girlfriend's garden. In the evening he watches television or listens to music. One evening a week he plays volleyball. He sees his girlfriend on Wednesdays and at the weekends. He likes going out, good food and vacations.

PSYCHOLOGICAL TESTING

On the WAIS, the social worker has a verbal IQ score of 119 and a performance IQ score of 96; a total IQ score of 110 puts him in the "normal—high" range. The verbal score is consistent with his level of education, meaning he has an adequate level of functioning for his profession as a social worker. His low score on the performance test is indicative of a deficiency in practical skills, probably owing to the fact that his education primarily emphasized verbal skills and also because of his level of uncertainty in performing the action tasks of the test. Furthermore, the precision and exactness that he demonstrates keep him from completing tasks on time. Attention and concentration deficits are not present.

During this part of the psychological testing he presents himself as helpless; fear and suspicion dominate. He is uncertain in answering the questions, although with patience and the support of the tester his fear diminishes, while the uncertainty remains.

For symptom and personality testing, the following tests were administered: SCL-90, Scale for Interpersonal Values (SIW), MMPI, GLTS, NVM, Inventory list of Daily Occupations, PMT, Sentence Completion Test and Four Pictures Test.

On the L and K scales of the MMPI he scored 73 and 60 respectively. Furthermore, he shows a two-top profile: the *Psychasthenia* scale with K correction is 78 and the *Depression* scale is 74. This is a common profile for people who feel depressed, agitated, restless and nervous. Such patients show perfectionistic traits, their thinking is of an obsessive nature, and most often they experience a whole series of fears and phobias. From an interpersonal point of view, such patients do not stand up for themselves, feel quickly self-critical, are self-punishing and are often passive-dependent. The social worker's conscience is, generally speaking, strong and inflexible, he worries a great deal, overreacts to small stressors and anticipates that situations will have a negative outcome. He received a remarkably low score of 36 on the *Hypomania* subscale. Together with the elevated score on the *Depression* scale, this is indicative of an avital functioning.

On the NVM, no profile in particular is evident and furthermore he has left too many questions blank to allow for calculation of a reliable score. On the GLTS he scores 10 on *Emotionality*, 9 on *Response tendency* and the lowest score of 1 on *Extroversion, Authority* and *Carefreeness*. On the SIW he scores very high on *Conformity* and low on *Recognition, Independence* and *Leadership*. On the Performance Motivation Test he scores a maximal score for *Performance motivation* and a maximal score for negative *Fear of failure*, while for positive *Fear of failure* his score is minimal. On the SCL-90 his score is very high on practically all scales except for the subscale *Hostility*.

In the Sentence Completion Test he indicates having a great need for support from his mother and that he misses his father in this respect as well; he describes his family as being protective in his youth. He shows a tendency to project his dependence onto others for whom he plays the role of saviour and comforter. He is always available for others in need. He cannot handle authority figures and wants to keep everyone as a friend. When things are not going his way he is quick to hang his head down and feel inferior and insecure.

On the Four Pictures Test, he writes a short story in beautiful and neat handwriting in which loneliness is the central theme. The main character of the story feels lonely and abandoned by everyone and longs for a life of coziness and security. He knows, however, that this is not his lot. The main character presents himself as dependent and resigns himself to the circumstances. He lets his head hang low.

The personality testing show an introvert, a worrisome, sombre, dependent man with a strong conscience. Remarkable is his low vitality. He has a tendency to let his head hang low and to give up. He comes across as submissive and shows personal inadequacy in contact with others. He cannot handle authority; as soon as conflict arises, he avoids the issue at hand by behaving subserviently and he does not feel the need to exercise influence over the situation. Thus, in order to avoid conflict, he conforms. He reacts more sensitively to stress than he would like to and caters too much to the needs and wishes of others.

In his experience and action, we see a man with an exaggerated unease who continuously worries and expects the worst. He has a need for support and presents himself in a dependent manner. We further see the defence mechanism of reaction formation; the person under examination is dependent and wants to be taken care of, but cannot handle these feelings, therefore he stands ready for everyone else and feels for other people's situations. The PMT shows a very high motivation to perform at work. At the same time, we see a low resistance to stress; stressful situations are avoided. The examinee needs a great deal of structure, clarity and support.

DSM-IV DIAGNOSIS

Axis I   No diagnosis
Axis II   Obsessive-compulsive personality disorder
Axis III   Physical factors: asthma
Axis IV   Psychosocial stressors: 3 (average)
           Chronic overburdening in work situation
Axis V   Current GAF: 70
           Highest GAF past year: 70

DSM-IV AND ICD-10 CRITERIA

In the DSM-IV, the obsessive-compulsive personality disorder is characterized by a pervasive pattern of preoccupation with orderliness, perfectionism and mental and interpersonal control, at the expense of flexibility, openness and efficiency. It begins by early adulthood and is present in a variety of contexts, as indicated by at least five of the following criteria:

1. Preoccupation with details, rules, lists, order, organization, or schedules to the extent that the major point of the activity is lost.
2. Perfectionism that interferes with task completion (e.g. inability to complete a project because one's own overly strict standards are not met).

3. Excessive devotion to work and productivity to the exclusion of leisure activities and friendships (not accounted for by obvious economic necessity).
4. Overconscientiousness, scrupulousness, and inflexibility about matters of morality, ethics, or values (not accounted for by cultural or religious identifications).
5. Inability to discard worn-out or worthless objects even when they have no sentimental value.
6. Reluctant to delegate tasks or to work with others unless they submit to exactly his or her way of doing things.
7. Adopts a miserly spending style toward both self and others; money is viewed as something to be hoarded for future catastrophes.
8. Rigidity and stubbornness.

In the ICD-10 the anankastic (obsessive-compulsive) personality disorder consists of eight criteria of which three have to be present to a marked degree:

1. Feelings of excessive doubt and caution.
2. Preoccupation with details, rules, lists, order, organization, or schedule.
3. Perfectionism that interferes with task completion.
4. Excessive conscientiousness, scrupulousness, and undue preoccupation with productivity to the exclusion of pleasure and interpersonal relationships.
5. Excessive pedantry and adherence to social conventions.
6. Rigidity and stubbornness.
7. Unreasonable insistence that others submit to exactly his or her way of doing things, or unreasonable reluctance to allow others to do things.
8. Intrusion of insistent and unwelcome thoughts or impulses.

As applicable to no other personality disorder, the obsessive-compulsive personality disorder in the DSM and the anankastic personality in the ICD-10 have a long history of clinical descriptions, especially in psychoanalytic writing. In the anal phase of experiencing lust, according to Freud (1908), lust acquired through handling and playing with the faecal matter was strongly warded off, and through reaction formation permanent character traits develop such as orderliness, connected with physical purity, thriftiness and stubbornness. A strict conscience forces these people to act conscientiously, fulfilling duties and being trustworthy. Abraham (1921) also furnished contributions to this theme. In the changes in the description of the disorder and several of the criteria of the DSM-IV in relation to the DSM-III-R, we can observe more of the classic psychoanalytic concept: more emphasis on orderliness, control and stubbornness.

Only limited empirical research has been done on the DSM criteria (Pfohl & Blum, 1991). Criterion 5 from the DSM-III-R was removed on this account; for the rest of the items which applied an acceptable level of support was available, given the limited number of studies. The same type of research also indicates that the majority of patients with a DSM diagnosis of obsessive-compulsive disorder on Axis I do not meet the criteria of the Axis II personality disorder. These patients instead meet the criteria of the avoidant and dependent personality. From an empirical view, there is still a great lack of clarity about the co-morbidity with other Axis I disorders.

Our clinical experience, however, indicates another position. In the obsessive-compulsive disorder, compulsive personality traits are almost never absent; these are far from always so outspoken in the descriptive view that makes applicable the diagnosis of obsessive-compulsive personality disorder of the DSM. The personality pattern rather shows itself as latent and during psychotherapy becomes more clearly visible. From the etiological perspective aggression, in stunted and burned-out form, plays an important role. Because of this, this personality disorder clinically receives a clearly distinct place, to be well separated from the dependent and avoidant personalities. The latter does not rule out people with obsessive-compulsive personality disorders having dependent and avoidant traits, as the case in this chapter shows. The compulsiveness mostly serves as avoidance and the dependency, although usually warded off, is strong.

Furthermore, we find a strong relationship with the dysthymic disorder of Axis I. With many obsessive-compulsive patients we have identified a depressiveness and gloominess that appeared almost characterological in origin and came close to a depressive personality disorder. Since it is difficult to establish a hierarchy between both patterns, the combined diagnosis seemed to us most accurate. In this view it goes without saying that discussion of whether or not the compulsiveness is the result of the mood disorder is important. The effect of antidepressants in these cases was in our experience not strong enough to bring about clinically significant and, for the patient, relevant improvement. The combined existence of a dysthymic disorder and an obsessive-compulsive disorder leads, in our professional practice, mostly to diagnoses related to work disability. Often this concerns middle-aged men who, through a combination of both patterns, increasingly became stuck in their work situation. They could not keep up with the pressure from work any more, and also developed more and more somatoform complaints. Retreating from their work did not solve their problems, as the character aspect was stronger than the effect of the surroundings.

It remains the case that in clinical practice, as well as in much empirical research, the obsessive-compulsive personality is clearly recognizable.

CHAPTER 2.11 Personality disorder not otherwise specified (NOS): the staff member

A 44-year-old staff member of a cultural council had been absent from work for a year. His employer proposed a psychological examination in order to obtain insight into his stress resistance and his suitability for his function. He agreed to co-operate.

FIRST IMPRESSION

On first contact we see a sturdy, corpulent man whose estimated age corresponds with his calendar age. Orientation in time, place and person is undisturbed. His awareness is intact. The staff member displays a cynical and offensive attitude and says he does not "have much confidence in the examination", although he is co-operative. His speech is elaborate; he is often difficult to curb and comes across as tense. The affect is very clearly dysphoric. Serious disturbance in thought and perception is lacking. Growth in contact is present to a limited extent during the testing session.

SYMPTOMATOLOGY AND PERSONALITY

The assessment of complaints points to fatigue, listlessness and a tendency towards worrying and fretting. In addition, tension, sleeping difficulties and diffuse feelings of anxiety are mentioned. Moreover, we see hostility and feelings of inadequacy, as well as decreased libido. The staff member says that he often feels dizzy and suffers from tachycardia: probably owing to an essential hypertension. He mentions hyperventilation and back problems, diverticulitis and a spastic colon as well. At the time of the examination he states that he has been suffering for some time from bouts of flu and colds; during the assessment, however, he gives the impression of being very tense but not ill. Psychotic symptoms, in the restricted sense, are not present.

The staff member gives the impression of an intelligent, strongly negativistic, resentful personality, full of inner tension and aggression. He describes himself as "someone who has cultivated being negative into an art". In essence, we are dealing with a probably extremely sensitive man with a high stimulus sensitivity. In the course of a neurotic development, he seems to have adopted an attitude after puberty in which there is no room for tender feelings. As a child, the situation was the other way round: his parents wanted to have a girl and stimulated feminine behaviour including doing the shopping and helping with the housework. He feels that boyish and masculine behaviour was suppressed. For instance, he was not allowed to work on the farm: "I wasn't even allowed to point a finger at a tractor." As a child his masculine, active ambitions were suppressed; from adolescence on, it was more feminine, passive ambitions that seemed to be repressed, at least on a behavioural level. In the form of defences, these passive ambitions are clearly observable in the contact, however.

He presents a somewhat diffuse identity. In interpersonal relationships, passive ambitions, in particular, seem to be repressed. Generally, defence mechanisms are developed in character, although we also recognized from time to time some (lightly) primitive defence in the form of splitting. The reality testing is intact, so that we can speak of a predominantly neurotic structured personality organization. The staff member appears to flirt from time to time with his pessimism.

BIOGRAPHY

The staff member was born as the youngest child in a family of three boys. His brothers are four and eight years his senior. No information is available about the pregnancy and delivery.

His father used to be employed as a foreman and later started his own business. His mother worked in the home. Both parents have now died, his father after having a heart ailment and his mother from lung disease. The children were raised as liberal Protestant. The atmosphere at home, according to the staff member, was reasonably good; but his father was quick tempered and beat the children regularly. His mother was very submissive to his father. The two eldest sons helped on the farm; he was not allowed to do "outdoor work" but helped his mother in the house and did the shopping. "I read a great deal and had to be nice to my mother."

After the staff member had gone to elementary school for several months, the family moved. He was able to adapt to the new surroundings but had few friends in the beginning, however: "We were imports." The elementary education was completed without academic problems. After this he went to high school because his parents thought he ought to develop himself intellectually. He cannot share anything concrete about the period between the ages of 12 and 18. At home there were no problems, although when his father became self-employed the family lived for some time in a caravan (he speaks here about the "hunger winter"). As a result he had to repeat a class. During this time he was a member of a music club and a gymnastic club. Enquiry into this period does not produce any information: "It certainly was not a carefree time, I think I have repressed a great deal."

For a long time, problems existed in his father's family. The nature and the cause remain unclear. He does remark on his aunt, however: "I used to go there from time to time and then they tried to indoctrinate me. Later, she got cancer fortunately and the last year in particular she suffered a great deal. I am still happy about that."

He graduated from high school. Although he wanted to go in an artistic direction, his parents wanted him to study medicine. After a year and a half, it was evident that he could not handle it, he left and went to work in a music store for eight months. This period was experienced by him as very pleasant. After this he started doing something that he had always wanted to do: go to music school. He quickly, however, came into conflict with the director in connection with a compulsory brand of piano that had to be bought. The conflict escalated to a physical confrontation between the director and the examinee. Following this incident, he received poor grades and he eventually left his education there. In 1968, the staff member went to the social academy with a scholarship from the Department of Justice, to study child welfare. In practice, he choose the area of cultural work. He experienced it as pleasant but confronting work. During this period he openly admitted his homosexuality.

During his education, he gave psychology lessons to nurses. He finished the social academy with good results and went to work in a town as a cultural staff member. His function as "civil servant between civil servants" gave rise to friction; he often found his involvement with culture difficult to combine with what he calls a civil servant institution.

In 1977 he changed jobs, and went to work as a staff member with the cultural council. His tasks consisted of co-ordinating, advising, regulation and supporting the management in connection with music and the visual arts. From the beginning, he appeared to have a hard time fitting into the "straight and narrow". He felt responsible for the management and wanted to bring art among the people. This enthusiastic attitude interfered frequently with the more difficult attitudes of colleagues. Also he gradually experienced more discrepancy between his input and the final result. He had difficulty separating his work and private life. Outbursts, usually owing to a supposed lack of input and/or involvement of colleagues, occurred frequently. One or the other has led to the fact that he now finds his work futile. He increasingly began to focus his attention on negative affairs, not only in his employment but also in his private life. For years he has suffered from intestinal complaints, and his level of tension has been unusually high. After a short period of sick leave, he has now been completely absent from work for the last six months.

The staff member never received sex education and at home sex was not discussed. Since the age of 11 he has masturbated, and for the first few years this left him with strong feelings of guilt. In the course of puberty, the examinee noticed that he felt attracted to boys. The heterosexual experience he had with a girl did not appeal to him at all. His first homosexual experience, however, gave him satisfaction. At the moment that he told his parents about his homosexuality, his father kicked him out of the house. Intervention by a sister-in-law caused his father to resume contact with him a week later and in tears he offered his excuses. The examinee met his current boyfriend and partner at a choir club. Although particularly his mother had a difficult time with this, as time went by a better understanding grew and the relationship was accepted. The examinee has lived with his partner for approximately 15 years now. The relationship can be called a good one. The partner is a singer and actor.

The staff member has an important hobby: singing. At this moment he would prefer to make this his profession, but this is not very easy to achieve.

PSYCHOLOGICAL TESTING

The staff member's intelligence is measured using the abridged Groninger Intelligence Test. On this test, he scores an IQ of 126. This score corresponds to his educational level.

On the SCL-90, his scores are all very high in comparison to the normal population, except for *Hostility*. In comparison to the norm group of psychiatry patients, his scores are mostly high.

The MMPI profile shows, next to an L of 51, an F of 70 and a K of 38, an elevated neurotic triangle: *Hypochondriasis* 89, *Depression* 84, and *Hysteria* 84 (with K correction). Except for *Social introversion* (54) the other scores are almost all around 70, with *Paranoia* as the highest (79). The picture that emerges from this profile is of a man who is under a great deal of inner tension, who is very vulnerable and not very stress resistant. He has a tendency to somatize his tensions, and moreover to regulate them in relationships with others. In contacts, he is very sensitive and has a tendency towards projection. The elevations on the neurotic triangle appear necessary to keep under control the vulnerability that is evident from the psychotic scales. His fears and his aggression quickly build up under pressure and he reacts with these symptoms.

On the NVM we see a comparable picture: *Negativism* is very high in comparison to the normal population and above average for the norm group of psychiatric patients; *Somatization* is very high for both norm groups. *Shyness* is high for the normal population and average in comparison to the psychiatric group, with similar scores for *Psychopathology*. He scores low on *Extroversion* in comparison to the normal population and below average in comparison to the psychiatry group. So here also we see a picture of a very tense man, weighed down by a great deal of worries, who partly somatizes these and partly takes them out aggressively on relationships. The low tolerance level makes his situation difficult.

On the Achievement Motivation Test his scores are very high on *Achievement motivation*, maximum on *Fear of failure* and low on *Fear of success*.

On the Scale for Interpersonal Values, he considers *Leadership* and *Conformity* unimportant, *Social support* and *Recognition* very important. On the GLTS, his very high score on *Sensitivity* is striking. On the Scale for Interpersonal Behavior, he scores as assertive.

The psychological testing shows a talented man, with a very high sensitivity to stimulation. His achievement motivation is high, but this goes hand in hand with an extreme fear of failure. Furthermore, we see someone who is not particularly conformist and has a strongly individualistic attitude, which go together with a strong wish for recognition. The high inner tension is partly somatized and partly warded off in manipulative contact with others. Moreover, we see an excess of feelings of anxiety and a low ego-strength. Stress resistance is low and he appears to hide this under an assertive attitude in interpersonal contacts.

DSM-III-R DIAGNOSES

Axis I   Dysthymia, secondary type, late onset
Axis II   Obsessive-compulsive personality traits
          Personality disorder NOS (impulsive personality)
Axis III Hypertension, diverticulitis, spastic colon
Axis IV   Psychosocial stress factors; dysfunctioning at work
          Seriousness 3: moderate
Axis V   Current GAF: 46
          Highest GAF past year: 44

The personality disorder "not otherwise specified" is a left-over category, in which disorders of personality functioning are classified that do not meet the criteria for a specific personality disorder. The presence of features of more than one specific personality disorder can apply here, without the person meeting the full criteria for a diagnosis. What is in question is the significant impairment in social and occupational functioning, or the cause of marked distress. This category can also be used when the clinician judges that a specific personality disorder not included in the DSM classification is appropriate. In the example above, this is the impulsive personality disorder. Other examples are the depressive personality disorder, the immature personality disorder, the masochistic and the negativistic personality disorder. In these cases, the specific personality disorder follows in parentheses. In the ICD-10 there is a similar left-over category.

PART 3

Theoretical Approaches

CHAPTER 3.1   The psychoanalytic approach

In his essay "Some character types in psycho-analytical work" (1916), Freud argues that the analyst's interest is not primarily directed at the character of the patient. Rather, the meaning and the history of the symptoms are central. However, an analyst who has started with a new patient is quickly confronted with resistance. Freud considers this resistance part of the character. Here, he warns, character traits are often of such a nature and intensity that one would not have previously attributed them to the patient. Thus, he refers here not so much to the manifest, descriptive traits, but rather to deeper patterns revealed only during analysis.

DESCRIPTIVE AND STRUCTURAL POINT OF VIEW

Psychoanalytic theory on character types and personality organizations has been expanded. The descriptive characterizations that rely on clinical practice began with Freud (1931). The erotic, compulsive and narcissistic types fall under this heading. The hysterical, infantile, oral-passive, oral-aggressive, anal-sadistic, anal-masochistic, genital, phallic, obsessive-compulsive, as-if, sadomasochistic, hypomanic, inadequate, paranoid, schizoid, borderline and passive-aggressive characters have been worked out by many authors since Freud. Various attempts have been made to obtain empirical support for these characters, with varying success (Hoffman, 1979).

Apart from the development of theories on this descriptive level, attempts have been made to organize patterns and structures on a more profound level, as is typical for the psychoanalytic method. In this context, the adaptive, dynamic and structural points of view are discussed in turn. One cannot speak of a strict separation between descriptive and structural development of theories. Character descriptions usually consist of both components; in one case, the accent lies more on the descriptive and in another case more on the structural. We can almost speak of a dimension with the description of overt behaviour on one extreme and the abstract constructions of ego structures on the other. From a structural point of view, theory is on a more abstract level and further removed from observation. From an empirical standpoint, this means that validation and objectivity are not, or are only in a very limited way, possible. Structural contributions are the most valuable for clinicians who run an open psychotherapeutic practice.

The relationship between descriptive and more structural theory is complex in nature. That is, there is a relationship, although not a direct one. Reasoning from the psychoanalytic framework, we could suppose that this connection between appearance and structure and the dynamics that lie behind it is comparable to that between manifest and latent dream material. What we dream is in itself meaningful, but at the same time there is also another deeper meaning concealed and unveiled in the manifest dream. Direct expression of wishes and desires is blocked by mechanisms of the primary process such as displacement, condensation, secondary processing and reversal. Exposing these processes occurs primarily in clinical practice. Empirical research fits in best with the descriptive point of view. Given the connection between the two, restricting oneself to just one means shedding light on only part of the phenomenon.

The contribution of psychoanalysis to character disorders is integrated in a theory of the genesis of these character types, the mechanisms that preserve character traits, and the accompanying conflicts that occur here. Various points of view have also been worked out in relation to symptomatology. In the classic psychoanalytic vision, the character is interpreted as the basis of neurosis. In addition, there is a point of view that sees the character as an alternative to neurosis. Finally, we distinguish the conceptualization of the character as parallel to neurosis.

In the last decade, much attention has been paid to narcissistic disorders in the psychoanalytic professional literature. Here, at least four ways of using the concept of narcissism play a role:

- narcissism as a developmental stage (primary narcissism);
- narcissism as a trait (secondary narcissism);
- psychological conflicts that relate to narcissism;
- narcissistic forms of transference (the grandiose self and the idealized parent image).

Furthermore, borderline disorder has received a great deal of attention. In this context, Otto Kernberg has described three organizational levels of the ego: the neurotic personality organization, the borderline personality organization and the psychotic personality organization. Kernberg's work has acquired the most recognition in recent psychiatric and psychological literature on personality disorders.

Kernberg (1975, 1976, 1984) classifies character pathology into three levels and in his attempt makes a connection between descriptive and structural theories: "high level, intermediary level and lower level" character pathology. In particular, the hysterical, obsessive-compulsive and depressive-masochistic characters fall under the first group. The second group comprises the better functioning narcissistic people, as well as some infantile and passive-aggressive characters. The "lower level" or borderline personality organization comprises for Kernberg most cases of infantile and narcissistic character disorders, and practically all schizoid, paranoid, hypomanic, as-if and antisocial personalities. His later division of the ego into three organizational levels prompts the question of what the intermediary level is: does it belong to the neurotic personality organization or to the borderline personality organization?

The many contributions in the psychoanalytic literature organize clinical experience in particular within this framework. This tradition has also been taken into account somewhat in the revised versions of the DSM, exclusively concerning the descriptive contributions. The structural, dynamic and adaptive approaches are not connected to the conceptual framework of the DSM.

The rest of this chapter presents a personal interpretation and arrangement of psychoanalytic contributions in the field of personality disorders (see also Derksen, 1990c). This approach is quite different from that of Salman Akhtar (1992), who contributes especially to the phenomenological and psychoanalytic description of the following selection of personality disorders: narcissistic, borderline, schizoid, paranoid, hypomanic, antisocial, histrionic and schizotypal. In his book he focuses on an overview in the psychoanalytic tradition. The approach in this book is much broader and, as far as the psychoanalytic point of view is concerned, there will be an attempt to analyse the basic structure of the personality disorders in a new way.

The modern term personality disorder is used instead of character disorder, although the concept of character is traditionally used in psychoanalysis (Kets de Vries & Perzow, 1991).

THREE AXES

The personality as well as the person's disorder can, psychodynamically speaking, be diagnosed on three axes:

- the drive axis;
- the ego axis;
- the self axis.

The concept of axis refers to an independently existing psychological function that forms a structure in relation to the other axes. Thus, there is an underlying mutual relationship influence. The sequence here is not coincidental: it is a genetic arrangement. In regard to psychopathology, a disturbance of the ego is the most serious.

The Drive Axis

In the first place, there is the drive axis. The terms with which this axis has been adorned are: oral, anal, phallic, latent and genital (Freud, 1905). This is a contribution of classic psychoanalytic theory to the personality disorders, and the axis was omitted in various theoretical developments following Freud. For example, Greenberg & Mitchell (1983) made a distinction between two psychoanalytic models: the drive model and the relationship model. The latter model radically departs from all drive-related explanations and postulates that all motivation originates from our experiences with other people.

The aversion of many Anglo-Saxon psychoanalysts to the classic drive theory often appears to be a consequence of language use. Concepts such as oral, anal, etc. are considered outdated. Rejection of drive, as has happened, occurred after the drive concept was erroneously interpreted as a purely biological concept. Furthermore, we see that theorists of the psychology of the self, as well as proponents of object relations theory (for example Greenberg, 1991), reintroduce the drive. The latter is labelled differently, however, and has less to do with aggression and sexuality and, in any case, with the unconscious. The unconscious is actually stripped of a part of its strength in such theories.

Without neglecting the contribution of the object relations school, I think that this school can exist in addition to the classic drive theory. Eliminating the latter would mean to me closing my eyes to an aspect of psychological reality, as this drive is revealed to us in clinical practice and in everyday human interaction. These clinical phenomena can provide rational insight and be rendered coherent through the explanatory force of drive theory. Every attempt at reducing all motives to a few drives is obviously incompatible with the dynamic and complex character of psychoanalysis. The same objection to reductionism also applies to the reduction of sexual and aggressive behaviour to vicissitudes in interpersonal relationships, as is proposed by some representatives of the object relations school.

Object relations theory has made a significant contribution to clinical practice. In psychotherapeutic and psychoanalytic practice, object relationships constantly assume a central position. Disturbed early relationships result in such things as fixations in certain phases of the development of drive. Furthermore, these disturbances can also be responsible for structural damage to the ego. After all, internalized object relationships are a part of the ego. Narcissistic disturbances are often the result of failed interaction between child and caretaker. In this case, it remains a question of content; object relations do not directly contribute to the form in which this content is poured, that is, the personality patterns that are of interest. Identification of the objects as they were observed, experienced by the child and fantasized about by the child, can provide a considerable contribution to the symptomatology.

In the course of psychosexual development, the libido lets itself be structured under the successive erogenous zones and finally arranges itself under the primacy of the genitals. This says something in particular about the development of libido and aggression. In this context, we often find a striking typology that is the consequence of fixations in these phases (Freud, 1913). These fixations are the consequence of the combined role played by biological, psychological and social factors. Within classic psychoanalysis, the drive takes the place of the boundary concept between body and psyche; a messenger of body to psyche with a mandate, as Freud expressed it.

The (innate) quantity of drive energy plays an important role in the development of fixations. If a baby is equipped with a predisposition towards strong aggression and/or sexually excitable reactions, the building up of the ego, ego ideal and superego is burdened to a larger extent than when this particular predisposition is not as apparent. The conditions during these phases play a role alongside the biological aspect. The predisposition is formed through human interactions. The drive is called to life, so to speak, only within psychological relationships in the form of a wish. Without these relationships there is no drive, but without drive these relationships do not exist. Both interlock and give each other form. To consider them separately is comparable with studying a fish while it is not in water.

A baby during the oral phase can basically receive too much or too little satisfaction. This can lead to fixation. Furthermore, a disturbance can occur also through an external circumstance during a phase, for instance separation from the mother during the oral phase. Particularly if insufficient compensations were offered, these processes can promote fixation in the phase concerned. Psychosexual energy remains behind. A comparison derived from Freud (1917) clarifies this. During a war the army advances and repeatedly encounters enemy troops. A battle is fought and the heavier the battle, the more troops stay behind to decide whether to fight. The remaining men advance further. Depending on the resistance, a number of soldiers remain who ultimately reach their goal, i.e. besieging a town in the territory of the enemy. In a similar way, because of fixations, libido stays behind. The comparison falls short in that it is not necessarily about fighting a battle: spoiling and neglect can be a factor as well. This type of fixation gives rise to personality traits that are rather stable. These characteristics also come more "from within" than the two that will be discussed next.

Ideal development goes hand in hand with as few fixations as possible and as rapid a growth towards the genital phase as possible. The psychological structure of early interactions (such as in the oral phase) is simpler than that of later ones (for example during the phallic phase). During the later phases the child has at his or her disposal more mental functions and structures and so is capable of working through more complex interactions.

Children can be confronted with more or fewer fixations in different phases. The phase in which the fixation occurs receives an accent in the personality; when several fixations take place, several accents result. The more accents, the more complex it is to maintain psychological balance. An extensive description of these types has been given elsewhere (Derksen, 1983a; 1983b). In brief, the following phenomena occur. A fixation in the oral phase and a dominance of oral themes in the person result in a personality with strong dependent characteristics. Being loved is of the greatest importance and the fear of losing love dominates all experience. The most important drive demands are accepted by the other structures (ego, superego). With a dominance of the anal phase we see a superego that has separated itself from the ego under high pressure. Anxiety of the conscience and inner dependence dominate the clinical picture of the person. A fixation in the phallic phase results in diminished tension between the ego and superego. No excessive erotic needs exist in this person, the main interest lies in self-preservation without many limitations and independence. A fixation in the latency phase leads to a personality profile in which sexual and aggressive feelings remain in the background. The adult with these fixations makes a quiet, shy, child-like impression and is overly adapted to the outside world. The genital phase represents the ultimate goal and with that also a sort of ideal; without marked fixations, all energy is available for heterosexual relationships, a productive professional life and sufficient possibilities to enjoy. In clinical practice as well as in daily life we can recognize these accents in the personality of people once we have some proficiency in determining them.

With regard to the relationship of this typology to symptom neuroses, we find here the basis of neurosis. Nobody is totally without symptoms and nobody has only symptoms, thus suffering from symptoms is a question of summing them up. The type of fixation gives form to the symptomatology. Examples are anxiety disorders, phobic complaints and conversions with oral fixations; compulsive-neurotic symptoms with anal fixations; acting-out behaviour and disturbed relationships related to problems with aggression and sexuality with phallic fixations; relationship problems and unassertiveness with fixations in the latency period. These fixations form a predisposition to the development of these symptoms. Each fixation can vary in strength; dimensions thus range from a little to a great deal. Moreover, the contribution of each phase can be diagnosed for each person.

In a structural sense, the psychotherapeutic influence of this type of fixation is doubtful. There are several reasons for this. A strong biological—genetic component is involved. Furthermore, it concerns a process that starts very early in a person's life, at a moment that a large part of ego activity has still to come into being. The chances of influencing oral fixations are lowest for that reason. The possibilities become slightly greater with fixations later in development. Furthermore, a condition for influencing change is that the process of development is actualized within the transference relationship. At this dimension it does not concern a psychological conflict, but rather a trait. From a psychotherapeutic point of view, it is more realistic that the ego becomes conscious of the nature and intensity of the fixation. As a rule, this consciousness stimulates the ego to choose to oppose these tendencies. Such a development produces other behaviour; the basic tendencies are met with more resistance, although they do not essentially change.

Axis of the Ego

In this context, the axis of the ego particularly concerns the structural diagnostics of the personality organization developed by Kernberg

(1981, 1984) and his colleagues. These clinicians have expanded the commonly used descriptive diagnostics with a structural diagnosis within the context of their research on the borderline personality disorder. This was a requirement since, according to Kernberg, the borderline disorder cannot be adequately distinguished from the psychotic and neurotic personality disorders on a symptom level. From a structural point of view, the personality is seen as composed of the three components as described by Freud (1923): id, ego and superego. Structural analysis refers to implementing this view. In the development of psychoanalytic thinking, however, structural analysis has been given more meanings which are integrated in the work of Kernberg (1984). Furthermore, he uses the concept of structure in his own way as well. In addition to Freud's classic structural position, he elaborates on the ego psychology of Hartmann (Hartmann, Kris & Lowenstein, 1946; Rapaport & Gill, 1959). Hartmann describes the ego as a structure which helps channel and shape psychic processes. The ego also provides stability to the psychological system.

The structure of the ego integrates substructures such as cognitive functions and defence mechanisms. Kernberg adds to this the substructure that comes into being through the internalizing of the object relationship. Here the quality of the object relationship determines to an important degree the level of development to which the substructures of defence mechanisms and cognitive functions belong. Kernberg views the development in the organization of the substructures of the ego not as linear or continuous, but rather as a discontinuous process. According to his theory, there are several levels of organization of the ego which need to be distinguished, which qualitatively differ from one another. Each level of organization is called a structural organization by Kernberg and is constituted by the dynamic integration of the substructures. In addition to psychological functions, Kernberg also distinguishes biological factors that contribute to the ultimate structural organization of the ego. Kernberg takes no notice of the manner in which biological and psychological factors go together. He conceives the structural organization as a link between etiological (psychological, biological) on the one hand, and behavioural mani-festations on the other. From this matrix, symptoms develop.

Structural diagnosis is thus focused on the personality organization that is underlying the manifest behaviour. Borderline is a level of functioning for Kernberg. In particular, he considers the following ego functions to be central: defence mechanisms, identity integration and reality testing. Kernberg distinguishes three types of organizations: the neurotic, the borderline, and the psychotic personality organization. In principle,

Table 3.1.1 Kernberg's criteria

	Identity diffusion	Primitive defence	Reality testing disturbed
Neurotic organization	−	−	−
Borderline organization	+	+	−
Psychotic organization	+	+	+

each individual can be placed within one of these categories. In structural diagnosis, three structural characteristics dominate, which together differentiate the neurotic, borderline and psychotic personality organization. These characteristics are the following:

1. Identity integration versus identity diffusion (and the related total quality of object relations). Patients with an identity diffusion have a non-integrated or very poorly integrated concept of themselves and of significant others; they have contradictory images of themselves and show inconsistent behaviour. These inconsistencies are denied by the patient.

2. Developed versus primitive defence mechanisms. Within psycho-analytic theory, defence mechanisms protect the individual against demands of drive, conscience demands and the outside world. Developed defence mechanisms are repression, rationalization, reaction formation, isolation and the like. Primitive defence mechanisms as a rule are used by the still immature and not autonomous ego of the young child, but can be institutionalized as a dominant defence, for example through a trauma. The most important mechanisms here are splitting, projective identification, primitive idealization, devaluation, omnipotence and denial.

3. Presence versus absence of reality testing. This mainly pertains to the capacity to evaluate one's own affect, behaviour and thoughts, and, if necessary, to correct these on the basis of observations and cognitive processes. A patient with psychotic symptoms which do not worry him or her demonstrates in the interpretation a disturbance in reality testing. For an overview, see Table 3.1.1.

The ego develops gradually in the course of infancy and toddlerhood. If a disturbance in development takes place at a very early stage, for example in the first year of life, the developing ego becomes fixated in that phase. This early period is characterized by an ego that is not yet capable of separating sufficiently his or her inner world from the outside world, or subject from object. The line of thought here is that a disturbance at this time predisposes a person to a psychotic personality organization. A disturbance in the development of the ego further on in development produces the borderline personality organization. The phase in the development process that is mentioned here is most often referred to as the "phase of the renewed approach" and is described extensively by Mahler and her co-workers (Mahler, 1971; Mahler, Pine & Bergman, 1975). This phase begins between the 16th and 24th month and coincides roughly with Freud's anal phase. A disturbance of the ego at the moment that it is intact structurally, roughly speaking during the oedipal phase, does not damage the ego. It goes without saying, however, that this can have consequences for the development of neurotic symptoms. The disturbances that lead to a psychotic and borderline ego usually have more to do with external influences than those with a neurotic development. In the case of the borderline disorder, much has become known through research on the importance of physical and psychological abuse as well as sexual abuse (Zanarini *et al.*, 1989). In comparison to the drive axis, where the disturbance comes especially from within, at the ego axis disturbances come about mainly externally.

In regard to the relationship between symptom and personality, the relationship of the parallel between personality disorder and neurosis applies. All three personality organizations can be accompanied by a broad range of symptoms that show a great deal of overlap among themselves. The connection between symptom and personality is certainly the least visible here. The fact is, however, that psychotic symptoms with an ego-syntonic character are only found at the psychotic personality organization. Furthermore, healthy, normal people fall under the neurotic organization. Each organization can exist without considerable symptomatology. Adaptation to social surroundings is of overriding importance here.

The foundation of these organization types is formed not through conflict, but through a deficit. Since we are concerned here with classes — qualitatively different organization levels — and not a dimension, the question remains: to what extent is change possible? Theoretically speaking, psychotherapy could in fact result in a structural change taking place. An example is someone who initially functioned on a borderline level but is able to function on a neurotic level after having terminated treatment. This does suggest, however, that the conditions that were responsible for the damage to the ego can be actualized during the course of the treatment, reshaping the ego. A change of such a drastic nature is not often encountered in the literature and in research on the borderline disorder. What is often feasible is a lessening of symptoms, an ego that is more in touch with itself and reality, improvement in developing relationships. Adaptation is better, but the borderline core is not changed.

Axis of the Self

In my view, the self consists of self representations and object representation with accompanying affective dispositions. This self is a gradually developing content (no structure) within the psychological apparatus, situated within the contours of the preconscious and conscious ego. A baby does not have a self yet; the self develops as a reaction to and dependent on the development of the ego. The development of the ego dominates this process. Disturbance can occur in people's perceptions of themselves and of others and in corresponding feelings. In this case, such a disturbance does not lead to a fixation but rather to disequilibrium in feelings of self-worth and thereby also in the experience of important objects. Feelings of superiority or inferiority come into being here: idealized and devaluated images of the self and of significant others, with the corresponding affects. The ego contains this imbalance and, consequently, the struc tural quality of the ego is essential to the precise form the disturbance takes.

In normal development, the self takes a definite form after the ego has become structurally intact; in the phallic phase, just before the oedipal phase. At a much earlier phase in development, the toddler knows the experience of desire to succeed in certain activities, such as sitting, standing and walking. Such narcissistic fun forms the self. All kinds of failures in this process (falling down, bumping the head, not being able to reach something that is too high up, etc.) are potential threats to having pleasure in their own ability. They are only potential threats, since they depend to a large degree on how the child's caretakers handle such events. In this complex process, an adequate relationship has to be established between feelings of self-worth, the ideal self and the ideal object. Self-worth, strengthened by the phallic experience of pleasure, counterbalances the realization that the ideal self lies in the future. The ideal object becomes an example for establishing the ego ideal, the latter being added to the superego.

In disturbed narcissism, the self and the ego ideal are either merged or have such a great distance between them that the ideal seems unattainable. This type of narcissistic disorder is based on a relationship disturbance which the child has had with one or more significant caretakers. Disturbance in feelings of self-worth influence every relationship, because the more psychological energy is required to keep the disturbed self in balance, the more is absent from the relationship with the other person. Accordingly, the relationship and partner are partially used for bringing feelings of self-worth into balance. These disturbances present themselves in a form that has been worked out by Kohut (1971) among others: the grandiose self and the idealized parent image. Kohut's work concerns the less serious forms of narcissistic disorders which are more serious·when the ego shows a borderline or psychotic organization. In addition, fixations of drive play a role.

These types of pattern are rather stable and show in contact with others, and for that reason have come to be associated with personality disorders. In relation to symptoms, we can discover here the personality as an alternative to neurosis. Symptoms are not tolerated by the person, as they constitute an injury to vulnerable feelings of self-worth. The problems of a patient with a narcissistic disturbance manifest themselves directly in a relationship and are usually ego-syntonic. If these patients develop symptoms, they behave in regard to these symptoms just as they do with respect to their personality traits. That is, symptoms are trivialized, rationalized and denied at critical moments. A brief case example will clarify this point.

Example

A 39-year-old teacher sought psychological treatment for a sleeping disorder and his problems with keeping order in the classroom. Furthermore, he was troubled by a spastic colon. During the first session, he showed more or less tacitly that he was not very impressed by the work that the psychologists at his school had been doing for years. His general practitioner and his wife had advised him years ago to seek psychological help. This help should be directed at his reoccurring fear that his wife, his children or he, himself, would become seriously ill.

In the sessions that followed, the patient barely went more deeply into these fears, if at all. Instead, he focused on regaining control of his class and the fact that he thought that his wife was having an affair with someone else. From a heteroanamnesis with his wife, a whole list of complaints came up. The patient had terrorized his family for years with his fear of diseases. If one of the children had a minor bout of flu the father suspected a serious tumour. He seldom or never accompanied his family to social events. Whenever he did, however, he would first stand in front of the mirror for a long time and examine his skin for blemishes. His abdominal complaints also dominated family life and if they were absent, he would come up with another symptom. The patient would trivialize complaints and refer to the possibility of yet undiscovered organic causes.

Confronted with his wife's remarks he would put the symptoms into perspective, place them in the past and make no attempt to go more deeply into them. The way he formulated his complaints, he gave the impression that I could not say anything meaningful about them either. He was not open to the influence of psychotherapy. In the mean time, his sleep disorder diminished and he was less concerned about his wife's imaginary extramarital affair. At that point, the therapeutic relationship ended.

This patient's defence fitted with the disorder of the self and served to maintain his self-worth. A symptom or disturbed personality trait threatens an unstable equilibrium. This used to be called a neurotic character, in which the patient does not personally suffer, in contrast to the character neurosis in which he or she does (Hoffmann, 1979). Within the context of an ego with its own manner of functioning, the disorder of the self can be understood as a dimension with varying degrees: the continuum of the narcissistic personality disorder. The degree of conflict is greater for this disorder than for the drive axis. Interpersonal dynamics have led to patterns which are considerably stable.

On the basis of the typology as it has been worked out for the narcissistic personality disorder by Kernberg, Kohut and Burston, Gabbard (1990) arrives at a description of the two opposite extreme types. Gabbard starts from a descriptive point of view and particularly describes the developmental relationship of these types. The "oblivious" narcissist appears at one end. These people are not aware of other people's reactions, and they are arrogant and aggressive. At a reception, they talk with others as if they were addressing a large audience, they seldom make eye contact and appear to look over the heads of those they are talking to. These narcissists are wrapped up in themselves and need to be the centre of attention. They have "a transmitter but no receiver", they talk *at* others and not *with* others. They are not susceptible to the fact that they have hurt other people's feelings, and are very insensitive to the needs of others. In their stories, they keep coming back to their own merits and do not notice other people's boredom.

In contrast to the "oblivious" type, Gabbard describes the "hyper-vigilant" type. These narcissistic disturbed persons are extremely sensitive to other people's reactions. Their attention is constantly focused on the other, in contrast to the type that is wrapped up in him- or herself as described above. They listen very carefully to what others say and — comparable with a paranoid attitude — they immediately detect the slightest criticism. Their feelings are quickly hurt, they rapidly feel ashamed and are easily humiliated. For example, in treatment they read the therapist's minimal facial expressions as evidence of disinterest, boredom or being made to feel tired by the patient. These patients are shy and inhibited in their behaviour. They avoid being the centre of attention and instead direct attention towards others as quickly as possible.

Both types struggle in their own way to maintain their self-worth. The "oblivious" type does this by impressing others with his or her own accomplishments and extinguishing other people's reactions as protection against narcissistic injuries. The "hypervigilant" type does this by avoiding potentially vulnerable situations and by studying other people's reactions in order to adjust his or her own behaviour accordingly.

In the model presented by Gabbard, these two types can be further explained. The first type of narcissist with the grandiose self comes about by merging a disorder of the self with a drive fixation in the phallic phase. In the second type, the disorder of the self is combined with a fixation in the oral and/or anal phases. Because of that, the dependent and avoidant traits are very apparent. Furthermore, the role of the superego is greater. The first superego core emerges in this anal phase, and particularly in combination with oral fixation we see a "critical" dependency on others.

Psychoanalytic treatment of a narcissistic disorder can be successful. However, this depends greatly on the extent to which the patient can commit him- or herself to the treatment. It goes without saying that the control the therapist has over feelings of countertransference plays a big role in the process. A narcissistic patient with a grandiose self reduces the analyst to a public audience. Therapists must be able to tolerate the devaluations and offensiveness that they encounter. Overly sensitive types idealize the therapist and avoid manifesting themselves. If these patients function on a neurotic ego level, psychoanalysis and psychodynamic therapy are possible.

Group therapy is also a possibility, but requires the patient to be more tolerant of frustration. "Oblivious" narcissists like having a potential audience but do not readily share time with others. Furthermore, they can easily end up in the role of co-therapist. Not getting exclusive attention for their unique problems is something such people may not tolerate very well. The group can offer them a lot, however, in terms of feedback on how they come across to others and the experience that others have desires of their own. The overly sensitive narcissist may try to remain in the shadows in the group and leave disappointed after several years. The extremes on this dimension are more difficult to deal with than those towards the middle.

With a borderline ego, a narcissistic disorder takes on another structural character and is much more pathological in nature. Kernberg (1984) mainly writes about this type of narcissist. He integrates the libidinal and aggressive aspirations but, in my opinion, makes insufficient distinction between the ego axis and the self axis. With borderline patients, it should be borne in mind that they may also have a healthy dose of narcissism.

COHERENCE BETWEEN THE AXES

This brings us to the relationship between the three axes. Diagnosis of a personality disorder takes place on all three axes separately. There is a particular connection, such as a phallic drive fixation and a narcissistic disorder, or a borderline ego and a narcissistic disorder. This is not a rule, however, and diagnoses of the different phenomena must occur independently. Many patients have an oral fixation, a neurotic ego and no disorder of the self. The linking of fixations on the drive and the ego axes with disturbances of the self complicates the clinical picture and has implications for treatment.

TREATMENT

Among the very first analysts who contributed to a psychoanalytic vision of the character and particularly to the treatment of character disorders, Reich (1928) took an outspoken position. According to him, no neurotic symptoms existed without a neurotic character. Thus, every analysis is necessarily character analysis. Resistance is rooted in the neurotic character and requires intensive analytic work. In addition, the structure of a symptom, according to Reich, is simpler than that of the character.

From this standpoint, psychoanalytic treatment begins with analysis of characterological resistances. Emphasis is placed more on the form in which the patient presents something than on the content: the *how* is more relevant in analysis than the *what*. The manner in which the person in analysis resists must be analysed extensively and in detail. Character analysis is education *for* analysis *by* analysis. The analysis is initially directed towards the patient's ego. During the second phase of treatment, analysis of early childhood experiences takes a more central position. Overcoming resistances that result from the character is not really the same as changing the character. The latter assumes an analysis of early childhood sources. We can recognize the approach of more recent authors in the field of personality disorders, such as Kernberg and Kohut, in the working method described by Reich in the first decades of the twentieth century.

The writings of Reich and other theorists from that time in the field of psychoanalytic characterology, such as Abraham and Fenichel, must not be seen as a reflection of the prevailing working method in the practical field of psychoanalysis at that time. The classic symptomatic transference neuroses formed the principal role in a positive indication for psychoanalytic treatment. Only gradually did a change come about, as Leo Stone described in his 1954 article, "The widening scope of indications for psychoanalysis". The indication field was extended to delinquents, addicts, psychosomatic disorders, character neuroses, borderline and narcissistic disorders. Even schizophrenia became the subject of analysis. The pendulum swung back, however, and groups of analysts kept warning about the broadening of the indication field (Anna Freud, 1954). They argued that psychoanalysis was developed on the basis of treatment of transference neuroses and is most successful with such psychoneuroses. The findings of the Psychotherapy Research Project of the Menninger Foundation (Wallerstein, 1986) also pointed in the direction of a limited indication field and stimulated the omitting of so-called "heroic indications".

In current psychoanalytic clinical practice, analyses of symptoms and character go hand in hand. On theoretical and clinical grounds, it is inconceivable for symptoms and character to be diagnosed and treated independently, although the accent can be different in the complaints which patients present. Either a symptom disorder or a character or personality disorder can be primary.

In principle, "classic" psychoanalysis appears, owing to its high frequency and intensive character, to be particularly suitable for problems of a more complicated nature which require lengthy treatment. Character disorders or personality problems are relevant in this respect. At the same time, couch analysis demands a great deal from patients. They must feel comfortable in aiming at a structural change in which the first matter of importance is not relieving specific symptoms. Patients must be motivated to acquire insight into themselves, to be able to and have the courage to handle this process. They must have the capacity to begin an emotionally meaningful, longlasting relationship with someone, in this case the analyst. In particular, patients with a personality disorder often do not meet these requirements, or do so only to a limited extent. One of the characteristics is that they finally experience their own behaviour as ego-syntonic and have the tendency to blame problems that occur in their interaction with other people on those others or on circumstances. Their defence and resistances, which are rooted in the disturbed character, lead to their frequently not seeking treatment. If they do, however, it is usually because of accompanying symptoms, and they only want to be free of the complaints. In short, it is not a favourable starting point for high-frequency psychoanalysis that will extend for several years.

Many different labels are used for individual psychotherapy on psychoanalytic grounds (Thiel, 1986): psychoanalytic psychotherapy, psychodynamic therapy, focal psychotherapy, psychotherapy "on analytic lines", and expressive psychotherapy. In addition to these are couples therapy and group psychotherapy performed on the basis of psychoanalytic principles. Every variant uses the psychoanalytic frame of reference. The setting differs from classic psychoanalysis because the patient sits rather than lies down. The ground rule of free association is used explicitly in many variants, however. The psychoanalytic therapist is often more directive than the analyst and the duration of analytic therapies is often shorter. In a variant such as that developed by Malan (1979), psychotherapeutic treatment lasts about 20 sessions. In view of the emphasis on short-term treatment in many non-psychoanalytic forms of treatment (i.e. behaviour therapy, client-centred therapy, cognitive therapy), the appeal of therapy with an analytic basis has increased. This development is also determined by factors beyond any clinical considerations, such as the policy of insurance companies.

Many patients with a personality disorder, as described in the DSM-IV and ICD-10, are, according to a psychoanalytic frame of reference, equated with patients having a borderline level of functioning (Kernberg, 1984). This is true in particular for Cluster B of Axis II of the DSM. These are the antisocial, borderline, histrionic and narcissistic personalities. The concept of "borderline disorder" has developed on the basis of psychoanalytic practice, in which a category of patients appeared to be suitable for couch analysis. These patients experienced a regression that was often too deep and no longer productive. A transference psychosis was often lying in wait (Derksen, 1990a). Their borderline ego structure was not solid enough to bear the classic psychoanalytic process.

Owing to changes in psychoanalytic techniques, these patients turned out to be more treatable. With more serious personality disorders that, in Kernberg's view, function on a borderline level, it is advisable to replace the classic setting of couch analysis with face-to-face psychoanalytic psychotherapy. This is also referred to as psychodynamic therapy (Kernberg et al., 1989). Much more than psychoanalysis, psychoanalytic therapy can also be directed towards influencing specific symptoms and complaints. Because of this, it can more readily relate to needs as they are experienced by many patients.

For years, many clinicians have observed an increase in narcissistic and borderline disorders. All kinds of symptoms can form a clinical picture, but a personality disorder is considered as primary. The development of psychoanalytic or psychodynamic psychotherapy can be seen in this context as an attempt to formulate an answer to the problem of an increasing category of patients requesting help, who show an inability to start or complete couch analysis. Adjustments in techniques, in the sense of a face-to-face setting and emphasis on certain interventions, are necessary here for building up a good working relationship, as well as for developing an effective strategy for influencing the disorder, in order to improve reality testing and bring about better adaption (Derksen & van der Mast, 1993).

A FEW COMMENTS

The psychoanalytic approach always entails some problems, which primarily concern the recognizability of the psychoanalytic conception of unconscious processes. What is essential for psychoanalysis is not in line with what most other schools of psychotherapy consider essential. The reconstruction of the unconscious only begins after many other therapeutic processes cease. Secondly, the structural, dynamic and genetic views of psychoanalysis are not, or are only to a limited extent, suitable for examination with a scientific empirical approach. At the same time, the empirical quantitative approach is quite dominant in research centres and universities. Psychoanalysis has never offered an alternative to the experimental empirical tradition with sufficient persuasiveness. As long as this remains the case, psychoanalysis cannot make a sufficient claim to scientific theory in the eyes of the scientific mainstream (Derksen, 1983b).

Furthermore, there is also a conceptual problem. The concepts with which drive theory has been indicated since Freud do not appeal to everybody and certainly not to every analyst. Except for these concepts, the drives themselves were also considered as obsolete by extreme representatives of object relations theory. Others (e.g. Greenberg, 1991) realize again that without a drive theory this does not work and make a courageous, but in my opinion failed, attempt to construct alternative drives. In France, Jacques Lacan tried to give psychoanalysis another conceptual basis, but his theory posed more problems than it solved.

It has not been made sufficiently clear to what extent the different psychotherapies derived from classic psychoanalysis can claim to be part of psychoanalytic treatment methods. How analytic are the different therapies and what exactly do they contribute to the treatment of personality disorders? These and other questions still await a satisfactory answer.

CHAPTER 3.2 The behavioural approach

In the behaviour therapy tradition, the assumption that behaviour is situation specific has been a predominant influence. It is likely that this theme of behavioural consistency is still viewed in this traditional sense by many behaviour therapists and researchers. Daily and clinical experience, however, points to the fact that at least a large part of behaviour is consistent across various situations. Empirical studies in the behaviour therapeutic tradition also start with this viewpoint (Bowers, 1973; Turner & Turkat, 1988). It is likely that with the increasing acceptance by behaviour therapists of a classification system of disorders such as the DSM, this type of research will bring about an increase in the number of publications in the area of personality disorders. To date, a start has been made, chiefly by Ira Turkat (1990), on the development of a behaviour therapy approach to treating personality disorders.

CASE FORMULATION

Turkat finds the DSM classification useful and employs it as a framework for his approach. In what he calls "case formulation", he starts with a diagnostic phase in which the therapist makes a behaviour analysis. The therapist pays special attention to interaction with the patient. He recodes every word, gesture, action and manifestation of the patient, on the basis of which he tries to formulate provisional hypotheses on the dominant personality traits. From these hypotheses, behaviours and symptoms not yet observed are predicted. Furthermore, the patient is questioned over and over about these behaviours and symptoms until an exhaustive list of symptoms has been obtained. On the basis of this material, a hypothesis is formulated about the central mechanism that may be responsible for the symptoms.

In "case formulation", a hypothesis is included about the etiology of the complaints and a prediction of the patient's future behaviour. Problem behaviour is extensively analysed, in which its history plays a large role. Predisposing factors are mapped out. All this information forms the basis for an individual, specific, custom-made treatment programme. The information mainly serves to test the hypothesis in regard to the central mechanism. An example of a central mechanism is the lack of empathy characteristics in the narcissistic personality disorder. This is one possibility, although the diagnosis of a narcissistic personality disorder can also be the cause of various other central mechanisms. This extensive "case formulation" is characteristic of Turkat's approach. Other authors in behaviour therapy (Alden, 1989; Renneberg et al., 1990; Stravynski et al., 1989) use this sort of technique to a lesser degree and seem to associate themselves more with the symptom disorders that often go hand in hand with personality disorders.

THERAPIST AS TEACHER AND GUIDE

In contrast to many insight-oriented psychotherapies, the therapeutic relationship in the mainstream of behaviour therapy is not of crucial importance. The effect of therapy is mostly due to the strategies with which problems are approached. The therapist is a teacher and guide. This learning process supposes a good therapeutic relationship, to which end motivation strategies may be applied. These motivation strategies can be especially important in the case of a patient with a personality disorder. Kiesler's (1986) interaction styles are used to create successful contact with the patient. Often this consists of initially matching — to a limited extent — the behaviour that the patient evokes in the therapist (for example, submissiveness with a narcissistic personality). Gradually the therapist breaks through this interaction style. Group therapy with the same type of patients can also be used to increase motivation.

The treatment strategies of the behaviour therapy approach are more easily applied to symptom disorders. Turkat is explicit, however, about how to work with personality disorders. He believes that the central mechanism must be modified. In his work, we can observe three aspects of intervention. First, there are strategies for controlling anxiety. These are useful, for instance, for a paranoid personality's fear of criticism or a dependent personality's fear of taking decisions independently. Relaxation training, formulating an anxiety hierarchy, breaking through avoidance behaviour and exposure techniques are applied in such cases.

A second type of strategy is applied in patients who lack impulse control, such as those with an antisocial personality. The main strategy is a response-prevention programme, often applied by means of a hierarchy. A third group of techniques concerns acquiring new skills and developing or refining existing skills: social skills training, cognitive training, sensitivity training. Patients lacking these skills, such as those with an avoidant personality, can particularly benefit from this. But even narcissistic patients are trained by Turkat to improve their empathic abilities. For a behaviour therapist he uses remarkable techniques, such as having a narcissistic personality read a book about Rogerian therapy. Family members of the patient are often involved in treatment as well.

DIALECTIC BEHAVIOUR THERAPY

Turner (1989) developed a structured cognitive behaviour therapy programme especially for the borderline patient population, while Linehan (1987) developed a dialectic behaviour therapy programme for out-patient borderline patients. Turner combines cognitive therapy focused on problem-solving skills, self-control desensitization focused on stress-evoking situations, supportive psychotherapy and "state of mind" modification. Individual treatment is combined with participation in a psycho-educational group. Linehan (Linehan & Heard, 1992) practises an extensive diagnostic method and uses a broad range of behaviour therapy techniques. Her accent on a dialectic process appears to refer to occupying oneself simultaneously with the various and contradictory characteristics of the borderline patient; change, synthesis and interconnection are emphasized during the assessment as well as the treatment. She has particularly worked with suicidal borderline patients and also does research on the effect of treatment.

A FEW COMMENTS

In contrast to the stimulating influence of behaviour therapy on the treatment of symptom disorders, the influence on interventions for personality disorders is limited. In this regard, there is a gap between practising behaviour therapists and researchers in the framework of learning theory. The former, by working in a clinical setting, automatically pay attention to the importance of personality. The latter appear to be for the most part imprisoned by the dominant models.

If there were to be a breakthrough leading to closer attention to treatment of the personality, and so not only focusing on the symptoms of somebody with a personality disorder, behaviour therapy would start to resemble cognitive therapy more and also other forms of insight-oriented psychotherapy. Owing to a potential loss of identity, there is perhaps a reticence to make developments toward such a breakthrough.

CHAPTER 3.3   The cognitive approach

The cognitive approach has received an important place in academic psychology. In some cases, the "cognitive revolution" has replaced learning theory, while in other cases they have existed simultaneously or complementarily. In the field of psychotherapy, cognitive therapy has developed relatively independently from behaviour therapy. One can think of such developments as rational emotive therapy, as developed after 1955 by Albert Ellis, and cognitive therapy initiated in the early 1960s by Aaron Beck (Perris, Blackburn & Perris, 1988). Ellis (1962) places the roots of his orientation in the tradition of psychoanalysis (Derksen, 1983b). The accent shifts from the unconscious to the cognitive, mainly conscious, side of a person. In the course of the development of cognitive therapy, behaviour therapy strategies have come to form part of cognitive intervention protocols. Among psychotherapists, the interest in cognitive therapy has increased sixfold since 1973 (Beck & Freeman, 1990).

SCHEMAS

An important point of departure at the basis of cognitive therapy is the thought that the most important source of dysfunctional behaviour and affects lies not so much in the motivational and response aspects of behaviour as in the incorrect attributions that people have. Personality is considered as a relatively stable organization of structures that fit together. They take care of the handling of external and internal stimuli and also direct behaviour. Beck and Freeman (1990) consider a personality disorder as a remarkable illustration of the "schema" concept. Schemas are specific rules that regulate information processing and behaviour; they can be compared with what George Kelly (1955) called "personal constructs". People can have all kinds of schemas, including personal schemas, familial schemas, cultural schemas and religious schemas. There are cognitive schemas responsible for making abstractions, interpretations and memories; affective schemas that generate feelings; motivational schemas that relate to wishes and desires; instrumental schemas that prepare actions; control schemas that take care of self-observation and inhibit actions. Schemas develop throughout life. The schemas that exist during childhood undergo a process of assimilation and accommodation, such as has been described by Piaget (Freeman, 1988). For a variety of reasons, certain schemas do not evolve in childhood but remain stuck at a particular level of development. In this is seen the start of a personality disorder.

These schemas co-operate as a sort of conveyer belt with different stations between perception and behaviour. Beck and Freeman (1990) state:

> Schemas can be inferred from behaviour assessed through interview and history taking. With the axis II patient, the schematic work is at the heart of the therapeutic endeavour. The position of particular schemas on the continuum from active (hypervalent or valent) to inactive (dormant or latent), and their position on the continuum from impermeable to changeable, are among the essential dimensions for the therapist to use in conceptualizing the patient's problems and developing a treatment strategy. (p. 8)

Schemas are difficult to change. Even if the patient realizes that his or her schemas are dysfunctional, bringing about change is often an immense task. "They [the schemas] are held firmly in place by behavioral, cognitive, and affective elements" (Beck & Freeman, 1990, p. 10). The therapeutic approach must also fit with all three levels.

COGNITIVE ATTITUDES

Personality traits are preferably called strategies, which have developed from the interaction between innate disposition and environmental influences. The dependent personality shows attachment as a strategy that is connected to a typical cognitive attitude, a fundamental belief, expressed in the sentence "I am helpless." These people consider themselves as needy, weak and incompetent and the other person as a competent caretaker. In a problematic situation, the schema "I need help" is activated. They believe they need a strong (significant) other to be able to survive.

The strategy of the avoidant person is avoidance and the cognitive style is "I can be hurt." They see themselves as incompetent, and have the fundamental conviction that they are worthless and unloved. They see the other person as potentially critical and disinterested.

The paranoid person employs caution as a strategy and the cognitive attitude is "People are potential adversaries." The key word is "suspicion". They see the other person as an imposter and manipulator, themselves as righteous. They believe that they are vulnerable in relation to other people.

The narcissistic personality's strategy is to do everything possible to increase its superior status, to build up the self. The cognitive style is "I am special." These patients see themselves as special and unique, feel superior and think they are entitled to special favours. They seek primarily the admiration of others in order to establish their own sense of grandiosity. One of their essential convictions is that they deserve special dispensations and privileges because they are special. They feel superior to others and above the law.

The histrionic personality dramatizes, accompanied by the cognitive attitude "I must make an impression." These people see themselves as very attractive and impressive, deserving attention. They start intensive relationships with others, but under the condition that they are the centre of the group and that others take on the role of listening audience. Their essential conviction is that they are fundamentally unattractive. They often need other people who admire them in order to feel happy.

The strategy of the obsessive-compulsive personality is perfectionism, whose cognitive message is "Mistakes are bad. I cannot make mistakes." Key words are "control" and "must". They consider they are responsible for themselves as well as other people. They see others as irresponsible or incompetent. Their basic convictions contain the following thoughts: "I am fundamentally poorly organized, I need order, a system and rules to be able to survive."

The strategy of the antisocial personality is one of attack and the cognitive style is "People exist to make fun of me." They see themselves as loners, autonomous and strong. The other person is an exploiter and deserves to be exploited. Furthermore, the other person is seen as weak and deserves to serve as prey. This is part of their essential conviction that they must be the aggressor if they do not want to become the victim.

The strategy of the schizoid personality is isolation and the cognitive style is "I need a great deal of room." They see themselves as autonomous and as loners. They like to take decisions alone and do solitary activities. They see others as pushy and perceive the openness of other people as an attempt to hedge them in. Their essential conviction is "I am fundamentally alone." Close relationships with other people are considered undesirable and limiting.

According to Beck & Freeman (1990), borderline and schizotypal people are not as easily typified, since they possess a great variety of typical styles. Their dysfunctional attitudes and behaviours are generalizations that are inflexible and difficult to change. Their attitudes usually stem from childhood and are the result of a typical sensitivity to such things as rejection during the learning process. Their generalizations lead to a particular way of processing and storing information, in which their behaviours are founded.

ECLECTIC THERAPY

Seen from the frame of reference of cognitive therapy, the irrational thoughts and dysfunctional opinions that form the basis of the Axis I symptom disorders are treated rather easily with rational therapy. A personality disorder pertains to persistent dysfunctional beliefs that have taken a structural place in the person's cognitive organization. Treatment is intensive and takes more time than treating depression, for instance. In addition to challenging, making explicit and replacing irrational cognitions, the therapist applies behaviour experiments in order to effect the desired change gradually. Assignments for performing all kinds of activities, assertiveness exercises, role playing, relaxation training and exposure techniques can be considered in this connection. Experiences from the past also play a role in discovering and working through irrational schemas. Irrational ideas are unravelled and related to the original situations in the past: the meaning of traumas discovered in the course of life get a place. Experimental techniques such as reliving childhood experiences and imagery are used to obtain material. "A rule of thumb is that cognitive change depends on a certain level of affective experience" (Beck, 1987). Furthermore, a good working relationship between patient and therapist is considered crucial. Beck & Freeman (1990, p. 65) describe the use of transference reactions. negative feelings in regard to the therapy situation and the therapist are seen as distorted interpretations that provide information about the patient's specific cognitive patterns. The therapist's role is that of adviser, teacher, re-educator and sometimes friend, who makes a great deal of use of his or her own life experiences to help the patient.

In a technical respect, cognitive therapy for personality disorders is an eclectic type of treatment. Use is made of all types of interventions developed in totally different traditions and directed towards cognitions, affects and behaviours. The conceptualization of the individual case is fundamental in the choice of techniques. It is assumed, however, that the development of new schemas and the changing of old, irrational and dysfunctional beliefs is the core of the treatment. It is also presumed that this aspect of treatment results in the greatest effect.

A FEW COMMENTS

Cognitive therapy, as it has been worked out particularly for the benefit of treating personality disorders, is fundamentally eclectic in nature. All kinds of techniques and approaches are applied without hesitation by psychotherapists who obviously want to be known as "cognitive". The question arises of what this label still means. The integration of a multitude of behavioural, experiential and psychodynamic techniques, without a critical basis in terms of a cognitive theoretical framework, greatly reduces the meaningfulness of this approach. The use of an extensive arsenal of techniques appears to prove the position that the cognitive approach alone is insufficient for the processes of change necessary for patients with a personality disorder.

If cognitive therapy wants to retain its identity, an expansion of the theoretical aspects of the cognitive reference framework is urgently required. Questions quickly raised when reading the literature include: What is the difference between schema, attitude, or basic belief and strategy? At this level, there is a great lack of definitions and demarcation of concepts.

Besides behaviour therapy, cognitive and rational therapy at least offer a valuable addition that has made its contribution to symptom disorders which are not too complex in nature. At first sight, the different cognitive patterns with the various types of personality disorders evoke the impression of a creative contribution. Clinical practice concerning the treatment of patients is much more complicated, however, and there we witness the expansion of an arsenal of techniques. For the time being, it can be said that the cognitive approach can provide its own contribution to the process of treating personality disorders. Reducing this treatment process to a cognitive one is contrary to what appears to be clinically necessary.

CHAPTER 3.4 The interpersonal approach

Interpersonal theory, in the tradition of Sullivan (1953) and Leary (1957), presents itself in the so-called "second generation" (Kiesler, 1986) as a scientific and clinically rich alternative to the DSM personality disorders. The interpersonal circle is, according to Kiesler, a theoretically derived, operationally grounded taxonomy that is not only able to generate reliable diagnoses, but also offers distinguished therapeutic approaches.

ABNORMAL BEHAVIOUR

Abnormal behaviour is defined as an inadequate manner of interpersonal communication. In contrast to what has often been done in systems theory, Kiesler assumes that an abnormal individual has a rigid, limited and extreme communication pattern. Others are often unconsciously involved in this. The person becomes more or less locked into this pattern as he or she elicits aversive behaviour in others and is not aware of his or her own contribution to this process. The central point for interpersonal taxonomy is the assumption that anyone who interacts continuously deals with two themes: affiliation (love−hate, friendliness−hostility) and control (dominance−submission, higher status−lower status). At an early point in development, a person acquires a certain interpersonal style, adopts certain roles and develops a definition of self. This leads to a certain type of behaviour in respect to others and also to certain claims on others. This also includes the nature of the relationship a person engages in, the degree of intimacy that characterizes it, the extent of control over it and the extent of dominance in it. From this point of view, everyone sends out a force field to which others are forced to react with complementary and also limited behavioural possibilities.

The themes of affiliation and control have been made into axes of an interpersonal circle that usually, as in the 1982 version, has 16 segments

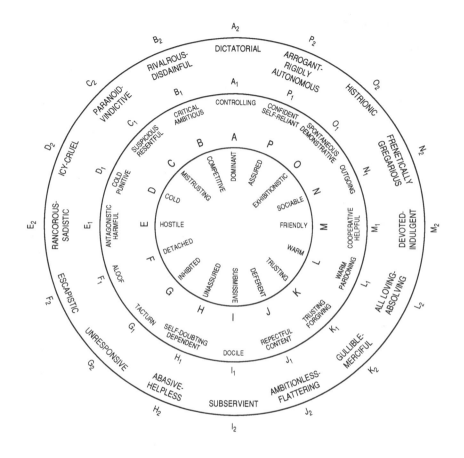

Figure 3.4.1 The interpersonal circle, 1982 version. Reproduced by permission from T. Millon & G. Klerman (Eds) (1986) *Contemporary Directions in Psychopathology: Toward the DSM-IV*. New York: The Guilford Press

(see Figure 3.4.1). An expanded version of 64 segments with 350 bipolar interpersonal items has also been developed. The segments are classes of interpersonal behaviour. Human behaviour is generally based on a merging of two or more of these segments. The outside ring indicates the most extreme variant of the axis concerned. In the centre this is zero. Interpersonal behaviour is abnormal if it takes on one or both of the following forms in the circle: rigidly stuck in one or more of the 16 segments; extreme scores on one or more of the outside categories. Diagnosis using this circle is solely directed towards overt, observable, interpersonal behaviour of abnormal people (Kiesler, 1986, p. 585). It does not concern motives, emotional states and cognitions, etc.

TRANSLATIONS

Over the course of time, various successful attempts have been made to translate the circle into the DSM personality disorders. One cannot expect this translation to go smoothly, but it is possible to achieve it in such a way that the information in the circle will produce a prototypical profile of interpersonal variables that can be associated with the DSM categories. A one-to-one relationship is not within the realms of possibility.

In Kiesler's translation, five personality disorders end up in two adjoining segments: the histrionic personality in N_2, O_2; the narcissistic personality in O_2, P_2; the dependent personality in H, J, without specification of levels; the obsessive-compulsive in F_1, G (without specification); and the passive-aggressive in E_1, F_1. Two personality disorders are translated into one segment only: the schizoid personality in F_2; and the antisocial in E (unspecified). The following are found in three of the adjoining circle segments: the paranoid personality in C_2, D_1, E_1; the avoidant in F_1, G_1, H_1. Two disorders are characterized by segments of different quadrants: the schizotypical personality in C_1, F_1, F (unspecified), while the borderline personality shows dramatic changes between segments in opposite quadrants: B_2 to J_2, E_2 to M_2.

The intensity of abnormal interpersonal behaviour varies with different disorders; some are only found in the centre ring, others in the middle and in the outer rings, while others, such as the narcissistic personality, are positioned only in the outer ring. A division into three clusters, as made in the DSM, cannot be maintained in this system. In this translation, the degree of complexity can be read in the locations occupied in the circle. The DSM personality disorders are also to be placed primarily in the "hostile" left half of the circle, most in the lower left half, the hostile—submissive quadrant. Although the remaining possibilities which the circle offers do occur, they are seldom found in psychiatric settings.

From the viewpoint of interpersonal theory, the DSM classification does not include a specification of the situations in which this type of behaviour occurs — a specification that is, however, necessary for this approach.

INTERPERSONAL THERAPY

According to Kiesler, the power of the interpersonal circle lies in the prediction of therapeutic interventions for personality disorders. He puts this as follows: "Indeed, the real promise of the Circle is that, having identified prototypic segments which define a particular disorder, theoretically derivable interventions can be systematically designated" (1986, p. 593). An objective of treatment is to promote behaviour that is contrary to the behaviour that currently dominates. For instance, with the obsessive-compulsive personality, N, O behaviour should increase in frequency and intensity. In this way, the person is detached from a rigid behaviour pattern. That can best be achieved by training in the opposite behaviours. The expected complementary behaviour elicited from the therapist by the patient can be predicted on the basis of the circle. Dominant behaviour evokes submissive behaviour and vice versa. Hostile behaviour evokes animosity and friendly behaviour evokes friendly behaviour. Transference reactions are charted in advance in this way, all the advantages of which are used in the treatment. The therapist can, for instance, specifically not exhibit behavioural reactions that evoke cool and suspicious responses from compulsive patients, but instead another type of behaviour pattern so that patients gain an entirely new experience in the interaction. This type of intervention based on the circle is extensively described in interpersonal therapy.

A FEW COMMENTS

A fundamental point of departure in interpersonal theory is that interpersonal behaviour means continuously negotiating affiliation (love – hate, friendliness – hostility) and control (dominance – submission, higher status – lower status). In fact, this reduces interpersonal behaviour to (1) a negotiation situation and (2) a pair of dimensions. How fundamental is this? Upon further consideration, the negotiation perspective and the two dimensions are possibilities in human behaviour, but certainly not the only foundations. After all, people often come together just for fun, pleasure, amusement and enjoyment. Negotiating, even if a deeper construct is implied, does have a definite cognitive connotation. This does not fit in with emotional processes and with considerations such as an attachment process that may precede a negotiation.

The theme of "affiliation" undoubtedly has broader implications than the theme of "control". Love and hate also reflect the two drives from psychoanalytic theory. These usually do not allow for such negotiation, however; cognitive dominance is seen as a fallacy. The tendency to control seems a phase-specific need; some people have this much more strongly than others, and there are also people for whom this theme is not at all relevant. Moreover, the need for control is very situation specific. In a situation with more unfamiliar people, one may have a tendency to control, while this declines in situations with acquaintances.

The circle is interesting within the framework of more general psychological theory on the personality. By the translation of the DSM categories into this circle, an effect is obtained comparable to translating concepts from one language into another. This process does not necessarily furnish more insight into the concepts. In this case, the increased complexity even augments confusion. We do not need the translation derivations in regard to treatment; they can also be derived from the DSM language.

CHAPTER 3.5 The biological approach

INTRODUCTION

If we posit that behaviour is the result of person and environment, then the person is in turn the product of biology and environment. The human personality comes into being and exists in the dialectic process between culture and biology. The personality demonstrates behaviour that is sometimes more situation specific and consequently variable (diachronic) and at other times more person specific and constant (synchronic). The relationship between diachrony and synchrony is complex and very few theories exist about it.

The relationship between psyche and soma is also relevant in this respect. An interaction between psychological and somatic factors is often discussed. The somatic and psychological appear to be placed on an equal level in a causal relationship. This line of thought is the basis of a concept that can be called with Ryle (1949) a category misconception. Thinking, feeling and acting resolutely are incorrectly described in the same language as physical, chemical and physiological processes. Like the somatic process the psychological is a complex organized whole, but fundamentally different in nature and structure. The somatic process is constituted by a field of causes and effects, which is also true for the psychological process, although the relationships here are non-mechanical. In regard to the psychological process, we therefore prefer speaking of determinants (Derksen & van de Loo, 1986).

The somatic process is a necessary but insufficient condition for the functioning of the psychological process. Conversely, brain physiology presupposes acting and perceiving. A disturbed metabolism of neurotransmitters such as serotonin, dopamine and noradrenaline can be a necessary condition for a specific type of aggressive behaviour. A suppressed psychological conflict can be a condition for the conversion of psychogenic blindness. However, it is a conceptual error to assume that one is the cause of the other. A necessary condition is still not a sufficient condition. In terms of causality, it is a question of the sufficient condition. Psychological and somatic factors differ in nature, validity and reach, and it is generally very difficult to think about them in hierarchical terms.

Research in the somatic and psychological fields differs, since their research goals fundamentally differ. Just as research goals differ, psyche and soma also impose on researchers a specific way of conducting research. Psyche and soma are not susceptible to being known in the same manner, and an adequate understanding of psyche and soma demands methodologies specifically geared to them. The research of the anatomical substratum differs radically from exploring a subject's feelings, experiences, motives, thoughts and desires. Experimenting and quantifying in the former area is weighted in a totally different way from that in the latter field. Physiological examination of a stomach ulcer does not do any harm and is no less valid than the psychological significance of discovering the ulcer in a psychotherapeutic relationship with the patient. The development of pharmacotherapy for ulcers is based on an entirely different research tradition, which is not influenced by psychology. Therefore, it is indeed incorrect to say that psychological, physiological and biochemical factors are together a constellation that determines the personality. Just as one does not cause the other, they can also not be summed up in an explanatory series. Physiological causes are different from psychological determinants. We have to learn to live with that conceptual difference on a theoretical level. We cannot combine the information from both research traditions in a collective language, a base language or metalanguage. This is fundamentally impossible.

In research the concepts of innate versus acquired are still usually seen in opposition, resulting in conceptual confusion. The pendulum swings towards the empirical and biological approach and away from the psychodynamic and psychological approach: a movement which should have been scrapped long ago. The remainder of this chapter should be understood against this background.

HEREDITARY DETERMINATION

Evidence for genetic contributions to individual personality differences is derived from three sources (McGuffin & Thapar, 1992). The first two are indirect: animal research on differences in temperament and psychophysiological research on biological correlates of personality. The third source is personality measurement with the aid of questionnaires. Comparisons are made in particular between relatives raised together and separately, and pairs of identical and fraternal twins.

In the area of personality differences, genetic research carried out using studies on adoption and twins claim that about half is determined by heredity (Kilzieh & Cloninger, 1993; Zuckerman, 1991; Tellegen *et al.*, 1988). Various personality traits, studied through correlations with identical twins, more or less produce correlations of between .40 and .60. The two factors expressed most powerfully in this are extroversion and neuroticism. Intellectual interests score almost as highly as neuroticism. Persistence also produces relatively high values, especially for women but not for men. Conversely, cynical attitudes produce high values with men and not with women.

Hans Eysenck (1947, 1957) was the first modern theoretician who occupied himself with the biological basis of the personality. It is impossible to imagine personality theory without his three fundamental dimensions: introversion—extroversion, neuroticism (or emotional instability), and psychoticism (or antisocial tendencies versus socialized humanity). As shown above, two of them appear in recent research.

McGuffin & Thapar (1992) are more cautious and state that despite problems in definition and measurement, the results of animal research, psychophysiological research and research using questionnaires suggest that the personality probably has a partial genetic basis.

PERSONALITY DISORDERS

In the field of personality disorders, the antisocial personality, previously called psychopath, has in the course of time received particular attention. McGuffin & Thapar (1992) come to the following conclusions on personality disorders. In terms of the antisocial personality, in studies on twins and adopted people usually defined in terms of being "guilty of criminal actions" and repeated convictions, a partial genetic etiology can be considered. The strongest evidence for heredity exists for petty crimes and the destruction of other people's property. This evidence does not exist for violence against other people. Given the fact that the research in this field does not make use of the DSM and ICD description of the antisocial personality, one still has to examine whether the same relationships can be found for this operational definition.

Just as for Eysenck's concept of neuroticism, anxiety is also currently viewed as partially determined by genetics, which is based on studies of twins. McGuffin & Thapar (1992) relate these studies on anxiety to the avoidant personality. They make a very convenient switch, however, from symptom to person. The same applies to what they report on obsessive-compulsive disorder and obsessive-compulsive personality disorder. In relation to the latter, the little research that exists is contradictory. The same applies to the histrionic personality. As already mentioned, some genetic evidence can also be found for extroversion as a trait. Histrionic personalities are also characterized by extroversion, but this trait alone is absolutely insufficient to characterize the total picture. People with a minor personality disorder can also be very extroverted.

Much more research has been done on disorders in the schizophrenic spectrum. For this a genetic component is no longer doubted. The extension of schizophrenia to schizotypia and schizotypal personality disorder is problematic, given the DSM description of a stable personality. It does not seem very advisable to examine the schizotypal personality for a genetic component and at the same time connect the schizotypia to genetic determinants and biological correlates. With regard to molecular genetics and the biological basis of personality disorders, McGuffin & Thapar (1992) conclude:

> In summary then, the explanatory power of cytogenetic techniques is limited, and biochemical markers of the sorts of psychophysiological measures which we discussed earlier can at best provide us with "endophenotypes" which lie a step closer to the abnormal genotypes than do clinical descriptions, but still represent vague and indistinct sign posts on the complicated pathway between abnormal genes and abnormal behaviour. A more attractive proposition might be to utilize the techniques of recombinant DNA research and go straight for the genotypes themselves. (p. 20)

PSYCHOPHYSIOLOGY

Psychophysiology is considered as a branch of psychology in which physiological parameters are used to study psychological phenomena (Kilzieh & Cloninger, 1993). Central in this are individual differences in sensory perception of stimuli from the environment, the processing of information and the organism's response to this. Some of the frequently used physiological parameters are: electroencephalography (EEG), evoked potentials (EP), event related potentials (ERPS), electrodermal activity and heart rate. These measures have been used a great deal among psychopaths in particular. The DSM and the ICD personality descriptions are, however, proportionately much too descriptive and abstract. For this type of research, dimensions such as introversion, extroversion, impulsiveness, anxiety and aggression offer greater possibilities.

In empirical research, a relationship has been established between aggressive behaviour and diminished serotonin function (Siever, Trestman & Silverman, 1992). The effects of tri-monoamines have been repeatedly connected with the emotions and general behaviour. The three-dimensional model of "novelty seeking", "harm avoidance" and "reward dependence" proposed by Cloninger is interesting in this context as well. Harm avoidance is connected to the serotonin system. This leads to behaviour inhibitions, cautiousness, indecisiveness and anxiety. Reward dependence is related to the norepinephrine system. This concerns dependency, emotional warmth, attachment and sociability. Novelty seeking is connected to dopamine which concerns exploration, interest in the environment, activity and energy. These dimensions can easily be determined by observing young children. They are theoretical psychological conceptualizations of supposed dimensions that can be coupled to biological correlates as conditions, without this relating to sufficient conditions.

A FEW COMMENTS

The biological approach is complex, but interesting and promising. Pharmacotherapy, which goes hand in hand with this approach, has provided relief for suffering patients in many respects. Everything points to the fact that neither the DSM nor ICD categories are suitable for this type of research. Interesting are fundamental dimensions of the personality, many versions of which have been developed over the years beginning with Eysenck, and which are also expressed in the five-factor model which is discussed separately.

In daily clinical work with patients with and without (relatively speaking) a personality disorder, we are impressed with the importance of dimensions such as extroversion, introversion, neuroticism, anxiety, impulsiveness and others. At the same time, we observe the significant contribution of the rearing and socialization of a child with a strong hereditary component in whatever respect. Impulsiveness can undergo development that is not inhibited by upbringing and poses many problems for the person's personality and environment. Moreover, an entirely different method of upbringing, especially adapted to such a child, enables the child to control the impulsive drive. Reflection on the impulses and their sublimation are among the possibilities and make a contribution to adequate adaptation. In this process of upbringing, not only do the strategies and child rearing of the parents dominate, they are also observed by an experiencing and imaginative child and adopted as a model without the parents' noticing this. In this identification process, children integrate their parents' personality traits into their own psychobiological structure. A child with a neurotic predisposition will be extrasensitive to these sides in one or both parents and easily identify with them. The reinforcement that occurs because of this cannot be attributed purely to heredity.

The biological contribution to personality and to the disturbed person never frees the person or the psychotherapist from the responsibility of helping to influence the negative aspects of this. Biological input has a favourable effect on the definition of psychotherapeutic possibilities and putting them into perspective. The psychotherapeutic impact on the fundamental functioning of the personality gives biological research a place in the area of human behaviour.

CHAPTER 3.6 Millon's biosocial learning approach

Millon calls his theoretical contribution the *biosocial learning* theory. The following three polarities are essential for this part of Millon's work:

- pleasure−pain
- self−other
- active−passive

Millon emphasizes a certain universality in these polarities, which reappear in the work of many theorists more or less identically.

> First, personality may be conceived as a complex of structures and functions designed to essentially maximize comfort and minimize discomfort (pleasure−pain). Beyond this, these structures and functions reflect where the individual looks to achieve these aims (self−other) and how he or she behaves in doing so (active−passive). Pathological deficits or imbalances that occur in the *nature* (pleasure versus pain), *source* (self versus others), or *instrumental behaviours* (active versus passive) that individuals employ will result in any of ten clinically-relevant, *basic* personality patterns, as well as three, usually more severe variants. (Millon, 1986, p. 653)

PLEASURE−PAIN

Millon also calls this pleasure−pain dimension the pathology in the nature of reinforcement. In this dimension, he summarizes energies, drives, feelings, emotions and affects. On the other hand, he refers to aspects of environment, such as events and objects. He mentions in this connection sex, sport, art and money. What is pleasurable to one person can be painful to another.

In relation to personality disorders, Millon distinguishes three possibilities. In the first place, it is possible to conceive of patients for whom both motivational systems are deficient; their capacity to experience events of life as either pleasurable or painful is lacking. They do not appear to be interested in personal enjoyment and social satisfaction; they do not seek positive reinforcement and do not make an attempt to avoid negative reinforcement. Interpersonal difficulties, however, do not seem to cause them real discomfort. In the DSM and ICD, this is called the schizoid personality. In Millon's framework, such people are called passive-detached personalities. Their fate is usually isolation and alienation. Millon believes that both constitutional factors and problems of upbringing play a role in the genesis of this.

Secondly, there are patients for whom only a single aspect of the polarity is present or abnormally dominant. These patients experience much in life as painful and very little as pleasurable. They experience anxiety and displeasure, but not happiness. In the DSM and ICD, they correspond to avoidant personalities. These are the active-detached types in Millon's framework. In the genesis of these types, Millon refers again to neurological as well as biochemical disorders and to traumata during childhood.

Finally, there can be patients for whom "normal" relationships that are associated with pleasure and pain are confused or reversed. They seek out that which is objectively aversive and experience it as pleasurable. Pain as a preferred quality of experience is recognized in the DSM *masochistic* or *self-defeating* personality. The counterpart to this is the aggressive or sadistic personality, for which pain, stress and cruelty form the preferred attitude of life. These individuals seek an active role in dominating, controlling and competing with others. Millon compares another variant of the same type with the competitive type A personality. He does not connect the obsessive-compulsive personality with type A behaviour as is the case in the DSM. A problem with this that cannot be explored further is that the literature on type A does not speak of personality but of behavioural disposition, which is essentially different. These two groups are termed discordant to indicate, on the one hand, the dissonant structure of their pleasure–pain dimension and, on the other hand, the conflictual nature of their interpersonal relationships. Masochistic personalities in this framework are called passive-discordant and aggressive personalities active-discordant. In relation to the background of these disturbances, Millon refers particularly to social learning processes and developmental problems.

OTHER–SELF

Millon extensively connects the subject–object polarity with the psychoanalytic theory regarding narcissism versus object relations, as developed by Freud as well as by object relations theorists and theorists of the self. This pathology in the source of reinforcement means that some people turn to others for this reinforcement, and other people turn to themselves. These distinctions go together with dependent and independent personalities.

Dependent people have learned that, in short, all good comes from other people; they have a great need for external support and attention. Frustration of this need evokes uneasiness and anxiety. In the DSM and ICD, this is called dependent personality disorder. Overprotection during upbringing can form the seed-bed for this. This concerns passive dependency problems. Those who also turn to others, but do this by a series of manipulative, seductive and attention-seeking behaviour, represent the active variant. In the DSM, this is called histrionic personality disorder.

Independent people have learned to maximize pleasure and avoid displeasure by exclusively seeing themselves as its source. The narcissistic personality represents the first line of development. They possess a superior self-image learned against a background of parental admiration. They represent the passive variant, as they already have everything they need. The active variant is called the antisocial personality in the DSM and ICD. They turn to themselves to avoid the pain they expect from other people. As compensation, they provide themselves with rewards which they generate. They have learned that they cannot count on other people, but only on themselves. They compensate for humiliations in their past here and now, misusing other people in the process. The balance in obtaining reinforcement from the other and from the self is disturbed. Clear distinctions between the other and the self are not made either by dependent or independent types.

In Millon's theory, a third group is distinguished in this context: the ambivalent. These patients experience a severe conflict about whom they should turn to for reinforcement: the other or themselves. In the DSM-III-R, they were called passive-aggressive personalities; one time they behave obediently, another time abnormally. They experience serious conflict regarding whether to turn to other people or to themselves. Millon calls these patients active-ambivalent, which includes a broader category than that described in the DSM. If they fail to meet other people's expectations, they feel guilty; if they meet other people's wishes, they become stubborn and negative. Passive-ambivalent patients are represented in the DSM and ICD as the obsessive-compulsive personality disorder. They give the impression of being oriented toward other people and adjust socially, which can be perceived from their learning history; they are accustomed to discipline. This front of adjustment, however, conceals a strong tendency toward rebellion which comes down to the acquisition of independence and acting on impulse. To avoid punishment, they have learned to deny these tendencies and comply with the values and norms of others.

ACTIVE – PASSIVE

The dimension passive versus active refers to what Millon calls the pathology in the instrumental coping style. This dimension refers to a whole range of behaviours that have to do with taking initiative in relation to changing or giving form to life events. In contrast to this attitude, people can also be reactive and largely adjust to their social environment. The latter category does not display overt manipulative behaviour; they appear inert and lack ambition. They seem to await circumstances before proceeding to adjust to them. Temperament and early life experiences can be the basis for this. They do not feel adequately competent and passivity is their strategy. Those with an active orientation are described as alert, vigilant, persevering, decisive and ambitious in relation to purposeful behaviour. They develop strategies, seek alternatives, manipulate events, all in view of obtaining pleasure or reward and avoiding punishment or rejection. They are constantly energetically engaged in influencing circumstances.

Millon has expanded his subdivision to a 5 × 2 matrix: the active – passive polarity being applied to the dependent, independent, ambivalent, discordant and detached orientations. He adds three dysfunctional variants to the 10 basic types that result from this and derives 13 personality configurations from the theory. The three dysfunctional variants represent serious pathology, expressed in problems of social adjustment and frequent psychotic episodes. Such people are especially vulnerable to the stressors of everyday life. He compares the dysfunctional detached variant with the schizotypal personality disorder of the DSM and ICD. Such people prefer social isolation, minimal attachment and obligation. They can react autistically or be cognitively confused. Eccentric behaviour makes a strange impression on others. Their pattern can be both active and passive, because of which they may seem in the clinical picture to be "hypersensitive" or "deficient of affect".

Borderline personality corresponds with the dysfunctional dependent, dysfunctional discordant and dysfunctional ambivalent orientations. All three are characterized by the dislocation of affectivity: an unstable and unsteady mood.

The DSM and ICD paranoid personality corresponds to the dysfunctional independent and to a lesser degree to the dysfunctional discordant and ambivalent orientations. Mistrust of others is a central feature, as is a sharp defensiveness towards anticipated criticism. Irritability and the tendency to perceive anger in others are strong. These people express a fear of losing control and independence.

SEVERITY

Millon connects the severity of a personality disorder to the estimated probability of a certain personality orientation fitting into some typical sociocultural niche in Western society. The less pathological, the more the personality style is able to maintain its structural coherence and function in a rewarding manner. Millon arrives at three categories.

The first and least severe group consists in DSM terms of the dependent, histrionic, narcissistic and antisocial personalities. Their needs and traits ensure that they manage their social environment and maintain relationships because they need them. They maintain their structural cohesion.

The second group represents an intermediate level of severity: the obsessive-compulsive, passive-aggressive, aggressive (sadistic), masochistic, schizoid and avoidant personalities. These types demonstrate less social adjustment.

The third group consists of the borderline, paranoid and schizotypal disorders (Millon, 1981; Millon & Everly, 1985). All three are functionally problematic, and often isolated, hostile or confused.

INTEGRATIVE THERAPY

In his book *Toward a New Personology* (1990), Millon gives a short description of integrative therapy for personality disorders. This concerns theory-based treatment techniques that must particularly transcend methods based on empiricism. Just as behaviour therapy techniques are most efficient in modifying certain actions, cognitive techniques are optimal for reforming phenomenological distortions. Intrapsychic techniques are especially suitable for influencing unconscious conflicts, as integrative psychotherapy is, according to

Millon, the most suitable for personality disorders. It goes without saying that empirical support for this still has to be collected.

Integrative therapy is more than eclecticism; it is rather post-eclecticism. Millon was not considering a new school of therapy. On the contrary, existing therapeutic techniques are suitable for patients' problems. No single school of therapy has the right approach, however, for all pathology. A co-ordinated strategy is necessary in psychotherapy for the application of a multitude of techniques to attune consecutive and combined treatment effects. The general philosophy behind integrative therapy is that specific treatment techniques are selected as tactics to achieve goals connected with the three polarities. The goal of therapy is to improve the lack of balance that in Millon's theory constitutes the core of the personality disorder. For instance, in relation to the pleasure – pain polarity, the aim of treatment of schizoid personalities must be to increase pleasure. Part of the treatment programme can be pharmacotherapy directed towards activating the dulled emotional life. Behavioural and cognitive techniques are more suitable for the avoidant personality. The same type of suggestions are applied to the other dimensions.

In many respects, this approach is the logical and pragmatic result of a diagnostic process. It remains the central goal of the therapy to bring more harmony to the disturbance on the level of the three polarities.

THE MCMI-III

Millon has designed a diagnostic instrument, the Millon Clinical Multiaxial Inventory (MCMI). It concerns a self-judgement scale with 175 true/false questions. The MCMI-II (Millon, 1987b) was a revised and expanded version of the original MCMI and contained, apart from several scales for clinical syndromes, 13 scales attuned to the DSM-III-R personality disorders. The MCMI-III (Millon, 1994) is the revision made for the DSM-IV. The MCMI-III is, compared with other self-judgement questionnaires intended for personality disorders, qualitatively the best. For an overview of the research, see Craig (1993).

A FEW COMMENTS

In essence, Millon's theoretically well-founded classification extracts some dimensions from the complex structure we call personality. In fact, his theory is particularly descriptive in nature and less concerned with describing mechanisms that make functioning of personality possible. The explanatory strength of his contribution is not nearly as great as the force of the system that adds clarity to classification. From a clinical standpoint, it could be wondered what insight Millon adds to the narcissistic personality, for instance. This insight seems to remain limited to the dimensions on which he focuses, and we are not able to know much more at this time through clinical practice. The connection between the active and passive ambivalents (the obsessive-compulsive and the passive-aggressive) is easily recognized in clinical practice. The advantage here is that the theoretical link complements the clinical association. This is an advantage of the descriptions Millon derives from the theory. He arrives at a broad group for the borderline that is clinically very recognizable.

Because Millon conducted work with the MCMI in the area of theory and classification and in the empirical field as well, his contribution in the field of personality disorders remains unique.

CHAPTER 3.7 The psychological test approach

In Part 2 a variety of test results were discussed in relation to a description of the various personality disorders. This chapter is based on the perspective of psychological testing and analyses the manner in which an assessment of personality psychopathology can be obtained by means of these techniques. In principle, this is not related to a classification system. As a rule, assessment of personality and psychopathology inherent to the test has also developed independently from major classification systems. In view of the frequent use of these techniques, a separate discussion is relevant here.

Traditionally, clinical psychological testing of patients consisted of three aspects: an intelligence test, primarily with use of the WAIS; a personality investigation using a questionnaire, usually the MMPI; and a projective technique, very often the Rorschach. Today, clinical psychologists have many more tests to choose from, and their choices will depend on their orientation and familiarity with the material. The more empirically oriented psychologists often prefer brief questionnaires that are well supported by research. Clinicians will supplement their assessment tools with projective material. Given the great quantity of testing techniques, it is frequently claimed that there are as many different tests as psychologists, although users mostly concentrate on a relatively limited number of techniques. Thorough knowledge of a limited number is preferred to a more superficial use of many different methods.

Within the framework of the subject of this book, a brief discussion of frequently used tests follows, based on interpretations that can be attached to the material in determining personality psychopathology. For research on intelligence, the Wechsler Adult Intelligence Scale (WAIS) is referred to and for personality questionnaires, the Minnesota

Multiphasic Personality Inventory 2 (MMPI-2). Finally, the Rorschach test will be discussed as one projective technique.

WAIS

Intelligence is an abstract concept, partially because it is difficult to give a generally acceptable definition. In personality psychology, intelligence receives the significance of a personality trait. In clinical practice, intelligence assessment of the patient contributes to the process of formulating indications for treatment. In addition to the complaints, personality and all sorts of hypotheses regarding underlying mechanisms that are often initially diagnosed, it is advisable also to obtain an indication of intelligence, introspective capacities, degree of suffering and social support. On the basis of these data, a specific intervention can be proposed. More insight-oriented forms of treatment largely require a certain level of intelligence and, consequently, a certain learning capacity in the patient. Cognitive development is a relevant variable in this regard, but in view of insight-oriented psychotherapy, emotional development is of equal importance.

With respect to personality disorders, a combination of research findings and clinical experience displays a number of relationships that must chiefly be considered as hypotheses. Given the specific objective and defined tasks of an intelligence test, the results do not in themselves offer specific, more complex information on the personality, which is why a brief impression is offered here of the relationship between the various subtests of the WAIS and the recognized personality disorders. The MMPI and Rorschach are examined in this chapter more in the light of their contribution to diagnosing personality.

The WAIS consists of a verbal section containing the subtests *Information, Comprehension, Arithmetic, Similarities, Vocabulary* and *Digit span*. The performance section consists of the subtests *Digit symbol, Picture completion, Block design, Picture arrangement* and *Object assembly*. Verbal IQ, performance IQ and total IQ scores are calculated.

During the intelligence test, many patients with a personality disorder tend to obtain higher scores on the action or performance section than on the verbal section. Their general tendency to act out could account for this. The behaviour of these people is more practised and less subject to disturbance than their verbal capacity. The verbal section puts the patient into more contact with the therapist than the performance section. The patients' relationships are, after all, often disturbed.

In the antisocial personality disorder the performance IQ is noticeably higher than the verbal IQ (often a difference of more than 15 points). This also applies to the classic psychopath and the behaviourally disturbed adolescent. In fact, this is often true for the histrionic, classic hysterical and, to a lesser degree, narcissistic personalities as well. In contrast, the verbal IQ score can be higher than the performance IQ in avoidant and dependent personalities. This is particularly the case if these people experience their relationship with the one who administers the test as positive and supportive.

Histrionic personalities often obtain remarkably low scores on the *Information* subtest. Paranoid and compulsive personalities quite often obtain high scores on the subtests *Similarities, Picture arrangement* and *Picture completion*. Their rigidity and suspicion contribute to this. Schizotypal individuals, on the other hand, can obtain lower scores because of their peculiar traits. A higher score on *Arithmetic* and *Digit span* is related to detachment (Meyer, 1989) and is something we often see in the schizoid and schizotypal personalities. Being closed off to the outside world can give rise to an imperturbable concentration. Narcissistic personalities usually obtain lower scores on scales where a detailed and more precise assignment has to be performed, such as the *Object assembly, Arithmetic, Vocabulary, Comprehension* and *Block design* subtests. With a highly structured test such as the WAIS, borderline patients usually receive better scores than on less structured tests, such as projective techniques. Furthermore, it is conceivable that borderline patients will have particular difficulty with the subtests *Digit symbol, Digit span* and *Arithmetic*. Their emotional instability is incompatible with the frustration tolerance required for these subtests. Obsessive-compulsive and passive-aggressive personalities can show diminished achievement on subtests in which speed is a factor, such as *Digit symbol, Block design, Object assembly* and *Picture arrangement*.

MMPI-2

The original version of the MMPI, published by Hathaway and McKinley in 1943, has become the world's most commonly used questionnaire for assessing psychopathology and personality. There are more than 10 000 publications on this extensive test of over 500 items. The original test has been translated into 60 languages. In the 1980s, the MMPI was improved and a newly standardized version published (Butcher *et al.*, 1989). The revision, which took almost seven years of research and development, has resulted in modernization of the content and language used in test items, elimination of items to which objections have been made, compilation of nationally representative normative data for the US population and development of new content scales. In the area of scale construction, various improvements have also been introduced (Graham, 1990; Butcher, 1990). The revision of the test, which now contains 567 items, was carried out in such a way that the enormous amount of research available, particularly on the clinical scales, can for the most part remain in use. Most of what is known concerns these scales, which are described in more depth below.

The Clinical Scales

The clinical scales are preceded by what are called the validity scales: the L scale, the F scale and the K scale. In the MMPI-2 the *Back Side F scale*, *Response Inconsistency Scale* and *Variable Response Inconsistency Scale* have been added to this. The L scale, the "lie scale", consists of 15 questions which, like the rest of the test, are answered with "agree" or "disagree". These questions will bring to light a rather naïve effort on the part of subjects to show themselves favourably. The items reveal the willingness of the subjects to confess small character weaknesses, such as, "I do not read all the editorials in the newspaper every day." The F scale is designed to single out people who interpret the test in a different way to that intended by the test designers. If a large number of the 60 items are answered more or less positively, this indicates a problem with the instructions of the test for this person. Finally, the K scale is comprised of 30 items and is intended to determine the extent of clinical defensiveness. The K scale is also used to make a correction in a number of clinical scales. The clinical scales are as in Table 3.7.1.

In the MMPI-2, the psychopathological concepts referred to under "original name" are replaced by scale numbers. The significance of these concepts is, after all, for the most part obsolete.

Scoring and interpretation of the MMPI-2 can be done by hand as well as by computer. Considerable attention is paid in the literature to the interpretation of the MMPI-2 profiles, in which the validity and clinical scales are represented graphically.

Profile Interpretation

The profiles can show no, one or several "tops". If the validity scales lie within acceptable limits, these tops can be interpreted. The code types

Table 3.7.1 MMPI-2 clinical scales

Scale number	Number of items	Original name
1	32	Hypochondriasis
2	57	Depression
3	60	Hysteria
4	50	Psychopathic deviation
5	56	Masculinity – femininity
6	40	Paranoia
7	48	Psychasthenia
8	78	Schizophrenia
9	46	Hypomania
0	69	Social introversion

are indicated with numbers. A T-score of 50 is average and the standard deviation is 10. The score on the clinical scales that is considered to be high varies among authors and scales. A score above 80 is often viewed as extremely elevated, between 70 and 80 as high, between 60 and 70 as moderately elevated and between 50 and 60 as slightly elevated. In a one-top profile, there is only a question of an elevated scale. In that case, the elevated scale is higher than all the other scales in the profile. In a two-top profile, for instance 2−7, scale 2 is the highest. Both scales differ by at least 5 T-scores from the rest of the scales. Reference to personality problems has been made particularly in two-top profiles (Graham, 1990). Table 3.7.2 shows the tops which are distinguished.

Of all of the scales that relate to personality problems, scale 4 consistently recurs. The items on this scale cover a wide variety of

Table 3.7.2 Personality problems and two-top MMPI profiles

Neurotic problems	Characterological problems	Psychotic problems	Undetermined problems
1−2/2−1	1−4/4−1	1−6/6−1	1−9/9−1
1−3/3−1	2−4/4−2	1−8/8−1	2−6/6−2
1−7/7−1	3−4/4−3	2−8/8−2	2−9/9−2
2−0/0−2	4−6/6−4	3−8/8−3	3−6/6−3
2−3/3−2	4−8/8−4	6−8/8−6	3−7/7−3
2−7/7−2	4−9/9−4	6−9/9−6	3−9/9−3
7−0/0−7	—	7−8/8−7	6−7/7−6
—	—	8−9/9−8	7−9/9−7
—	—	8−0/0−8	—

subjects: little or no fulfilment in life, problems with relatives and family, delinquency, sexual problems and difficulties with authority. Often the scale is seen as a measure of rebellion: a moderate elevation reflects socially acceptable rebellion and a very high score indicates criminal behaviour. Low scores indicate conventionality and blind acceptance of authority. Graham (1990, pp. 64−5) characterizes people with high scores as follows:

1. They have difficulty incorporating values and standards of society.
2. They may engage in asocial and antisocial behaviour, including lying, cheating, stealing, acting out sexually, excessive use of alcohol and/or drugs (especially if $T > 75$).
3. They are rebellious toward authority figures.
4. They have stormy relationships with family members.
5. They blame family members for their difficulties.
6. They have a history of underachievement.
7. They tend to have marital problems.
8. They are impulsive and seek immediate gratification of impulses.
9. They do not plan their behaviour well.
10. They tend to act without considering the consequences.
11. They are impatient, have a limited frustration tolerance.
12. They show poor judgement, take risks.
13. They tend not to take advantage of experience.
14. They are seen by others as immature and childish.
15. They are narcissistic, self-centred, selfish and egocentric.
16. They are ostentatious and exhibitionistic.
17. They are insensitive to the needs and feelings of others.
18. They are interested in others in terms of their usefulness.
19. They are likeable, create good first impressions.
20. They have shallow, superficial relations.
21. They seem unable to form warm attachments to others.
22. They are extroverted and outgoing.
23. They are talkative, active, adventurous, energetic, and spontaneous.
24. They are considered by others to be intelligent and self-confident.
25. They have a wide range of interests but lack clear direction.
26. They tend to be hostile, aggressive, resentful, rebellious, antagonistic, and refractory.
27. They have sarcastic and cynical attitudes.
28. They may act in aggressive ways.
29. If female, they may express aggression in more passive, indirect ways.
30. They may feign guilt and remorse when in trouble.
31. They are not seen as overwhelmed by emotional turmoil.
32. They may admit feeling sad, fearful, and worried about the future.
33. They experience absence of a deep emotional response.
34. They feel empty and bored.
35. If psychiatric patients, they are likely to receive antisocial or passive aggressive personality disorder diagnoses.
36. They have poor prognosis for psychotherapy or counselling.
37. They may agree to treatment to avoid something more unpleasant.
38. They tend to terminate treatment prematurely.

39. In treatment, they tend to intellectualize excessively and blame others for difficulties.

Reproduced by permission from J. Graham (1990). *MMPI-2 Assessing Personality and Psychopathology.* New York: Oxford University Press.

In combination with an elevation on scale 1, we see people who do not easily come for treatment on their own initiative. They do mention non-specific physical complaints. Their aggression is present, but not expressed directly. Alcohol use is often a factor. Problems with work and family frequently go hand in hand with alcohol abuse. In school and work, they are unmotivated and lack purpose. They go through life disappointed and pessimistic and are demanding and irritable in relationships.

In combination with an elevation on scale 2, we often see that a request for help occurs after there are problems with relatives, family members or the authorities. Impulsiveness is strong and enduring delayed gratification of needs, desires and impulses is difficult. They have many conflicts with social norms, acting-out behaviour, and alcohol and drug abuse. After periods of acting out, they experience feelings of guilt, self-reproach, depression, anxiety and worthlessness for a long time. These feelings, however, often seem not to be genuine. Acting-out behaviour occurs repeatedly. Suicide is common among these patients. Significant others frequently feel partly responsible for this.

If they are not experiencing difficulties, high scorers on scale 2 and 4 are energetic and social. They make a positive impression on others. Behind this façade of competence lie feelings of inadequacy, worthlessness and passive dependency. These people tend to feel uncomfortable in relationships, especially with someone of the opposite sex. Their prognosis for therapy is limited and they often terminate treatment prematurely.

The combination 2−4 coincides quite often with 7: 2−4−7/2−7−4/ 4−7−2. Here the diagnosis of passive-aggressive personality disorder is often made. Moreover, this code type is often found among addicts.

In combination with scale 3, we see people who are chronically very angry. They cannot give adequate form to their animosity and aggressive impulses. If scale 3 is higher than 4, the expression of anger is particularly indirect and passive. If scale 4 is higher, periods of aggressive acting out can occur. These people have a great lack of insight into the "how" and "why" of their behaviour. They are very sensitive to rejection and react aggressively to criticism. Family problems and promiscuity occur frequently. These patients are relatively free from feelings of depression and anxiety. They do, however, have psychosomatic complaints. They often receive a passive-aggressive personality diagnosis.

In combination with scale 6, we see immature, narcissistic, hedonistic people. They are passive-dependent and require enormous attention and sympathy from others. They can be very resentful of the most minor requirements which others make of them. They do not manage very well in interpersonal relationships and have problems particularly with the opposite sex. They are suspicious in regard to the motives of other people and avoid deep emotional relationships. There are problems in their work and in their marriage. Suppressed anger and animosity play a role. These people deny the presence of psychological problems and attribute their cause to others. They unrealistically overestimate themselves. In psychiatry, these patients often receive the following diagnoses: passive-aggressive personality, paranoid personality disorder, or paranoid schizophrenic.

In combination with scale 7, we see people who alternate between periods of intense feelings of guilt about their behaviour and periods of intense insensitivity to the consequences of their behaviour toward others. Their acting-out behaviour can be related to alcohol use and sexual promiscuity. Self-reproach does not lead to a lessening of acting-out behaviour.

In combination with scale 8, we see people who do not fit into their environment. They are experienced by others as strange and peculiar. They are non-conformists and critical of authorities. Their behaviour is unpredictable and they have problems with impulse control. In terms of criminal behaviour, we often see sexual offences. Their achievements are low and adjustment to the social environment is marginal. Their self-esteem is low, they feel insecure and avoid intimate relationships. They do not have basic social skills, are isolated and withdrawn. In psychiatry they often receive the diagnosis of schizophrenia, as well as the following diagnoses: paranoid personality disorder, antisocial personality disorder, and schizoid personality disorder.

In combination with scale 9, there is a striking, deliberate disregard of social rules. They come into contact with the authorities because of their antisocial behaviour. They are unscrupulous and possess a weak sense of morality and changing ethical standards. Alcoholism, quarrelling, marital problems, sexual acting out and a great deal of delinquent behaviour are among the possibilities. These individuals are narcissistic and egoistic, they do not learn from experience, and they seek emotional stimulation and tension. In short, the traits described for an elevation of scale 4 often recur here further magnified. The diagnosis of antisocial personality is often made.

In summary, we see the following behaviour problems in patients with an elevation on scale 4 in combination with various other scales: placing the blame on others, poor performance at school and at work, problems with intimate relationships, little or no insight, acting-out behaviour, having little regard for norms and values, and poor performance in psychotherapy.

THE RORSCHACH TEST

Of all the so-called indirect techniques, the ink blot test, developed by Hermann Rorschach, is the best known. The Rorschach test consists of ten plates, each 170 × 244 mm in size. A nearly symmetrical ink blot is printed on each plate. Five blots are achromatic and consist only of shades of black, white and grey. Two plates also have shades of red, and the remaining three plates contain more colours. In general, recognizable forms can be observed in the blots, which are to a great extent individually determined. Individual differences have resulted in the plates obtaining significance as a psychodiagnostic instrument. An important assumption is that the differences in perception are systematically related to aspects of the personality.

After a period of frequent use of the test in clinical practice, it greatly decreased in the 1960s. Lack of reliability and validity played a large role in the diminishing interest of clinicians and researchers. In the 1970s the American psychologist John Exner (1986) integrated the most valid elements from various Rorschach scoring and interpretation systems. He did this primarily on the basis of quantitative empirical research. Furthermore, he initiated a great deal of experimental research on the blots. His "Comprehensive System" is today the most widely used system for administration, scoring and interpretation (Derksen, Cohen & de Ruiter, 1993). A computer program is available for calculating structural summaries, as well as for interpretation. This saves considerable time when using this already time-consuming method of personality testing.

A Structural Vision

The Rorschach test offers a totally independent vision of the personality. The test is a so-called "wide band procedure" (Exner, 1986, p. 301) and can provide information that can be relevant for a great many clinical decisions. This differs from the view obtained with personality questionnaires such as the MMPI. If it can be assumed that a particularly descriptive picture of the patient is obtained through the use of questionnaires, the administration of the Rorschach test particularly contributes to a structural view. From this structural point of view, aspects of the personality − such as needs, feelings, stress tolerance, extent of control, cognitive functioning, defence mechanisms and interpersonal attitudes − are coherently presented very specifically. Some examples of this are discussed briefly below.

People in a more defensive position often appear to give responses in which pure form (code = F) is used as a determinant. These people use simply and solely the contours of the blot for their interpretation. Furthermore, many pure F answers indicate an extremely simplistic and economical way of dealing with the environment. These people tend to avoid, ignore or reject the complexity of a stimulus field as much as possible and because of that often have difficulties with their social environment.

Even Rorschach himself pointed to people's preferred response style as can be indicated by the test. What is of concern in this regard is the relationship between the sum of human motivation responses and the sum of the weighted chromatic colour responses. The manner of problem solving that emerges from this is a rather stable personality trait and falls into three alternative styles: the introversive, the extratensive and the ambitent. A person with an introversive style reviews the various alternative solutions to a problem in advance and subsequently solves the problem with a limited number of actions. An extratensive person approaches a problem with the "trial and error" method. He or she arrives at a solution in a process of interaction with objects or with the environment, thereby requiring more actions and, consequently, making more mistakes. These methods do not differ much in terms of the end result or the amount of time they require. Ambitents, on the other hand, do not exercise consistent problem-solving skills and sometimes use the extratensive style and, at other times, the introversive style. This means that they need more time, make more mistakes and are the least efficient of the three. These types are encountered quite often among patients with a mood disorder who do not optimally benefit from psychotherapy.

Patients (and non-patients) who give more passive than active movement responses are striking for their tendency for passive-dependent behaviour. The movement with which they animate the static blot in their perception, for instance a sleeping princess or two climbing bears, indicates in itself elements of reasoning, imagination and higher forms of conceptualization. Those who give a great many movement responses with a passive dimension, scored according to a table, avoid the responsibility of making decisions and choose to be dependent on others in order to give direction to their actions.

The variables that are part of the structural summary result in a number of indices, such as the suicide, depression and schizophrenia indices. The egocentrism index comes about by a summation of the reflection responses and the pairs, divided by the total number of answers. Research has mapped the range of these types of responses, and the interpretation of this index tends to be a measure for a psychological orientation concerned with oneself and self-interest. A low score on this index indicates feelings of inferiority, while a high score denotes narcissistic overevaluation of self-worth.

There is also a research tradition that employs the Rorschach test to study DSM personality disorders. This particularly concerns borderline and antisocial personalities (see Erdberg, 1993).

A FEW COMMENTS

Research on intelligence measures a rather stable personality trait, even though it is still not exactly clear how it should be defined. In the discussion of the five-factor model (Big Five), intelligence is mentioned as a possible sixth model. In all probability, this cannot, however, be limited by the result produced with the help of the WAIS. That is, IQ is a rather limited representation of a number of cognitive activities expressing someone's capacity to learn. It predicts rather well someone's school performance, but in the case of a personality disorder IQ can be quite high and educational performance and career proportionately very poor. Social and creative intelligence are not really covered by this measurement.

The questionnaire method for personality research depends on statements made by the individual. With an empirically developed technique, such as the MMPI, connections can be determined on empirical grounds. The advantage of the MMPI-2 is that it is a very extensive questionnaire based on a great deal of acquired experience. Its disadvantage is that its psychometric aspects on, for instance, the scale level are weak. What the various clinical scales measure has not been consistently determined by means of psychometrics, although extensive clinical experience has been gained. In regard to personality disorders, the MMPI-2 particularly measures acting-out behaviour with scale 4. We observe this trait mainly in Cluster B personality disorders. Because scale 4 is so significant in this respect it is in fact impossible to speak of a strong basis. Its capacity to differentiate is not great.

Morey, Waugh and Blashfield (1985) applied a rational—empirical strategy when creating the MMPI scales for DSM-III personality disorders. Ultimately they used 164 MMPI items for the 121 scales and compiled empirical support. Their positively biased reports have still been insufficiently set off against DSM-III diagnostics as a criterion (Morey et al., 1988). For instance, the data in a Flemish population were much less optimistic than those in the studies of Morey and others.

The MMPI scales 4, 6 and 8 measure principally a person's adaptation to the social environment. On these scales, the degree of adjustment to the environment, the degree to which a person has problems with the social environment, becomes quickly visible. Symptoms usually play a role in this but not necessarily a leading role. In other cases, one is very dependent on the symptoms which the patient reports. If we consider symptomatology as a defence and accordingly propose a theory-based interpretation of the test, we can observe neurotic, borderline and psychotic defences. The neurotic triangle is marked by an elevation on scales 1, 2 and 3. In comparison, we speak of the psychotic valley: scale 6 and 8 elevated and scale 7 lower than 6 and 8. With borderline defence, the neurotic triangle and the psychotic valley elevation are present. Research could also be related in this regard to Kernberg's personality organizations. Dependence on the reporting of symptoms is also present here. If this is absent, elevated scores are seldom encountered with, for instance, a psychotic personality organization, as is evident also from clinical experience.

In individual personality disorders, such as borderline disorder, a significant amount of research has been conducted in relation to the MMPI borderline profile. This usually concerns the "old" MMPI, but because of the way in which this has been restandardized, this research remains applicable to the MMPI-2. Examples of this type of profile have already been mentioned in the case studies in Part 2.

Projective Research versus the Questionnaire Method

In comparison to the Rorschach test, the MMPI-2 produces data that are more on the level of a descriptive classification. Someone with a depression on Axis I is more likely to have a high or elevated score on scale 2 of the MMPI-2 than on the depression index of the Rorschach test. The starting point of the MMPI-2 is totally different, proceeding from the perception of a person and not from the statements which an individual gives about his or her condition. The test draws information out of the person in a certain respect, so that he or she oversees how this comes about. In an ethical sense, this raises a special problem. Both the perception and the projection aspects of the test provoked and still provoke more mystery about the Rorschach than about the questionnaire method. With the MMPI-2, this is even less the case than previously. The discussion of the subtle versus the obvious items has in the meantime also been decided in favour of the obvious items (Butcher, 1993). The obvious items provide the greatest contribution to a scale. It is also true of the MMPI that the respondent cannot oversee the meaning attached to answering the items.

In clinical practice, it is striking that the Rorschach test has much more to offer when the MMPI profile does not yield much clinically significant information. As soon as the person cannot or does not want to make relevant statements about him- or herself, a projective technique offers more perspective. An example in this regard is the antisocial personality: hypotheses on the seriousness of the gaps in the area of conscience and in the quality of object relations can probably best be generated with the use of projective psychological tests. It remains true, however, that empirical support is largely lacking for certain tests, such as the Thematic Apperception Test (TAT), the Sentence Completion Test and the Four Pictures Test. Clinicians proceed here on the basis of their own experience or that of other clinicians. Furthermore, the lack of an interpretative framework for the above-mentioned tests renders clinical interpretation significant only when it is largely supported by theory. The extensive psychoanalytic theory is particularly suitable for giving meaning to material that is gathered using these methods. For instance, in the story of the Four Pictures Test and several stories in the TAT, themes are identified that can be related to drive development (oral, anal, phallic, oedipal and latency themes). Furthermore, the theory of object relations provides a source of inspiration for con- templation of the relationship patterns which patients incorporate in their stories.

The drawback of the Rorschach test is the high degree of complexity in administering, scoring and interpreting it, which is at the expense of reliability. Moreover, not every Rorschach protocol is equally rich in information.

Cross-cultural Information

With respect to personality disorders in general, people do not experience themselves as the chief problem, but largely blame their difficulties on others or on circumstances. The scores on a questionnaire cannot be expected to offer much when this is the case. On the other hand, the MMPI-2 collects a great deal of information on personal interests and lists many points of view, ideals and perceptions, and generates patterns on the basis of this which, although ego-syntonic for the one who fills it out, provide striking pictures with regard to scales. It helps that a great deal of empirical research is available from which correlations have emerged on all sorts of complaints or personality traits. An example of such a correlation is an elevation on scale 2, 4 and 7 with alcohol abuse. The validity scales, six in number in the MMPI-2, make a particularly unique contribution in relation to the attitude with which the patient has filled in the questionnaire. It is quite possible to ascertain defensiveness versus receptivity to psychological influence from these scales.

The original MMPI has been cross-culturally used in many countries and the MMPI-2 has also been or is being standardized in some 20 different countries (Derksen et al., 1993). This renders it possible to compare normal populations, which is not yet the case for the Rorschach Comprehensive System. The results of the MMPI-2 so far indicate that a comparison of the test data is certainly possible.

Comparison of the MMPI-2 administered to a representative sample of the Dutch population and one administered in the United States (Derksen & de Mey, 1993) furnishes some empirical support for hypotheses on cultural differences and shifts in personality, such as are developed in Part 4 of this book. Significantly in a statistical sense, but not surprisingly in a clinical sense, the Dutch score was higher on the neurotic scales 1, 2, 3 and 0. Americans obtained higher scores on the rest of the scales. In other words, defence patterns in the Netherlands concentrate on an "inwardly directed" coping style and in the United States we see a more "outwardly directed", extroverted orientation. On the lie scale, the Dutch obtained, in comparison to the Americans, quite an elevated score. Psychotic defence, vulnerability and personality disorders appear to stand out more in the United States. According to Fowler (personal communication), the differences observed when using the MMPI-2 have in fact become less than they used to be. The shift that is further analysed in Part 4 becomes ascertainable here. The psychological style is becoming more extroverted, more open, more impulsive and less restricted.

CHAPTER 3.8 The contribution of personality theory

In recent years personality theory, a subdivision of academic psychology, has made increasing contributions to personality models. The study of personality disorders may be able to benefit from this in the future. This renewed interest in the personality as a constant factor remained for the most part in the background in the 1960s and 1970s.

In the psychological theory of personality, there has always been an empirical tradition related to learning theory in which little consistency is attributed to behaviour. In this tradition, personality traits have always been considered as cognitive fiction. These views seem more the result of insufficient suitable research methods than of characteristics of the object of study itself. In fact, the tradition of emphasizing situation-specific aspects of behaviour results in an isolated existence; it has no place in day-to-day human interactions, in which practical insights into people and their peculiarities are very extensively employed. Many terms and concepts are used to refer to personality. Like Horatius, the philosophical tradition considers the person as stronger than any theory that intended to undermine it.

BIG FIVE

In this context, the discussion will be limited to a brief overview of the five-factor personality model called the *Big Five*. Not only does this model appear to make it possible for the empiricist to revalue the personality as a valid object of study, it also offers an interesting perspective on personality disorders. These five fundamental factors are also found in many empirical studies and may be used to explain a great deal of the variance in the broad domain of personality theories.

In 1961, according to Tupes & Christal (cited in Costa & McCrae, 1992), five factors appeared to form a reasonable reflection of all the concepts used in the English language to indicate personality traits. Studies with personality questionnaires also revealed five factors. Questionnaires that measure personality disorders, such as the Morey scales of the MMPI, were also used for this purpose. Today, these dimensions are no longer considered to be fiction, but observable differences in patterns of behaving, feeling and thinking. This concerns dimensions and therefore not categories as in the DSM and ICD. The advantage is that there is a continuum in the variation of normal personality traits. Moreover, a continuum can be created between normality and a pathological form of traits.

Below are the factors as they are often described, together with adjectives that relate to the dimensions (see also Costa & McCrae, 1992). The abbreviations used are: N, E, O, A and C.

- N stands for neuroticism: negative affectivity versus emotional stability. Quiet − concerned; even-tempered − moody; content with oneself − self-pitying; easy-going − self-conscious; non-emotional − emotional; thick-skinned − vulnerable.

- E stands for extroversion: passionate, socially active versus introversion. Reserved − warm; loner − gregarious; quiet − talkative; passive − active; frugal − hedonistic; insensitive − passionate.

- O stands for openness to experience: intellect, cultured versus narrow-minded. With both feet on the ground − imaginative; uncreative − creative; conventional − original; preference for routine − preference for diversity; non-inquisitive − inquisitive; conservative − liberal.

- A stands for agreeableness: friendly, co-operative, socialization versus antagonism. Ruthless − gentle; suspicious − trusting; stingy − generous; antagonistic − agreeable; critical − merciful; irritated − good-natured.

- C stands for conscientiousness: will to achieve, compulsive versus non-directive. Negligent − conscientious; lazy − hard-working; unorganized − well-organized; careless in agreements − precise; aimless − ambitious; quitting − persisting.

RELATIONSHIP TO PERSONALITY DISORDERS

A very promising beginning has been made with research on the reliability and validity of these factors. Moreover, initiatives have been taken in validity studies in other language areas and among various age groups. Some biological basis for the five dimensions is also supposedly present (Costa & McCrae, 1992). Several instruments have been developed to measure the five dimensions and the adjectives: Revised Interpersonal Adjective Scales — Big Five version (JASR-B5, Trapnell & Wiggins, 1990); Hogan Personality Inventory (HPI, Hogan, 1986); NEO Personality Inventory (NEO-PI, Costa & McCrae, 1985, 1989).

The relationship between personality disorders and the five factors has in the mean time become a subject of study as well. Initiatives for empirical exploration have been taken and a conceptual analysis made. Costa & McCrae (1992) presented a proposal for changes to Axis II: the addition of (a) a description of the personality; (b) the diagnosis of related problems. In regard to (a) the five factors can be used; and for (b) the pathology related to these factors can be considered. So (a) contains dimensional information and (b) categorial information. The idea behind these proposals is that Axis II used in this way becomes more flexible and applicable to a larger group of patients than the current categorial system. Treatment should suit the symptoms. A personality profile produces information indicating the best treatment. For example: average on N and C yields a relatively good prognosis; low on A means suspicion regarding the therapist and an attitude directed towards one's own self (narcissistic probably); high on E indicates insight-oriented group therapy; low on O reflects little tolerance for unconventional methods and probably a preference for a direct and behavioural approach (Costa & McCrae, 1992, p. 354).

Costa and McCrae further suggest that a sixth dimension should be the intelligence of the person. This suggestion is in line with the current practice of placing mental retardation on Axis II.

A FEW COMMENTS

Based on clinical experience with personality disorders, it is possible to foresee the following problems. The five factors are complex in nature and it is quite easy to create all kinds of subtypes that can be problematic for deriving a particular score on a dimension. For example, a person whose score is low on extroversion need not necessarily be passive in any way, but rather a type that is reticent and hard working. Insensitivity does not have to fall under this category either. On the contrary, the introverted personality can have very profound feelings. It is precisely in the process of inhibition that feelings intensify.

The N factor can relate to someone who is depressive, which is often reflective of a state rather than a trait. A depressive person is usually worrying, moody, vulnerable, self-conscious and emotional. Research should be able to indicate whether this dimension does not primarily measure a mood disorder.

The dimension described under O appears partly to overlap that under E. In addition, a lack of openness can surely also be related to intellect and cultural interests. Under A are people who are agreeable on contact, but can certainly behave antagonistically in certain situations. The exterior frequently conceals an interior that has much sharper edges.

Under C, we see people who, owing to their conscientious attitude, are much too detailed and therefore poorly organized. Strong ambition can also go hand in hand with a much less precise and perfectionist attitude. Because of ambition, the person often rushes, wants too much and operates too broadly.

PART 4

Management of Personality Disorders in Clinical Practice

CHAPTER 4.1 Psychodiagnostics

The first contact with a new patient can be in writing, by telephone, or face to face. The psychodiagnostic process begins with this first contact. The manner in which it is handled by the patient will offer meaningful clinical information. Some patients with a personality disorder telephone and make a great fuss about the time and day of the appointment. The extent to which a person is willing or able to accept the rules of the practice, institution or clinic becomes clear at the beginning of this first contact. As a rule, it is possible to tell quickly from the reactions of the psychological assistant who answers the telephone how well somebody is adjusting to the times that are reserved for intakes. Some patients already make demands about the treatment and its costs during the very first telephone conversation.

Nowadays one meets many people who describe their symptoms in professional jargon during the first contact. An example of a 20-year-old girl: "I've got anorexia nervosa, I have almost all the characteristics, but I am not yet down to a third of my weight." A 25-year-old man: "I have agoraphobia and for this I would like behaviour therapy." The following is heard considerably less often: "I have a personality disorder"; or "I am bothered by my obsessive-compulsive personality and want to be treated with psychoanalysis." There are two possibilities here: either personality disorders are still insufficiently understood by the public; or these diagnoses are much further removed from the experience of people themselves. Both are likely to apply. In any case, many symptoms are more concrete than in the condition we call personality disorder.

If the request for help relates to one or several concrete symptoms, there may be a personality disorder on Axis II, without the patient in question formulating this as such or being bothered by it at all. With some patients, a personality disorder is apparent fairly quickly in the contact. If patients only ask for help about a symptom, it is advisable to exclude personality problems in the assessment. When an entire range of Axis I disorders is presented, a more extensive evaluation of the personality is indicated.

During the intake, patients can be questioned fairly easily about symptoms for the purpose of gathering descriptive information. Diagnosis consists of gathering information about the patient. Apart from the complaints, an assessment is made of mood, somatic and psychosomatic disorders, as well as life history starting from birth and ending with expectations for the future. As a rule, this requires at least two one-hour sessions. Particularly with patients who request help for vaguer complaints, such as failures in their work, problems in relationships or other adjustment problems, a personality disorder is often diagnosed. In the remainder of this chapter, it will be shown more concretely how the diagnostician can go about determining a personality disorder during the session. This method of working is not only appropriate when a personality disorder is suspected, but is also often recommended for a diagnostic assessment of symptom disorders. The description of the psychodiagnostic approach given here is meant to be relatively independent of psychotherapeutic orientation. It goes without saying that during the diagnostic phase one makes use of many approaches that have been developed in the various mainstreams of psychotherapy, psychiatry and psychological treatment.

The diagnostic contact with a new patient begins with observation, which is followed by therapeutic sessions supported by observation and may subsequently be supplemented by follow-up examination. A complete psychodiagnostic process stretches over several sessions, if necessary supplemented by psychological tests, physical examinations, laboratory results and an observation period. The diagnostic examination can be performed by one and the same therapist, but contributions from several disciplines can be provided as well. This varies with the setting.

All the information gathered during the assessment process is brought together and interpreted with the help of a theoretical frame of reference, leading to hypotheses that can be put to the test during the treatment phase.

OBSERVATION

An advantage of the diagnostician personally going to the waiting room to meet a patient is that the latter can be observed. Some patients seat themselves in the middle of the waiting room and quietly read a magazine. Others find a corner, during the winter keep their coat on and stare tensely ahead. Some make contact with other patients and we have to interrupt them before we can go to the consultation room. Yet others have difficulty waiting their turn, walk towards the consulting room and knock on the door.

The way in which patients move about, shake hands and introduce themselves provides information about their condition. Sometimes, after a sturdy handshake, one is happy if one's hand emerges un-injured. In other cases, it seems as if a soft, wet cloth is being placed in one's hand. One of my patients refused to hang his coat on the coat rack in the hallway in case it should be stolen. Some patients start with remarks about the clinic, the practice setting, or the wall decorations.

No far-reaching conclusions can be drawn from these observations. It is just material that is part of the data from the assessment process. This material is all generated by the personality which, in whatever form, produces this behaviour.

INTAKE

Intake is understood to mean the first contact with the patient. As a rule this is the first session − and sometimes the only one − of a psychodiagnostic assessment.

The various psychotherapeutic schools usually adopt their own methods for an intake; they approach the patient in a manner which they expect to be useful in view of the treatment. A behaviour therapy approach emphasizes a concrete analysis of the undesired behaviour(s). In the psychoanalytic tradition, so-called trial interpretations can be used to investigate if patients are capable of benefiting from coherence and interpretation being presented to them concerning statements they have given about themselves, their complaints and their history. In psychiatry, many anamnestic checklists are in circulation. As is usual in the medical model, all kinds of life areas and symptoms are inquired about. Working from a systems approach, it is helpful if the entire family is present and the members' complaints are described within the family context.

No separate method exists for doing an intake against the background of a possible psychological, psychotherapeutic or psychiatric treatment (Jong, 1987). Empirical scientific research is lacking.

In clinical practice, the intake is often the patient's first contact with a therapist in the field of mental disorders. In the case of a referral for admission to or part-time treatment in a psychiatric or psycho-therapeutic institution, an intake is a sort of review exercise for the patient. Depending on the type of treatment setting, specific aspects of the intake are distinguished. After all, the indication is also often connected with the specific treatment strategies that are available in the setting concerned.

The following description of the subjects that are relevant for the intake is inspired by an out-patient treatment setting and a first contact with a new patient. It is my conviction that the subjects that are treated here are also valuable for an intake in another clinical situation.

The intake and the entire diagnostic process are characterized by the investigator's attitude. The assessor examines the symptomatology presented and the person of the patient, together with the social context in which the person finds him- or herself. This assessment in itself already forms an intervention and is never entirely separate from the treatment. If the presence of psychological help is brought to the attention of a potential patient, this is already an intervention. The patient has to make the decision either to make use of this or not (Derksen, 1986).

Before the intake, the patient usually forms all sorts of ideas about what is in store for him or her. In the inner world of the person, a great deal has already been going on before he or she shows up at an appointment. Already during the first contact, this may be evident from the following types of statement: "I could not get no sleep, because I was constantly thinking of my visit to you." "Because I had an appointment here, I have talked much more with my wife and now I see much more clearly what the problem really is, so that I don't know exactly what I am doing here." "Now that I sit here I feel even sicker than before I thought of this possibility."

Controlled empirical effect studies on psychotherapy often demonstrate improvement of the experimental condition — compared to controls — before treatment starts. This expectation effect on the part of the patient is usually already in effect prior to the intake. Before the patient is seated in the consulting room, the assessor has already gained a certain impression. For instance, the patient has had previous contact with the treatment setting on the telephone and at that time made a particular impression. Some patients already ask over the telephone or even before they go for an appointment to describe more about their complaints: "What is this going to cost me?" Sometimes the husband calls for his wife or the other way around. The patient is sent, brought or comes by him- or herself.

If the patient is accompanied by a partner or a member of the family, it sometimes happens that the patient's companion goes in the direction of the consulting room. If the patient has no objection to this, nor do I for the duration of the intake. This is known to have more advantages than disadvantages. For some patients, the presence of the partner gives a feeling of security. Of course, it can also be an obstacle for the free expression of deeper considerations, but there will be enough opportunity for these to be expressed at a later stage of the diagnostic phase. In cases in which a partner is present, the diagnostician has the opportunity to do a concise hetero-anamnesis at the same time. Particularly for patients with personality problems, the sight of a partner can be refreshing.

In a number of cases the patient who comes accompanied by his or her partner can show dependent and/or avoidant personality traits. After the assessor's opening question, the patient's eyes go − either consciously or subconsciously − in the direction of the partner, who usually takes over the talking from the patient. Often this pattern has already existed for a long time. In this case, it is usually advisable to intervene right away and give the "floor" back to the patient.

It is often clinically interesting to observe how the patient describes his or her own problems and what phraseology he or she uses. The direction here is in the hands of the diagnostician. In the course of the session, the partner can be asked to take a seat in the waiting room for a little while, so that the patient can be seen alone. In itself, it is already meaningful that the partner, a parent or somebody else from the system is accompanying the patient. Often this means that the former is genuinely concerned about the complaints and offers a helping hand. A psychological or psychotherapeutic treatment of somebody with a supportive, empathic partner in the background has a better prognosis than when the partner is indifferent towards the therapy or even re- jects it. The latter frequently occurs. With children and the elderly, assessment of the system is recommended in all cases.

The following is a discussion of the essential ingredients of an intake and subsequent sessions that together form the diagnostic phase (Derksen, 1982).

Actual Symptomatology

In the first place, the diagnostician wants to know what complaint or complaints, or what manner of suffering, have led the patient to seek help. The prevalence, the frequency and intensity of each separate complaint are formulated as clearly as possible by the patient with the help of the assessor. Sufficient information is gathered to gain a perspective on provocative stimuli and consequent factors in order to make a functional analysis. The complaints of patients suffering from an obvious symptom disorder are easiest to deal with. These form the foreground in the contact and the personality forms the latent background. The same can apply to people with a personality disorder; they can struggle with one or several symptoms or syndromes and request help for these. If the patient with a personality disorder does not request help for a complaint but for his or her way of functioning, the request for help is usually formulated in a more complex way. For the patient as well as for the diagnostician getting a clear picture of the problems requires more of an effort.

After the diagnostician's opening question, such as "What can I do for you?", it is best in all cases to wait and show an understanding of the exact manner in which the patient translates his or her problems into words. Patients who tell their story rapidly have sufficient time to tell it during the first session; additions to what they have to say can be obtained with concrete questions. Patients who, apart from their complaints, show striking personality traits often find it difficult to fill in the time given to them and show this in a somewhat conspicuous manner. It often happens that compulsive patients want to be very complete in what they have to say from the start of the contact. In order to accomplish this they start at the beginning: their birth and family. After 45 minutes they usually still have not said anything about their complaints and, although necessary, interrupting their story is not always easy.

In view of the ego-syntonic character of a personality disorder, these patients are often directed to the diagnostician by a general practitioner, another mental health worker, or their partner. They usually do not report this right away but it is evident from the way in which they express themselves. They are recognizable by the aloof manner in which they speak about themselves. For instance, in explaining their problems they very often quote other people's statements about themselves. In these cases it is wise to devote the first session to dealing extensively with the feelings with which they have come to the consulting room, their dissatisfaction with the referral, their shame or uneasiness, their sense that they are a victim of other people or of circumstances. Since a certain level of co-operation is necessary for a good diagnosis as well as for treatment, it is sensible to put clearly into words the forces within the patient that co-operate with this and those that oppose it. In this respect, the intake also constitutes a diagnostic examination and stimulates motivation.

To somebody who has rigid thought patterns as a consequence of personality psychopathology, it is very discouraging to find exactly what he or she expected. This can, for instance, relate to a whole series of factual questions about complaints and history without an appeal being made to other than cognitive personality traits. A sympathetic and empathic way of presenting the deregulation of these patterns offers a better chance of a successful intervention phase. This means that the patient is challenged to put his or her perception and experience processes into words. Particularly for more compulsive patients this is quite a task, but it is also a new experience and it prepares them for the features of possible treatment. In all cases, the communication of understanding and empathy is necessary without giving superficial or false reassurance in the process, introducing values or norms, or allowing for personal disclosures by the diagnostician.

Complaint History

It is best to give extensive attention to the history of the complaint in the first consultation. This applies also if the patient displays a poor behaviour pattern or interaction problems. Many patients are not conscious of the exact time frame and the course of the complaints. Especially if the complaint had a very insidious onset, this is more difficult to trace than when it is a question of an acute breakthrough of symptoms. The problems that arise from a personality disorder can be difficult to trace as well. It can be helpful to look back, together with the patient, to a point in time at which there was no question of a complaint and to examine the history from that point on in detail.

In this context it is sensible to integrate the connection between the phenomena of anxiety, depression and somatoform complaints into the diagnosis:

Particularly in the outpatient setting, these three ingredients occur with various degrees of coherence and overlap. It is helpful to attempt to bring about a hierarchy: is it primarily a question of depression, of anxiety or of physical complaints? Patients can react to a sombre mood with anxiety and subsequently present the anxiety as a complaint. Physical experiences can evoke anxiety or gloom. Depression can also form part of a reaction to a panic disorder. It is necessary to localize the time and place at which this complaint occurred, as well as drawing an up-to-date "cross-section" as soon as complaints are felt. The patient is

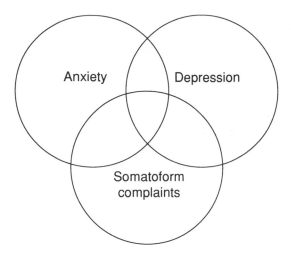

Figure 4.1.1 Connection between anxiety, depression and somatoform complaints

actively involved in this searching process and ideally this should result in meaningful insight into the disorder for the patient as well.

The complaint groups discussed here are interesting for the diagnosis of personality disorders. An affective disorder can manifest a certain character pathology that, without the mood disorder, would not result in a notable typification of the person. For instance, in the discussion regarding the validity of the diagnosis of borderline personality disorder, Akiskal (1981), Klein (1977) and Liebowitz (1979) in particular have put forward the hypothesis that it concerns a subclinical variant of an affective disorder. This has, however, not been confirmed in subsequent research. The diagnostician must try to gain insight into the profile of the personality such as it was before the influence of the mood disorder. We can see a similar process with an anxiety disorder and a dependent or avoidant personality. Strong dependency and avoidance can occur as a consequence of the anxiety. These are, however, conditions that usually disappear with the diminishing of the symptoms; in other words, they concern a *state* instead of a *trait*. Somatoform disorders can evoke anxiety and dependency as well. The avoidant and dependent personality disorders are common among patients who at first present anxiety or somatoform complaints.

Typical of a personality disorder is the fact that striking characteristics exist independently of a mood disorder or panic disorder. The confusion regarding the borderline disorder is also caused by the empirical data showing that a mood disorder is often present in these patients, while anxiety disorders are frequently present in avoidant and dependent personality disorders, leading to a request for help (Stein, Hollander & Skodol, 1993).

Apart from the request for help, one can consider the occurrence and the history of physical illnesses and psychosomatic phenomena at length during this phase. Many patients are so accustomed to their migraine, neck and shoulder complaints, back pain or spastic colon that they do not mention it on their own initiative. The importance of these complaints for forming hypotheses during the diagnostic phase is evident to every clinician. Theoretically speaking, we could expect a connection between more generally formulated physical complaints and personality pathology. Etiologically speaking, both go back to childhood. For the physical complaints, one is referred to the pre-verbal phase, in which the baby and toddler still have to communicate with the body, especially since not enough language is available. According to the theoretical hypothesis, disturbances during these years stimulate somatoform and psychosomatic complaints. The personality disorders are also rooted in disturbances during and following these early years of life. It is also possible that one disturbance stimulates the other.

On completion of the assessment of complaints, one tries to gain an impression of the degree of suffering experienced by the patient. To what degree does the patient suffer in terms of the symptom or the disturbed personality traits? Indications for this are found in the manner of speaking about and dealing with the complaints, in the attempts to request help, the intensity of the accompanying anxiety symptoms and the depth of any accompanying depression. People also present themselves very differently in their adjustment to the possibilities and impossibilities of the treatment setting. If at a certain time a patient is not available because he or she has to play golf, this also naturally says something about the importance assigned to the undertaking. Patients with passive-aggressive and/or masochistic traits quite often inform the intaker spontaneously that they "want to do anything to get rid of those miserable complaints". In the course of treatment this turns out to have been a spontaneous denial; he or she makes an extreme effort to show the therapist that there is nothing that helps and every attempt to assist is sabotaged.

PERSONALITY ASSESSMENT

The next step during the first meeting relates to the study of the personality. With the assessment of the personality, one is, in simple terms, interested in how somebody is. Quite often this is evident from how he or she usually acts. In this context, it is relevant to examine the person's adaptation to the various circumstances; first of all, to the circumstances at home during the first few years of life. This is followed by adaptation to elementary school, puberty and secondary school and finally, adaptation to the work situation and to intimate relationships. Personality problems become evident in these adaptations in a descriptive way. This does not mean that the patient's relationships are all constantly disturbed. For instance, with the dependent, avoidant and schizoid personalities, one notices that there often appears to be too little conflictual tension. This information is obtained in a normal anamnesis.

DSM Criteria

The DSM-IV and ICD-10 criteria for each disorder can be introduced in the session in question format. We can establish a number of problems here. In the first place, there are almost 100 relevant criteria for the 10 personality disorders. In clinical practice, the clinician usually does not do a careful diagnosis of all 10 disorders (Widiger, 1991). Doing this in addition to all that has to be done during an intake is asking too much. This is especially true for assessments for which semi-structured interviews and self-report questionnaires are available. In clinical practice, the use of these questionnaires is usually seen as too time consuming. In the second phase, these patients, when asked about the various criteria such as those that are mentioned in the DSM-IV and ICD-10, typically react with denial. If we present the same questions to their partners, we have a chance that the latter notice problems more frequently. In view of the ego-syntonic character and the typical defence of these patients, the assessment of pathology in the personality is more difficult than the assessment of symptom disorders. In many cases, significant others suffer more from the personality disorder than the patients themselves. The latter are so familiar with their own behaviour repertoire that they do not question it.

The emphases of the diagnostician's strategy for Axis I disorders are different from those for Axis II disorders. When asking concrete and detailed questions related to Axis I disorders, the experienced diagnostician as a rule obtains a fairly reliable picture. With Axis II disorders, it is recommended that a stronger emphasis be placed on what one experiences in the contact with the patient. On the basis of this experience in the relationship, the diagnostician formulates a hypothesis for himself (Turkat, 1990). Even minimal information is used to arrive at a hypothesis regarding one of the three clusters. Furthermore, one looks for affirmation or refutation of this in the course of the discussion. A few examples follow.

Examples

Upon meeting, a 35-year-old lady gives a clammy, soft handshake, seemingly without muscular strength. As soon as invited to, she starts talking about her complaints and problems. She looks around helplessly. She says, "I don't know either, if only I knew. I just can't handle it, it doesn't work. I keep falling back. I don't think I will manage it this way." This type of phrasing by a new patient gives a lot of information about their personal style. In an absolute sense, the words and sentences somebody uses demonstrate their limitations in the vocabulary of the person concerned. Within those limits everyone chooses their own concepts. Some are so dependent that they draw their partner in and by means of a quick glance have the partner determine the words in which the difficulties of the patient are expressed. They themselves, at least at that moment, do not have the required language at their disposal. The above-mentioned woman apparently wants to express something like: "I can't cope with life so well, I am not able to deal with the circumstances in which I find myself." This may also be the core of her problem.

On another occasion, a lot of noise and thumping sounds are heard coming from the waiting room. In the hall, a somewhat lanky man approaches with an attitude of "Well, how about it?" After he has explained for several minutes that he wants to get a better picture of who he is himself, loud rock music is heard coming from the waiting room. The young man explains the noise: "That boy I met in the bus, I hadn't seen him for a long time and I thought I'd bring him along." He relieves the situation by going to the waiting room and during the remainder of the assessment session it is quiet. As a diagnostician, one is especially surprised by the fact that he has come of his own free will and so I decided to inquire about his contact with the law. "Do you want only to know what I've been convicted of or everything that I've done?" He tells an impressive story, especially in view of his age.

In the case that somebody, like the woman mentioned above, acts dependently, one formulates the hypothesis of a dependent personality disorder. Over the course of the contact, one can confirm or refute this hypothesis. The young man evokes the suspicion of an antisocial and/or narcissistic personality disorder, and more information can be obtained about this.

Viewed from the interpersonal approach of Sullivan, Leary and Kiesler, the diagnostician notices that a patient with a personality disorder communicates in a rigid, limited or extreme manner. He or she can become entangled and be tempted to react in a complementary manner, for instance showing submissive behaviour with an authoritarian patient, warm behaviour with a suspicious patient, exhibitionistic behaviour with an inhibited patient. By means of Kiesler's interpersonal circle, which was explained in Chapter 3.4, one can detect this trap in advance. Through this approach the diagnostician, as well as the therapist, gains valuable information about interaction style. The guidelines for the treatment follow fairly directly from these interpersonal reactions.

The cognitive approach contributes to the psychodiagnostics in a similar manner. The diagnostician tracks down the dysfunctional schemata by listening attentively to the way in which the patient expresses him- or herself. The more the patient starts feeling free in the diagnostic discussion, the more the cognitive attitudes usually get free play as well. It goes without saying that one can also question the patient about irrational fundamental convictions. An explicitly neutral and positively interested attitude on the part of the diagnostician facilitates research into these schemata.

Structural Diagnosis

An impression of the personality can furthermore be obtained by this sort of approach: "You have told me a lot about your complaints, now I would like to hear some more about you as a person. Can you describe yourself, your personality in such a manner that I can get a good impression of you?" The more structured, descriptive part of the session is now alternated with a much less structured phase. The patient is burdened with this open-ended question and the diagnostician waits and looks at how he or she deals with it. Is the patient successful in giving form to such a task with little to hold on to? Which wording does he or she choose? Does the patient include subjects such as hobbies, having contact with others, sexuality? Ideally, the patient who has a good intrapsychic structure comes along in a fairly relaxed, self-reflective mood and spontaneously vents thoughts, feelings and experiences about him- or herself that the diagnostician can integrate into a coherent picture. The patient who has a weak internal psychological organization has visible and noticeable difficulty with this type of question. In this respect, diagnosis can benefit from insights and techniques developed within the psychodynamic orientation. The descriptive level of the classification in the DSM is supplemented by the psychoanalytic structural point of view; the organization level of the ego is examined.

Apart from the self-description, one can inquire who is the most important person in the patient's life at this moment. The patient is asked to describe this person in such a way that the diagnostician can obtain a good picture of the significant other. Again, the diagnostician wonders if he or she will be successful in constructing an integrated picture of that significant other on the basis of that data. Does the material evoke the contours of the person? More weakly structured patients, who function on the borderline or psychotic level, are not able to do this well (Kernberg, 1981, 1984). They describe themselves and the other (self representation and object representation) as if the following apply (Derksen, 1986; Derksen, Hummelen & Bouwens, 1988; Derksen, Hummelen & Bouwens, 1989):

- they consist of strongly contrasting qualities;
- there is no connection present in that person, there seems to be some sort of pool of loose pieces;
- the person him- or herself and/or the significant other seem to keep changing with the circumstances;
- not infrequently the patient totally fails this assignment. If insisting helps here, one notices that the other and the self cannot be distinguished from each other.

Apart from integration of identity, the quality of the defence mechanisms is also examined during this phase (see also Chapter 3.1).

Countertransference Reactions

In the patient's description of him- or herself, we encounter material that can be used in the diagnosis of a possible Axis II personality disorder or personality trait. During the entire discussion, but perhaps in particular during this unstructured phase in the psychodiagnosis, the diagnostician also listens to him- or herself and considers his or her own perception of the other. The questions one can ask oneself as an aid are:

- Do I feel sufficiently free in the contact to ask every question that I can think of?

- Do I notice that I prefer avoiding certain subjects such as sexuality and aggression in the form of maltreatment by the patient?
- Do I find it difficult to enquire thoroughly about antisocial behaviour and confrontations with the law?
- What type of fantasy does this person sitting in front of me evoke within me and what is my reaction to my own fantasies?
- Do I get a feeling of substitute outrage, shame or anger?
- Do I tend to go and help this person, do I remain busy gathering advice?
- Why do I start showing certain tendencies and feel less free in my work as a diagnostician?

Such questions can be more technically formulated as: Which defence mechanisms do I detect in the contact? A feeling of uneasiness is usually indicative of the occurrence of primitive defence mechanisms: splitting, projective identification, denial, omnipotence, devaluation or idealization. In contrast, the developed pendants of this are: repression, projection, denial, rationalization, isolation and reaction formation, which allow themselves to be identified less easily as they reveal themselves in more subtle ways during the contact.

If we look at the three clusters of Axis II on the basis of this information, we can roughly hypothesize that the Cluster C personality disorders are found mostly within the neurotic range, with developed defence mechanisms, an integrated identity perception and intact reality testing. Cluster B functions mainly on a borderline level and is characterized by primitive defence mechanisms, a diffuse identity perception, but constantly intact reality testing. The borderline concepts that are used here refer to the functioning of the person; more specifically as a certain structure of the ego, in Kernberg's sense (Derksen, 1990b). Personality disorders of Cluster A are characterized by a primitive defence mechanism and diffuse identity. Reality testing, however, often has gaps in it and this means that the patient functions on a psychotic level. This applies in particular to the paranoid and schizotypal personality and, probably to a much lesser degree, to the schizoid personality disorder. The diagnostician's countertransference reaction is different for each cluster.

With Cluster A, we frequently experience what Rümcke called the praecox feeling: "a peculiar, unique uncertainty and a feeling of peculiarity that is connected with the interruption of the normal being-related-to-each-other. That which is called the approach-instinct is one-sidedly disturbed" (Rümcke, 1954). Through a considerable adaptation, this praecox feeling can be very light, but for that reason all the more important to notice. The ego of these patients is structurally damaged and, under pressure, the decompensation receives a psychotic expression. The paranoid personality is often defensive in the contact. The diagnostician is suspect and thought to be hostile from the very start. Through the mechanism of projective identification the patient tries to control those feelings and impulses in the diagnostician that he or she cannot keep under control. Often this expresses itself in critical questioning of the diagnostician: "What are you writing down there? What are you going to do with everything I tell you here? Is there somebody else listening behind a screen?" With the schizotypal person, the peculiarities and the paranoid thoughts sometimes remain hidden behind a mask of rationalizations. They often give the impression that they have special relationships with others and exclude the diagnostician from this. A 25-year-old man kept emphasizing that he knew what I wanted to say and took the conversation over from me. In such a case one feels superfluous as a conversation partner.

In Cluster B disorders, we often find a structurally damaged ego that works out the difficulties in a much more emotional and impulsive way. The disturbance of the ego took place later in development than with Cluster A disorders and differentiation between self and other, outer world and inner world is better but not good. In direct contact, one often notices an unbalanced self-esteem with these disorders. In the contact with the assessor and therapist, the patient attempts to mend his or her defective self-appreciation. After a discussion of 45 minutes, the above-mentioned young man indicated that he was cleverer than anyone else he knew, he had everybody under his thumb and only came for an intake to ask a few questions regarding what he called his unlimited laziness. With such patients, one often has the experience of feeling less free to ask what one would like. The need for control of the other can be so strong that as a diagnostician one is influenced by this and feels fearful of breaking through that control.

Depending on the degree of suffering, narcissistic and borderline people will have a tendency to devaluate or to idealize the diagnostician. This indicates the domination of splitting mechanisms in the constellation of defence mechanisms. In the first case, this can evoke irritation and the tendency to prove oneself. In the event of idealization, one can start feeling so flattered that the patient is no longer asked critical questions and/or confrontations. Particularly with self-esteem disturbances (narcissistic disorders), the problems of the patient aggravate rather quickly in the relationship which he or she starts. So the contact is informative, but also very difficult.

With respect to Cluster C, the diagnostician often feels the urge to help, support or protect the patient. One does not experience constraint caused by fear for the other person, but by pity, substitute anger or sadness. The lady in the example given above evoked the urge to function as some kind of prosthesis for her. Many people would feel the inclination to take her into their home to protect her against all fears and dangers. She appeals strongly to the diagnostician's fatherly and/or motherly feelings. One can imagine that it is exactly this counter-transference reaction that explains dropping out, on the one hand, and treatment lasting for years without results, on the other. With the obsessive-compulsive person, one often feels the urge to start quarrelling. Long-windedness and numerous irrelevant details mentioned by the patient cause irritation. They cannot get started on their own role in the whole. The disturbances in the contact are less rough than with Clusters A and B. The diagnostician experiences more freedom in dealing with these patients, but more feelings and urges are evoked than with people who we think do not have a personality disorder.

Gathering information on psychodynamics is obviously also valuable with patients who do not meet descriptive and structural criteria for a personality disorder. In this manner, one obtains an impression of the possibilities for uncovering psychotherapy. Several trial interpretations may be part of this phase, by means of which the diagnostician brings coherence to the material which the patient has produced. It is crucial that such an interpretation leads the patient to deepening of the material, new insights, experiencing of feelings, etc.

The information that is obtained in the manner mentioned above is supplemented with data on cognitive and emotional development. Cognitive development covers the educational history of the person involved, the employment career and the development of skills, talents and hobbies. Through emotional development, insight is obtained into the integration of basic drives, such as aggression and sexuality, in behaviour and experiencing. Furthermore, the possibilities of the patient for recognition, differentiation and expression of the familiar arsenal of human feeling modalities are subject to examination.

A final aspect of the personality assessment concerns the lifestyle of the patient:

- For how long and how hard does the patient work?
- What does he or she smoke, drink and eat and how much?
- How much does the patient move about and rest?

The answers to these questions are evaluated in the light of the research in health psychology in these areas.

PARTNER RELATIONSHIP AND FAMILY LIFE

During the intake, one briefly enquires about the patient's living situation and intimate relationships. If time permits, one goes deeper into the family and into psychological and somatic disorders in immediate family members and in the more extended family. If this makes the intake too burdensome, the subject is postponed to the following session. The same obviously applies to themes such as those that have been discussed in the preceding section.

OBSTACLES TO TREATMENT

The intake is of great importance to what happens afterwards. The patient gains his or her first impression of the treatment setting and the therapist. This exchange inspires trust or suspicion and it can set the tone for what follows. Questions are asked about the patient's attitude toward treatment. This is especially relevant with patients with a Cluster B personality disorder.

Given the frequent occurrence of narcissistic damage in patients with a personality disorder, idealization or devaluation of the therapist and treatment setting are obvious dangers. Making these aspirations more explicit is not an easy task, but it is often very helpful in the process of establishing a working relationship. The devaluation can take place more or less in a direct way. A patient, such as the elementary school teacher mentioned in Chapter 3.1, was very open about his devaluation of the work of the psychologist who was affiliated with the school. With regard to the question of how he thought the psychologist functioned, he adopted a superior attitude and reported that he, as a teacher, usually knew the children much better. In the course of the assessment and monitoring, it turned out that this man did his utmost to demonstrate that I could not really change anything, particularly in connection with his physical complaints. He cut himself off from the psychological contribution and its influence. Moreover, he trivialized his symptoms.

In other cases, a patient may repeatedly emphasize that you are the expert, the doctor who knows what has to be done, and that he or she likes to leave it up to you as the therapist. The devaluation that is hidden behind this is usually less easy to bring to light. Brushing aside this obstacle of a narcissistic nature and getting to work can in some cases actually be the best solution. The patient will gradually become attached to the therapist after all, because he or she feels the effectiveness of therapy. Often this is not the case, however, and one has to try to grin and bear it. Needless to say, the therapy has then already started.

Motivation is further examined by presenting the patient with observations that relate to critical aspects of his or her behaviour. The possibilities of the patient's undergoing further diagnosis and treatment are charted. Limitations may be found in the personality itself, but also in the financial field, the time someone can or wishes to spend on therapy, or, in the absence of the necessary rest, on receiving help. If the treatment is to be continued after the intake, this usually takes the form of a continuation of the psychodiagnostic assessment.

Resistance or opposition to psychological help can show itself in various ways during the intake, particularly with personality problems. Some of the most frequent ways of resisting are discussed below.

1. *Unclear and vague descriptions of complaints and problems*. It can be very useful to confront the patient with these in the course of the discussion, which can bring to light the resistance to receiving help. Given ego-syntonic personality traits, concrete complaints often cause intense suffering. If the complaints are not that strong, the pressure to seek treatment can stem particularly from the partner, parent or from another important person in the system. It is advisable to observe and reflect on this during the intake together with the patient. This avoids misunderstandings in the future. The manner in which one can communicate about this is as follows: "Something within you seeks help for the problem, something else doesn't want to be helped, doesn't find this necessary and wants to try on its own. Let's together look a bit further at the side of you that doesn't allow a second captain on the ship." In some cases this leads to a conscious decision on the part of the diagnostician and the patient not to start treatment yet. This can be postponed to a point in the future at which it is possible to meet the conditions that it is agreed must first be present in the person. In other cases, these interventions are more successful than previously in helping the patient to overcome the aversion to therapy and assessment. One must nevertheless remain watchful for the return of the same tendencies in a later phase.

2. *The patient gives very short responses*. Sometimes one frequently hears "yes" or "no" and the patient does not take a deeper look into the

problems. After some time the diagnostician can confront the patient with this observation and ask if he or she always communicates so little or if this has to do with the present discussion. If the latter is the case, conscious resistance often plays a role. The patient may feel like a loser as he or she sits there, with hurt pride, angry about the dependence this situation brings with it. Always used to sitting behind the wheel, the patient now has the feeling that he or she must hand over the wheel and is degraded to the status of passenger. The diagnostician can go deeper into this by enquiring if the patient is usually a good or a poor loser. In the first case – the patient does not say much – we are concerned with poor cognitive skills, a personality problem or both. Obviously, the problem can also be the result of depression.

3. *No deepening of the contact during the intake session.* Usually one expects the patient to be capable of and prepared to give more intimate and more emotionally meaningful statements over the course of the session. Trust in the relationship then grows. In such cases, the hope and expectation are directed towards the treatment and the patient invests in this. Some patients, as a rule, will never invest in psychotherapeutic help, they do not play the game but wait and take only from the session what they find useful. They will often deny that they do this, however. Others do not behave in this way because of certain things they do not like. Many people with a personality disorder have difficulty reacting neutrally; they are quickly touched in a positive or negative sense by, for instance, the treatment setting, the way in which appointments are made, the personality of the diagnostician, etc. Reflection on the lack of contact can clarify the possibilities and limitations of a future intervention.

HISTORY

If the patient's complaints permit it, a number of investigation sessions can be held following the intake, in which the complaints or difficulties presented end up somewhat in the background. These diagnostic sessions can, if necessary, be supplemented by psychological or somatic testing.

This is not always the most practical way of proceeding. This comment applies to psychotic or borderline-psychotic patients, patients under the influence of psycho-active substances, or patients who apply for help in a crisis atmosphere and do not have the concentration to provide information about their history. In these cases, quick interventions of various kinds (psychological as well as medical) are necessary. With a panic disorder that has recently emerged for the first time, the patient is often preoccupied with the symptoms. Just as in a crisis situation, there is no energy left at that moment to delve deeper into the past. The informative discussions directed at the patient's history must then be postponed, although not cancelled.

We often find that patients with a narcissistic personality disorder or with strong narcissistic traits of a certain type consider their past to be irrelevant. In their experience, they are not bothered by something that is in the past — their focus is directed toward the future. They even deny the influence of the past. If they have complaints, it is often easier for them to bear the symptoms if they come "out of the blue" and "are not connected with anything". If no therapist can figure them out, their unique character is established. Even the here and now receives limited attention. If the diagnostician wants to give extensive attention to their history, this can cause them to drop out, as they regard this as nonsense. As a rule, their behaviour serves in defence of narcissistic injuries that frequently occurred in the past. The attention of these people is held by an ideal instead of by the reality in which they live. From an outsider's viewpoint, the ideal is often still far removed from the reality of the here and now. In the future, they expect to identify with this ideal, which is why present and past are difficult to bear.

The diagnostician gets to know a great deal about the narcissistic disturbed personality by a careful analysis of the here and now interaction with the patient. Transference hides the mechanism that covers the essence of the problems: the attempt to maintain self-esteem through the other person. In this context, the patient often allows devaluation and injuries by the diagnostician without being very aware of it. The dependence at that moment is difficult to bear. Experience with the occurrence of transference and countertransference with this type of patient is necessary for an adequate diagnosis and motivation of the patient for treatment. A great deal of information can be obtained from hetero-anamnestic assessment. If the working relationship has improved, it is desirable then to come back to the patient's life history.

In patients who have a structurally damaged ego, functioning at a borderline or psychotic organization level, information about their history often suffers from more gaps and distortions than that in patients with an ego that is intact.

Example

A typical example is a borderline female patient who told of an event that had occurred when she was five years old. She and a boy living close by were playing in the street on tricycles. They tried to cross the street in front of an approaching car. She managed to get across but the boy was hit and eventually died. She remembered hearing her father say to the neighbour that he was sorry that the latter had lost his only son and that it would have been better if fate had struck his own daughter. After all, he had three more children. In the course of treatment she reformulated this information as follows. All attention went to the dead boy and the neighbour. She felt that nobody cared for her, and in her fantasy her father's opinion was that it would have been better if she had died (see also p. 247).

The relationship these patients have to reality is problematic. They often distort reality and confuse inner and outer world, fantasy and reality to a greater extent than neurotics.

In other cases it happens that patients can recall nothing or only very little of their childhood years, often to the age of ten. It is necessary to reflect on this particular situation and to evaluate if it is a question of resistance, repression and denial, or serious memory problems that may be indicative of a very limited intelligence or organic damage.

There are many psychotherapists who let themselves be tempted by their orientation toward symptom treatment to start quickly with a complaint-directed intervention. That can work well with appropriate patients. For patients with a personality disorder it can also quickly end in failure and cause the termination of the therapeutic relationship. Furthermore, it happens quite often in out-patient treatment settings that help is sought by couples who have become caught up in a complicated relationship pattern and find themselves in a crisis. In such cases it is often desirable to turn quickly to discussions about the relationship. A better alternative is usually first to offer both partners a series of individual sessions. In these assessment sessions, the individual symptomatology and the personality can be examined. After all, personality problems, often without noticeable symptom disorders, frequently lead to relationship disorders.

As a rule, there is time and space to examine the life history of the patient. This happens in one or, if necessary, several sessions. If there is no anamnestic material about the patient, this phase becomes especially important. In many cases, a discussion about his or her past is a unique experience for the patient. The manner in which this session is held is crucial. In the medical tradition, too much emphasis is placed on asking questions from a checklist with specific points of attention, while too little emphasis is placed on the development of a dynamic understanding of somebody's life history. As a consequence, an extensive report is made of the events in the life of the patient, but insight into a person's functioning is lacking. Integration of an anamnestic and psychodynamic working method is by far the best method and elaboration is especially useful in the diagnosis of a personality disorder.

Gathering information about the mother's pregnancy, conditions during the patient's birth, infancy, development of functions such as eating, potty training, walking, talking, playing and social behaviour, form a fixed part of the assessment. Also of importance are temperament, child-rearing style, family composition, interrelationships, school periods. This material can usually be gathered through concrete questions.

A discussion about the past becomes interesting in view of perception if it is opened with the following question: "Could you try to tell me your earliest memory?" Ideally this produces a reflective attitude and the patient comes up with associations which he or she has not previously put into words. The emotional colour of such an early memory is informative. For a patient with anxiety complaints in connection with going somewhere alone or going home alone, it is quite usual for it to turn out that the first memory concerns the transition from home to kindergarten. This memory mostly reflects signs of anxiety and resistance as part of the reaction to separation from the mother.

With the paranoid, schizoid and schizotypal personalities of Cluster A, the life history is extensively examined in view of the occurrence of psychotic experiences. Except for manifest psychotic symptoms, bizarre affect, behaviour or cognition can indicate one and the same psychotic personality organization. If the latter is discovered in a certain period of the life history, evaluating the attitude of the patient with regard to this is essential for gaining insight into the strength of the ego. Often these events are denied and there is no real sense of the severity, nor has special attention been given to this episode.

With the borderline, antisocial, narcissistic and histrionic personalities, aggression, impulsiveness, emotional instability, a tendency towards self-destructive behaviour, suicide and substance abuse play large roles. These traits have to be examined in the context of the life history. According to a study by Herman, Perry and van der Kolk (1989), 81% of adult borderline patients have been traumatized during their childhood by physical or sexual abuse or because they were witness to serious violence. With antisocial personalities, we often see a pattern of total neglect. The study by Raczek (1992) confirms a concentration of these personality disorders among abused patients. This reasoning cannot be turned around: many studies have shown that in the large category of psychiatric patients, physical and sexual abuse is fairly frequent; however, only a small percentage of abused children become psychiatric patients. For these "lower-level" personality disorders, as Kernberg called them, the reliability of the patient's statements is usually not very great. This type of patient often sketches a dramatic past with much physical punishment and unacceptable child-rearing conditions. Hetero-anamnesis is especially recommended here.

With the dependent, avoidant, obsessive-compulsive and passive-aggressive person, the role of abuse and/or neglect in early childhood is usually more limited, or even absent. Here, too, one examines the life history to check when the patterns typical for the personality disorder became noticeable. This manifestation may apply to the patient, but more often to the social environment. As a rule, one can discover a pattern starting in the early childhood years, but sometimes this is not the case. In the patient's experience, a change in the person appears to have occurred mostly in puberty and sometimes even later. In these cases, one can wonder if it is not more a matter of personality traits that are based on a conflict rather than a trauma, a fixation or an early learning experience. The perspectives for treatment are different if the change in the psychological style at a later age is based on a conflict.

In short, by examining the life history, one can find out if the person, before the difficulties that have given cause for the request for help were present, was already characterized by traits that give the diagnostician cause for diagnosing a personality disorder. The premorbid personality is assessed in detail. In this way, an important problem in psychodiagnostic assessment can be dealt with adequately: the influence of symptom disorders on personality. These may involve mood disorders and anxiety disorders as illustrated above. In these cases it concerns a state instead of a trait and that is a real, but often difficult distinction in the assessment of personality. In some cases, somebody who knew the patient before he or she requested help can offer valuable extra information.

In further examining the life history, one continues with the school period, puberty, integration of sexuality and aggression in behaviour, adolescence and the transition to living, working and/or studying independently. It is a good idea for the diagnostician to let patients who work outside as well as inside the home describe concrete behaviour as a consequence of the interaction between person and situation. This can take the form of letting the patient describe exactly what he or she does during an average day. Methods of behavioural assessment can be of help here. An example of this is keeping a diary during a fixed period in which detailed notes are made of behaviour and the thoughts and feelings the patient experiences in various situations in the course of the day. Besides concrete activities, questions are asked about the patient's ambitions and fantasies in various areas of life (such as a partner relationship, relationships with friends, work and career).

In the context of these diagnostic sessions it is essential, certainly with a patient with a personality disorder, to see the partner or other important person separately. This can, of course, only be done if the patient agrees. It is recommended that the therapist approach the partner in person for an appointment. The manner in which the partner reacts to the request is indicative of the nature of the relationship. Somebody with a personality disorder quite often chooses a partner with personality difficulties. In the case of a qualitatively good relationship of two emotionally involved people, the diagnostician would expect a co-operative and interested attitude from the partner. Very often something quite different is found. In view of the ego-syntonic character of the problems and the fact that the relationships of these patients are usually especially burdened, the partner's attitude to the problems is interesting and often illuminating. At the same time one gets to know the person in the background who, after all, is often mentioned during the session. In the best case scenario, one wins from the partner co-operation that can be a decisive factor in success with a more concrete treatment programme. Moreover, during the discussion with the partner, one can anticipate a willingness to participate in possible future discussions about the relationship.

As always, but especially strongly at this point, the diagnostician's attitude during these anamnestic sessions must be characterized by empathy and neutrality. In the best case scenario, discussions that are relatively isolated from attention to possible symptoms stir up a process in the patient in which he or she begins to reflect about him- or herself and because of that arrives at new insights and/or feelings. If this happens, the patient will say things like: "As a result of our discussion in the previous session, I've been thinking about the question of whether I don't react to tension in exactly the same way as my father and I've noticed that made me angry. I want to deal with it differently and I think I've already made a small beginning." In such a case, the treatment already takes effect during the assessment period.

In other cases, it becomes clear that this way of working has no influence on the patient. If the personality traits are rigid in character, no influence at all appears to emanate from the assessment sessions. In this case it is helpful to suggest to the patient: "How could it be that our sessions up to now seem to have so little influence on you?" Often the patient not only closes the door of the consulting room behind him or her but also appears to pull up some sort of handbrake to stop the self-reflection which one attempts to evoke during this phase. One must not underestimate the conscious or subconscious resistance to influence and change by an external professional.

We usually only see a spontaneous reflection that marks the beginning of a psychotherapeutic process with neurotic patients without strong personality pathology. In these people, introspective capabilities are noticeable, and often they have a well-crystallized emotional life, which is typically lacking in the case of a personality disorder. This makes them excellent candidates for insight-oriented psychotherapy. Further, if the DSM criteria do not apply, this absence of reflection draws attention to personality pathology. What is typical of the disturbed personality is that certain aspirations are lived out and so this part of the person looks unconsciously for satisfaction instead of change or restraint. As a result, the part of the ego that wishes for change is weakened. The diagnosis charts both aspects of the ego, providing an important prognostic factor for treatment.

SUPPLEMENTARY ASSESSMENT

If the course of the psychodiagnostic phase goes more or less according to schedule, one can decide to continue the assessment, e.g. by continuing the somatic assessment. In many settings a general physical examination is part of the initial assessment. This can be supplemented by specialized examinations and a laboratory test.

Psychological test examination can make a significant and decisive contribution to the diagnosis of a personality disorder. In Chapter 3.7 the psychological testing approach was illustrated more extensively. At this point in the assessment, a choice is made from the available psychological instruments, depending on the previous results. If there are few questions concerning the cognitive functioning, for instance because the person concerned has a good education and work performance, this part can be left out or remain concise. Emphasis can then be put on the part of the assessment which uses personality questionnaires and projective techniques. If there are doubts as to the quality of the cognitive functioning, one can start by assessing this.

For less co-operative patients with a personality disorder the assessment using personality questionnaires quite often shows a defensive attitude. This is expressed in a repressed complaint profile and elevation on possible test attitude scales measuring defensiveness. This is useful extra information. In the projective examination, such people usually find fewer clues for formulating their defence. On the Rorschach test, they offer few responses and tend to give banal answers. Stories on the TAT are kept short. However, on the level of instruction, something can be done about this by stimulating them to be more elaborate. Moreover, it does not always go this way; the material can appear to be unexpectedly rich.

The information obtained with the help of tests and questionnaires supplements the remaining data. So far, statements have been obtained that are controlled to a certain extent by conscious functioning. The cognitive control has more effect on certain questionnaires and less on others. However, sometimes the picture the diagnostician gets of the person is quite limited. The expert clinician "worms" out of the patient more than the latter has been willing to put forward. Because of a certain empirical connection, a questionnaire can deliver much more than the person who fills it out actually wanted to confide. It is therefore useful.

Projective material is usually somewhat less sensitive to the patient's conscious intention. The way in which information is gathered here, for instance by means of perception in the Rorschach test and projection in the TAT, is not controlled consciously. We can take advantage of this, particularly with personality disorders. The following comparison is not entirely parallel, but does clarify what I want to say about this. If one wants to know more about a certain house, all kinds of questions about the year of building, construction, the material used, etc. are relevant. This is anamnestic data. A structural diagnosis offers information about the quality of the house's foundations. Questions can be answered such as: Is the foundation intact? If it is damaged structurally, is there not a danger of collapse? Is the house on the brink of collapse or is this partly already the case? The psychological examination adds information about the interior of the home: the upholstery, furniture, interior decoration, the atmosphere created, etc. Thus to return to our patients, this type of information can be crucial for a successful approach, particularly in view of the extra difficulties with the establishment of a working relationship and the treatment of patients with a personality disorder. If it is feasible in practice, and the patient is co-operative (in the case of a patient with a personality disorder), a more or less elaborate psychological test examination is always indicated.

CONCLUSION OF THE DIAGNOSIS

Every psychodiagnostic process is concluded with an indication, hypothetical conclusions, and eventually a prognosis. The results are discussed in depth with the patient as far as is possible and advisable. In many cases the diagnostic process naturally changes into a treatment strategy. As a rule, this concerns neurotic patients who, as a result of the assessment session, are already on the path of change. With patients who, apart from symptom disorders, may also have a personality disorder, the transition is mostly not so smooth. Benefit can be gained by going more extensively than usual into the findings and into what would be desirable in view of the interventions, what is perhaps absolutely necessary and what is feasible. Arguments should be direct and forceful. The patient should be asked his or her reactions to the assessment that has been presented.

It is especially important to formulate exactly where the typical personality traits of the patient are functional and where they become dysfunctional. The adaptation of the individual to the social environment can be involved here. Furthermore, one can also formulate exactly which personality traits co-operate with a possible treatment and which stand in its way. With a treatment plan that is directed towards certain symptoms, the personality is also evaluated from this point of view. To the above-mentioned teacher who trivialized his complaints and fought every form of influence, it was explained clearly and in plain words that could not be misunderstood that he could get help for his complaints, but that something in his personality did its utmost to avoid treatment. He was advised not to seek any further treatment now but to come back as soon as he felt that he could accept this type of help. In other cases, this kind of discussion can be helpful for a patient with a personality disorder as a motivation for psychotherapy. Sometimes it is a good idea to invite the partner for this discussion. The latter often supports the diagnostician's plan, but obviously the patient him- or herself must agree as well.

CHAPTER 4.2   Several starting points in treatment

Special attention is required for the management or treatment of patients with a personality disorder. Whatever psychotherapeutic orientation prevails or whatever treatment technique is chosen, co-operation of the patient him- or herself is assumed. If the personality has been harmoniously shaped and adaptation to the social environment is without marked conflicts, the patient usually co-operates adequately with treatment. As a rule, this usually concerns a symptom disorder. Remarkable personality traits also play a role in the cases of many people who ask for help. The more the personality is based on or involved in psychic conflicts, the more directly it influences the manner in which the treatment relationship is handled. Without the patient exactly meeting the DSM or ICD criteria for a personality disorder, the working relationship can already be made difficult by certain relatively strong features of personality.

According to any classification system, personality pathology is, in many cases in daily life, synonymous with "difficult people". They may be, for instance, very stubborn, overly precise and perfectionistic, very dependent and constantly in need of support, incessantly busy making trouble, continuously critical with respect to others. During work or a project, they may back out at the last minute. They evoke strong positive and negative feelings, they repeatedly give people the feeling that they are insane, and one never has the impression that one is making contact with them. In the end, everybody is busy doing odd jobs that the person with the character traits concerned leaves unfinished or delegates to someone else without consulting anyone, and so one gets the feeling of being used and abused, etc. If therapists want to be successful, they must recognize this type of behaviour pattern and bear it in mind during the treatment. This does not mean that the therapy programme will necessarily be very different from those involving patients without a personality disorder.

First, two misconceptions in the field of treatment of personality disorders will be discussed in this chapter. Then three treatment methods will be distinguished.

MISCONCEPTIONS

A radical separation of complaint and personality, symptom-directed and person-directed psychotherapy, can only be made at the writing desk. We cannot find this sharp distinction in clinical practice. Psychotherapeutic interventions, inspired by any therapy model whatsoever, always influence personality. A person's complaint, symptom, relationship conflict or problem of purpose is within the individual, like a system constantly connected with other subsystems. A simple clarifying example: a symptom-directed, behaviour therapy based treatment of panic attacks during shopping, and the consequent avoidance of the city, also has consequences for a person's feeling of self, if it has a sufficient effect on the symptom. Appreciation of oneself increases, one feels more self-assured, less gloomy and, as a result, often takes further steps that enhance self-confidence. The person takes the plunge in a quarrel with a relative that has dragged on for years and experiences relief as a result. In this respect, the complete individual can change favourably through therapeutic attention to a single symptom. Subsequent discussions about the causes of the complaints become purely academic.

During this kind of treatment, which will often be indicated in the out-patient clinic, the complaint is the manifest element in the foreground and the individual is the latent element in the background. In another case, this can also work in reverse: by means of conversational therapeutic exploration of and influence on the self-confidence which a person lacks, phobic complaints can disappear. As soon as that person feels more self-assured, they dare to show themselves to others again. We often see fear of other people, a social phobia, going together with a period in the person's life in which adversities set the tone. In such cases, these symptoms are of a passing nature. If the latent background is shaped by a dependent or infantile personality, the fear symptomatology can be more structural. Given this difference, it is relevant, diagnostically speaking, to diagnose the complaint and individual jointly as well as separately.

In the initial phase of treatment, however, a difference is made between the complaint-directed and the person-directed approach. In the practice of treatment this distinction is not really satisfactory. In the out-patient sphere, one form can change into the other almost spontaneously. Sometimes a symptom-directed approach can be started and gradually the personality, someone's perception and experience of the world, begins to assume a position more in the middle of therapeutic attention, often with the complaint disappearing into the background. The distinction between insight giving and symptom oriented is not adequate either. A complaint-oriented approach can result in many insights for the patient.

Another misconception is that treatment of a personality disorder is essentially different from treatment of someone with complaints, but without a personality disorder. Several of the DSM-IV and ICD-10 categories related to personality instead of symptom or syndrome cannot be distinguished qualitatively from a situation which we consider normal. Normality blends smoothly into certain personality characteristics. The more characteristics we have, the closer we come to the disorder in that classification, so this particularly concerns a difference in intensity. Incidentally, someone's personality can contain a great number of psychic conflicts without it meeting the required classification criteria.

It should be noted here that the proposition that personality pathology and normality are in the same dimension does not apply to all personality disorders. I am thinking specifically of the borderline, paranoid, schizotypal, antisocial and, in some cases, the narcissistic and the histrionic person. With these and sometimes other personality disorders, we can speak of a qualitative difference found in the structure of the ego. A structural defect makes possible a type of personality disorder that, although varying in seriousness, generates a differently structured mental experience. In these cases, the patient functions on a borderline or psychotic level. This does not refer to symptomatology but to the structural and integrative capacities of the ego. Quite often, clinical or day treatment is preferred for this type of disorder. In practice, different types of treatment are applied over the years that all make a contribution to recovery. In any case, these patients also end up spending quite some time in out-patient treatment settings.

To formulate an indication for treatment, the personality always has to be diagnosed. In contrast with the past, this is common today in almost all schools of therapy. It concerns the extent to which the personality shows characteristics that cause non-adaptation. In this case, the social context also has constantly to be taken into account, as behaviour is, after all, a function of the individual and the environment.

If, in this context, there are severe personality problems, usually in addition to symptoms and syndromes, experience and research tell us that the treatment will be more difficult and take a long time to achieve a sufficient result. People with a personality disorder without symptoms are found outside treatment settings more often than inside. They are frequently submitted for psychological and/or psychiatric evaluation by their boss, company medical service, certification bureau or court. Their suffering is not great and self-reflection is not their most obvious characteristic. Given these special difficulties, it is relevant to introduce a certain emphasis in treatment. The remainder of this chapter deals with these differences in emphasis.

A DSM and ICD classification for a symptom of personality disorder does not offer sufficient information to the clinical psychologist to formulate an indication for treatment. Much more extensive diagnostics are necessary than this descriptive classification alone. An analysis of the patient's course of life, a study of the cognitive and intelligence aspects of the personality, insight into the patient's tolerance and stresses, an assessment of his or her ego functions and suffering, social support and introspective capacities are all necessary. This in fact presupposes a psychological test or evaluation.

A refinement of the psychological nuances of the patient can be obtained with the questionnaire method as well as with a projective study. Fortunately, the projective part is not a question of taking a kind of psychological X-ray, as it was once perceived. The material which people with a personality disorder produce with techniques such as the Sentence Completion Test, the Four Pictures Test and several TAT plates turns out to be very helpful for obtaining a good impression of what keeps them engaged with respect to content, how they view their social environment, which norms and values are considered important, or what is going to offend them. This is extremely valuable for starting a treatment relationship and preventing drop-out. A detailed picture offers perspectives for more effective treatment. For this reason, it also seems advisable to perform a psychological evaluation of anyone classified in DSM-IV or ICD-10 terms preceding each attempt to intervene in out-patient practice.

THE AIM OF TREATMENT

What is the aim of treating a patient with a personality disorder? This is not a simple question. The purpose of the treatment can be easily formulated in the case of people who are asking for help themselves for a symptom that does not exist in addition to, or is not based on, a personality disorder. This means that they want to be bothered less by the complaint. The way in which this goal is reached not only depends on the patient but also on the therapist who is approached. The aim toward which the therapist inclines may well deviate from that of patients with a personality disorder coupled with one or more symptoms.

Usually, the patient wants a reduction in symptoms and furthermore has some wishes concerning his or her social environment. Certain people or situations need to be changed. The willingness of the patient to strive for changes within him- or herself is crucial. Psychotherapy, psychological and psychiatric treatment are primarily aimed at realizing changes in the individual. These changes are expected to lead to better adaptation to the social environment and to dealing with interpersonal relationships more productively. As a rule, the desirability of certain changes in someone with a personality disorder and its feasibility are rather divergent. In practice, this always has to be solved for each patient. No two people are the same, and entirely different treatment goals and strategies can result from the same DSM Axis II diagnosis. It can also happen that symptom-oriented treatment is started and in the course of this process the patient becomes more capable of self-reflection, more introspective and starts feeling the need to work more on personality characteristics that used to be ego-syntonic. No single model covers this complex clinical practice completely, which is also true for the model discussed below.

THREE TREATMENT STRATEGIES

In view of the treatment strategies that can be applied to the management of patients with a personality disorder, and in most cases also for a number of symptoms and/or syndromes, we make a somewhat artificial but hopefully instructive distinction between three variants. They might be combined or applied together. The distinction made here particularly relates to the differences in the point of application of the treatment, in the objective and in many cases also in the emphasis of the methods. The treatment method with the least far-reaching objective is called here the adaptation-promoting treatment. Secondly, cognitive-behavioural treatment is discussed, and thirdly structure-changing treatment. The last has the most far-reaching objective and is characterized by the attitude of the therapist, who imposes well-defined limitations on him- or herself. The choice of one of the three types of treatment obviously depends on the results of the psychodiagnostic process and the possibilities of the treatment institution.

Adaptation-promoting Treatment

Most patients who want help but do not wish to change much will only allow help if they have concrete symptoms. If they suffer little on account of their symptoms, but have many difficulties in relationships, the outlook for treatment, including personality changes, is usually sombre. In adaptation-promoting treatment, emphasis is not placed on introspection or reflection on psychic qualities, but on directive influencing of the critical aspects of patients' adjustment to their surroundings. It is assumed here that better adaptation leads to a decrease in symptomatology and to a reduction of the problems that are the result of the personality pathology.

Interventions based on adaptation may be complemented to some extent by techniques that reduce the symptoms. Such a treatment usually has a great deal of structure. Limiting oneself to treatment of complaints produces insufficiently stable effects, as clinical experience and the sparse research have so far indicated. The complaints often quickly return as soon as the balance between individual and environment again becomes disturbed. This treatment modality presupposes a therapist who, given the nature of the personality, co-operates to accomplish a more suitable adjustment. Sometimes this treatment takes the form of advice, for instance not to start a certain relationship, not to exercise certain wishes or demands. In many cases, it is meaningful to involve not only the patients but also their partners and family in the treatment. Because personality disorders frequently express themselves in disturbed interpersonal relationships, family sessions are often indicated.

For someone with a dependent personality disorder who ended up in difficulties after having started his or her own company, such an approach can consist of advising the patient against continuing the company and advising a return to salaried employment. In this respect, guidance is often necessary in handling the disappointment. Adaptation is improved in such cases, people are advised to choose the environment that better suits their own idiosyncrasies, shortcomings and needs. They generally already take care of that themselves, but certain experiences can make them decide to take another step.

Consciously prescribing rest and relaxation can work as a relief for an obsessive-compulsive personality. Often advice does not work well, whereas an assignment might be helpful.

Example

For an elderly, narcissistic, disturbed detective, adaptation-promoting treatment meant that discussions were particularly aimed at recovery of his self-confidence. The disturbance of his self-confidence was the result of narcissistic injuries owing to conflicts at work and subsequent rejection on medical grounds. In this case no attempt was made to make the grandiose self aware, but in fact some satisfaction was offered of which he had been deprived in another context. As often happens with these types of patients with a narcissistic personality disorder, who function on a neurotic level, they are bothered by depression and inhibited anger and complain of poor cognitive activity. They experience their thinking as disturbed, their concentration as diminished and their condition is usually accompanied by a series of physical phenomena without sufficient physiological cause. In the sessions, the accent was placed on everything he had done well, on what he had achieved and on the fact that he had served very intensive years in his work. His being turned down on medical grounds did not look that bad in this light. He was rather quickly able to continue in the indicated direction and his psychological balance was restored.

Broadly speaking and more abstractly formulated, the factors responsible for the disturbed balance or the surfacing of complaints are discovered in this type of intervention. Expressed more technically, an extensive functional and topographical analysis is made. Clarifying this point shows the vulnerabilities in the person—environment system. How one then deals with these vulnerabilities depends on many factors. In the example of the detective, it is practically unwise and probably clinically infeasible to aim at a structural change in his narcissistic problems. In such a case, a covered approach will be chosen, and the personality is, relatively speaking, left alone. This is never entirely the case, as indicated before, since clarification of vulnerabilities is sometimes a type of very confronting feedback that in most cases influences the patient.

Cognitive-behavioural Treatment

With this approach, the accent initially lies more on changing the person than on regaining better adaptation. It is assumed that the change will result in better adjustment. In many cases, a symptom-specific treatment is started.

ample

nple is a female patient, six months pregnant and inhibited by a f obsessive-compulsive neurotic symptoms, such as checking the gas knobs, repeatedly checking whether the doors in the house are locked, etc. Furthermore, she appeared to have an obsessive-compulsive personality. The compulsive symptoms were treated with a programme of exposure and response prevention, and regarding her personality problems, she was taught to deal with feelings differently and to rest more. Her irrational, rigid and perfectionistic thought process was challenged through cognitive therapy. This combined approach involved a busy therapy programme and homework project, but she improved considerably in six months.

In certain cases, cognitive therapy can cause a lot of material from the past to surface and the person realizes the origin of basic cognitions. This has revealing aspects but is not necessarily aimed towards this end, which is the case in the third type of treatment. The treatment is directive and the sessions often have the character of a lesson, but the personality can be greatly influenced. The accent does lie more on learning than on emotional growth. This is not to say that the latter necessarily fails to occur. With such a treatment, it is usually a good idea to involve the patient's social system, for instance his or her partner or other family members. Parts of the treatment may consist of family therapy.

In this mode, a strong emphasis is placed on training the social skills of the dependent as well as the avoidant personality. A lack of assertiveness can practically always be found in these individuals, and they can benefit from extensive training in this area. This type of training usually and preferably takes place in a group, which is very instructive for these patients. They get a chance to learn from the models in the group; whether they use them is another matter. Offering only assertiveness training is usually inadvisable in this method, but it can be combined very effectively with individual treatment. During individual consultations, symptoms and problematic behaviours can be worked on by means of an actual treatment programme. It is often a good idea to involve partners or family members in this type of treatment. This combination is also productive in trying to keep patients motivated and in preventing them from giving up through avoidance, particularly in skills training.

Structure-changing Treatment

In this mode of treatment, the purpose of intervention is to influence the core of the personality structure; symptom disorders are also considered to be treated effectively in this manner. Psychotherapy is usually intensive, lengthy and demands a great deal from patient and therapist alike. As a rule, we are talking about psychodynamic therapy (Brown & Pedder, 1980; Derksen & van der Mast, 1993; Lynn & Garske, 1988; Masterson, Tolpin & Sifneos, 1991; Pierloot & Thiel, 1986).

This form of treatment is usually indicated when the patient asks for therapy as a result of symptoms and/or syndromes. Except for symptoms in the sense of anxiety disorders, mood disorders and somatoform complaints, it also frequently happens that a person reaches an impasse in a situation: work or study do not proceed as smoothly as they used to, relationship problems emerge that the person can no longer solve him- or herself. These patients ask for help themselves, mainly because of their symptoms, but also because they have discovered that their behaviour and experiences produce problems in relationships with others.

These patients make the connection between a complaint and a symptom or, on the other hand, between suffering and their personality. In the diagnostic contact, they already look ahead of their symptoms and experience problems intrapsychically, and have the feeling that they should be occupied with these problems. The need for insight with these patients is greater than the motivation to get rid of a complaint. They are already more focused on their inner world than on the outside world. Their experience and conceptual world are different, with usually more diversity, to those of a type of patient who wants to get rid of a problem. This orientation can be observed in the stories of the individuals themselves.

We do not immediately expect these types of characteristic from the patient in someone with a personality disorder. Defence patterns are, after all, usually more rigid than in patients with a predominant symptom neurosis. Patients without a specific personality pathology essentially respond with more relief and positive experience to a psychotherapeutic and psychodiagnostic conversation than those with a personality disorder. This probably particularly applies to Cluster A and

Cluster B disorders. Patients from Cluster C are likely to react more positively towards therapeutic contact. For such cases, the treatment discussed in this section is more suitable. This also applies to patients with a more rigid defence but who have already had various treatments and gradually made progress.

In principle, family members and partners are not involved in this treatment. This type of therapy can be managed from several frames of reference, including psychoanalytic, psychodynamic, Rogerian, inter-actional, and certain variants from the cognitive frame of reference as well. It goes without saying that who the therapist is, is often more important than the framework he or she uses. Whatever type of treatment is used, the therapist must have a broad psychotherapeutic experience and a thorough knowledge of personality and psycho-pathology. The guiding principle of treatment is the theory that a per-sonality disorder is an inhibition in early childhood development, a piece of childlike feeling and experience that is isolated in the adult individual and must be developed by therapy.

Example

An example of such a case is a 33-year-old student of US literature. He came for treatment in a crisis-like state. Because of a holiday at the time, he did not make immediate contact and left a panic-stricken message on the answering machine. He asked for treatment because he was not making progress with his studies. He was sitting over his books for his third year but was too tense to study so that he was unable to complete his studies. He never showed up for exams. In the morning, he would feel panicky and think of unpleasant things. During the day, he would feel depressed, a feeling which would lessen in the evening, certainly when he had contact with acquaintances and friends. He ate, drank and slept too much, and weighed over 200 lb. He was bothered by pains in the chest and shoulders. He thought himself too passive and did not recognize in himself the ambitions his fellow students seemed to possess. He felt inferior in relationships with his peers, did not have enough self-confidence and was afraid of abandonment.

His problems increased after the study programme became less structured and depended more on his completing it himself. He had failed several other courses in the past. This often had to do with an atmosphere of too much freedom, which oppressed him. He said that others described him as a nice, hospitable young man, but not very assertive. He did not have specific hobbies, did not keep up to date with his profession and read only recreational magazines for fun. He had lived with a male friend for two years. He considered the relationship a safe one; people usually liked his friend. He mentioned the fact that his friend could be very aggressive. Except for this friend, no one else knew of his problems. With respect to the outside world, he kept up the appearance that everything was going normally. His homosexuality was not a problem for him, but he had had a great deal of trouble broaching the subject at home. His father had passed away about ten years before, which was a relief for him as now he would not have to inform him of his sexual preference. A process of mourning his deceased father seemed to have been out of the question. Life at home used to be dominated by his father's construction company. His parents were always busy with the company and he hated the home atmosphere. This applied to a lesser extent to his older brother and sister.

The diagnostic investigation further indicated that this patient had strong dependent and avoidant personality characteristics. He always avoided any negative tension in relationships, would sacrifice himself time and time again and was consequently often taken advantage of. The way in which he allowed himself to be used became significant within the contours of the self-defeating (masochistic) personality disorder. He lived in a fantasy world most of the day, where everything proceeded much more nicely and better than in reality. He avoided practically every social interaction that could pose tension or a threat. He had a lot of difficulty expressing anger or rage. Whenever something upset him, it was only noticeable in his fantasy world. This then took the form of bombing entire cities, particularly those in which his family members lived.

His motivation for psychotherapy was the pressure to which he was subjected on account of the years he had avoided taking care of his duties and because everything was now beginning to get stuck. In fact his whole life was in disarray. The relationship with his friend was also of poor quality and increasingly in a state of crisis. He was a sort of housekeeper, while good contact and meaningful intimacy were lacking. He appeared to have a strong need to be liked. He preferred to stay at home and wanted to be taken care of himself, without obligations. His desire for treatment was also intensified by his dependent structure. Most of all, he wanted to transfer his problems to the therapist and have the weight taken off his own shoulders. He would have gladly put his whole life in the therapist's hands and looked on passively. He would have appreciated the therapist's advice and possible opinions. He obediently pushed aside the frustration which he had to deal with when this was not forthcoming. He still behaved like a schoolboy in his relationship with his mother, and was at her beck and call. He avoided all tension in this apparently symbiotic relationship.

The patient had been treated with psychoanalytic psychotherapy for five years, which unfortunately could only take place once a week. He had finished his university studies but afterwards sought and found training and work in another sector that was more in keeping with his personality. He himself broke off his poor relationship and went to live alone. Towards the end of treatment, he was in a new, steady relationship that was much more fruitful, but continued to live alone. He was capable of taking life into his own hands much more than before and could benefit more from the integration of his aggressive feelings. This was not to say that he did not remain a nice, gentle "teddybear" in many respects. His relationships with his mother and also with his friends and acquaintances had become much more realistic; he could distance himself from others and express his own desires.

This can be seen best in the following incident. A colleague at work had heard from someone that the patient had completed a university course before starting this job. This man asked him one day if that was really true. Our patient replied that this was indeed the case. Walking away, the colleague added that our patient had certainly failed, since he worked here now. Before therapy, such a remark would have put him off balance for days. Now he felt hurt, but reacted by thinking that this was rather mean of his colleague, nasty even, and said more about his colleague than about him. We can consider this shift in the experience structure a structural improvement.

I do not mean to imply with this example that other types of therapy, for instance cognitive therapy developed by Beck & Freeman (1990), could not also lead to such a change. We need not have any illusions, however, about the duration of that approach, if it were to produce this type of result; it would take a long time.

Exploratory psychotherapy is an advisable solution, particularly with a complex disorder consisting of a serious personality disorder within the neurotic range and a series of symptoms. This should not be expected to provide solely insight and material for analysis. Supporting aspects will be represented abundantly in Cluster C problems. Revealing an exploratory psychotherapy has analysing and supporting dimensio Analysing means traditional intervention: clarifications, confronta and interpretations, which are preferably directed towards asp the relationship between patient and therapist. Needless to say, this takes place in an empathic atmosphere, and empathy alone is already supportive. In a treatment where support is the focus of attention, less analysis takes place. What support means only becomes tangibly clear with each individual patient. In some cases, this means giving compliments as soon as the patient shows progress. This can also mean that advice is given, that the patient is encouraged to confront him- or herself with a frightening situation. In the example of the student mentioned above, these elements were also present in the exploratory therapy at critical times during the completion of his studies.

This supporting and stimulating approach could be integrated into psychotherapy without any problem. Interventions aimed at giving support are commonly used, particularly with the dependent and avoidant personalities, and in any case much more often than when these types of personality traits are not dominant. Giving support can also take the form of a corrective emotional experience. In treatment, the patient can experience what was previously lacking in life. These types of aspect also always mark structure-changing therapy, for instance the healing experience accompanied by empathic understanding and good listening. All attention focused for three-quarters of an hour on the person exclusively can be a powerfully effective factor, and this is confirmed by research. Group psychotherapy is another type of treatment that aims at structural change.

MEDICAL TREATMENT

In popular speech as well as in scientific research on personality, the biological base, often called temperament, has always played a role. This is referred to briefly in Part 5 when constitutional disposition is discussed. In contrast to what we would initially expect on the basis of consensus on the biological correlates of personality, developments in medical treatment of personality pathology are not impressive. Pharmacological treatment of symptom disorders and syndromes such ssion, anxiety and impulsiveness is much more highly the treatment of DSM and ICD personality disorders. the problem of the descriptive approach in essity for dimensional diagnostics for treatment

ation of treatment of personality disorder is to be pplication of medical therapy for unambiguous Although it sounds paradoxical, medical treatment of Axis II starts at Axis I. Two areas that for many reasons develop independently of each other in clinical practice are condemned to rely on each other here: biological psychiatry and clinical psychology with psychological testing. Research on psychological testing offers a treasure trove of information about dimensions in individuals. The progress of biological psychiatry is better served in this way than with descriptive classification.

CHAPTER 4.3 Tips for treatment

We can use the existing cluster arrangement of DSM personality disorders to make a number of observations about relationship formation and patients' potential willingness to accept help. Establishment of a relationship with the therapist is a prerequisite for every treatment. At this level, we can roughly distinguish the clusters. Furthermore, we make a number of general observations per cluster that relate to diagnosis and treatment. Separately, most of the DSM classifications say little about treatability. Descriptive diagnosis alone is insufficient for that.

The indications for treatment below are based mainly on literature in which clinical experience is systematically presented and also on my own experience with these types of patient. In the main, this still requires further empirical research. These indications stem particularly from the personality, not from any potentially present symptom disorders.

With regard to Cluster A, a treatment relationship does not usually arise on the basis of the patient's wishes. Patients often lack a notion of and insight into their illness. Certain symptoms may compel them to recognize their illness to a limited extent and temporarily. Before starting, tolerance of the treatment relationship must be diagnosed and under no circumstances overestimated. This means that the therapist must operate extremely cautiously and carefully.

Cluster A patients may struggle with dormant or manifest psychotic disorders, but this does not have to be the case. This is much more obvious with the paranoid and schizotypal person than with the schizoid personality. During diagnosis, whether and the degree to which reality testing has been lost must be checked carefully. Furthermore, the patient's relationship to reality, including emotional and cognitive components in a broader sense, must be examined (Frosch, 1983). With these patients, the demand for treatment only crops up when intense symptoms are apparent. If the situation is stable, they usually do not seek help.

PARANOID PERSONALITY DISORDER

With the paranoid personality, trust can generally only be won very gradually. In any case, this means that the therapist has to avoid being experienced as hostile or seeking to humiliate or offend the patient. The therapist has to be very empathic in order to win trust, but must not start participating in the disturbed patterns (Meyer, 1989). In order to find out how to avoid these pitfalls, it is important to gain insight during diagnosis into the patient's precise preferences and often stereotypical critical points. Careful psychological study can contribute in a positive sense to the treatment relationship, as the patient gets the feeling of being taken seriously. The diagnostician's empathic attitude also contributes to this. Furthermore, insights into personality that follow from this are suitable for establishing a productive treatment relationship.

As Gabbard (1990) describes, a low feeling of self-esteem in the patient creates the need to accuse others of incompetence. Diagnosticians and psychotherapists can also feel under attack and tend to defend themselves. This defensive reaction reinforces the aggression of paranoid patients. They tend to interpret the therapist's defensiveness as a sign of the fact that the therapist really has something to hide. Openness, empathy and fulfilling a container function for the patient's projected negative feelings are necessary. Otherwise, dropping out lies in wait. A subtle approach for each individual also costs a lot of time and energy. This can never be hurried. Broadly speaking, this applies to all personality disorders, but particularly to these three. Group therapy or group treatment can never be considered for the paranoid personality. In this environment, interpersonal relationships cannot be adequately guarded, and the only option is individual sessions. In view of the paranoid's level of suspiciousness, group treatment is inadvisable.

Influencing concrete symptoms has the greatest chance of success after sufficient trust has been established in the treatment relationship. Furthermore, one has to keep in mind that in the complaint-directed approach, the patient is usually lost to possible further treatment as soon as complaints diminish. A more far-reaching objective resides in the area of the patient's relationship to reality. Perception of reality is to a large extent affectively loaded and should become more neutral. Step by step, the therapist can offer help in establishing doubt about the accuracy of perceptions.

Cognitive therapy can play a meaningful role in improving perception of reality. But the fact is also pointed out (Beck & Freeman, 1990) that these paranoid cognitions are difficult to influence just like that. Before an attempt is made, the patient must be helped to become more skilled in coping with his or her problems and to be able to feel more relaxed. Becoming more skilled can consist of learning better problem-solving strategies, but can also mean changing the underestimation of his or her possibilities or the overestimation of the problems that a situation contains. For this, the careful building up of a working relationship is a chief point. Turkat (1990) emphasizes diminishing the paranoid personality's sensitivity to criticism. Gradually, the anxiety the patient experiences owing to negative feedback is diminished, followed by modification of social behaviour. Turkat is optimistic about the behavioural treatment of these types of patient.

SCHIZOID PERSONALITY DISORDER

The schizoid personality has great difficulty in sustaining an intimate relationship. In descriptive diagnostics, it is assumed that the individual does not want intimate relationships and is therefore also disinterested in a therapeutic relationship. From a psychodynamic point of view, this lack of wanting a relationship can be seen as the surface in this respect. At a deeper level, there is an inability based on inadequacy, rather than on conflict. In contrast, we would sooner speak of a conflict in the avoidant personality. From an empirical standpoint, the schizoid personality is also considered as a certain subtype of the avoidant personality. Gabbard (1990, p. 321) describes the task of the therapist with the schizoid patient as follows:

> The task of the therapist is to "thaw" the patient's frozen internal object-relations by providing a new experience of relatedness. The schizoid style of relatedness emerges from inadequacies in the patient's earliest relationships with parental figures — what Epstein (1979) referred to as primary maturational failure.

In this view, the therapist's responsibility is the complex task of finding a way of dealing with the patient that can break through his or her tendency toward social isolation.

A problem, however, is that this can be more the objective of the therapist and of a particular therapy than that of the patient, who is often not very interested in all the possibilities for total change. The motivation for help often remains limited to a change in a well-defined complaint. With these types of patient this complaint rather frequently takes the form of a sexual perversion. Exhibitionism is particularly mentioned in this context (Gabbard, 1990). Because of this, the patient may feel forced to seek treatment. The majority of schizoid patients, however, never cross the threshold of the consulting room.

If one succeeds in gaining the patient's faith in the treatment, the "dosage" of the therapist's interventions is of overriding importance. Feedback and confrontation in an initial phase lead to dropping out. If an individual, supportive treatment gets off the ground, the aspect of the therapeutic relationship is of fundamental significance. The patient probably profits less from insight and working through, and more from the possibilities for growth offered in the relationship with the therapist.

With schizoid patients who display a neurotic personality organization on a structural level and are willing to undergo treatment for a longer period, dynamic group psychotherapy can be considered. Basically, they can profit from the socialization process that can take place. An immediate problem is, however, that they usually do not speak in the group and thus contribute little or nothing to the group process. They grow silently, nourished by observing the other members and by experiencing the group atmosphere. Group treatment evokes family associations much more readily than individual psychotherapy. These processes are of potentially great therapeutical value, particularly for disorders with a basis in early childhood. Individual psychotherapy can evoke such a process, but certainly not as easily nor as intensively. A combination of group and individual psychotherapy is conceivable as well and can even be strongly indicated. Other group members can start protesting against this and work the schizoid patient out of the group literally and figuratively. So the group and the group psychotherapist must be able and willing to work with these patients. They cannot be in group therapy with only schizoid patients, although this may be possible in a combination with some schizotypal patients.

If affective or psychotic symptoms necessitate treatment, the advisability of medical treatment must be considered. In addition to this, adaptation-promoting treatment can be appropriate, as is applicable for the entire A cluster.

SCHIZOTYPAL PERSONALITY DISORDER

The schizotypal patient usually equals the schizoid patient in terms of difficulties in interpersonal relationships. Apart from the social isolation of the schizotypal patient, the fact that he or she acts "crazy" plays a large role — certainly in the eyes of those closest to him or her — because of which the patient is largely avoided. The schizotypal patient's cognitive non-organization has more effect on people close to him or her than the schizoid's tendency to withdraw. Affective reactions can also be much stronger and show a varying pattern: aggressive outbursts and paranoid characteristics are not uncommon. Assessment of the ego organization is particularly relevant in this case. A psychotic personality organization generally appears obvious. In view of its relationship to schizophrenia, a medical treatment approach is often preferred.

The way these individuals are handled can be very similar to the way psychotics are treated. Confrontations on the level of reality testing are usually contra-indicated. Schizotypal characteristics can be an attempt to regain a grip on reality, instead of the patients displaying the disorder themselves and having to change. If these patients seek treatment, a combination of medication and supportive structuring discussions is indicated. As is often the case with Cluster A, great changes should not be expected and the shifts are usually minimal in those areas where the therapist would prefer to see them.

Group psychotherapy is contra-indicated, because the nature of therapy is too revealing and because these patients with their characteristic traits do not fit into such a group. This is not to say that they cannot participate in a discussion group in which, for instance, there are more post-psychotic or borderline-psychotic patients. Family therapy sessions are frequently a necessary supplement to the treatment programme. Moreover, improving social skills is mentioned in cognitive and behaviour therapeutic treatment.

The narcissistic and antisocial patients from Cluster B in the DSM are generally not to be expected to come into the consulting room of their own accord. This is fairly often forced on the antisocial personality by the judicial system. Not seldom, the narcissistic personality appears for a session after being pressured by his or her partner. Most of the suffering usually occurs in the borderline and histrionic personalities.

With patients from Cluster B, we can generally speak of a disorder in their self-esteem. This constitutes part of their problem, but they do not see this themselves. Their problems are expressed immediately in the treatment relationship. In more technical terms, the narcissistic disorder we can observe in the narcissistic, borderline, antisocial and, in many instances, the histrionic personality manifests itself in contact with the therapist from the first moment. Consider, for instance, a male entrepreneur who is dragged in by his wife to discuss their marital problems. Within the first five minutes, he begins to insert remarks to the effect that he does not highly esteem psychologists, psychiatrists and all those other "-ists". He has acquired sufficient insight into human nature in his work and all the rest is nonsense.

The self-esteem of these individuals is so disturbed that they can only feel good by putting down potentially threatening others. Jealousy and depression are held within bounds by their making themselves the key figure and convincing others in a more or less subtle manner to assume the role of applauding audience. The therapist has to monitor the relationship carefully and be used to handling such problems. If he or she is not skilled in this and, for instance, cannot tolerate the humiliations and devaluations, the treatment relationship can quickly become disturbed. In the above example, this could happen if the therapist grew angry at the insults and took the wife's side.

Furthermore, it is necessary to study the ego structure of patients from Cluster B thoroughly. The question is whether they function in a psychoanalytic sense on a borderline, psychotic or neurotic level. This has a number of elementary consequences for treatment. If they function on a psychotic level, one abandons psychotherapy but provides the function of a "help-ego", probably in combination with medication. If they function on a borderline level, treatment may possibly start with repairing the ego. In the case of a neurotic organization, a much broader arsenal of treatment possibilities is available in principle.

BORDERLINE PERSONALITY DISORDER

More has been written about the borderline personality disorder than about other DSM personality disorders. There are various figures on the occurrence of this disorder, ranging between 15% and 40% (Derksen, 1990; Gunderson *et al.*, 1989). It is of great importance, certainly in out-patient practice, whether the DSM concept or Kernberg's structural concept is used in the diagnostics. The latter is considerably more comprehensive. Given this situation, the present discussion of tips for treatment of borderline patients is more extensive than those for the other personality disorders.

The borderline patient is heart and soul a product of psychoanalytic practice. Couch analysis has an important place in this practice. With neurotic patients suitable for this type of treatment, one becomes accustomed to the fact that they are gradually or quickly able to overcome their symptoms. The analysis process was especially directed towards the unconscious cores of their symptoms as well as towards those of their personality. These patients could become sufficiently attached to the analyst, and they were capable of developing a transference relationship and transference neurosis.

What we would nowadays call a subgroup of borderline patients was also found suitable for classic couch analysis. Descriptively speaking, they made a neurotic impression, exhibited many symptoms and personality problems, but were not suspected of having a psychotic core or foundation. Once on the couch, it appeared that this process, in which regression is stimulated, was too much of a burden for them. They showed extreme reactions in relationship to the analyst. In one case, the patient became especially chaotic and extremely anxious; in another, transference psychosis arose and treatment had to be discontinued. With others, it was particularly a question of a negative therapeutic reaction. The main thing in many cases was that the patient seemed to regress rather than make progress. Working on emotional reactions from early childhood demanded too much of the patient's ego. This fact inherent in experience has started a rich tradition of research on borderline patients and alternative methods of treatment.

Several points of view have developed in the psychoanalytic tradition on what is considered the most suitable treatment. These points of view are generally accompanied by different accents on the borderline concept and accordingly on the diagnosis of this disorder. Some authors mainly point out certain types of character patterns, others a certain level of functioning of the personality, while others place the accent on a combination of typical symptoms in borderline syndrome. In view of etiology, practically everyone refers to a disturbance in the separation—individuation process, resulting in the various accents in treatment. In any case, the borderline concept is so broad that many clinical psychologists, theoreticians and researchers find a position under it. Since publication of the DSM-III in particular, the descriptive classification of the borderline patient has gained in significance. Following the DSM description, other psychotherapy traditions, such as behaviour therapy, cognitive therapy, client-centred therapy and family therapy, have contributed as well (Clarkin, Marziali & Munroe-Blum, 1992; Grotstein, Solomon & Lang, 1987).

Psychoanalytic clinical practice has been the greatest stimulant for treatment strategies of the borderline personality disorder. In the psychoanalytic tradition, various opinions have developed regarding the changes that are necessary in the treatment technique for an optimal approach.

The treatment methods developed by Kernberg *et al.* (1989) have been highly influential. They call their treatment method expressive psychotherapy. This is distinguished from psychoanalysis on the one hand and from supportive psychotherapy on the other hand. In contrast to psychoanalysis, expressive psychotherapy does not take place in a horizontal position but sitting in a face-to-face situation. The patient is instructed to communicate openly and continuously about what goes on in his or her head. The frequency is two to three times a week.

In contrast to psychoanalysis, the here and now is a focal point during the main part of the treatment. In psychoanalysis, genetic interpretations are frequently offered early in treatment. In contrast to psychoanalysis, transference analysis is constantly related to events in the daily life of the patient. Neutrality is abandoned more often by the expressive psychotherapist than by the psychoanalyst. This is caused by the acting-out behaviour of borderline patients. In contrast to supportive therapy, technical neutrality is maintained as much as possible in expressive psychotherapy. Patients can be praised in supportive therapy, encouraged, convinced and advised, and the environment can be influenced. This is avoided in expressive therapy. Of three interventions used in analysis and in expressive therapy (clarifications, confrontations and interpretations), interpretations are lacking in the supportive variant.

In Cluster B, borderline patients usually experience the greatest suffering. As this is a broad disorder, however, all kinds of subtypes can be differentiated. In all probability, out-patient treatment of borderline patients has three variables: the type of out-patient setting, the type of therapist, the (sub)type of borderline patient. The majority of treatments of borderline patients start on an out-patient basis and get through a phase of clinical treatment. As is to be expected, the treatment is continued on an out-patient basis, usually after a short admission, and possibly also terminated. One notices in determining the borderline personality disorder diagnosis that more patients meet Kernberg's structural criteria than the DSM-III-R criteria in an out-patient setting, as is also to be expected. The latter is more frequently encountered in clinical settings (Derksen, 1990d).

When the descriptive and structural diagnosis of borderline is finished, as well as a study of the course of life, a heteroanamnesis and a psychological test study, the subtype of borderline patient that is concerned can be determined. I recognize with some regularity the following subtypes: infantile, histrionic, obsessive-compulsive, masochistic, narcissistic, as-if, schizoid, paranoid, hypomanic and the antisocial borderline. Speaking more schematically, we can say that the borderline patient can in a structural respect be adorned descriptively with Cluster A, Cluster B and Cluster C characteristics. Except for the co-morbidity of Axis I disorders, special attention is required to suicidal tendencies, quality of interpersonal relationships, level of social adaptation, tendency to acting-out behaviour, supporting network, intelligence, motivation to change and capacity to maintain a therapeutic relationship. All these aspects contribute to formulating an indication. We can present these step by step.

Step 1.   The structural diagnosis of borderline personality organization gives relevant information about the organization level of the ego. This means that treatment initially has to be directed toward the ego. Exploration is avoided of deeply rooted affects or experiences from early childhood that have not yet been dealt with. Discovering the drive-related roots of sexual and aggressive aspirations is avoided entirely. Instead, primitive defence mechanisms, diffuse identity aspects and weak spots in the person's relationship to reality are the central issues. Regression is avoided. Treatment always takes place in a sitting position and the frequency of the sessions is adjusted to the needs of the patient, as well as to usefulness in regard to the treatment objective. Acting-out behaviour is indicated as quickly as possible, and there is an attempt to prevent outbursts of aggression. Clear agreements are made regarding time, length, payment and limits of the sessions. If this treatment has an effect in terms of an improved level of ego-integration, a more exploratory psychotherapy can perhaps follow.

It can happen that the patient fits the criteria for borderline personality disorder in a descriptive, DSM respect, but shows a neurotic personality organization in a structural sense. For these patients, the above-mentioned limitation of the treatment basically does not apply. Their ego is capable of tolerating more. This is not to say that the indication cannot amount to the same, however; it depends on the steps which follow (Derksen, 1991).

Step 2.   The indication mentioned above only applies if the picture is not complicated by other factors. Clinical practice, however, is usually complex. The following factor is the co-morbidity of Axis I disorders. In the out-patient field, borderline patients' symptom disorders demand a lot of attention. Most of the time, these were responsible for the request for help. Taking the basic indications described under Step 1 into account, attention is given to reducing the symptoms. In some cases, for instance a major depressive episode or an anxiety disorder, it is recommended that the treatment package be expanded with pharmacotherapeutic support. In addition, symptom-directed techniques from the behavioural therapy tradition can be an advisable approach.

It is sometimes assumed that symptom shifting occurs, especially with borderline patients, as soon as a symptom is under control. However, this has not been confirmed systematically by my clinical experience. Symptom shifting has occurred with certain neurotic, borderline and psychotic patients. Usually it concerns an extensive pattern of rather passing symptoms that had already shifted before treatment. Diagnosing this tendency to shift influences the formulation of an indication as well. With some borderline patients, simultaneous occurrence of symptom disorders can provide an advantage in that they aspire to change more than they otherwise would have.

Step 3. The subtype we can diagnose in each borderline patient indicates many (im)possibilities for treatment. The chances of success are greater the more the subtype corresponds to Cluster C personality traits: dependent, avoidant, obsessive-compulsive, passive-aggressive and self-defeating. The therapeutic relationship is more productive with these patients than with borderline patients with Cluster A and Cluster B traits. Regarding characteristics from Cluster B, we think of narcissistic, histrionic, antisocial, but also infantile, as-if and hysterical traits. There are few possibilities for treatment, particularly in the antisocial subtype. In Cluster A, we think of the schizoid, paranoid, schizotypal and also hypomanic traits. A limited dose of a neurolepticum can offer support particularly in the latter cases, but sometimes in patients with a subtype from Cluster B as well.

Step 4. The other personality characteristics are now relevant, such as intelligence, introspection, tendency toward acting-out behaviour, suicidal tendencies, quality of intimate relationships, level of social adjustment, and not only the desire for change but also the motivation to change. This concerns dimensions on which the patient scores to a certain degree.

Step 5. Finally, social support is important. If the patient has a qualitatively good intimate relationship from which support can be derived, there is a better prospect for treatment and change. Support can also come from a well-structured work situation and from a good circle of friends. Most of the time, however, the problems themselves are in these areas.

In connection with the steps mentioned above, another division can be made in the three levels that are mentioned more often in literature:

"lower-level", "intermediary-level" and "high-level" borderline disorder.

The following patients can be arranged in the lower level:

- structural and descriptive borderline patients (Step 1);
- many symptoms in the form of vaguely defined anxiety complaints, mood disorders, sexual disorders, etc. (Step 2);
- subtype according to Cluster A characteristics and possibly also antisocial and narcissistic traits (Step 3);
- poor intelligence, little introspection, a constant tendency towards acting-out behaviour, suicidal impulses, poor intimate relationships, poor social adjustment (Step 4);
- limited or lacking social support, very little motivation to change (Step 5).

Intermediary-level patients:

- meet the descriptive and structural borderline criteria;
- have many symptom disorders;
- have Cluster B traits;
- score better, but not well on the personality variables described in Step 4;
- usually impulsiveness is very present;
- social support is present to a limited extent;
- the motivation to change is limited.

High-level borderline patients:

- generally only fit the structural criteria and the descriptive criteria also become visible at moments of extreme stress;
- co-morbidity is limited to one or more well-defined complaints;
- Cluster C traits prevail;
- the personality variables from Step 4 are quite favourable, impulsiveness and suicidal tendencies become visible under stress only;
- have reasonably good social support;
- have sufficient motivation to change.

When does out-patient treatment take place and when is clinical treatment preferable? This question is continuously relevant during out-patient diagnosis and treatment of the borderline patient. At several points, the feasibility of ambulatory treatment is reconsidered. A number of characteristics are crucial here.

1. Suicidal tendencies of the patient. Previous suicide attempts point to the danger of repetition.

2. Acting-out behaviour can disturb treatment. This can take the form of not coming or coming late, coming under the influence of substances, destroying furniture, making threats, etc. It is a good idea, and more pleasant, to make a prior agreement with the patient that, if this kind of behaviour begins to predominate, he or she will be referred to a mental hospital.

3. Another important aspect is social adaptation. If the patient has a job and derives support from this, because it often provides structure, admission to the hospital is greatly disadvantageous as the pattern of working is broken.

4. The patient's social environment must also remain capable of providing support. This volunteer aid requires the attention of the therapist(s) at various times.

5. In the case of strong antisocial traits, out-patient treatment is usually not feasible.

In view of the treatment strategies that can be applied in managing patients with a borderline disorder and generally a number of symptoms and/or syndromes as well, we make the same distinction that has also been made in Chapter 4.1: adaptation-promoting treatment, cognitive-behavioural treatment and structure-changing treatment. It can also happen that these treatments overlap or are applied together. As already emphasized, the distinction particularly relates to the difference in starting point of the treatment, the objective and in many cases also emphases in the working method. These three treatment modalities fit in with the three levels on which we have classified borderline patients: adaptation-specific treatment with lower-level borderline patients; cognitive-behavioural treatment with intermediary-level borderline patients; and structure-changing treatment with high-level borderline patients. Divisions are made here on the basis of feasibility, not desirability.

This is not to say that it always works like this. The division is only schematic and still has to be studied. Experience in practice is, however, that it is helpful with diagnosing, formulating indication and treatment as well. In some cases, there can be a switch to the next level in the course of the treatment. It also happens frequently that a treatment is started but not completed. Serious suicidal tendencies can necessitate admission to a mental hospital; acting-out behaviour during a certain, usually typical phase in treatment leads to dropping out.

Three cases follow that refer to this triple division of borderline patients and treatment viewpoints. First a lower-level, then an intermediary-level and finally a high-level borderline patient are described.

The poultry butcher

Psychotherapeutic treatment is requested for a 37-year-old male by a social worker. The patient has problems with relationships; he has been unsuccessful in building up a relationship, particularly with a woman. Furthermore, he has a series of other complaints that are diagnosed as a serious major depressive episode, an undifferentiated somatoform disorder and a social phobia. In addition to borderline personality disorder, antisocial characteristics, narcissistic and histrionic personality disorders are also diagnosed. He scores 94 on the IQ test. He has an elevated F scale on the MMPI, and a high score on scales 6 and 4. Furthermore, he exhibits an elevated neurotic triangle.

The patient works in a poultry slaughterhouse, but he ends up on sick leave because of fights with other workers. In conversations, he complains about his low professional prestige and wants help, especially in finding a suitable wife and a better job. He arrives at the practice several times with stories about quarrels and fist fights he has had on the way. Alcohol use plays a role. At times, when aspects of his personality become the focus of attention, he falls back on his physical complaints or becomes aggressive. An attempt is made to improve his poor social adjustment with a psychological test evaluation and advice from the Employment Office. This leads to nothing, however. The patient wants work in the welfare sector, but this does not correspond at all with his lack of schooling and his personality traits. Furthermore, an attempt is made to teach him social skills so that he will have more contact possibilities. This is done by means of participation in assertiveness training. Soon, however, he gets very angry at the way things work in the group and leaves the training. He breaks off the individual contacts as well, and blames us for poor assistance.

The manager

A 28-year-old manager/owner of a transport company is referred to us after examination by a colleague. During this psychological testing, he refused to fill in questionnaires, because after all anyone could read them. During testing he shows depressive complaints, loss of initiative, rapid fatigue, anhedonia, difficulty in falling and remaining asleep. The test cannot be concluded. Hypothetically for the time being, we think of a paranoid disorder, a dissociative disorder or an impulse-control disorder in regard to his complaints. Traits of the narcissistic and borderline personality disorders are considered with respect to Axis II. In continuing the assistance, he is tested for his concentration problems and intelligence at his own request. He has an IQ score of 110 on the WAIS.

His request for help six months after the examination is related to the fact that he says he has not recognized himself for a year and a half. He feels alienated, very hostile and aggressive towards others. He cannot concentrate in business meetings, does not perform adequately and is bothered, in his opinion, by serious memory problems. He often has the feeling that a "carousel is turning round in my head". Sometimes he feels like a 50-year-old and sometimes he feels barely 10 years old. He is very brief about his past, information about which does not come across as solid. He has two younger sisters who are married. His parents were divorced ten years ago and he experienced his childhood as pleasant. He was always a difficult and aggressive young man, however, who did not let anyone push him around. The patient is single and lives with his mother. When considered from a financial standpoint, his company is healthy. He particularly wants help for his complaints.

Structurally, he shows a borderline personality organization. In addition to this he has narcissistic, but certainly also antisocial traits. During contact, the most descriptive criteria of borderline disorder turn out to apply to him as well. After a certain time, it appears that he often uses a great deal of alcohol and cocaine. Taking his suspiciousness into account, a successful treatment relationship is built up. This is often difficult as he repeatedly asks the therapist for things that are not proper: to write a letter giving evidence that his sick-leave benefits should be continued, while he works full time; to write double expense declarations and to share them with him. Confrontations with these antisocial traits made him run away in anger once and not resume contact for several weeks.

His complaints bring him back to the consultation room, however. His complaints in these sessions are grounded in his ways of dealing with women. He has a pattern of changing relationships and in fact experiences considerable difficulty with this. His defence mechanism, splitting, is repeatedly indicated in this context. With the support of treatment he gradually gets a better grip on his symptoms. Prozac is used to support the sessions. In times of intensification of the complaints, he comes once a week, otherwise once every fortnight. Treatment is still ongoing.

The housewife

A 45-year-old detective asks for help for his complaints. He suffers from disturbed moods; in recent months he feels gloomy, washed-out and does not accomplish anything. He is on sick leave and does not see a way out of his problems. During the first few sessions, he says that his wife is not doing well either. She had been admitted to a psychiatric hospital in the past for depression and has not been feeling well again during the past year. The couple quarrel a lot and this greatly influences the family atmosphere. They have three children, the oldest of whom has just entered puberty.

During the diagnostic phase, we called his wife for an orientation meeting. On the telephone, she reacts explosively: "How ridiculous that now you are only now contacting me, while my husband has already seen you a number of times. That is no way to treat someone." As soon as she shows up at the appointment, however, she behaves rather timidly and subdued. She is almost 40 years old but looks about 10 years younger. At this time, she is a housewife again. She worked in a store for a while but left when she proved unable to continue making the extra effort that her boss continuously required from her.

Ultimately, both come for treatment. The detective initially receives a short period of individual therapy directed at clarifying his personal conflicts and conflicts in his marriage and work. Marital therapy follows for about a year. This is combined with the detective following assertiveness training.

As soon as things are going better with him and the marital problems become manageable, the wife's situation worsens considerably. A more personal diagnosis indicates not only her depressive moods, all manner of fears and psychosomatic complaints, but also a personality disorder. She appears particularly to show characteristics of borderline personality disorder: instability of moods, identity and interpersonal relationships. Her feelings vary between anxiety and sadness on the one hand, and extreme irritation and anger on the other. These can change quickly. Her self-esteem is mostly negative and her relationships with people are characterized by many quarrels; she almost never has emotionally positive or neutral contacts for a lengthy period. She frequently brings up her suicidal plans in the sessions and sometimes uses them as a threat. The attempts she undertakes are rather easily stopped by her environment. Her estimated intelligence is high average and she is sufficiently capable of introspection.

In her experience, her home situation used to be very unsafe. She talks about a trauma at the age of four: she was playing with a tricycle on the pavement together with the boy next door. They both crossed the road suddenly, she a little ahead of him. She just avoided a fast-driving car, but the boy was hit and died on the spot. She says that she remembers her father saying to their neighbour in her presence: "If only my daughter had been run over. Because I have five anyway and you only have two." As is common with borderline patients, this turned out in a later treatment phase to be a distortion of reality by her imagination. What she really seems to remember is that she did not get enough attention for dealing with the shock; everyone concentrated on the neighbours. Furthermore, from nine to eleven years old, she had been abused by her two older brothers in their sexual games. At the age of 18, she had several boyfriends who forced her to give herself sexually. One of these young men beat her and would constantly force her to adjust herself to him. In spite of this, she did not leave him.

Her present husband seems nothing like an aggressor, but makes a timid and submissive impression. At work, she was constantly put under pressure by an aggressive boss who humiliated her. She does not resist and never gets angry. Furthermore, it looks very much like she has built up a circle of acquaintances which consists of people who constantly have problems. She starts caring for them in all kinds of practical ways and gives away many things that are actually precious to her. She gives the impression that she allows herself to be abused masochistically in relationships and, in spite of this, she continues them. She evokes feelings of irritation within the therapist with this. Also, the tendency to reject her must be held firmly under control.

As soon as her ego functions improve due to treatment, and her relationship to reality becomes more solid, things go better. She feels fine more often for a period, but this frightens her. "Oh, it cannot last," she seems to say to herself inwardly. Suddenly something happens which causes her to fall back on complaints. It requires a lot of skilled analytic work to have her experience that she is not allowed to feel good, that she is more familiar with misery than happiness, and that she unconsciously creates circumstances that cause unhappiness as soon as she starts feeling good.

She undergoes treatment for four years. During the first period, the treatment is accompanied by many crises. She disappears several times from home in a suicidal mood and the therapist is called in to help. Institutionalization is only barely avoided. Another time, her marital conflicts get completely out of hand and help is requested in the middle of the night. However, gradual progress is shown in accordance with "three steps forward and two steps back". In the last phase, treatment is combined with her participation in group therapy. The treatment is supported for quite some time with antidepressive medication. Six months after individual therapy has been satisfactorily completed, she is also able to leave group therapy. Her complaints have been reduced considerably and in many respects she has much healthier relationships than before. Her family situation and marital relationship have stabilized into a satisfactory balance.

Comments

A few considerations for putting things into perspective. As we have seen, *the* out-patient treatment for borderline patients does not exist. During the psychodiagnostic phase it is advisable and necessary to formulate a differentiated picture of the borderline patient. Furthermore, the model presented is a way to deal with all data. This model turns out to be helpful in clinical practice, but it still lacks an empirical foundation, which could be the next step.

Freud noticed in the psychoanalytic construction of theories that the most complete diagnosis coincides with a successfully concluded psychoanalytic treatment. Psychodiagnosis, as described above, can be extensive, profound and nevertheless insufficiently able to predict the behaviour and reactions of borderline patients during the treatment phase. Borderline patients, and not only borderline patients, can mobilize unexpected psychological sources for making progress in the intervention phase. The part of the ego that is healthy turns out to be larger and stronger than expected. All the same, these areas can be disappointing and contrary to what was expected during diagnosis. Freud solved this in his time by agreeing upon a trial analysis of three months. During this phase, treatment could be stopped by the analyst as well as by the individual being analysed.

In out-patient treatment of borderline personality disorder, this is, in fact, a good idea. Treatment is started but remains non-committal. In this initial phase, one usually gains a clearer idea of the possibilities and impossibilities of out-patient treatment. This clinical practice reveals which ingredients in the treatment package meet expectations as well. The search process that characterizes diagnosis remains current throughout the treatment phase. All efforts are aimed at offering the kind of help that is effective and works best on a difficult group of patients.

HISTRIONIC PERSONALITY DISORDER

The histrionic personality usually asks for help when the total pattern of starting and maintaining relationships has deteriorated. In some cases, an actual complaint can be the cause, for instance a disorder in sexual functioning. Furthermore, these patients can show up for treatment for couple therapy, encouraged or not by their partner. If there are insufficient complaints, these patients do not usually ask for help themselves. When their relationship patterns can be continued, in spite of multiple failures, their motivation to seek help is limited.

Histrionic personalities expect a dramatic and exaggerated treatment approach (Meyer, 1989). For them therapy must be intense, although it can easily take the form of a placebo. A high-frequency start can initially connect these patients to the treatment. Afterwards, it must be possible to make a transition to an approach in which their way of dealing with others becomes the focus of attention. At those times, the treatment relationship does not usually break off.

Histrionic patients may also come for psychological help with more or less vague anxiety complaints. If a complaint-specific approach is applied, it has a fair chance of failure. It is often difficult to render complaints tangible, as is necessary in a behaviour therapy framework for functional analysis. Furthermore, it generally turns out afterwards that the patient approaches the treatment programme with little enthusiasm. In the latent attitude, we do not encounter a remarkable amount of interest in the actual work needed to improve the complaint pattern. The anxiety complaints are trivialized after some time; they seem to move into the background and weeks or months later can be presented by the patient as before. The relationship of the histrionic personality with the type of therapist who wants to help reduce the complaint is superficial and artificial.

The histrionic patient has a tendency in the relationship with the therapist to get rid of the objective that is inherently related to that relationship: the influencing of a complaint pattern. Instead of a working relationship aimed at the problems, the relationship is sexualized, particularly if the patient is female and the therapist male.

Example

In the intake session, a 20-year-old histrionic patient, who appeared with anxiety complaints, announced that she preferred relationships with men at least 15 years older than she was. She guessed, from a socially desirable perspective, the age of the diagnostician. It emerged from the treatment which followed, which she received from a female psychotherapist, that her remark was not particularly a reflection of her actual relationships. Because of the way she looked, the eroticization of the relationship had already started as far as she was concerned. This eroticization disappeared immediately when she received a proposal for some assessment sessions at which her parents would be present.

In this case, obtaining what one has one's mind on plays an important role. Physically attractive male and female histrionic personalities have learned to use their forte to the fullest; seduction starts to play a leading role in their social identity. In treatment practice, it is usually a question of female patients who are in love with male therapists. The reverse, male patients who are in love with female therapists, receives considerably less attention. With homosexual patients, there is an extra dimension for the heterosexual therapist: dealing with one's own homosexual feelings. Therapists must learn to deal with the feelings of these patients, which means being able to tolerate and analyse them and not allowing them to continue or enjoying them. Countertransference and acting-out on the part of the therapist are expressed in initiating an erotic relationship with the patient. Apart from the therapist's personality traits, insufficient education and training play a role in this. Therapeutic management of these feelings is a complex but worthwhile matter (Gabbard, 1990).

Because of the histrionic patient's acting-out behaviour, the more profound feelings that accompany intimate relationships and attachment processes are pushed into the background or wear off in the course of this process. As a consequence, an inability to build up a real intimate relationship often occurs.

If the treatment takes the form of uncovering psychotherapy, beginning with an emphasis on the way in which these patients present themselves, start relationships and perceive reality is obviously the best.

Most of these aspects are revealed by the patients' egocentrism, exaggerated expression of emotions, shallow contacts and suggestibility. As soon as they have become somewhat attached to the therapist and the therapy, a great deal of time may be necessary to reflect these traits. In this way, their attention is gradually directed to their behaviour, which can be a stimulant to distance oneself from ego-syntonic traits.

The here and now in the therapeutic relationship plays an important role in this insight-producing co-operation. The therapist's attitude must be sufficiently empathic and will often also display supporting elements. Cognitive therapy can contribute in such a case as well; holding emotions and interactions against the rational light of therapy can, if adequately applied, plant the patient's feet more firmly on the ground. The detailed and concrete working method offers a good contrast to the vague, general psychological style of histrionics.

If the histrionic patient is suitable for individual exploratory psychotherapy, group therapy is usually a possibility. The group atmosphere must be such that these people can be incorporated. After they have initially taken a central place in the group, helping others and basking in admiration, the reversal that goes hand in hand with feedback on other aspects of their behaviour can surpass their capacity. The group atmosphere must be optimal for continuation of this necessary step in the treatment process to be possible.

NARCISSISTIC PERSONALITY DISORDER

Narcissistic personalities usually do not show up for treatment before certain symptoms cause so much suffering that they have no choice. When they appear, they are up to their neck in difficulties. They are sometimes coaxed by their partner, often threatened with termination of the relationship. The degree to which these patients have dependence needs is usually crucial for treatment possibilities. With a (quantitatively) severe narcissistic disorder, there is little attachment to others and the social environment. So we can expect little from attachment to the therapist. With the first type of narcissist ("oblivious"), as described in Chapter 3.1, this is manifested perfectly. The relationship with the therapist is more easily established with the second type ("hypervigilant"). These patients' oral and anal fixations contribute. They are able to avoid their narcissistic vulnerability, however, and the therapist must realize what type of conflicts and vulnerabilities this concerns. Influencing this second type is easier than influencing the first type and can often also happen in the context of a shorter therapy.

The dependency strivings of narcissistic personalities, which are as a rule sparse, are evoked by symptom disorders to a greater extent than by relationship difficulties. Diagnosis of the degree to which these feelings of dependency are active prevents disappointment during the treatment phase. They can be detected by studying the patient's tolerance of feelings of mourning, guilt and depression.

The narcissistic person does not in many cases want to accept treatment of the complaint. Complaints frequently turn into physical symptoms, in which mainly mental factors play a role. All kinds of psychosomatic, somatoform and hypochondriacal symptoms and traits can occur. For this reason, a complaint-specific, behavioural approach may be indicated. If this treatment diminishes complaints, it keeps pace with a decrease in motivation to change. In the eyes of the narcissistic personality, the therapist has to be brilliant. Such patients consider themselves to be so special that they may keep feeling the need for a special approach. Nothing is more annoying to the narcissist than to struggle with the problems of an ordinary mortal. As Kernberg (1984, p. 197) indicates, the therapist should not be too brilliant either, because that evokes jealousy and irritation in the patient. The narcissistic disorder is also displayed in the manner in which patients talk about previous therapy. In a case which Gabbard (1990, pp. 387–8) describes, the patient had forgotten the name of the previous therapist and described the treatment as a waste of time.

The degree to which patients allow themselves to be influenced is under their own control. In many cases, narcissistic problems are exhibited rather directly in contact with the therapist. A self-esteem disorder sooner or later manipulates the other in the relationship into the position of an admiring audience. The pathological, grandiose self of the patient exercises a compelling effect on the social environment. These patients evoke a support-giving form of treatment, and the support must be directed toward their self-esteem. The psychotherapist has several possibilities: he can assume this role himself; he may choose not to; he may do this partially; he may do this to varying degrees during treatment. When the therapist provides this support less than the patient (unconsciously) asks for, tensions develop in the contact. Then the question is always whether this tension will have a therapeutic effect which will lead to a worsening of the treatment relationship. The therapist must constantly be aware of and consider this question. In clinical practice, it is usually tested step by step. The ability to reflect, the capacity for introspection that is fed by pressure of suffering, determines the outcome of this process. If building up a treatment relationship is successful, psychoanalytic psychotherapy or psychoanalysis becomes a possibility. In these cases, interpreting the transference relationship is a large part of the work.

In the category of patients suffering from a narcissistic disorder who come for help but are not motivated or able to begin lengthy exploratory psychotherapy, we can distinguish several groups. The first group is formed by people who have lost their mental balance because of narcissistic injuries. They have lost their self-confidence, are full of anger and resentment, and feel depressed. Psychological guidance of this group for a short period of time can focus on the recovery of self-esteem together with self-confidence. In such a case, the therapist helps the patient recover his or her balance by finding a favourable interpretation for the patient of incidents that have played a role in the injuries. This usually turns into a support-giving, covering treatment. In many cases, this is even possible in a very limited number of sessions (Millon, 1981, p. 180). Talking about themselves, recalling and elaborating on their achievements to a therapist who listens well, has a very healing effect. The grandiose self is offered a chance to recover and is also changed to a limited degree in the sense of being rendered somewhat less pathological. The focus, however, is particularly on the recovery of the old mental balance. It is best to choose this approach if the patient is middle-aged or older and has evidently not previously suffered from his or her narcissistic vulnerability. In fact, the old balance is largely recovered and, in the most favourable cases, the patient learns from the crisis and becomes a little less vulnerable.

With the second group of patients, more can be accomplished. They gradually become able to reflect on their complaints and their personality, acquire insights through therapy and make progress in their functioning. This insight is partial, however, and usually does not relate directly to the core of their narcissistic problems. Self-esteem remains vulnerable and they recognize this problem now, but it is not analysed by means of the transference relationship. In a structural respect, little or nothing has changed. They can also profit from a cognitive approach and learn to put their tendency constantly to make the rules themselves into perspective. This type of treatment usually does not last very long. They do not relinquish the controls for long and quickly want them back again. This group is usually younger than the previous one and has more complaints in connection with the narcissistic disorder.

The last group comes for a longer period of time especially for exploratory psychotherapy. In therapy, they behave similarly to patients with a more differentiated personality profile. This is probably particularly so because of adequate dependency strivings that make starting a treatment relationship easier.

Problems in partner relationships can be worked on with success in couple or family therapy. In a severe narcissistic disorder, group therapy often fails owing to the predominance of feelings of jealousy, rivalry and devaluation. Being in a group for treatment damages the patients' feelings of being special and unique. The insults which group members constantly hand out to each other wear out the working relationship. If the group therapists are skilled in working with these types of disorder, chances for significant improvements are greater. Since a disorder of self-esteem is manifest almost immediately in the group and usually appears to be intensive, the effects of well-directed group therapy can also be considerable.

In this respect, Horner (1990, p. 166) points out that the usefulness of group therapy depends on the quality of the narcissistic problems: is a character defence or a character structure concerned? Unfortunately, Horner is very brief in his description of this difference: a character defence is overt or covert behaviour that can have a series of objectives. It can ward off anger or disapproval. One objective may be to win love or arouse pity. It can prevent individuals from becoming conscious of aspects of themselves about which they would start feeling guilt or shame. It can help to keep certain impulses under control, of which they are afraid to lose control and which would then lead to guilt, punishment or retribution. In group therapy, the narcissism that functions as defence can be analysed meaningfully.

> When we speak of character structure, however, we are dealing with the very fibre of the personality, and confrontation may not only not help, but unless handled carefully within the context of transference, may make matters worse. (Horner, 1990, p. 166)

If individual psychotherapy has been successful, follow-up in the form of group psychotherapy may be advisable. Working in parallel is also possible: individual and group therapy together.

ANTISOCIAL PERSONALITY DISORDER

Diagnostically, antisocial people often combine a borderline personality organization and a narcissistic disorder in themselves. More or less serious antisocial traits are added to this, which can turn into a DSM disorder. This particularly concerns the criminal type, which can be determined quite easily in the diagnostic contact, even if previous information is lacking. Owing to their typically extrovert attitude and rather primary narcissistic traits on the surface, and if combined with limited intelligence, the patients reveal a great deal of antisocial behaviour in the long run. Furthermore, tension can be felt during confrontations; impulsiveness and aggressiveness (narcissistic anger) surface quickly.

A seemingly better adjusted antisocial personality also exists. These people display a superficial type of adjustment in relationships and go along with the needs of the diagnostician and the therapist. The more intelligent individuals initially give the diagnostician the impression that he or she is dealing with someone who functions well and is even pleasant in the contact. This "mask of sanity" conceals an enormous amount of pathology characterized not so much by intrapsychic conflicts but particularly by the absence of mental functions which we implicitly assume that everyone has. Examples of these are inner inhibitions, personal observation, real empathy, capacity to tolerate feelings of guilt and shame, a differentiated emotional make-up, the capacity to learn from experiences, etc.

Sometimes, albeit uncommonly, an antisocial personality asks for out-patient treatment. Usually the request for help is stimulated by a symptom disorder or syndrome. In exceptional cases, this may also be prompted by relationship problems and substance abuse or dependency. Not only is diagnosis of the complaint extremely relevant in these cases, but study of the personality as well. Questions one has to ask include:

- Considering the balance of the total individual, is it really advisable to treat, for instance, an anxiety complaint?

- Should a certain lack of assertiveness and clumsiness in social situations really be corrected?

- If feelings of depression and guilt are present and the patient asks for relief, should one respond to this or would it be more advisable to let these experiences exist and help increase tolerance of them?

Besides strictly psychological reasons, ethical motives also play a role. This makes formulation of an indication more complicated. The same type of unintended consequences are perceptible in delinquents in prison, a home or institution. They have the opportunity to participate a great deal in sports, which improves their physical condition and vitality and also serves them well later on in their thieving activity.

Furthermore, these individuals' partners occasionally come and ask for help. It is usually difficult to involve the antisocial person in the therapy. What remains in this case is to guide the partner in a process of becoming conscious of the nature of the relationship and making a new choice regarding its continuation or termination.

If out-patient treatment gets under way it usually fails, with patients quitting at crucial moments. Clinical treatment may offer more perspectives. A reason for this is that acting-out behaviour can be broken by institutionalizing. Action-directed people do not come into contact with their emotional sides as long as they can keep transforming their impulses into behaviour. Between impulse and behaviour, emotion and cognition are lacking. A high degree of refinement, a caring, empathic atmosphere, and a strict confrontational approach are necessary to handle the impulses and manipulations. Involving the family is usually indicated. Successful treatment is lengthy, since it concerns a process of correcting emotional experience. New patterns of relationship formation must become rooted intrapsychically as well as interpersonally.

A final remark on this cluster concerns frequent relationship problems. These often have to do with antisocial and narcissistic traits in one or both partners. The interaction and communication problems that are presented, and often treated, are rooted in deeper intrapsychic problems related to self-esteem and poor control of impulses where sex and aggression are concerned.

CLUSTER C PERSONALITY DISORDERS

With Cluster C, the treatment relationship usually gets off to a smooth start. This type of person has sufficient dependency needs to start such a relationship, often has a longing for the relationship and cherishes the care that patients can receive. Problems express themselves *indirectly* in the treatment relationship.

Cluster C traits occur frequently in both out-patient and clinical psychotherapeutic practice. Depending on their symptoms, the seriousness of their personality disorder and also their capacities, these patients are eligible for a large variety of psychotherapies. In this group the diagnostician certainly does not only encounter personalities who function on a neurotic level. Borderline and psychotic personality organizations can also be found, which exist relatively concealed behind the more superficial adjustment strategies found in this cluster. The seriousness of the dysfunctional personality traits sometimes indicates underlying structural problems of the ego. At other times, this becomes clear only during treatment, in which case one has to limit oneself in the treatment approach.

With neurotic patients having Cluster C personality disorders or traits of this, exercising a psychological influence is mainly directed towards strengthening the capacity for emotional and cognitive expression, increasing independence, decreasing anxiety and guilt feelings, and learning to handle aggression more productively. In many cases, cognitive therapy will be chosen, combined with assertiveness training in a group. These choices of treatment are certainly also made because of the short-term character of the assistance. These people's personalities require certain therapeutic strategies, however (Horowitz *et al.*, 1984).

Dependent people carry their pattern of dependency and insecurity with them into therapy. Already during the first consultation, this type of patient asks a great deal. The request for help is intense, because the need for support and reassurance is great. They do not start a conflict with the therapist, and they are happy because they expect to see their dependency needs satisfied in this future relationship. The out-patient therapist may have a tendency initially to give advice. Because of this, however, he or she stimulates even more questions and pretty soon it seems a bottomless pit.

Frustration of these dependency needs may be indicated, but there is no rule. During treatment, the therapist often feels a tendency to become or remain active, starts feeling responsible and tends to assume parts of the patient's burden that are too heavy for him or her. The patient's dependency can go hand in hand with a critical attitude. If one listens carefully to the accusations, they basically concern the fact that not enough is received. The therapist does not fulfil his or her role of the giving and nourishing other. Gabbard (1990, p. 474) mentions as a rule of thumb in treating these patients that what they say is probably not what they need after all. Influencing dependency is usually not what prompts them to come and not what they ask for. These needs are so ego-syntonic that they try to satisfy them in practically every relationship.

Treatment can start with a symptom-specific approach, but this is again not a rule. Sometimes it is decided to give no special attention to symptoms and to direct the interventions towards the person. In other cases, a combination of complaint- and person-specific therapy is found.

Anxiety disorders are quite often the reason the dependent person asks for help. Panic attacks with and without agoraphobia, phobias and social phobic complaints stand out. We can usually discover separation problems in the course of life of the dependent person with anxiety complaints. This often starts in early childhood. The patient can most often still remember that the transition from home to school was accompanied by a lot of anxiety. For whatever reason, the children made an anxiously attached impression (Bowlby, 1973).

The obsessive-compulsive personality with a neurotic personality organization can also profit from a wide range of therapeutic approaches. Cognitive treatment often fits in well with their dominance of cognitive processes. The intellectual attitude alone is a basis which makes it possible to profit from insight-oriented therapy. There is also a pitfall in this: rationalizations are heavy and often dominate relationship formation. Interpreting rationalizations and isolation of affect and content is a necessary phase.

Owing to their characteristic defence mechanisms, some obsessive-compulsive people switch off the dynamics in the human contact and consequently in the therapeutic relationship as well. In this respect, directive actions from the psychotherapist are necessary to break through these processes. In some cases, the compulsive traits are so strong that the treatment relationship is coloured by conflicts of autonomy and dependency. The patient starts quarrelling endlessly with the therapist about details, is very stubborn and keeps intimate thoughts and feelings to him- or herself as much as possible. This pattern is often reinforced by passive-aggressive traits. We also frequently see depressive episodes and dysthymia appearing in combination in the obsessive-compulsive person. This combination tends to make them feel incapacitated. If they are declared unfit for work and work less or not at all, this does not really take a burden off their shoulders. This also indicates that the personality is more responsible for the complaint pattern than the work situation.

The following rule of thumb can be applied in the course of therapeutic treatment: patients with this personality disorder have not come close to their true mind. There is always more intimate information to be obtained than is actually presented during the first phase of treatment. This becomes clear as soon as experience of sexual and aggressive feelings is more deeply examined. Specifically, concerning the theme of sexuality, we often see a complex structure of cognitions, fantasies and mental conflicts. It constantly plays a role, they work it out introvertly and cannot give these themes tangible form in their intimate relationships. After a period of individual therapy, group therapy can be an advisable possibility for these patients, if they have benefited from individual treatment. Furthermore, symptom disorders must be in the background in the clinical picture compared to personality problems. If the symptoms require a therapist's separate attention, individual treatment is a prerequisite.

A combined treatment is usually applied with the avoidant personality: psychotherapy and behavioural exercises. Most avoidant people can benefit from training in social skills and assertiveness. In the diagnosis, it must be determined whether a lack of skills or a psychic conflict that suppresses certain behaviour is particularly involved. These patients often suffer from social phobia and successful treatment keeps pace with the diminishing of avoidant traits. Depending on the personality and what the patient wants, exploratory psychotherapy can be applied. In these cases, one must have obtained the impression from psycho-diagnosis that the avoidant behaviour is less a consequence of a lack of skills than of psychic conflicts.

Where the ego lacks skills due to underdevelopment, training these skills can be a rather efficient solution. If suppressed aggressive feelings place a kind of restriction on individuals' ability to be themselves, discovery of these feelings and working through the conflicts that accompany them can create psychic space in a more structural sense, so that growth of the personality becomes possible. Then social skills still develop and do so more naturally. Using group psychotherapy for the avoidant personality poses a risk that the patient will take up a position on the edge of the group, thus being able to maintain avoidance behaviour by means of a superficial adjustment to the group.

PASSIVE-AGGRESSIVE AND DEPRESSIVE PERSONALITY DISORDERS

The passive-aggressive personality disorder has disappeared from the DSM-IV and is now on the reserve list. My clinical impression is that passive-aggressive traits are found frequently with other personality disorders such as the obsessive-compulsive disorder. The passive-aggressive traits, of which the patient is usually unaware, can sabotage every treatment. Remarkably, these patients are the ones who spontaneously claim during the intake that they "would do anything to get better". With this kind of remark, they keep the fact concealed from their consciousness that they have dug in with their complaints and will try to defend them at any length. All kinds of complicated disturbances of their aggressive structure play a part. If these patients are not able or prepared to benefit from exploratory psychotherapy, every treatment usually fails. A system approach in the form of a partner relationship or family therapy can offer a solution in some cases.

The sadistic personality has disappeared from the category of temporary personality disorders because it was not found often enough in clinical practice. The masochistic (self-defeating) personality has also disappeared from this classification system, particularly because it was under pressure from the US women's liberation movement. However, we can observe masochistic traits in many personality disorders from Cluster B (the borderline personality) as well as Cluster C (the dependent, avoidant and obsessive-compulsive personalities). Empirical support for this disorder was still weak at the beginning of the 1990s (Fiester, 1991). During therapy, this can express itself in what used to be called "negative therapeutic reaction" in psychoanalysis (Freud, 1933). As soon as things could start improving with the patients, a relapse occurs. They cannot tolerate the feeling of no longer having any complaints or bad luck. Their unconscious feelings of guilt are the foundation of a need for punishment, which evokes symptoms or other misfortunes. As a rule, this pattern has to be worked through repeatedly with the patient before the area succumbs.

The depressive personality has a long, rich history that goes back to Kraepelin (Phillips *et al.*, 1993). It now has a place, next to passive-aggressive, in the DSM appendix "Proposed diagnostic categories needing further study". This disorder is mentioned frequently in the clinical literature, but much less in empirical research. The problem so far is the definition of other personality disorders (the obsessive-compulsive, dependent, avoidant and passive-aggressive) on the one hand, and Axis I disorders, such as dysthymia, on the other.

Working with a patient with a depressive personality disorder is usually a weighty task for the therapist. These patients' moods are so down and gloomy, their self-concept so tinted by inadequacy and worthlessness, their attitude towards themselves and others so full of criticism and accusations, that the therapeutic contact suffers because of it. Depressive character traits are usually ego-syntonic and do not lead to a well-motivated request for help. These patients encounter relationship problems with their partners rather easily. Couple therapy can switch over to individual therapy after some time. Often a period of individual treatment is necessary to prompt the beginning of insights. Afterwards, the patient can be placed in group therapy for secondary treatment. When therapy takes hold we usually see that a lengthy therapeutic process stimulates a growth process. New identifications and introjections take place and the group members can be helpful with this. A mood disorder can, genetically speaking, be traced back to a disturbance in the very early relationship between mother (or father) and child. If exploratory therapy is not indicated, skills or assertiveness training can be considered.

CHAPTER 4.4   The personality of the therapist

Before now, attention has been focused particularly on the treatment strategy. With psychological, psychotherapeutic and psychiatric interventions, the therapist tries to introduce organization or structure into the interaction that develops between him or her and the patient. In order to go beyond the general level of human behaviour and to introduce this structure, information is drawn from scientific research and the development of theories in fields which best fit mental disorders and their treatment. As soon as the problem is in the psychological area, the stubbornness with which people tend to be influenced by the impression which the therapist makes on them is remarkable. Personal aspects are more closely involved in psychological treatment than in somatic medicine, for instance. The thing-like character of mental disorders and processes has virtually no place in the layperson's experience.

For a large part, the therapist's persona is his or her own instrument, especially in the eyes of patients. After ten years of specialistic training in psychotherapeutic treatment, a certain question may be asked at one point in the psychotherapeutic process and not at another point. The way in which an interpretation is formulated by the therapist can be the result of lengthy therapy training. Training and experience have a very subtle influence on the way the therapist presents him- or herself during treatment. For a layperson, this is not, or is barely, identifiable as a certain expertise. The manner in which the therapist forms the relationship with the patient reveals the expertise.

Usually the persona(lity) of the therapist treating a patient with a personality disorder is especially put to the test. Because of this, the therapist is his own instrument to an even greater extent than is generally the case. Owing to the typical traits of the patient, the psychotherapist is, as a rule, treated less neutrally by this type of patient than by a patient with a more differentiated personality. The therapy can fail, even in the first session. From the moment their eyes meet, the patient can feel antipathy towards the therapist. This can be nourished by intensely irrational sources in the patient, such as a dislike of the therapist's appearance, difficulty with the way the therapist dresses, criticism of the practice setting, the secretary, the institution, etc. In one case, a woman left treatment because there were "yuppie magazines" in the waiting room and consequently she believed that the practice did not suit her. This concerned magazines such as *Vogue*. She dragged her husband into her criticism of the practice. He wanted treatment for himself but was unable to stand up to his wife's aggression.

However, even if the first contact starts smoothly, the therapy can suddenly be broken off in any case. Up to that point the patient expected to find confirmation of his or her preconceived idea of how the therapist would react and behave. A certain question or utterance by the therapist can be in conflict with the patient's strong prejudices and give cause for discontinuing the treatment relationship. Diagnosis is all the more important, for this must help the therapist in mapping the typical personal style of the patient. If the patient gives the therapist this opportunity, it increases the chance of successful therapy. The more their symptoms cause suffering, the more individuals push their typical perceptions into the background. They return, however, the moment the suffering has for any reason decreased.

So a great deal is required of the therapist's personality. A point-by-point description of each aspect is given below; these are not all important to the same degree for the various personality disorders.

SENSITIVITY

Interpersonal sensitivity is of great importance. If the therapist easily feels what moves and drives the patient, he or she can use this to build up a relationship. People with a disturbed personality are very sensitive to diadic contact. They readily react to the moods and attitudes of the diagnostician and therapist. Non-verbal aspects of communication can greatly influence their perception of the therapist. Symbolic contents are often more in the background. Direct, non-verbal aspects in contact have a great affective value. The therapist's flexibility is especially relevant; this means the ability to notice the sensitivity of the patient as well as having the skill to keep this in mind in terms of one's own behaviour. More specifically, it means that the therapist can avoid hurting the patient and that he or she can press the right buttons in the patient in order to create a productive working relationship. Only after many years did a patient with a dependent personality disorder talk about sexual abuse by a boy next door and his friend. When asked why this was brought up, she said that the arrangement of the table and chairs in the consulting room was different and much better now. Before, her chair stood with the back close to the wall, now it was in front of a window. She had had the feeling that she was sitting with her back against the wall, and she felt so trapped that she did not dare begin talking about the abuse.

These remarks do not alter the clinical fact that the optimal distance between therapist and patient is relevant, especially with personality disorders. The patient's sensitivity to the dyad can disturb the distance which the therapist wants to achieve. Initially this seems to help contact, but chances are great that it will ultimately lead to failure of the treatment, which results in repetition of the frequent failures in relationships which these patients carry with them.

OTHER FEELINGS

A psychotherapist notices that patients with a personality disorder often evoke more and different feelings in him or her than people without a strongly disturbed personality structure. Personality disorders are expressed particularly in the way in which contacts are started and continued, for which primitive defence mechanisms may be responsible. Feelings of anxiety on the part of the therapist can be so strong that he or she starts reacting defensively. The patient's criticism of the therapist can be incisive due to his or her particular sensitivity and can throw the therapist off balance. Because of the early, pre-oedipal aspect of the disorder, the patient articulates relational aspects of the same kind as those that reside in the psychotherapist. If the latter has not become familiar with this through therapy training, it can lead to uncontrollable countertransference relationships. Anxiety, defensiveness, irritation, aggression and despair are amongst the feelings that can be activated in the therapist.

CONTAINER

Some treatment strategies require the psychotherapist to function as a "container" for the patient's feelings for a short or longer period. The question is whether the therapist is up to this. Due to mechanisms such as externalization, the therapist may feel a great deal of aggression towards significant individuals from the patient's environment. For instance, in such cases patients may extensively and repeatedly describe how they are offended and insulted by people close to them, without feeling aggressive or defending themselves. Anger on the part of the therapist can distort an accurate perception of the patient and his or her interactions. A masochistic patient can evoke considerable pity and protective impulses. The therapist must constantly be capable of and prepared to reflect on the feelings evoked within him- or herself and avoid action based on feelings on which he or she has not reflected. In this respect, psychotherapists educated in group therapy could have an advantage. They usually already have extensive experience in dealing with strong feelings evoked by group processes.

NARCISSISTIC ASPECTS IN THE RELATIONSHIP

Specifically with narcissistic disorders, the psychotherapist very quickly ends up in a role in which he or she is expected to help regulate the patient's self-esteem. He or she is involved as a narcissistic "extension" of the patient and is idealized and devaluated at the patient's discretion. The narcissistic vulnerabilities of the therapist immediately play a role here. Exploratory treatment usually demands that the therapist play the role of an audience for a while and must applaud to support the patient's grandiosity. The degree to which a therapist can do this is closely connected to his personal style and traits.

SELF-ESTEEM AND FEELINGS OF SUCCESS

The self-esteem or feelings of success of therapists treating patients with a personality disorder should not depend too much on achieving quick psychotherapeutic changes. Symptoms and difficulties that are the consequence of a learning experience or of a suppressed mental conflict, and which have not existed for several years, can usually be influenced more easily than deeply rooted personality traits. We also know from empirical studies that complaints accompanied by a personality disorder are more difficult to change than symptoms of someone with a reasonably balanced personality structure. The psychotherapist must often be content with providing a limited contribution to improving the problems and assume that in time the patient will ask for help once more. This may be with the same therapist, but there is a good chance that the patient will focus his or her hope and expectations on a new therapist. Switching to a colleague who obtains reports can be offensive. It is wise to realize at the beginning of treatment that the chance is very great that this will happen and that this can be the fate of many colleagues. Apart from the patient's own opinion about his or her former treatment, careful analysis often reveals that this completed or interrupted therapy was a necessary and useful step in the process of improvement. In short, the capacity to take an insult must be considerable.

ACTING OUT

The therapist must have a sharp eye for detecting acting-out behaviour in the patient, certainly in the case of Cluster B disorders. Giving feelings and conflicts free rein reduces the chance of influencing personal style. This acting-out behaviour is ego-syntonic and usually completely eludes the conscious experience of the patient. The therapist who focuses his or her attention on exploratory psychotherapy, regardless of the orientation, will have to handle very aptly the inability of the patient to reflect on ego-syntonic behaviour patterns in the first phase of treatment. Also, if the therapist makes use of a cognitive psychological frame of reference, it will take a great many well-planned technical interventions to inspire the patient to examine his or her own cognitions.

CHAPTER 4.5   Personality disorders at an older age

The concept of personality disorder does not imply something temporary in nature. On the contrary, it implies that the disorder will accompany the individual permanently. In mental health care practice, this diagnosis is usually made only after adolescence. Moreover, the frequency with which this diagnosis is made decreases in people over the age of 45. In literature about personality disorders so far, we can search in vain for articles or books that relate to personality disorders in children or the elderly. The American *Journal of Personality Disorders*, which made its first appearance in 1987 as a quarterly, has so far never contained contributions on personality disorders in elderly people. Some geriatric and gerontological contributions, however, are now making brief mentions of this subject.

The fact that personality disorder is diagnosed less readily in clinical practice in the elderly than in people of middle age or younger is interesting in itself. This may reveal characteristics of diagnostic practices as well as a decrease in disturbed personalities with increasing age. We (still) cannot fall back entirely on empirical research for this, although we can in part. It is, for instance, widely recognized that the antisocial personality subsides with age. The risk of repetition of criminal activities is considerably lower at the age of 40 than at the age of 20. It is frequently claimed in clinical circles that borderline disorder rarely occurs in people past 40. This contrasts with the frequent occurrence of this disorder in patients at a younger age (Derksen, 1990c; Derksen & Donker, 1990). First of all, a vignette.

Example

A 63-year-old man seeks help because he thinks he plays an unhealthy role in his family. When something is the matter at home, for instance when his wife is ill, he becomes so anxious that he makes everyone suffer. When his son had problems with his knee, the man was convinced it was bone cancer. He has the impression that he makes other people's lives impossible. An important issue for him is the fact that his oldest daughter is a lesbian. She started a relationship with a girlfriend ten years ago and they have a child together. He can accept neither the lesbian relationship nor the child, whom he has never seen.

He expresses his history of problems with the remark, "I came here forty years too late." He was the tenth child in a family of 11 children, and his father was a factory worker. The children had a strict Catholic upbringing and he has constantly had the feeling of being burdened by mortal sin. Guilt feelings, particularly about masturbation, played a big part in this. He was continually walking in and out of the confessional. He worked as a teacher of German for years at a small school and as director of a school community for the last few years, until he took early retirement. He feels he was never able to cope with this latter job. He describes himself as a melancholy man who worries all day and is plagued by guilt feelings. He is quickly irritated and reproaches himself a great deal. He says he never dares to be happy, because he expects to regret it. Furthermore, he describes himself as precise, perfectionistic and stubborn. In addition to these complaints, he is troubled by a disposition for rheumatism and by essential hypertension. He is diagnosed as having obsessive-compulsive personality disorder.

Personality disorders in elderly people will be discussed below, particularly on clinical grounds and with theoretical considerations, taking each cluster separately (see also Derksen, 1992a, 1992b).

CLUSTER A

With Cluster A (the paranoid, schizoid and schizotypal personalities) it is essential to consider the fact that this in many cases concerns a psychotic disorder, as has been discussed in Chapter 4.3. This applies with particular certainty to the paranoid and schizotypal disorders; it need not be the case for the schizoid, although it is possible. A psychotic disorder refers to disturbed reality testing. These patients have delusions and/or hallucinations, and at such moments usually have neither insight into nor a sense of their illness. In comparison to neuroses, a qualitatively different image is at issue with psychoses; the ego functions have been affected structurally and, when capacity is exceeded by the load, decompensation can produce a psychotic image.

This structural problem was already present and continues into older age as well.

In the case of an older paranoid personality, we rather often see a combination with the appearance of a delusion disorder (which is diagnosed on Axis I). Unlike a variant of schizophrenia, the contents of a delusion in a delusion disorder cannot be called really bizarre. An example is a surgeon of Turkish origin who, at the age of 55, was convinced that the Turkish secret police were infiltrating the hospital to eliminate him. This delusion proved incorrigible, but it did not influence his total behaviour: it was still possible to have reasonably good contact with him and exchange ideas in a normal manner about subjects other than those concerning the delusion. His total ego was not afflicted by the psychotic core. Some elderly people have the tendency to develop a more suspicious attitude. This can be reinforced by a developing deafness. If the paranoid traits are there already, it makes the pattern worse and gives an extremely rigid impression.

People with any of the three disorders in Cluster A have a strong tendency to isolate themselves and usually maintain few or no friendly contacts (especially in the case of a schizoid person). At an older age, this does not change suddenly, but rather becomes gradually more pronounced. It goes without saying that making this diagnosis in the elderly requires caution. The pattern must have been recognizable throughout the patient's life, which applies to all personality disorders. For instance, the isolation in which many elderly people end up, often depending on their social environment, education and financial possibilities, can erroneously be seen as a schizoid-like pattern. To diagnose a personality disorder in such a case would be wrong, together with all the consequences for treatment. The fact that the most desirable intervention comes down to an attempt to support and change the environment can be overlooked.

CLUSTER B

With Cluster B personality disorders (antisocial, narcissistic, borderline and histrionic) the dramatic, emotional and impulsive sides play a major role. These types of trait diminish with age, speaking from clinical experience. This means that, for these disorders, conspicuous traits can diminish, and the diagnosis is consequently made less frequently. Of the three clusters, this is the one in which a decreased prevalence among the elderly seems probable, although this remains to be confirmed by further empirical research.

For the antisocial person, we know that a decrease of antisocial behaviour in particular occurs after the age of 30. If the individual concerned has a steady relationship, has perhaps established a family and found permanent employment, there is a great chance that antisocial behaviour will not reoccur. At the same time this is a circular argument, as the antisocial traits were probably not that strong in the first place if such attachment has taken place.

Antisocial personalities usually do not suffer from their traits at all, but let their surroundings suffer. The moment they omit their antisocial actions, the problem, in so far as it is revealed, seems to be solved. How much the inner psychic structure has changed remains an open question. I have also experienced elderly people who even took their grandchildren out to steal. All characteristics that have to do with aggressive behaviour diminish with age, usually merely in the interests of self-preservation. Vitality decreases, and one cannot physically achieve what was once possible. More limitations also apply in the area of relationships. Apart from the possibility of increased wisdom and experience, elderly people may seem to grow wiser owing to natural limitations as well. Since behavioural characteristics are so much in focus, the frequency of diagnosis diminishes in any case. It should not remain unnoticed here that we can also detect a tendency among some elderly people towards more antisocial behaviour, even if they do not meet personality disorder criteria. With these elderly people, an attitude of "What can they do to me? I no longer have that long to live so I'll do as I please" seems to be dominant.

In the narcissistic person who has already retired or is in sight of retirement, the possibility for gaining admiration for achievements lessens with advancing age. Interactions with other people decrease and, accordingly, the problems that used to arise in these interactions are likely to decrease as well. With the elderly, the need to achieve and to compete gradually diminishes and, broadly speaking, this also applies to the narcissist.

In psychoanalytic literature, the enormous danger of depression in advanced age is constantly pointed out. Damage to their grandiosity fantasies has usually already occurred frequently and ageing alone can be experienced as a great humiliation. If these people do not have any other Axis I disorder, they generally will not have asked for help in the past. Given the fact that adjustment has proceeded reasonably well, this personality disorder may no longer be diagnosed as such at an advanced age, but these people will be classified under the depression diagnosis, which is made so often with elderly people. In these cases, their depression more often has its roots in a — now less clear — personality disorder.

It is often stated that borderline personality is not a "real" personality disorder, as the diagnosis occurs much less frequently after the age of 40, despite the fact that about 30% of people with mental problems are currently diagnosed as having this disorder (Derksen, 1990c). Anger, rage, impulsiveness, acting-out behaviour and unstable relationships can diminish with advancing age owing to changes in temperament. Snijder, Pitts and Gustin (1983) compared a group of patients over 40 with personality disorders with a similar group consisting of members under 40. They determined that the older group had a lower energy level. Ultimately, one adapts to relationships and certain working environments.

The so-called primitive defence mechanisms occur frequently, especially in borderline patients, but also with other Cluster B personalities. A chief mechanism in this is splitting; other people and things are categorized as either completely good or completely bad, which can alternate. People cannot tolerate ambivalence and this is aided by defence mechanisms such as idealizing, devaluation, denial and omnipotence. By using these defence mechanisms, borderline patients often make a mess of their relationships. People who have to deal with this type of defensiveness in the social environment usually develop a tendency to point this out to these borderline patients, if only to be less bothered by it themselves. If this process continues for several years, it could be assumed that it produces a therapeutic effect. Slowly but surely, the borderline patient becomes aware of the mechanisms and works on changing them. This could be an explanation for this diagnosis occurring less at an advanced age.

These changes and the less frequent diagnosis at an advanced age must be put into perspective, however. In my extensive clinical experience with borderline patients I have also had the opportunity to examine many elderly people whom I could often diagnose as borderline. However, one quickly runs up against the limitations of the DSM criteria. The traits described, again specifically within Cluster B, seem arranged with relatively younger patients in mind. It would appear advisable to come to a readjustment of the criteria regarding these disorders in elderly people. In this respect, Millon (1981) and Stone (1986) are also of the opinion that, although a shift of symptoms takes place, the underlying psychopathology does not change. Comparable to what I have observed in narcissistic patients, McGlashan (1986) in his research finds indications for a deteriorated functioning of borderline patients over 50 years old. Depressive complaints increase in particular. With borderline patients, another element is the fact that they usually have a great need for a stable social context, which supplements their poor internal psychic structure. Its reduction often evokes a crisis in elderly people and intensifies symptomatology. In contrast to the antisocial person, the borderline patient experiences intense suffering.

Histrionic behaviour in particular, the often extravagant emotionality and great variation in feelings of the histrionic personality grow less with age. Diminished physical attractiveness can evoke gloominess and depression. The tendency to be at the centre of attention can be expressed in older people in an acute concentration on physical problems, both large and small. These are accentuated and have the function of obtaining attention and care from the immediate social environment. Egocentrism, which we can often observe here, can further intensify the focusing of attention on the suffering body. The bodily complaints become central and draw attention, which means that the person is even less interested in other people.

CLUSTER C

Cluster C personality disorders are the most frequent in comparison to Clusters A and B, and this also applies among elderly people. Dependent and avoidant personalities often hide in a protected marital relationship for their entire lives. This only becomes a real problem when they lose their partner. Dependency, helplessness and social anxiety are then revealed to the fullest extent. What elderly people then have to ask of family or care systems is enormous. For elderly people with dependent and avoidant traits, who in spite of everything have tried to get by and prove themselves worthy in social life and society, retirement can also mean relief from the stress under which they have continuously had to live. The social safety net in which these people now end up offers security and rest, their burden decreases and their mental balance improves.

With the obsessive-compulsive personality (see also the case at the beginning of this chapter), a changing image can be presented at an older age as well. Because of these people's overadjustment and rigidity, they relatively quickly come under disability regulations. At an older age, rigidity and inflexibility increase rather than decrease. At the same time, there is less pressure, and indecisiveness and perfectionism are put less frequently to the test, owing to which stress can decrease. The compulsive pattern remains, however, and emerges as soon as more social demands are placed on these people. We also see the same developments with the passive-aggressive and depressive personalities.

LESS STRESS AT AN OLDER AGE

So far, we can give two reasons for the line of thought that personality disorders occur less frequently at an older age.

The first, and in my view the most important, is particularly imbedded in the area of social reasons. Considered abstractly, personality is expressed in the adjustment of the individual to the social environment. This environment changes for the elderly and, in many respects, puts less pressure on the individual. Children have left home, immediate responsibility for child raising and caring decreases. Active participation in work decreases, people retire early and take it easy. Because of this, a considerable amount of the burden falls away, particularly for people with a personality disorder who have trouble keeping up with the necessary adjustments. They enter a new psychic balance, daily demands on their psychological flexibility diminish, stress decreases and, as a result, traits we diagnose as the various DSM and ICD personality disorders fade into the background. This is not to say that they disappear. If these people for some reason become employed again, for instance, we can expect the same personality traits to reoccur. In other words, social input decreases, while the psychological constellation remains unchanged.

The second reason for the decreased diagnosis of personality disorders at an advanced age appears to hinge especially on biological factors. Vitality decreases, emotionality, impulsiveness and acting-out behaviour are reduced. This change has consequences, particularly for Cluster B. The rough edges become smoother, people are somewhat easier in contacts. The intensity of emotions that were formerly difficult to control and integrate decreases. The immediate expression of impulses is abandoned, partly owing to decreased vitality. In many cases, this does not mean that these people no longer want to express these impulses; their mental willingness remains, but they they are no longer able. Old age does not necessarily bring wisdom. It appears instead that the obstacles of old age have a positive effect. So mildness does not come from more insight and self-reflection, but from a change in temperament. Character and personality are built on the foundations of temperament, and because of this fundamental change the personality readjusts. Together with a decrease in social demands, the disturbed personality is drastically reorganized. Mental changes that become visible in elderly people with a personality disorder are more of an effect than a cause in both cases.

TREATMENT

For the Axis I symptom and syndrome disorders of the DSM as well as for personality disorders, it is not the case that this division alone immediately provides the clinician with the right treatment. For that to be so, a much more extensive diagnosis is necessary than this descriptive classification alone. Analysis of the course of life, study of the cognitive and intelligence aspects of personality, insight into the patient's capacity and burden, assessment of ego functions, as well as of suffering, social support and introspective capacities, are also urgently required where the elderly are concerned.

Therefore, this also means that specific therapy is not available for every type of personality disorder. From the viewpoint of psychotherapeutic influencing, global expectations can be formulated for each cluster. The previous chapters in this part can be referred to in relation to this.

Elderly people with a personality disorder will not often present themselves with the disorder to request help. If their adaptation to problems were the reason, we could expect them to end up in treatment at a younger age. The elderly ask for help when symptom disorders appear in addition to Axis II problems. In the primary health care system, I see quite a number of elderly women who come seeking help for panic disorder with agoraphobic complaints. Relatively in the background, diagnosis often reveals that this belongs to an individual with many dependent and avoidant traits. Changes in living circumstances, for instance a divorce at an advanced age, increased relationship conflicts or the death of a partner, prompt these changes.

As already mentioned, in clinical practice these elderly people mainly come when a symptom (anxiety attack, phobia, physical complaint without an organic cause) or a syndrome (depression) starts to intensify. In these cases symptom-directed treatment by means of, for instance, behaviour therapy techniques is combined with adaptation-promoting therapy. Finally, it must be mentioned that elderly people with a Cluster C personality disorder come rather frequently for help when unprocessed mourning is involved. Cluster C personality disorders particularly evoke a disturbance of the coping process that is considered normal in mourning. In these cases, therapy directed towards the mourning process is combined with the adaptation-promoting treatment.

Personality disorders correspond with gerontology in that both fields of study are enjoying a strong increase of interest. With gerontology, this is certainly related to the ageing of the population and the increased quality of health care. Personality disorders have received attention, because, among other things, increasing numbers of people are asking help from the out-patient mental health care system. They could no longer cope with what was expected of them in their work and relationships. In the near future, we can expect the two fields of study to come into closer contact with each other than has so far been the case.

PART 5

Sociocultural and Economic Backgrounds of Personality Disorders

CHAPTER 5.1 Determinants of personality disorders

Generally speaking, we can distinguish three aspects in the development process of a personality disorder, In the first place, constitutional disposition plays a role. Secondly, conditions during childhood form the personality. Thirdly, social context can make it more or less difficult for the personality to adapt successfully to social circumstances.

ASPECT 1: CONSTITUTIONAL DISPOSITION

The contribution of constitutional disposition to personality, and thus to personality disorders, has been introduced in theories of temperament. According to the Greek physician Galen, the "dominant mood disposition" was dependent on the mingling of body fluids: blood, yellow bile, black bile and phlegm. The many contributions to this area from the nineteenth and the first half of the twentieth century have explored the connection between biological aspects and character. In the Netherlands, Heymans (1929) made a contribution to, among other things, the construction of three dimensions: emotionality, secondary function and activity. Emotionality is related to the degree to which an individual gets easily upset about something, quickly becomes emotional. The secondary function is seen in contrast to the primary function. The latter case concerns individuals who think and act mainly on the basis of actual conscious content. Preferences and moods can produce a greatly changing picture. Impulsiveness is greater in the second case than in the first. The first case concerns people whose thinking and acting are strongly determined by previous experiences. Impressions have longlasting effects on them, they hold on to regularity, habits and principles. Activity refers to always doing something, always undertaking something, always showing an energetic attitude (Kouwer, 1977).

In psychoanalysis, the contribution of the constitution in psycho-neuroses and character neuroses was repeatedly pointed out by Freud. In more recent research (Siever, 1991) concerning biological correlations, a relation is sought to Axis I categories. This is not so much to do with categories as with dimensions. Dimensions relate better to clinical and empirical findings. As total descriptive unities, the DSM personality disorders are not suitable for connecting with biological correlations. They are too broad, too general and too descriptive. More psychological research into the functions and structures of the personality is necessary before successful biological relationships can be established. The dimensions that are considered relevant at this time in the study of personality pathology include cognitive disorganization (schizotypy), affective instability, anxiety and impulsiveness. It is remarkable that emotionality and Heymans' primary function (impulsiveness) are easily recognizable here. Research concerning biological correlations of personality pathology is still in its infancy, but it is very promising. At this level, cultural changes are the least influential.

ASPECT 2: CONDITIONS DURING CHILDHOOD

The conditions during childhood are considered relevant to personality development by practically all schools in the field of psychopathology. Very different processes are covered by this broad indication.

Rearing and caring for infants, toddlers and pre-schoolers fall under this category. It is perhaps superfluous to state that there are totally different styles of child rearing. On the one hand these differences are related to the parents' personalities, while on the other hand parents can also treat their children differently.

The traumata from external events that can influence the process of raising and caring are also part of these conditions. One can think of hospitalization of the mother during early childhood, an accident, a disaster in the form of a war, etc. Depending on the precise nature of the trauma, the age of the child and the manner in which it has been handled in relation to the child, this disturbance exerts its influence on the development of the person.

Parents or family members themselves can also be responsible for traumata. Empirical research has repeatedly pointed at the role of neglect, physical and sexual abuse of the young child, particularly in the development of borderline and antisocial personality disorders. More generally speaking, we can observe that traumata which disturb caretaking owing to external events or the behaviour of the parents can result in structural damage if they take place at a very early age. Structural damage is damage of the ego structure. In such cases, we have to take into account that it will be a case of a defect rather than of a conflict in personality pathology. The result of this can be found in a personality disorder of the Cluster A or Cluster B type functioning at the borderline or psychotic level. To a lesser degree, this applies to personality disorders from Cluster C.

Furthermore, the formation of a relationship between the child and the caretaker plays an important role. In the clinical literature on the genesis of borderline personality disorder, a disturbance in the separation–individuation process is indicated by many authors as a primary cause of the disorder. According to object relations theory, childhood relationships are internalized by the growing child: what initially existed between the child and parents exists later in the adult. More concretely, as the parents once spoke to the child, the adult now speaks to him- or herself.

In addition, the child's feeling and fantasy processes fall under this aspect. The small child's perception is highly directed by these processes and this perception in turn influences psychological development to a certain extent.

ASPECT 3: SOCIAL CONTEXT

Social context is an all-encompassing collective name for social structures as they actually exist. According to Berger and Luckmann (1966), we can distinguish the subsystems of techno-economy, social structure and ideology in the structure of society. We expect the ideological subsystem to play a particular role in the genesis of personality disorders. It is in this subsystem that the opinions which people have about themselves and their world are rooted. In other words, this is the level of legitimacy. We place the ideals and norms that keep each society and each group of people together on this level (von der Dunk, 1992).

Child-rearing practices are formed by these perceptions of the world and, in turn, shape personalities. It should be clear that the aspects of "conditions during childhood" and "social context" are linked. Not only can problems occurring during child rearing be compensated for by the working of certain social processes in which the adult finds him- or herself, but early childhood disturbances may be expressed owing to a lack of compensatory possibilities in the culture. Furthermore, the dominant ideology structures child-rearing practices to a large extent as they take form within a certain culture. On the other hand, child-rearing practices also influence culture. This influence takes form when the generation in question arrives at positions in which they can influence the culture. In general, there is no direct connection such as "adults that received anti-authoritarian education are anti-authoritarian educators". The process of the succession of generations has its own mechanisms; there are often breaks, changes and attempts to do everything differently.

DISCUSSION

A number of questions can be asked in regard to these three aspects. Do symptom disorders not come about within the same circles of influence? Even stronger, has this not been set up so broadly that every behaviour results from this? To a certain degree, the answer is yes, thus making the relevance of these aspects for personality disorders even greater. It is my impression that there are three reasons why these aspects are particularly relevant for personality disorders.

- First, the patient is familiar with the personality and also with its disturbances, which generally date from childhood. This is not always true for the concrete complaints which a person presents. As soon as it concerns the person more than the symptom, we are dealing with a long history.

- Secondly, in personality traits the accent lies more on constant than on variable factors. The notion "that's just the way I am" plays a role in a person's perception. In the clinical sphere, this evokes the biological — genetic sides.

- Thirdly, personality problems can be concealed to a certain degree if good adaptation to the social context takes place. Somebody with authority problems who reaches a high rank in the army is much better off than if he had become a teacher in a secondary technical school. Somebody who is very precise, perfectionist, overtly exact (obsessive-compulsive) will be better off as a chemical analyst, bookkeeper or accountant than as a builder. A person with an intense avoidance of relationships with others, owing to fear or a lack of interest, will do better in a profession such as forestry than as a group leader. Adaptation plays a greater role here than in symptom neuroses. Therefore, there is a closer relationship between the possibilities in the social structure and the manifestation of personality problems.

In the following chapters, a number of observations will be made about recent shifts in different social sectors with regard to the third aspect. Its influence on people's style of behaviour will be indicated later. It has to be taken into account that these are mainly speculations based on observations in clinical practice as well as in daily life. Wherever possible, empirical data are used as a basis. Many of the observations, however, lack an empirical basis which could well be available in the future.

CHAPTER 5.2   Techno-economic developments and individualization

The economic basis of our society has little stability and seems to be a prisoner of its own need for growth. If economic growth declines, there will be serious consequences for material existence. Economic growth is a stimulus that changes many sectors in the economic constant. The view is that economic growth cannot relax, can never achieve stability, but can only move forward and increase. Apart from the consequences of this for our ecological system and for the sharply increasing contrast between rich and poor, north and south, it influences the behavioural style of members of society. The systemic nature of society is such that shifts in the economy lead to changes in every other sector.

Today in Western society, we can observe that the social structure has been taking an important position in comparison to the techno-economy and particularly in comparison to ideology. Current society seems to consist solely of rules, laws, influence strategies, subsidies and other incentive measures. In a broad sense, we can observe a receding of ideological orientations since World War II. Furthermore, on a relatively smaller scale, we see this development in political parties. They are directed towards voters in a more pragmatic way. The social structure often serves to manage crises in the techno-economy. Pragmatism here supplants ideological inspiration.

Development towards increasing individualization in Western culture is being described by scientists from various disciplines (Sampson, 1988). A great deal of evidence is available for this development: the issue of rules is becoming increasingly differentiated in order to meet individual needs. For example, a drink before a meal in China means the same choice for virtually everybody. In contrast, if 30 Dutch people are given the choice of a drink before a meal, it is not unusual for 20 different drinks to be selected. As a further example, the consumer pattern in Western culture has room for a dozen "different" kinds of soap. The ego increasingly differentiates itself from its neighbour. In itself, this is an element of human choices already made at a young age: children like to stress their difference from one another. In our culture, however, these traits seem to be particularly highly developed.

The development and emphasis of the ego and the self take place against a background in which the forming of the person can no longer be completed in the nuclear family alone. Much more and on a much greater scale than in former times, the developing person needs to be helped to prepare to function in society. Education within family boundaries is considerably extended in the educational environment outside the family. In agricultural societies of the past, education within the family was sufficient for members later to earn a living from the land or by raising cattle. Today, families fail hopelessly in preparing young people for their place in society. The complexity of labour relations demands very specific educational principles. Thus our society is overflowing with courses and training projects. For the university educated, it is necessary to obtain supplementary education on a yearly basis. Today, people are looked down on if they do not draw on the training budget.

So the ego is shaped in a variety of ways and by a variety of people. Practical and technical knowledge has priority over ideological knowledge. Behaviour-focused training in order to acquire new skills plays a large role. The economy dictates a pragmatism that is being increasingly incorporated into training programmes. For several years now, university training programmes have been cut back and restricted, so that only the most necessary courses remain. Broader training comprising social and cultural aspects of education is becoming increasingly rare.

Techno-economic development, in connection with the social structure, stimulates individualization on the ideological plane. Individualization, partly made possible by the improved material conditions enjoyed by many people, makes demands on the production of goods and the political—juridical structure in society. This development in the West can be explained by referring to the sociopsychological processes that can be observed in Japan. In Japan, the influence of the ideological tradition is still strong, but is diminishing under the influence of the growth of the techno-economy and changes in the social structure. The type of psychological problems observed there are being compared to those in the West. The accents in the personality differ and consequently also the typical symptoms and characteristic personality problems (Derksen & Klein Herenbrink, 1991).

JAPAN

In Kobe, Japan, in 1990, a 15-year-old girl arrived a few seconds too late at the gate of her school. As usual, a teacher had closed the iron gate exactly on time, and as a consequence the gate hit the girl on the head. The girl died as a result. This incident gained a great deal of public interest and the teacher was fired. A professor researching physical punishment in high schools in Japan protested that what had happened was treated as an isolated incident rather than as a structural problem in the Japanese school system. The teacher himself sighed: "I have taken only two days off in the past year. Why does such a tragedy have to happen to me, I who work with such dedication?"

During the opening ceremony of the International Congress for Applied Psychology in Kyoto in 1990, we were surprised with a violin concert by 100 children, a great number of whom could barely even hold a violin. Some of the children had been trained in playing the instrument from a very early age. For infants, toddlers and pre-schoolers, the atmosphere is extremely child friendly. As soon as the child reaches an age at which education is going to play a more important role, a number of guidelines systematically fall into place. This is the reason that the pressure under which children and also adults live is much higher than we are used to in the West.

One of the rules is to be harmonious, not to quarrel or make trouble. A survey showed that 50% of Japanese report that one of the most important things in life is not to be a burden to someone else. They pray that this will not happen. Within this framework, there is hope for sudden death in old age. Being bedridden with a long illness or afflicted with dementia is seen as being a burden to the family.

The adult Japanese will seldom directly turn down a request. They hardly know what we call assertiveness in the West; they view themselves primarily as members of a social group and are oriented toward adjustment in this group. Another guideline prescribes that memory has to be trained well, and they have to learn everything by heart. Furthermore, it is of importance that everything that is started is also finished. The motivation to perform is keen and opportunities have to be utilized. They value creativity and spontaneity much less than we do in the West.

An entrance exam is given for some kindergartens. A good choice of school is of great importance. A good kindergarten increases the chance of getting into a good elementary school, which leads to a better prospective for a good high school and, after all, that is the best road to get into a high-status university. As soon as this last station has been passed through, it is a question of graduation, with which the right ticket for a good job in the business community is bought. The greatest pressure comes from the entrance exam. Parents assume that happiness equals a graduation diploma from a good school and this value is transferred to their children.

In the meantime, school phobia has grown into a real social problem. According to Hiroko Mori, who worked in the United States for seven years as a psychologist and researcher, this is a typical Japanese problem. School and parents demand conformity to rules and performance. The students are under a great deal of work pressure and heavy group pressure. The school uniform has to be of a specific length, and hairstyles have to meet specific requirements. In the West, the kind of problem is different in that children become drop-outs sooner, skip school more often, seek conflicts, etc. Japanese children develop a phobia and suffer more from it than young people in the West. The phobias usually last a long time (from one to three years) and are rather difficult to treat.

Another problem is "anthropophobia". In our terminology, we would probably call this a social phobia. People become fearful in social contact, they are often unable to cope with the requirements which this contact makes of them and the contradiction between these requirements and those they have traditionally learned from their upbringing. The poor social skills of the Japanese go hand in hand with worries about what others think of them. Harmony in contact must remain constant at all costs and, in order to achieve that, they have a great tendency to meet the expectations others are supposed to have of them.

This difference between the American and Japanese behaviour style can be illustrated by a small co-operative venture in Texas. In order to increase productivity, it was suggested to the employees that they should look in the mirror every morning before going to work and say a hundred times to themselves: "I am beautiful" (Markus & Kitayama, 1991). The Japanese counterpart of this anecdote can be found in a Japanese supermarket in New Jersey. Here the employees were given instructions to start the day holding each other's hands and saying to one another: "You are beautiful" (Markus & Kitayama, 1991).

Personality disorders found in Japan seem to have much more to do with compulsiveness, indicating a strong superego, than with the disturbed self, which we seem to encounter increasingly in the West.

Besides the tendency to adjust, the perfectionism of the Japanese is also well known. On an individual level, this is often too much to handle and, as a consequence, compulsiveness is a rather frequent personality disorder. However well one performs objectively, it is never good enough. Work always wins over relaxation, and there is an incapacity for enjoyment. Decision making is delayed. This problem exists on such a large scale that government-sponsored programmes are currently being launched that teach citizens relaxation techniques and aim at introducing a better lifestyle.

The Japanese go on holiday too infrequently. When they do go on holiday, they behave exactly like the Japanese tourists we are familiar with, travelling in groups. They apparently cannot really enjoy relaxation. The negative consequences of this are receiving increasing attention, as is evident from the phenomenon of sudden death at work. A committee of lawyers and doctors has opened a telephone line for this purpose and received 1350 telephone calls within a year. It has reached the point where women whose husbands die at work are taking legal measures against employers for placing demands which are too high. Some companies require their employees to work 3000 hours a year. In comparison, the average is 1655 hours in Germany and 1924 hours in the United States.

Another problem among women is an increase in eating disorders. Anorexia nervosa as well as bulimia (binge eating with weight fluctuations) are more frequently found than in the West.

The percentage of divorces is traditionally low in Japan: less than one in ten marriages ends up in divorce. Women have consistently been taught a submissive role. This is changing now under the influence of the feminist movement that is increasingly gaining ground in Japan. With a rising number of divorces, there are two peaks: young married people who reach the conclusion that they have made a mistake and break off their marriage after a few years; and, a more remarkable group, women between ages 50 and 60. Children have left home and husbands retire at the age of 55. The women have been used to focusing on the children and having their husbands at work. These men are mockingly called "cockroaches". They come home, are incapable of doing anything in the household, and do not do anything else either. They just sit around listlessly, to their spouse's increasing irritation. Their personal relationship turns out to be so poor that there are no subjects for conversation. This goes on until the woman of the house leaves. Her risk in doing so is not slight in view of the fact that the majority have to support themselves financially after taking such a step. Programmes are being designed by the business community to prepare men for these problems. This problem seems to apply to a lesser degree to the younger generation.

With regard to the mental disorders that are common in Japan, they are noticeably connected to the typical Japanese psychological style: introversion. In the West, we see more and more behaviour problems emerging where dropping out and acting out play an important role: here mental conflicts are increasingly manifested in social surroundings. Examples are skipping school, drug use, alcohol abuse and violent conflicts. Particularly in the United States, but also increasingly in Europe, this goes hand in hand with the typical extrovert psychological style that will be discussed in more detail below. In contrast with introvert characteristics, people with extrovert traits have fewer intrapsychic inhibitions, and are corrected more by their surroundings than by their own value and norm system. In Japan, this value and norm system is highly developed, which has consequences for psychological order and the development of disorders. Drug use and criminal offences are much less frequent in Japan. Dr Mori compared in a study the formation of identity among Japanese and American students. The Japanese turned out to score highly on identity conflicts; doubts between individualistic tendencies and the expectations of society (collectivism) were central. The Americans experienced many fewer identity conflicts, were more egocentric and less concerned about other people's problems. Around the age of 30, the Japanese turned out to be more able to integrate both attitudes into their personal life.

Superficially, there seems to be a lot of room for psychologists and psychiatrists to direct themselves towards diagnosing and treating mental disorders in Japanese society. Psychotherapy, however, is not very popular. In Japanese culture the family unit is strong; the individualization tendency that manifests itself sharply in the West is still not so operative. Problems are discussed within the family; people refrain from washing their dirty linen in public so as not to damage the family name. When treatment by experts is necessary, clinical psychologists and psychotherapists are in any case available only to a limited degree. There are about 10 000 psychologists for a population of 120 million. The number of psychologists concerned with mental disorders and their treatment is less than one-third of this figure.

Furthermore, modern psychotherapies are only rarely available, as training in this area is not very widespread among psychologists. They have, however, their own traditional therapies originating from Zen Buddhism. "Morita" and the "Nikan" therapy can be specifically mentioned. Both forms go hand in hand with the introvert style of the Japanese. Central themes are "finding yourself", introspection, and finding peace and rest. During this process, the therapist comes by from time to time to go through a few things with the client. It is not surprising that, of the Western therapies, Rogerian (client-centred) therapy has been particularly influential. However, it is not applied on a large scale.

The predominant mental problems, described above, appear to be connected rather directly with the social context. The entire Japanese society seems to be in need of social restructuring. Traditional Japanese values, inspired by the predominant religions of Shintoism and Buddhism, seem to have got stuck in the structures of a modern industrial superpower that has its own requirements. The economy has grown much faster than the forms of interpersonal behaviour could change, although they appear to have started trying to catch up. At the same time, this economic expansion was also enabled by the psychological characteristics of the "average Japanese". Japanese society is now faced with the complex task of preserving its obvious current advantages and, nevertheless, passing through the change necessary to keep up with other, Western superpowers. The question is whether this is possible without resulting in the behaviour problems and personality disorders normally associated with the process.

CHAPTER 5.3 Shifts in ideology and behavioural style

In cultural psychology and cultural sociology in the United States, a change in people's personality style from "inner directed" to "other directed" was described as early as the 1950s (Riesman, 1950). Relatively introverted, closed personality characteristics made room for a great capacity to react to environmental stimuli. The socially skilled salesperson type was emerging. The inhibiting conscience made room for an impulsive ego that was ready for action.

Instead of an inhibition of impulses through an inward deepening of feelings, longings, fantasies and mental conflicts, we see an extroverted other-directed individual that expresses him- or herself and points an accusing finger at unjust circumstances. Expressing these basic impulses and feelings renders experience of them superficial. Passion is no longer felt, as it happens after all, primarily during the inhibition process; rather, impulse is directly transformed into behaviour. The ego unquestioningly accepts the urge from the drives. Sexuality has become something that can be shopped for, superficial, quickly subordinated to the ego and added to the self. Aggression must be possible to get things "off your chest" and to show others immediately what is irritating you. In the place of a person who shows respect for tradition and authority, a person is emerging who knows his or her rights by heart and acts assertively with regard to everyone he or she meets.

During the 1960s in particular, norms were thrown to the wind. The prudishness of the older generation was confronted with openness, and individual freedom became highly esteemed. In Western Europe, this can be seen as a reaction of the new generation to the great post-war ideological controversies (von der Dunk, 1992).

The ego ideal is projected less into the future and appears to be fusing increasingly with the self. This means, in these people's experience, that they are already, in their feeling of self, the ideal towards which they should really be aspiring. They seem unable to tolerate the necessary tension between self and ideal, and will not permit delay in the fulfilment of their desires. Their experience of self coincides with their ideal self. Their behaviour radiates this in a more or less covert form.

The current economic set-up does not posit a person who is level headed, who has many inner reflections, inhibitions, strict norms and values. Much more in keeping with this situation is a person with strong desires, high performance motivation, and a restlessness in body and soul. Ambition, feelings of competitiveness, a striving for progress and mental flexibility are also essential characteristics of this personality. Quality is losing out to quantity. The less this person is acquainted with feelings of dependence, doubt in his or her own ability and ethical considerations, the more these characteristics get a chance to express themselves. The latter could also be called Cluster C characteristics. Except for the fact that the personality comes under more tension, we can also see a general shift in psychological style from Cluster C to Cluster B traits.

Certain objections are now worth considering. An objection to the above-mentioned argument on this point is not so much the question, in Riesman's terms, of a shift to the other-directed personality, but more the fact that these people are asking for psychological, psychiatric and psychotherapeutic help. In other words, they always existed, only not in the field of vision of the mental health care system. One can add to this that psychological and psychiatric help are offered more extensively today. Furthermore, this group of people has the material means to develop a distinct profile. Simply put, they have more and want more, now. Undoubtedly, there is an element of truth in these objections, but the process being discussed can be observed in numerous areas of our culture. A reduction to the observations of psychotherapists alone seems to be an oversimplification.

The narcissistic personality does not worry about the past, takes the present for what it is, and lives in the future. He or she does everything to make the future reality. As soon as this has been accomplished to a certain degree, the next challenge is necessary in order to ward off feelings of emptiness and gloom. Problems relating to concentration and discipline at school often indicate that students live neither in the future nor in the past, but only in the here and now. They do everything to avoid experiencing the here and now as dull or boring. Cognitive and affective processes between impulse and action are not allowed. The perspective of the future remains limited to "just living and being able to buy" and "getting rich" (Ree, 1992). Psychological health has to do with the capacity to allow past, present and future on the stage together. This also applies to the other functions of reality and fantasy. Cushman (1990) observes in this context that the so-called "empty self" emerged after World War II. This self lacks community, tradition and purpose shared with others. Consumption offers compensation for this emptiness. "I shop, therefore I am" reads a recent slogan (Kroes, 1992).

The ancient superego has little function with a view to achieving economic growth. Moral and ethical considerations and traditions mean a break in productivity. The space which this takes up is amply taken over by ego and ideal. With this, a part of the psychological basis of traditions, cultural values, religion, rituals, etc. falls away. It does not mean that cultural values disappear − people cannot exist without them − but they lose their emphasis. Solidarity between people who share the same values has made room for individual interests and competitiveness. Traditions that transcend material relationships crumble under fire from rational challenge. Doctrines from different religions have become very easy prey for criticism and rejection. With this, religiousness as a feeling is also trivialized. Old traditions have been inadequately replaced by new ones. The end of liberalism has already been announced by philosophers.

On the level of the ego, we encounter the counterpart expressed by Christopher Lasch (1979) in his book *The Culture of Narcissism*. The ego (or better formulated, a part of it, the self) has become more central to the human psyche than has previously been the case. The shift we can observe in the human personality varies coincidentally with the one in the social structure: the self, self-worth, self-preservation, egocentrism and individual performance are central.

Basically, this shift in mental machinery leads to a reactivation of our childish characteristics, as we have also seen above. In the United States, we can observe the behaviour of the child in the latency period (from 5 to 12 years of age) fully in adults. People begin short, superficial relationships (out of sight, out of mind), react impulsively, are always cheerful and emotionally superficial. People are all called by their first name. The Californian masses in trainers and running shorts would seem more at home in a large sandpit. They eat the same food a child in latency favours: McDonald's and Kentucky Fried Chicken. "Have fun" shout the men and women of middle age to each other, and they are perfectly capable of enjoying themselves in Disneyland. American restaurants and amusement parks are now increasingly overrunning the

European continent. Just as in the United States, borders in Europe will fade away and the continent will perhaps become one big nation, with its citizens increasingly addressing one another in English.

Critics have labelled the national culture that has been created in America a mass culture, eminently superficial (Kroes, 1992). Huizinga called it a "culture turned outwards". "In its conformity, in its slavish orientation to peer groups, in its constantly chasing after new stimuli and satisfaction, it offers an image of a ship without rudder or anchor" (Kroes, 1992, p. 37). Instead of a compass, people need radar with which to receive constantly changing signals from their surroundings.

Some time ago, we were able to follow the public hearing in the United States concerning the alleged sexual indiscretions of Judge Clarence Thomas, candidate for the prestigious Supreme Court, toward his subordinate at the time, Anita Hill, herself now a professor of law. From the standpoint of conscience, a gigantic superego seems to be monitoring what certain people say to members of the opposite sex. We do not know of a comparable tribunal in Victorian times.

In many respects, including economic ones, the United States is our future. What could this mean for Europe? Does this indicate the strictness of individual superegos or the very lack of an integrated superego at the individual level? As compensation for this deficiency on the juridical—political level, strict rules and laws are evoked collectively. Curiously enough, these types of debate in the United States always concern somebody else's conscience instead of one's own. It appears that we are dealing with a collective victim culture: all fully grown children who are innocent, gullible and victims of a brutal aggressor. The damage they have suffered must be paid for in hard cash.

Are these cultural elements not also sneaking into European societies? The diminished pressure of the superego stimulates childlike character-istics in adults. These infantile adults behave towards political—juridical authorities as a child in latency towards his or her parents. These parents are responsible for and have to take care of the child, but, misrepresented by their own fantasy processes, are criticized for being too strict. Our culture currently lacks adult narratives for its members. An elementary school that used to be named after a saint has been rebaptized into a primary school named Mickey Mouse. The saint used to be an example for former youth to imitate, but the same cannot be said of Mickey Mouse. In the above-mentioned childlike characteristics, we can recognize the impulsiveness, affective lability and histrionics of various Cluster B disorders.

These developments are partially supported and stimulated by the methodology of different modern psychotherapeutic systems. Many of these therapeutic strategies are, after all, intended to enlarge the person's possibilities of affective expression. This often means that the inhibitions to that expression are lessened. These inhibitions are frequently localized in the superego. The internalization of parental values and norms is experienced as overly restrictive. Under the influence of psychotherapy, one is increasingly liberated from this and so also from the traditions, values and norms that were expressed here. An individualized version of these values and norms must take their place.

In many cases, there are also fewer behavioural guidelines, and shifts of emphasis towards more affective and instinctive expression. The reinforcement of the ego often means more openness of this ego with regard to the affective and instinctive sides of the person and less pressure from the conscience and the ideal. The more extreme variables, presented in the 1960s and 1970s as humanistic psychology and psychotherapy, no longer include affective inhibition. In this case, one strives for an intrapsychic openness that contains a pathological absence of borders and inhibitions. Each affect must immediately have space so as not to be actually experienced. At the same time, one aspect of psychological functioning is centrally stressed at the cost of other psychic contents.

In the age in which we live, we are regularly confronted with the excesses of this behaviour in the form of petty crimes, soccer vandalism, gambling addiction and substance abuse. This concerns individuals who have fallen by the wayside in the same race. They have little to offer or are too blocked by external circumstances to keep afloat in the psychological orientation of the mainstream.

The tendency towards individualization refers to the aspect of destructiveness in instinctual life. Aggression stimulates an independent self. The development towards individualization facilitates the expression of aggression, partially owing to the diminished pressure of conscience. Clinically speaking, control of human aggression is the biggest problem of our time in this respect.

Many people are members of a large variety of associations, foundations and sports clubs, particularly in a country such as the Netherlands. There is perhaps no country in the world with so many clubs in which people socialize and feel mutual bonds in proportion to the number of inhabitants. This can be seen as an effort to fill in a gap on the ideological level. People belong to something, even if it does not sufficiently stimulate behavioural rules on a broader scale. Furthermore, we can observe a kind of "new reality" in the younger generations. One gets the impression that they are trying to give form to their life with very exaggerated rules of behaviour which are grafted onto reality. The economic recession and unemployment appear to have stimulated this development. The fact remains, however, that generations of young people grow up in a television, video and computer culture in which they are alone with a machine, experience superficial satisfaction and in which their personality is not offered any stimulus for growth.

This subject will be further illustrated in this chapter on the basis of common disorders relating to intimate relationships. Of course, these are also found among people without a personality disorder, but are particularly striking among borderline, antisocial and narcissistic people. The problem of the mourning process and psychosomatic and/ or somatoform disorders are included for the same purpose. The subject of mourning has been chosen because it particularly illustrates how the falling away of cultural help renders the mourning process a psychological problem. Clinicians classify the increase in personality disorders under the broader group of so-called "early disorders" (Derksen, 1990c). For the past 20 years, it has been asserted in clinical circles that their incidence has increased in comparison with symptom neuroses (Reiche, 1991). Psychosomatic and somatoform disorders also fall into this group.

RELATIONSHIP DISORDERS

When two people choose each other as partners, the role that tradition, family background, circumstances, etc. play has been reduced in comparison to at least half a century ago. Conscience, the carrier of tradition and attitudes in the person, usually plays an insignificant part. Sexual desires, components of basic instincts, are often given free rein with little inhibition in the initial phase of many relationships. This is greatly accepted by the conscience and ego ideal. Narcissistic motives play a significant role in the choice of a partner. Unconsciously, one chooses oneself in the other as one would like to be and/or as one hopes one already is. The ideal is brought even closer to the self and the necessary tension between both parties is further diminished.

After the first phase in the relationship, when these instinctual sides have subsided a little, the ego and the self become protagonists in the development of the relationship. Consequently, what keeps partners together is found especially in the area of psychology and particularly in the psychology of the self. How does the other person suit me? What kind of feelings does the other person evoke in me? Can I talk with that other person in such a manner that I feel good about myself? Does the other person understand me completely? Does the other person give me self-confidence, and does the other person support my insecurity? Egocentric themes are increasingly involved; the most prominent feature is not so much the other as another person and for that reason attractive, but the other in his or her function with respect to the self. If the other person does not fulfil these functions, the conscience offers little protest about switching over to a new relationship. Relationships have become almost as vulnerable as superficial moods.

Unconsciously, the relationship starts to play an important role in the maintenance of self-esteem, and accordingly functions as a defence against feelings of gloominess and inferiority. The person cannot tolerate a confrontation between his or her ideal image of self and the real self. In the absence of sufficient narcissistic support, the second current of instinct lies in wait — destructiveness that takes on the form of aggression. In many relationships, couples literally fight to the death. It is a well-known fact that most violence takes place in the home.

Conscience has lost some influence, as we have seen, and that is also expressed in the relative ease with which a marriage is dissolved and a new partner chosen who is more attractive for the moment. The ego encounters less opposition when it chooses the side of the basic drive. Many men choose a younger wife who not only refreshes their sexual life, but is also willing to give their self-esteem a face-lift which the former partner could no longer honestly do in view of their actual experiences. Only in that manner can intrapsychic issues remain concealed.

Exactly in line with a narcissistic disorder, the surroundings are adjusted to the self instead of the other way round. The narcissistic elements that dominate a choice of partner and intimate relationships result in emotional superficiality. The other facets of the psyche contribute little, so depth is lost. Superficiality in partner relationships has consequences for the children born from these unions. The emotional availability of the mother and father is less than it previously was. Their own narcissistic desires are incompatible with being emotionally available for the child. Lack of emotional availability weakens the development of an autonomous ego in the child.

The child's self is furthermore put under pressure at a young age by other aspects of current child rearing. Elementary school children often have many different kinds of activities in their schedule. All as a matter of course, they take physical education classes, join the hockey club, take swimming lessons, play soccer, learn to ride, take music lessons, have piano lessons at home and have Sunday morning singing lessons from a family friend. Everything must be possible. The neighbours' children do it too, and their parents are so very proud of their offsprings' achievements. It is no longer a question of enjoying these activities: the parent's self is built up and expanded through the achievements of the child. Parents give in to all the child's wishes, because they hope to experience satisfaction from that themselves. In fact the child, for whom too few limits are set, becomes overburdened. Because the ego weakens, the self merges more easily with the ego ideal and this process results in a narcissistic disorder. Due to the diminished influence of authority, supervision and hierarchy in the educational process, the generational differences become smaller for children. This teaches them to approach unknown adults as if they were peers of the same age.

The child keeps him- or herself occupied with television, video and computer games, allowing the parents to give priority to their own affairs. The world of the adult that is introduced to the child through these media is populated by superhumans who can withstand extreme conditions. Reality, in which it has become increasingly clear to the public at large that victims and witnesses of violence and disasters develop psychological problems and are in need of help, is presented to young people as a second-rate contest that they can no longer appreciate. Here an ego ideal is stimulated, the nature of which is predominantly imaginary, infeasible and therefore added to the self as the content of fantasy. An overdose of this type of entertainment stimulates a regression in the growing child towards early childhood, symbiotic and thus pre-oedipal themes, where omnipotence plays a big role. With that, the current generation runs the risk of enlarging their infantile personality traits to an even greater extent than is already the case. The Nintendo club in the Netherlands already has more than 300 000 young members around the age of ten. Books and sports are declining in popularity among Dutch youth. It is difficult to say whether technology in the form of microelectronics is connected to an already present tendency or arouses it to a great extent and stimulates it. The result is the same either way.

These and probably many other ingredients complete the circle and reproduce, among other things, a certain type of narcissistic problem.

GRIEF

The lack of tradition and rituals can be seen in no uncertain terms in the subject of grief. At the passing away of a loved one, there used to be cultural assistance to support mourners in working through their loss. Announcers went around and the necessary measures were taken. Clothing and jewellery were adapted to the circumstances, mourners were given special consideration and had the opportunity to withdraw for some time from society before re-entering it.

Former rituals have been lost and nothing has taken their place. The mourning process has become a very personal affair, and collective grief is shunned. How often do we read in the obituaries that "the cremation took place privately". One of the current consequences of this is that people in mourning become patients suffering from a stagnated mourning process and come daily for help from psychologists and psychiatrists. In the privacy of the consulting room, they have to work out feelings that have lost their place in the natural social setting. The bond between people that can be the consequence of collectively working through sorrow and pain is no longer present. This deprives many people of the opportunity to work out old sorrows of their own at the loss of another person. This purifying function has been lost.

Psychological, educational and psychiatric practices seem partly to fill the gap left by the disappearance of rituals. The ego has to finish the job alone or in a very small circle. People no longer know what the grieving process looks like. The inward orientation and the intrapsychic aspects of this are neglected. To allow sorrow and pain is at odds with the type of behaviour, inspired by economic interests, that has been allowed to flourish as a result of the breakdown of traditions, rituals, etc.

PHYSICAL SUFFERING

Instead of feeling sorrow or pain, we notice in clinical practice that people develop physical complaints, physical pain instead of psychological pain. Half the complaints that surface in the offices of general practitioners in the Netherlands are not of a physical but rather of a psychological nature. The body is used as a medium of expression, but not consciously: headaches, neck and shoulder complaints, pain in the chest and in the left arm, stomach and intestinal complaints, aching muscles, heart palpitations, high blood pressure, fear of contracting a serious physical illness, etc.

Particularly in middle-aged people, we often see an increase in physical complaints without a sufficient physiological explanation. The pressure they are under proves too much. Too much was expected of their mental resilience. Time and again this new personality, strongly emphasizing the ego, has to make new and creative adjustments to drastically changing circumstances, both in working conditions and in human relationships. This feat becomes more difficult with the passing of the years. At the same time, people are psychologically put together in such a way that every step backwards, every decrease in capacity and resilience, is experienced negatively, leading to feelings of inferiority and depression. As a consequence, this decline is fervently denied. The empty self has nothing to offer from within that compares with the challenges from outside. Physical suffering offers an escape from oppressive psychological power games.

CHAPTER 5.4   Implications for the personality

As a consequence of the developments discussed previously in this part, the personality is overburdened. More is asked of the ego's psychological flexibility than in earlier societies. Young children often have to make choices regarding their school and schedule that have far-reaching implications for their future education. Today, people have to assume many different roles in work settings. Owing to the incessantly changing social context and technological innovations, refresher courses are constantly necessary, and time and again a balance must be found between knowledge, performance and relaxation. Those who aspire to a career, particularly in business, must change jobs regularly. Disturbances in the development of a person and his or her identity are more easily exposed because of this. If people want to stay up to date with the constantly changing social context, they will be candidates for psychological help more often during these transitions. The demand for help here primarily concerns help for people with personality problems.

INCREASE IN BORDERLINE AND NARCISSISTIC DISORDERS?

From clinicians, especially psychoanalysts, but also from people like Theodore Millon, we often hear that borderline and narcissistic disorders are on the increase. Researchers observe an increase in the number of diagnoses of borderline disorders, but see at the same time a decrease in diagnoses of such problems as sociopathy and hysteria. It is likely that the clinical picture we now call borderline or narcissistic used to be classified under a different name. Both points of view seem justifiable. In any case, the study of personality disorders has greatly increased, which correlates with the interest in clinical practice. This merging of research and practice is often the exception rather than the rule. Something is the matter here.

Most clinical psychologists can agree that important factors for a disturbed personality of the borderline, narcissistic or antisocial type are traceable back to childhood. Biological – genetic baggage is equally relevant. In these early experiences, the first disturbances in psychological development appear that are consequently intensified or weakened, compensated or not compensated by the developments that follow, all of which has been outlined more extensively above.

In his comments regarding the genesis and prevalence of borderline disorder, Millon (1987a) distinguishes more or less the same etiological factors as were described in Chapter 5.1: constitutional disposition, problematic early care and current social changes. Of these three factors, only one has been subject to change during the last decade. To explain the increased incidence of borderline personality disorder, Millon concentrates largely on the fundamental and rapid changes in Western culture that have led to what he calls unharmonious and splitting life experiences. At the same time, the availability of bonding and healing social customs and institutions has decreased in a psychological sense. The current changes that Millon briefly touches on and rather directly connects with personality disorders are the following:

- The amorphous state of today's culture is reflected in the interpersonal fluctuations and affective instability we see in borderline patients. A society with fixed customs and institutions produces a psychological make-up with one and the same structure. Now, traditional values are exposed to erosion at a rapid tempo. Children are faced with constantly changing behavioural styles and norms that constantly come under pressure.

- Family patterns have changed drastically since World War II. For instance, children no longer have a clear idea of the work that their father does. Mothers shift attention more and more to activities outside the family. Traditional sex roles have become vague. Children can no longer take advantage of direct observation of adult activities. Owing to divorce, the family regroups itself. In the future, children will no longer be able to rely on the observations and convictions that were internalized in the past. Kicks in the here and now are more interesting than the uncertain future.

- At the age of 18, a child in the United States has put in more time watching television than going to school or having contact with his or her parents. Children with vague values and norms are particularly sensitive to the highly romanticized and idealized models which are served up to them on television.

- Use of drugs and alcohol affects the already weak internal psychological structures even further.

When there is a lack of corrective effects, disturbing experiences that took place early in life become firmly rooted. As an example of such a waning effect, Millon mentions religion and church. Furthermore, the extended family has for the most part disappeared. There are fewer children and the family is isolated more than before in a continuously changing environment. In instances of abuse or neglect, in the past the child could more easily find a parent substitute such as a grandmother, older brother, sister, uncle, aunt or neighbour. Dependency on parents in childhood has become greater. Healing of damage sustained in the parent–child relationship is much more restricted than previously. Millon further comments that in an economic respect, children used to be a kind of provision for old age. Fortunately, this is now no longer necessary. Being needed, however, also gave direction and purpose to the life of children. Economically speaking, children are now often a burden.

LACK OF IDENTITY

To date, our Western culture has not been able to produce one or more collective ideologies to accompany economic growth and individualization; that is, a comprehensive world view with an explanatory system that is acceptable to these times, in which people can feel rooted and from which they can derive their identity. In this context, the revival of nationalism observable in and outside Europe in recent years fits this picture. Von der Dunk connects the consideration of individual, often regional traditions that are beginning to surface to the increased internationalization of politics, Europeanization and levelling of lifestyles and the large-scale manner of operating in the economic and technological fields: "These developments generate opposing forces" (1992, p. 11).

The traditional values and norms of liberalism, confessionalism and socialism have disappeared like a thief in the night. The vacuum left behind has never been filled. The social customs and institutions mentioned by Millon, which bring about coherence and reparation of what was damaged in early childhood, have not yet returned in another form. One of the consequences is that individuality seems to be reduced to egoism (Spence, 1985) and identity to narcissism. In that vacuum, we see a jumble of behavioural problems emerging, which care providers and researchers recognize as personality disorders.

The same process can also be observed in Germany. The road from a fatherless to a motherless society has already been travelled (König, 1988). Consumption-directed character has replaced authority-bound character. By motherless is meant the idea that the mother role has been taken over by a technological mother: television, video, walkman, Nintendo. The Frankfurter Schule tradition has for many years cleared the way for this type of view.

We have established identity problems on a sociocultural as well as an individual level. Developments in the direction of a narcissistic interpersonal style reduce interest in one's past and focus attention on the future: what is yet to come, or what one still has or wants to accomplish. The openness, democracy and ideology of equal opportunities support this. The identity as an area of content in the ego is, however, rooted especially in the personal and social past. The possibilities and limitations of the person become visible from his or her past. The narcissistic person would like to think of him- or herself as free from this. On a national level, an attempt is made to recover identity through nationalism, regionalism and the revival of traditions. So far, no parallel process can be indicated for the individual. The main task of social institutions and social structures, specifically on the ideological plane and considered from the viewpoint of the individual, is to develop, stimulate and anchor the superego. Ideals and norms hold society together and also build a foundation of personal identity; they hold the individual together. In individual development, the ego ideal and the conscience need reinforcement from the culture. If this reinforcement is not forthcoming, we run the chance of one of the following reactions:

- childlike traits;
- antisocial traits;
- egocentric traits;
- aggressive and sexual acting out.

These personality traits can best be characterized as Cluster B traits on Axis II of the DSM-IV. The psychological balance in DSM Clusters B and C is disturbed. In Cluster C personality disorders, the activity of the superego contributes to fear, shame and avoidance. This concerns a contribution of the superego that is much too rigid or conflictual. In Cluster B, we observe diminished pressure from the conscience, and a disturbance of idealization. The distance between the self and the ideal has become much too small.

These personality traits (childish, antisocial, egocentric or narcissistic) form the baggage in the personal care and educational styles of new generations. Under this trend, the emphasis on education, traditional child rearing and culture is disappearing. Taking its place is an individualistic, impulsive style of education that is not inspired by a particular line of thought but rather by a personal, an individualized and accordingly mainly egocentric orientation. The distance between child and parent is growing smaller; parental tolerance for the behaviour and impulsiveness of the child is lessening; and the chances of parental outbursts of irritation, aggression and sexual impulsiveness are increasing. Too few affective and cognitive buffers are built up between impulse and action.

One more speculative illustration may be worthwhile. Seen from the standpoint of the psychoanalytic tradition, the development of "basic trust" is an important task in the first period of childhood. This basic trust develops because the child can rely on adequate feeding and care, and the child gets the notion that he or she has wound up somewhere where it is possible to thrive. In a climate where impulsiveness, unpredictability, egocentrism and antisocial characteristics make an indelible contribution, we can imagine that basic trust develops in a less stable manner. If we transpose this to the level of society, it can be noticed immediately that safety, and also a lack of safety, has become one of the greatest concerns of contemporary Western humanity. People feel unsafe and ill at ease. People fear robbery, violence, rape and, on a larger scale, war, natural disasters and destruction of the environment.

Individualization, in individual psychological development, appeals especially to aggressive affect sources. This is in contrast to the forming of close bonds (symbiosis and collectivism), where an appeal is made particularly to love (libido). Relationship patterns seem to be increasingly characterized by more superficial narcissistic patterns, in keeping with individualism. In this regard, one may suppose that aggression is the primary psychological style. Given its extrovert and impulsive characteristics, this could mean that human aggression will further increase in the future development of psychological styles. Reassuringly, people often speak of counterreactions that surface in culture "on their own". I have not, however, been able to observe structural counterreactions in the Western world as yet.

It goes without saying that the above hypotheses are still in need of empirical support. In this respect, it has been more the intention to produce ideas than to validate them.

PART 6

Personality Disorders in the Future

CHAPTER 6.1   Towards the DSM-V and ICD-11

INTRODUCTION

Nowadays, many psychotherapists in the United States and in a number of Western European countries are given the DSM diagnosis to read along with the psychodiagnostic assessment report when a patient is referred for psychotherapy. As a rule, this does not impress therapists very much. More often than not, the indication for treatment is more closely related to (deeper) personality traits than to symptoms. Naturally, there are exceptions in the field of psychotic symptomatology. If one of the psychotic disorders applies, it usually limits (psychotherapeutic) treatment. In view of medical treatment, the classification does indicate the direction (for instance, neuroleptics), although not much more. In many other cases, a DSM Axis I diagnosis, or rather classification, does not mean much more than a ticket for a theatre performance. The owners of these tickets can differ greatly, in spite of a similar interest at that moment in a cultural event. Apart from a descriptive contribution, the DSM and ICD could have more significance for a clinician if a number of changes were introduced.

In the future, the DSM and the ICD will probably come to resemble each other more closely. The DSM multi-axial system generally seems to be an improvement. How would Axis II look in DSM-V? We assume that the descriptive approach, the limitation of a theoretical basis and empirical testing possibilities are maintained. Below, the perspective of psychotherapeutic, medical and psychological treatment is largely adopted. With that, a bold and very temporary attempt is made to re-evaluate the classification system for therapists. This is done not only in terms of tradition in the Anglo-Saxon countries, but the way in which this system could receive more acceptance and appreciation in countries such as Germany, France, Spain, Italy, Belgium and the Netherlands is also taken into consideration. These are proposals that require further research. They originate from the conviction that this classification system currently provides a useful contribution to research and clinical practice, but that even more is possible for practice in particular.

Axis I remains the axis of symptom and syndrome descriptions on the behavioural level, having a descriptive nature and a minimum of theoretical references.

With respect to Axis II, the first change is the result of an attempt to operate consistently. The term personality disorder must be deleted from this classification system, not because personality disorders do not exist, but rather on account of the theoretical basis which this term requires. Axis II becomes the axis of disorders in intrapersonal relationships. This axis could be called *interaction disorders*.

As has also been asserted in Part 1 of this book, the majority of the criteria refer to relational rather than intrapersonal aspects. The conceptualization of interaction disorders is less abstract and requires less theory. Interaction between people can be better established descriptively than can someone's personality. After all, personality, whether we like it or not, always involves layers, and we cannot avoid a depth dimension. Furthermore, a personality disorder usually comes to the clinician's attention only when problems have emerged in interactions with the social environment.

Moreover, interaction disorders could be registered on the basis of criteria, which would form steps on a dimension of severity: the more criteria applicable, the more serious the situation of the person in question. Thus, this axis becomes dimensional instead of categorial. The number of criteria is indicated with a figure. In this respect, more justice can be done to interaction disorders that lead to relationship, marriage and family difficulties. In clinical practice, therapists are flooded by requests from people with disturbed relationships, marriage crises and attachment problems. These disorders are related to personality disorders and can often be lumped together. With the disturbance of interactions, these relationship disorders receive more direct interpretation. This means that more room becomes available for classification of these types of disorder. Furthermore, this means that they could disappear from the V codes, a difficult remainder anyway, so that the number of V codes could be restricted. This would be an advantage.

As with the previously described personality disorders, interaction disorders must be stable and observed over a longer period of time. This concerns stable interaction patterns of the person at issue. It is not the personality that is diagnosed, but rather interactions that remain constant and observable in various situations. All this seems to fit the overall idea of the DSM better. No restrictions need be made with respect to age. Such disturbances can be determined in children of five years and older, for instance.

FIVE INTERACTION DISTURBANCES

In view of the large overlap between personality disorders, their number could be reduced. Cluster A might then appear as follows.

An Interaction Disorder as a Result of Psychotic Traits

This disorder has paranoid, schizoid and schizotypal traits. The criteria of the old disorders, in which interpersonal behaviour plays a large role and which originate from the DSM-IV, can be copied.

From the paranoid:

1. Suspects, without sufficient basis, that others are exploiting or deceiving him or her.
3. Is reluctant to confide in others due to unwarranted fear that the information will be used maliciously against him or her.
4. Reads demeaning or threatening meanings into benign remarks or events.
6. Perceives attacks on his or her character or reputation that are not apparent to others and is quick to react angrily or to counterattack.
7. Has recurrent unfounded suspicions regarding the fidelity of spouse or sexual partner.

From the schizoid:

1. Neither desires nor enjoys close relationships, including being part of a family.
5. Lacks close friends and confidants other than first degree relatives.
6. Appears indifferent to praise or criticism from others.

From the schizotypal:

8. Lacks close friends and confidants other than first-degree relatives.

9. Suffers from excessive social anxiety that does not diminish with familiarity and that tends to be associated with paranoid fears rather than with negative judgements about the self.

The remaining criteria are either no longer applicable, or are classified on Axis I within the schizophrenic disorders or the delusion disorder. Reformulation in a more relational respect and a merging of the criteria could lead to a limited set. The ICD criteria for the paranoid and the schizoid person could be involved in this enterprise. Empirical research must be the decisive factor in this instance. The remaining criteria form a dimension: the more they are applicable, the greater the disturbance of interpersonal relationships.

Cluster B becomes as follows.

An Interaction Disorder due to Antisocial Behaviour

All except criterion 4 can be used. Extension to the classic psychopath concept is obvious. ICD-10 criteria can be reviewed and empirical support must be the deciding factor.

An Interaction Disorder due to Narcissistic Behaviour

For this disorder, criteria are gathered that relate to the interpersonal behaviour of the borderline, narcissistic and histrionic personality disorders, which could be the following:

From the borderline:

1. Frantic efforts to avoid real or imagined abandonment.
2. A pattern of unstable and intense interpersonal relationships characterized by alternating between extremes of idealization and devaluation.
4. Impulsiveness in at least two areas that are potentially damaging to the person's self (e.g. squandering money, sex, substance abuse, reckless driving, binge eating).
8. Inappropriate, intense anger or lack of control of anger (e.g. frequent displays of temper, constant anger, recurrent fighting).

From the histrionic:

2. Interacts with others in ways that are often characterized by inappropriate sexually seductive or provocative behaviour.

4. Consistently uses physical appearance to draw attention to him/herself.
7. Is suggestible, i.e. easily influenced by others or circumstances.
8. Considers relationships to be more intimate than they actually are.

From the narcissistic:

1. Has a grandiose sense of self-importance (e.g. exaggerates achievements and talents, expects to be recognized as superior without commensurate achievements).
3. Believes that he or she is "special" and unique and can only be understood by, or should associate with, other special or high-status people (or institutions).
4. Requires excessive admiration.
5. Believes that he or she is entitled to certain things, i.e. unreasonable expectations of especially favourable treatment or automatic compliance with his or her expectations.
6. Is interpersonally exploitative, i.e. takes advantage of others to achieve his or her own ends.
7. Displays lack of empathy: is unwilling to recognize or identify with the feelings and needs of others.
8. Is often envious of others or believes that others are envious of him or her.
9. Has arrogant, haughty behaviours or attitudes.

Here, we can also arrive at a selection. Common characteristics are interaction disturbances because the other is constantly involved in order to maintain the feeling of self-worth.

The following remain in Cluster C.

An Interaction Disorder due to Anxiety Traits

The criteria of the avoidant and dependent personality disorders are integrated for this disorder. The following criteria are incorporated from the avoidant personality disorder:

1. Avoids occupational activities that involve significant interpersonal contact, because of fears of criticism, disapproval, or rejection.
2. Is unwilling to get involved with people unless certain of being liked.
3. Is restrained in intimate relationships due to fear of being shamed or ridiculed.

5. Is inhibited in new interpersonal situations due to feelings of inadequacy.
6. Is unusually reluctant to take personal risks or to engage in any new activities because they may prove embarrassing.

From the dependent personality disorder:

1. Is unable to make everyday decisions without an excessive amount of advice and reassurance from others.
2. Needs others to assume responsibility for most major areas in his or her life.
5. Goes to excessive lengths to obtain nurturing and support from others, to the point of volunteering to do things that are unpleasant.
7. Urgently seeks another relationship as a source of care and support when a close relationship ends.

Again, the best criteria relating to interaction from DSM and ICD can be selected and chosen for the dimension on empirical grounds.

An Interaction Disorder due to Rigid Traits

Some criteria can be selected from the DSM-IV obsessive-compulsive personality disorder and some from the DSM-III-R passive-aggressive personality disorder.

For example, from the obsessive-compulsive disorder:

1. Preoccupation with details, rules, lists, order, organization, or schedules to the extent that the major point of the activity is lost.
3. Excessive devotion to work and productivity to the exclusion of leisure activities and friendships (not accounted for by an obvious economic necessity).
6. Reluctance to delegate tasks or to work with others unless the others submit exactly to his or her way of doing things.
7. Adopts a miserly spending style with regard to both self and others; money is viewed as something to be hoarded for future catastrophes.
8. Rigidity and stubbornness.

The following from the passive-aggressive disorder:

2. Becomes sulky, irritable, or argumentative when asked to do something he or she does not want to do.

4. Protests, without justification, that others make unreasonable demands on him or her.
5. Avoids obligations by claiming to have "forgotten".
8. Obstructs the efforts of others by failing to do his or her share of the work.
9. Unreasonably criticizes or scorns people in position of authority.

Here too, further elaboration and integration on empirical grounds are necessary. Depending on the outcomes of empirical research, the depressive personality disorder, which has now been temporarily admitted, could receive a place in the future under the title of *interaction disorder due to depressive traits*.

A more theoretical elaboration is offered by the interpersonal approach. It has some disadvantages, however, one of which is the limited dimensions that are given prominence in interpersonal behaviour. In interpersonal taxonomy, the basic assumption is that those who interact are constantly negotiating two issues, i.e. affiliation (love−hate, friendliness−hostility), and control (dominance−submission, higher status−lower status). Furthermore, the entire model is rather complex without generating much more insight. A better formulation could be the dimensions distinguished by Millon: pleasure−pain; self−other; active−passive.

BIOLOGICAL AND PSYCHOLOGICAL DATA

Axis II becomes twofold: *biological and psychological data*. In the first place, physical disorders and conditions are recorded, as is common practice. The results of a physical examination and laboratory tests are stated here. Under these conditions, research results and acceptable hypotheses are incorporated in the area that used to be called the temperament. An example is perhaps Cloninger's three-dimensional model: "novelty seeking", "harm avoidance" and "reward dependence". In the second place, relevant psychological data are recorded, e.g. personality traits which are usually dimensionally constructed, where, incidentally, some biological basis is present.

In the future this could also apply to one or several dimensions of the so-called Big Five: neuroticism, extroversion, openness to experience, agreeableness and conscientiousness. In addition to these general psychological findings, which have relevance for clinical practice, results of psychological research that may have been conducted are stated. These can be divided into: cognitive assessment (intelligence and neuropsychological data); symptom assessment (results of various questionnaires); personality assessment (results of questionnaires as well as projective material).

A THEORETICAL AXIS

Axis IV could become the axis of *structural—dynamic conditions*. This has already been under discussion in a previous phase (Millon & Klerman, 1986). This axis is more theoretical and less empirical in character, less descriptive and more structural. A number of mechanisms in this axis are recorded that have been developed in a psychoanalytic and psychodynamic tradition and contribute to the whole of clinical practice. This particularly concerns the dynamic conditions that have received a broader acceptance by clinicians from various theoretical orientations. The relevance for clinical practice in the form of more clinical insight is shared by broad groups and suits the current school-transcending orientation.

The strongest areas of these mechanisms are the theoretical declarations of phenomena observable in treatment practice and the clinical insights that accompany them. In empirical respects, the basis is absent or very weak. Opponents of admitting these mechanisms may refer to this lack of empirical basis. With the same argument, they could also combat the current Axis II, and the lack of empirical support is absolutely true for the old Axis IV and Axis V as well. Another argument is that the empirical testability of these types of contribution is much more limited than that of Axis I and Axis II. This is because the descriptive level is usually not emphasized. At the same time, these mechanisms do form part of the baggage of a great many practicians throughout the world, and there is a gap if this is not accounted for in an internationally used classification system. Clinicians who do not feel competent in this respect can skip the notations on this axis. A possible gain is that the DSM is regarded more seriously and completely in the clinical world. Treatment is supposed to follow classification, but a DSM label is not much more than the previously mentioned ticket for a theatre performance, and does not say anything about the "inside" of the personality that is so important for treatment. How can Axis IV be filled in?

The following mechanisms can be recorded under the heading of *ego functions*:

1. *Defence mechanisms.* One or more of the following frequently occurring defence mechanisms can be recorded: repression, denial, projection, isolation, reaction formation, rationalization, sublimation, identifying with the aggressor, splitting, primitive denial, idealization, devaluation, omnipotent control, projective identification. Each mechanism is described as precisely as possible in an explanation in the DSM.

2. *Identity formation.* It is determined whether the identity is integrated, diffuse or fragmented. This is examined in relation to self-representation, as well as to object representation.

3. *Relationship to reality.* The quality of reality testing (intact or not intact) is examined and thus the capacity to distinguish self adequately from other, inner world from outer world. The relationship to reality (particularly the cognitive aspects) and the feeling for reality (de-realization and de-personalization) are charted as well.

4. *Introspection and suffering.* The extent to which the ego is capable of individual reflection is of essential importance to a psychotherapeutic treatment. Motivation for psychotherapeutic treatment is also determined by the pressure of suffering which is subjectively felt. The diagnostician tries to form an image of this for him- or herself. Both qualities can be recorded on a five-point scale in terms of the extent to which they are present.

5. *Disorders in the regulation of aggression and sexuality.* Both drive-like feelings are scored on a dimension with five points:

   Impulsive breakthroughs ——————————— Complete inhibition

6. *Superego.* The superego is classified in view of structure and intensity. How developed versus how lacunal is the function of the conscience and the ego ideal? How strict versus how flexible are both aspects of this superego?

On Axis V, the seriousness of the psychosocial stressors, which was previously recorded on Axis IV, is preserved. The previous Axis V, the general assessment of functioning, is no longer present. This information relates to adaptation. This will become clear, however, after the interaction problems of Axis II have been listed.

In summary:

• *Axis I*: Clinical disorders and other conditions that may be a focus of clinical attentions.

- *Axis II*: Mental retardation and interaction disorders.
- *Axis III*: General medical conditions, biological and psychological conditions.
- *Axis IV*: Structural—dynamic conditions.
- *Axis V*: Psychological and environmental problems.

A DSM diagnosis in the above-mentioned sense more closely resembles a diagnosis than a classification. The correlation between this diagnosis and treatment becomes more significant.

CHAPTER 6.2   Empirical research and development of theories

Most empirical research of the DSM and ICD personality disorders still has to take place. The categories have never been the result of empirical research, but rather the starting signal. Doing experimental, perhaps double-blind-controlled, empirical research with a group of patients, of whom it is assumed that influencing their disorder is difficult to initiate and can take a long time, is neither an easy nor an attractive task. A control group, necessary to be able to ascribe the changes possibly occurring in the clinical picture to the interventions in the experimental group, cannot be used for that long, owing to practical and ethical considerations. It is easier to influence a symptom disorder with certain treatment techniques and to compare it with a control group where this influence is missing. In Armand Loranger's words, "the evaluation of many Axis II criteria requires more clinical sophistication and judgment than most Axis I criteria" (1992, p. 323).

LONG-TERM EFFECT

Research on the process and the long-term effect on groups of patients with a personality disorder leaves a great deal to be desired (Stone, 1993; Perry, 1993). This type of research has so far been conducted largely with borderline patients, and to a lesser degree with antisocial, schizotypal and narcissistic patients. As a rule, these are studies with patients who had been or were being admitted to hospital. These studies are usually uncontrolled, the diagnoses obtained are often not very reliable, and the patients have been treated with various intensities and in very different ways. The conclusions obtained are equivocal; treatment appears to be effective, but after several years these patients still have many symptoms and function poorly socially. These naturalistic studies offer insight into the course of a personality disorder, but other empirical, scientifically responsible statements cannot be based on them. In any case, the out-patient population with milder personality disorders is missing in the long-term follow-up studies.

CONTROLLED STUDIES

Shea (1993) discusses nine controlled studies that took place within a relatively short period. The majority concern behaviour therapy treatments, in some cases psychodynamic methods and methods providing insight. Six studies are about the avoidant personality disorder, two are mixed groups, and one concerns borderline patients. In three studies, avoidant personalities were treated with gradual exposure, social skills training and systematic desensitization. Compared to a control group, they reported improvements, especially in the area of social contacts.

Other studies indicated limited improvements, for instance progress in the area of social skills, but this was superficial and the feeling of inner loneliness did not change. Linehan *et al.* (1991) concluded that cognitive behaviour therapy for female suicidal borderline patients appears to have an influence on suicide. In this case, a combination of individual and group therapy was practised over a one-year period. There are indications that psychodynamic therapy also has some effect on a variety of personality disorders (Shea, 1993, p. 173).

There are plenty of problems with these controlled studies, such as small numbers of patients, unclear diagnostic and classification procedures, a control group which did not come close to meeting the methodological requirements in all cases, effects of treatment which more often concerned symptoms or certain behaviours which were isolated for research purposes rather than the personality itself.

The latter comment immediately raises a problem that is part of this subject. The empirical tradition connected to the descriptive classification researches into effectiveness in the descriptive field as well and, therefore, mainly in relation to symptoms or personal behaviours. The question is what this really says about the influence of these interventions on personality patterns and the deeper layers that are part of it. In other words, it probably says nothing about structural change in the disturbed personality. The method of research inherent in Axis I disorders needs to be adjusted in order to be able to determine the effects of treatment on the Axis II disorders. The methodology for reliably determining changes at this level is perhaps not actually lacking, but is uncommon within the current empirical tradition. An intensive, experimental study of the individual would perhaps be a possible alternative (Barlow, Hayes & Nelson, 1984).

CASE STUDIES

Case studies described by clinicians provide useful hypotheses and valuable ideas, but make a very limited contribution to general knowledge. Empirical researchers should allow themselves to be inspired by case studies more than has normally been the case so far. This would result in research questions that, if researchable, would make a greater contribution than the usual superficial empirical relationships for clinicians.

Case studies can offer insight into the "inside" of the personality. Casuistry clearly and repeatedly states that the general patterns, such as dependency on others in dependent personality disorder, the grandiose self in narcissistic themes, and the characteristic cognitions in obsessive-compulsive personality, have a specific, individually different basis. Insight into the determinants of individual personality disorders can be obtained by means of an extensive case description. This concerns an exploratory psychotherapy case description, which offers insight into the specific core patterns that can be discovered in the various personalities. Those essential patterns have cognitive, emotional, drive-related and behavioural components, as well as specific defence mechanisms and other ego functions.

External validation research on, for instance, family backgrounds and biological indications is useful but always requires well-chosen groups for comparison. If people believe that borderline patients in their childhood were subjected or exposed to physical violence and abuse, this only acquires significance if it is not found in another type of personality disorder or in so-called normals.

INSTRUMENTS

There are a number of obvious suggestions regarding future research on methods which can be classified and diagnosed in a reliable manner. In the first place, it appears wise not to invest energy in fragmentation on the level of this set of instruments. If those occupied with the development of refining questionnaires and semi-structured interviews join forces, the chances for progress are greater. In view of the scant agreement between the various instruments, this is no superfluous luxury (Loranger, 1992).

It does not seem a bad idea to concentrate on Millon's MCMI, as far as questionnaires are concerned. In addition, an adjustment for the DSM-IV, see MCMI-III, was published in 1994 (Millon, 1994). This instrument can usefully be applied for screening larger groups.

In the category of semi-structured interviews, the IPDE appears to offer the best possibilities. In relation to the construction and dissemination of this instrument, co-operation is already found on a large scale.

At the level of an individual Axis II disorder, the *Diagnostic Interview for Borderline Patients* (DIB-R) is a good example. This type of instrument, which composes a core group of patients with a high degree of specificity and sensitivity, cannot be overlooked. Experience with the DIB is that clinicians are also interested in this and that they have, for instance, decided in staff discussions on the personality disorder diagnosis to use this instrument. In the proposal regarding interaction disorders, as presented in Chapter 6.1, only five instruments are necessary to chart interpersonal disorders.

DEVELOPMENT OF THEORIES

In conclusion, but not in the last instance, it is of great importance that a development be started in the field of personality disorders, in which broader, more encompassing ideas are constructed. Except for the development of subtheories from the various approaches, as we have seen in Part 3, it appears advisable to spend more energy on the integration of the subtheories into a greater whole, in which behavioural, interpersonal, cognitive, structural–dynamic and possibly other approaches go together. As far as this greater whole is concerned, the psychological level is primary. This is complementary to the formation of theory on the biological level, without being introduced on the same level or being confused with it.

CHAPTER 6.3 Conclusions concerning psychodiagnostics and treatment

Is there anything new for the clinician? Is the emphasis on personality disorders in recent years an old gift wrapped in new paper for the psychotherapist? The answer is probably yes, it usually is. Not all old news in a new package is superfluous, however. This emphasis also directs the attention of clinicians who have not yet reached this stage to this theme. Students of clinical psychology and psychiatry now receive a more complete presentation of psychopathology in their training. The DSM and the ICD have contributed greatly to this. Previously, there was a danger that the selection of themes had more to do with the personal interests of instructors than with clinical relevance and the incidence of the disorders concerned in the field.

PSYCHODIAGNOSTICS

Where the psychodiagnostics of patients with a personality disorder are concerned, inspiration must now come chiefly from clinical practice. As a rule, psychodiagnostics and treatment confront us with an extra problem: the ego-syntonic character of personality traits. This is not true for all patients, however. It is mainly the case when the personality disorder forms part of patients' defence or resistance. In many respects, these patients are especially difficult people for others, particularly others in their immediate social environment. A number of recommendations are given below that relate to the practice of psychodiagnostics and are inspired by diverse approaches.

Motivation

Start with a series of assessment sessions concerning the patient's course of life. For this, the patient will often have to be motivated. One way to do this is by proposing that advice will be given after the investigative sessions. At that point, the person can reconsider whether he or she wants something and, if so, what. The patient can be helped in this consideration by what the diagnostician has to tell him or her.

Empathy

Conduct the assessment sessions in a quiet, very interested manner. Empathy is the most important quality in this phase. This is not a superficial quality, but can signify the following. The diagnostician puts him- or herself in the patient's shoes and tries to spark the patient's awareness of feelings he or she might have had at certain moments in his or her life. For instance, a patient with a narcissistic disorder, who is reluctant to talk about the past, lets slip the remark that his parents had discouraged him from studying when he was younger. In order to persevere anyway, he locked himself up in a chicken coop in the garden. Although he had light, he had no heating. Often, his rival brothers tried to cut off the electricity supply so that he could not work. He tells this without displaying noticeable feelings. The diagnostician tries to generate reflection on the possible feelings. "You must have felt very thwarted at that time. Did you not feel discouraged once in a while?" Depending on the patient's reaction, further exploration can take place.

Often the patient will react defensively and deny any feeling. In order to continue to be effective, it is necessary to take very small steps, one at a time. The effectiveness lies in the fact that feelings not experienced at the time can still be experienced now. In this manner, the affective sides are deepened and introspection increases, especially in the narcissistic personality. This can positively affect attachment to the therapist as well. From a dimensional perspective, incidentally, a different approach is required for every type of personality disorder. This applies most to the treatment, but one must be able to profit optimally from thorough diagnostics.

The diagnostician wants to obtain detailed insight into behavioural aspects. This means that an effort is made to chart concrete behaviour. Self-reporting behavioural assessment techniques can be helpful in this. Through homework assignments, a diary or, for specific behaviours, through monitoring, little pieces of behaviour are charted, as is normally done with symptoms.

Cognitive aspects of the personality are made visible. Cognitive therapy models for obtaining insight into the manifest and deeper cognitions are also very useful during this phase.

Interpersonal aspects are charted as well. This is done by having the person relate very concretely how he or she acts in relationships. Hetero-anamnesis makes an essential contribution to this.

Intrapsychic patterns are clarified. Aspects relating to ego functions are: Which defence mechanisms are mainly used? What is the situation with regard to reality testing? How is the person's relationship to reality structured? The latter is further elaborated in the feeling for and perception of reality.

What does the integration of sexuality in the behaviour look like? How did the development history of the psychosexual aspects proceed, which components of sexuality are inhibited and which ones indulged in? What phase-specific early childhood fixations can we observe in the person's psychosexual development?

How does aggression in the behaviour take shape? To what extent is aggression used for separation and independence? What forms have inhibition, repression and sublimation of aggression taken? How have the sexual and the aggressive drive contributed to conflicts with which the person is struggling?

What parts do the conscience and the ego ideal play in the above? What is the quality of the conscience structure? What is its influence on behaviour? To what extent does acting-out behaviour relate to a poor presence or repressed aspects of this conscience? Is inhibition caused by the conscience experienced, authentic or based on fear? How great is the distance between the ego ideal and the self? To what extent is fusion involved and to what extent is there an optimal distance between the two aspects? How do these patterns continue to work in relationships with others?

What quality has the self adopted? In what way is the presence of feelings of superiority and/or inferiority involved? To what degree are other people used to repair this self, and what influence does this have on behaviour?

The contribution of the above-mentioned effects to psychodiagnostics and possible treatment is more important than the exact certainty that a person meets four or five criteria of one or several DSM Axis II categories.

Assessment by Means of Psychological Tests

Try to profit as much as is useful and feasible from the psychological test examination during the diagnostic phase. This has several advantages. In the first place, it always provides a surplus of information, which can serve to optimize the commitment to treatment in a person with relational problems. In the second place, a descriptive diagnosis has limited value as soon as it is no longer a matter, or only a matter, of treating a concrete complaint. In these cases, the nature of the personality traits makes or breaks each treatment. They must be examined and charted carefully in advance.

Never start the diagnostic examination with a test or short questionnaire, but always with an interview. Make sure the patient or the person who comes for an assessment evaluation knows perfectly well who the diagnostician or psychotherapist is. Let there be no lack of clarity about educational background, function and qualifications. The objective of the meeting must also be completely clear. Start with the actual complaints or questions, and then gradually explore the background. Take several sessions for this. Give the patient – diagnostician relationship a chance to grow.

After these sessions, the psychological test examination can take place. At that time, there will often be a specific presentation of questions that might possibly be answered better with the aid of test data. Needless to say, this psychological test examination is desirable, but by no means always feasible. In many cases, the patient will not make room for it; in other cases, there are limitations owing to the setting, financing or any other external reason. If there are no obstacles, a psychological test examination may appear as follows.

Start with an open assignment. Hand the patient a pencil and a sheet of paper and ask him or her to draw a person. Observe how the patient handles this assignment. After completion, enquire or judge whether a man or a woman has been drawn, and ask for a drawing of the opposite sex. After this, one can choose to continue with, for instance, a fruit tree, a dream tree, a fantasy tree, a house, etc. One can also proceed to another part of the examination.

An elementary examination of cognitive functions can now follow. It is advisable to administer a complete WAIS. In some cases, this will be supplemented by some neuropsychological tests.

A complaints list, such as the SCL-90 or the Amsterdam Biographical Questionnaire (ABV), can then be administered. This gives an impression of the co-morbidity of Axis I disorders and the tendency of the person to admit to complaints. The previous examples are more general lists. Separate questionnaires are available for specific complaints, such as depression, fear and impulsiveness.

One or several personality questionnaires are useful at this stage. The MMPI-2 is usually considered. In the Netherlands, the condensed version, the NVM, is often chosen. Combined use can also be beneficial. The Dutch Personality Questionnaire (NPV) is frequently used as well. Other comparable possibilities are Cattel-16 PF, and the Edwards Personal Preference Schedule (EPPS). Besides these general lists, a great many specific lists are available. The instruments used often depend on the experience which the psychologist in question has acquired with the instruments. Specialization in the use of, and limiting oneself to, certain tests is preferred in practice, probably rightly so, to the use of a large number of different methods. In this framework, questionnaires or semi-structured interviews can also be used to execute the descriptive diagnostics more thoroughly.

Projective assessments, for instance with the aid of the Rorschach test, the Thematic Apperception Test, the Four Pictures Test, or the Sentence Completion Test, will now be discussed. In this context, experience with a certain technique is possibly even more important. The Rorschach test, administered, scored and interpreted according to the rules of the "Comprehensive System", has the advantage of offering an empirical background. Except for the empirical effect, clinical judgement of the material must also be given an opportunity to contribute to the development of hypotheses. The interpretation process is particularly useful; a person's defence process can be studied in view of readings on this indirect technique. As a rule, the more prejudicial the social desirability revealed by the questionnaire method, the more rich and plentiful will be the material that emerges in this part of the examination.

Hetero-anamnesis

Administer a hetero-anamnesis with the patient's most important partner(s). Sometimes this will be the parents. Listen attentively to how they talk about the patient. Someone with an extreme personality structure consciously or unconsciously chooses a partner who has something to offer in this area as well. Try to obtain a picture of the partner's personality. If the parents come for the hetero-anamnesis, many questions that concern the course of the patient's life will be useful and necessary, although one must realize that the reliability of the information is often not too great. Consider how many parents summarize their offspring's childhood years with conclusions such as: "There were never many problems. Everything went smoothly. Development was normal." With this, they either omit the endless differentiation and nuancing that is present in relation to every child's developmental process, or they have never noticed it.

After the Physical Examination

Possible physical complaints that justify suspicion of a somatic cause and have still not been sorted out now become part of the diagnostic programme.

Theoretical Frame of Reference

Utilize a theoretical frame of reference to arrange all the data which has been collected and give it significance. Reports on psychodiagnostic examinations consist much too often of an extensive report which is full of facts and ends in a descriptive diagnosis. The course of life is worked out in detail, everything is recorded — except for one thing: insight. These types of report serve only a very limited function; they are insufficient for a well-supported indication position.

The objective in this regard is to interpret the material and develop a hypothesis supported by theory. In this respect, one can choose from various frames of reference. Sometimes, insights from different frameworks can be integrated. The more boldly the diagnostician dares to theorize about the patient in this phase, the greater the benefit to the therapist. One can theorize about connections between symptomatology and personality; the etiology and development of the symptom and personality pathology; the mechanisms that could be responsible for maintaining the problems; the development and integration of drive-like feelings such as aggression and sexuality; the contribution of narcissism; the integration of the superego; the quality and function of various personal relationships.

The advantage of extensive theories, such as psychoanalytic theory, is that they are comparable to a detailed map of a country that is to be visited for the first time. They offer many possibilities that can be treated as hypotheses in the treatment contact and can possibly be adjusted. Making use of psychodynamic theory does not necessarily exclude other approaches, such as the cognitive, interpersonal, biological and psycho-physiological approaches. Integration is desirable, but not always feasible for everyone. For the experienced clinician, many patients seem to evoke the approach that is most applicable to their personality and disorders of their own accord.

Communication

After the psychodiagnostic assessment, communicate openly with the patient about the results. If intelligence and level of comprehension are reasonable, the patient will usually also appreciate such open communication of results. The fact that all kind of research has been conducted by means of tests elevates a patient's perception of the objectivity of the event, which can be helpful.

Formulate the results in such a manner that the personality of the examined person is kept in mind. For instance, in the case of an obsessive-compulsive personality, one does well to indicate the character traits by beginning with a remark such as: "You have too much of a good quality." At the beginning of this explanation, concentrate on what has come forward as the essence of the examination, then dress it up with details. Give the patient ample opportunity to react.

The atmosphere of this discussion should reflect the data: this concerns hypotheses that could function as a guideline in a treatment or piece of advice and that require further testing. The openness which the diagnostician shows often also has a disarming effect on patients with a personality disorder. Directness in mentioning the patient's vulner-abilities and the manner in which this is formulated also work well with people who are strongly prejudiced, particularly in relationships with others, such as the category concerned here.

TREATMENT

As with every indication, a plan is drawn up for the treatment according to the hypotheses that have been obtained. A great deal of extra attention is given to *what* exactly the person does and *how* he or she deals with him- or herself, other people and the world around him or her, especially in the case of personality disorders.

Many sessions have the character of an examination of the precise manner in which the patient does something. For instance, take a patient who talks about his or her relationship problems. The way someone starts relationships and continues them, the conflicts that arise, etc., are usually connected with personality characteristics and traits. Many people with these types of problem have the tendency to point to others as the source of their difficulties, without their meeting the DSM and ICD categories. If instead of relationship therapy individual treatment has been started, the person is invited to describe very precisely what he or she does, thinks, feels and says in a concrete interaction with the partner. In the course of many sessions, the therapist studies in depth, together with the patient, how the latter dealt with a situation and with somebody else.

This degree of detail is very time consuming. Often, this is caused by the patient's resistance; he or she is unwilling to make concrete statements and does not readily "lapse" into details. This resistance has to be discussed and worked through first. The more successful this is, the more the therapist and the patient get the feeling that they are productively charting the course of an interaction.

If this searching process takes place as precisely as possible and with a great deal of patience, impulse and defence aspects become eligible as well. The therapist is helped by information that has been collected during the previous examination and by theories formulated in that phase. These theories in particular help the psychotherapist indicate directions in which to search, shed light on alternative possibilities or put the material in another light. For instance, the hypothesis may have shown a series of injuries to the patient's self-esteem that have occurred recently in relation to his or her boss, but which have a history in the course of the patient's life. The patient can be coaxed into his or her behaviour by the aggression evoked by this suppressed pain. This way of forming a hypothesis can be helpful in getting a grip on the interactions with the boss that are confusing for the patient.

During the treatment phase, psychodiagnostics are in fact elaborated further and further. The patterns that are initially recognized are corrected and supplemented. Some distinctions may be helpful in this.

Primary

In the working method recommended here, some personality trait is to the fore at virtually every moment. One can keep asking oneself the following question: *Is this personality trait primary or secondary?* In other words, are we dealing with the basis, the bottom, or is there yet another level underneath? Is this an original, direct expression of a certain affect, of a drive, of a cognitive pattern or of a form of relationship, or is it a total or partial reaction to one or more of these? Or again, does this personality trait have particularly a defence function or does it form one of the cornerstones of the total psychic organization?

An example is a patient's reticence and introversion. These can be primary, provided with a genetic base in early development, or a reaction to events experienced by the person. The latter may also have taken place very early in development. With the joint exploration of the introverted aspects, the therapist examines (like a diagnostician) the two options to discover which is the most probable. The significance of this lies in the fact that possibilities for intervention differ and the expected effect of intervention changes. If a basal trait is concerned, agreeing with what has been worked out in the various personality theory approaches and has also been incorporated in the Big Five, the therapeutic approach is limited to helping the patient become conscious of this trait. His or her ego is helped and also made capable of observing this trait. The distance between the observing ego and the personality trait is enlarged. Because of this, the person obtains, in principle, more freedom with respect to this trait. It becomes possible, for instance, for the patient to predict when a reaction, actuated by the trait, will take place again. More tangibly, the process may acquire this content: "As soon as the acquaintances that have come to visit start going into detail about their personal intimacies, I react by switching off."

Helping to enlarge the distance between observing ego and personality trait is often a painful process. The patient now sees much more clearly how he or she reacts and will start to experience negatively biased feelings in this regard, which can evoke feelings of guilt and shame. The individual's conscience or ego ideal becomes active. At this point, the basis for a growth process is formed. Something that was previously absent can be built up little by little. The patient's identification with the therapist, who is often considered to be less introverted, gets started.

In the case of a primary trait, we often see that this remains powerful and cannot be erased. The change consists more of a restructuring. Initially, something new with a more extroverted character is constructed in addition to the introversion, and afterwards a part of the introverted trait crosses over into the extroverted trait. Both continue to exist side by side. A new house is built, so to speak, right next to the old house, and the person now lives in both houses. Neither the old building nor the new is satisfactory by itself.

Secondary

More changes are possible for a trait which is considered as secondary. An example is impulsiveness, or possibly also introversion. Someone acts rather than feels and thinks. Initially, analysis of the *what* and *how* is most important. With that there is also the benefit of such behaviour, for instance in the form of the pleasure or kick this produces. The advantages are discussed extensively.

In addition, the therapist constructs a hypothesis about what is being avoided with the behaviour. What is the impulsiveness warding off? It could be painful feelings that in fact form a deeper foundation, even though they have not yet been felt. This foundation is brought to the attention of the patient by means of interpretation. If the patient can benefit from this, it becomes possible to place the entire trait on a second plane, at which time the underlying experience, trait or behaviour pattern becomes central. In this case, it concerns a conflict and not a structure. For example, we can arrange most narcissistic disorders under this secondary trait.

TWO PSYCHOTHERAPEUTIC CURRENTS

Many schools in the field of psychotherapeutic treatment converge in the area of personality disorders. However, significant differences in emphasis in working methods remain. From the standpoint of these therapeutic approaches, we can make some remarks. It seems possible, in view of the descriptions in Part 3, to subdivide the two main currents in the area of psychotherapy of personality disorders.

The first group (type 1) consists of psychoanalytic, psychodynamic and also Rogerian or client-centred psychotherapy, which have not previously been discussed. These approaches are characterized by the fact that the patient—psychotherapist relationship plays a vital role in treatment. In contrast to behaviour therapy, cognitive and interpersonal approaches, the psychotherapist does not just adopt the role of teacher. The relationship is used to reveal and to indicate transference processes. Providing insight and solving conscious as well as unconscious psychic conflicts are important objectives. Another difference from the other group is that advice is, in principle, not given. If this does occur, it is rather the exception than the rule. An important objective of this working method is the clearing up of aspects presented in the patient's interpersonal relationships that are not understood. The therapist's attitude and the interventions used are limited. The therapy situation is kept under close control.

The second mainstream (type 2) is formed by behavioural therapeutic, cognitive and interpersonal approaches. They are similar in that they are concrete, directed towards solutions and aimed at immediately influencing behaviour. The psychotherapist is a teacher, directive, advising and supportive. The objective is not to make unconscious motives conscious, but to influence undesired behaviour. A multitude of techniques are mobilized for that purpose.

Which of the two mainstreams is applicable depends on the diagnosis of the individual patient, of course. If we consider this subject apart from an actual patient and against the background of the new division of Axis II, Axis III and Axis IV proposed here, we can posit the following.

In principle, type 2 is applied in the case of interaction disorders caused by psychotic traits, antisocial traits and anxiety traits. This is the only advisable option for psychotic and antisocial traits, if treatment is possible at all. In anxiety traits, this approach usually suits perfectly the wishes such patients have themselves, because of the structure it provides. Type 1 may also be possible, and could even be more desirable, but type 2 is more easily achieved.

Type 1 is applied in the case of interaction disorders as a consequence of narcissistic and rigid traits. With these decisions, however, what can be seen on Axis III and Axis IV is continuously taken into consideration. Two examples follow.

Examples

A 25-year-old male patient has no Axis I diagnosis but does have an interaction disorder due to antisocial traits on Axis II. This is combined with a high degree of "harm avoidance" and "reward dependence", a good intelligence and elevated neuroticism on the Big Five of Axis III. On Axis IV, he shows developed defence mechanisms, integrated identity (thus a neurotic personality organization), acting out of aggression, inhibited sexual development, incomplete superego integration and a sufficient presence of suffering. Treatment with type 2 psychotherapy has a good chance here. This would be totally different if, with a similar Axis II classification, "novelty seeking" on Axis III were strong, extroversion in particular were noticed, primitive defence mechanisms dominant on Axis IV, diffuse identity, intact reality testing (borderline organization) and all remaining factors the same.

A female patient has an obsessive-compulsive disorder on Axis I and an interaction disorder because of rigid traits on Axis II. On Axis III she is "harm avoidant" to a high degree, her score is high on the neuroticism and low on the extroversion factor and she has a good intelligence. On Axis IV, she shows a great deal of rationalization and isolation (developed defence mechanisms), integrated identity, and inhibited development of aggression and sexuality. Furthermore, she has a very stringent superego and high pressure from suffering. Type 1 psychotherapy is advisable.

With respect to the treatment of patients with a personality disorder, changes in the working method occur frequently in clinical practice. Because of the strict rules with type 1 psychotherapy, it is easier to switch from type 1 to type 2 than vice versa. The effective psycho-therapist is characterized by the flexibility to change strategy and to bring about an integration of various treatment methods in the case of an actual patient.

PREVENTION

The prevention of personality disorders is no more feasible than the prevention of symptom disorders or, to make a comparison from a totally different field, the prevention of traffic accidents. In view of the complexity of the psychological development of the personality and the great number of factors that contribute to it, it is perhaps especially surprising that things do not go wrong more often.

In view of the discussion in Part 5, some remarks on the sociocultural aspects are relevant. If it is true that these shifts take place in ideology and behavioural style and more is required from people's ego and self, what contribution can be made on a preventive level?

The most important and feasible possibility is the influencing of child-rearing practices. A relevant basis for personality disorders is created in childhood, and the child-rearing strategy and ideology employed have, in any case, some influence on the development of the individual. It is relatively simple to try to make a positive contribution to this piece of the puzzle: by educating each citizen during his or her school years in the psychology and pedagogy of child rearing. A body of knowledge and experience is present in child and development psychology and pedagogy that is not conveyed to ordinary people, although they are the ones who raise the new generation. To teach someone to use a computer and not how to raise a child is a striking example of short-term thinking. Attention is directed towards the productivity of such a person on the job market in, let us say, five or ten years, but not towards the fact that this person will be adding a new member to the community in 15 years' time. The teaching of child psychology and educational strategies could be made part of the curriculum in elementary schools and continued in every high school.

It is up to psychologists and psychiatrists to point out these gaps to politicians and policy makers. If they omit to do this, they will be ignoring a part of their social responsibility. If the latter group does not react to this information, they will be failing to attempt to repair structural shortcomings that accompany human interactions now and in the future.

REFERENCES

Abraham, K. (1921). Contributions to the theory of the anal character. In: D. Bryan & A. Strachey, *Selected papers of Karl Abraham*. New York: Basic Books, 1968, 370–92.

Akhtar, S. (1992). *Broken Structures: Severe Personality Disorders and their Treatment*. Northvale: Jason Aronson Inc.

Akiskal, H. (1981). Subaffective disorders: Dysthymic cyclothymic, and bipolar II disorders in the "borderline" realm. *Psychiatric Clinics of North America*, **4**, 25–46.

Alden, L. (1989). Short-term structured treatment for avoidant personality disorder. *Journal of Consulting and Clinical Psychology*, **57**, 756–64.

Allport, G. (1937). *Personality: A Psychological Interpretation*. New York: Holt.

American Psychiatric Association. (1952). *Diagnostic and Statistical Manual of Mental Disorders*, First Edition. Washington, DC: American Psychiatric Association.

American Psychiatric Association. (1968). *Diagnostic and Statistical Manual of Mental Disorders*, Second Edition. Washington, DC: American Psychiatric Association.

American Psychiatric Association. (1980). *Diagnostic and Statistical Manual of Mental Disorders*, Third Edition. Washington, DC: American Psychiatric Association.

American Psychiatric Association. (1987). *Diagnostic and Statistical Manual of Mental Disorders*, Third Edition, Revised. Washington, DC: American Psychiatric Association.

American Psychiatric Association. (1993). *DSM-IV draft criteria*. Washington, DC: Task Force on DSM-IV, American Psychiatric Association.

American Psychiatric Association (1994). *Diagnostic and Statistical Manual of Mental Disorders*, Fourth Edition. Washington, DC: American Psychiatric Association.

Barlow, D., Hayes, S. & Nelson, R. (1984). *The Scientist Practitioner:*

Research and Accountability in Clinical and Educational Settings. New York: Pergamon.

Beck, A. (1987). Cognitive therapy. In: J. Zeig (Ed.), *The evolution of psychotherapy*. New York: Brunner/Mazel.

Beck, T. & Freeman, A. (1990). *Cognitive Therapy of Personality Disorders*. New York: The Guilford Press.

Berg, M. (1983). Borderline psychopathology as displayed on psychological tests. *Journal of Personality Assessment*, **47**, 120−33.

Berger, P. & Luckmann, T. (1966). *The Social Construction of Reality*. Harmondsworth: Penguin.

Bernstein, D., Useda, D. & Siever, L. (1993). Paranoid personality disorder: review of the literature and recommendations for DSM-IV. *Journal of Personality Disorders*, **7**, 53−62.

Bowers, K. (1973). Situationism in psychology: an analysis and a critique. *Psychological Review*, **80**, 307−36.

Bowlby, J. (1973). *Attachment and Loss: Volume 2. Separation*. London: The Hogarth Press and The Institute of Psycho-Analysis.

Brown, D. & Pedder, J. (1980). *Psychodynamische Psychotherapie*. Aplhen aan den Rijn: Samson.

Butcher, J. (1990). *The MMPI-2 in Psychological Treatment*. New York: Oxford University Press.

Butcher, J. (1993). *The MMPI-2 in court*. Paper presented at the 28th Annual Symposium on Recent Developments in the Use of the MMPI. St. Petersburg Beach, Florida.

Butcher, J., Dahlstrom, W., Graham, J., Tellegen, A. & Kaemmer, B. (1989). *Manual for the Restandardized Minnesota Multiphasic Personality Inventory: MMPI-2. An Administrative and Interpretative Guide*. Minneapolis, MN: University of Minnesota Press.

Clarkin, J., Marziali, E. & Munroe-Blum, H. (Eds) (1992). *Borderline Personality Disorder, Clinical and Empirical Perspectives*. New York: The Guilford Press.

Costa, P. & McCrae, R. (1985). *The NEO Personality Inventory Manual*. Odessa, FL: Psychological Assessment Resources.

Costa, P. & McCrae, R. (1989). *The NEO-PINEO-FFI Manual Supplement*. Odessa, FL: Psychological Assessment Resources.

Costa, P. & McCrae, R. (1992). The five-factor model of personality and its relevance to personality disorders. *Journal of Personality Disorders*, **6**, 343−59.

Craig, R. (Ed.) (1993). *The Millon Clinical Multiaxial Inventory, A Clinical Research Information Synthesis*. Hillsdale, New Jersey: Lawrence Erlbaum Associates.

Cushman, P. (1990). Why the self is empty: toward a historically situated psychology. *American Psychologist*, **45**, 5, 599−611.

Derksen, J. (1982). *Psychologische hulp in de eerste lijn*. Baarn: Nelissen.

Derksen, J. (1983a). *Over verlies en verlangen*. Deventer: Van Loghum Slaterus.

Derksen, J. (1983b). *Psychotherapieen in het geding. Een structurele analyse met behulp van de psychoanalytische theorie*. Baarn: Nelissen.

Derksen, J. (1986). *Structurele diagnostiek van psychische stoornissen: neurose, borderline, psychose*. Baarn: Nelissen.

Derksen, J. (1988a). *Het Diagnostisch Interview voor Borderline Patiënten, Nederlandse vertaling en bewerking*. Lisse: Swets Test Service.

Derksen, J. (1988b). *Het Diagnostisch Interview voor Borderline Borderline Patiënten: Handleiding*. Lisse: Swets Test Service.

Derksen, J. (1989). Borderline-stoornis: van patiënten in een grensgebied naar een welomschreven persoonlijkheidsstoornis. *Gedrag & Gezondheid*, **16**, 159−66.

Derksen, J. (1990a). Een overzicht van drie concepten in de diagnostiek van de borderline-stoornis. In: J. Derksen & F. Donker (Eds), *De borderline-patiënt: diagnostiek, behandeling en onderzoek*. Amersfoort: Acco, 12−33.

Derksen, J. (1990b). Enkele empirische studies naar de borderline-persoonlijkheidsstoornis in Nederland. In: J. Derksen & F. Donker (Eds), *De borderline-patiënt: diagnostiek, behandeling en onderzoek*. Amersfoort: Acco, 81−90.

Derksen, J. (1990c). Over de differentiatie tussen vroege stoornissen, borderline stoornissen, narcistische stoornissen en neurosen. In: J. Derksen & F. Donker (Eds), *De borderline-patiënt: diagnostiek, behandeling en onderzoek*. Amersfoort: Acco, 121−6.

Derksen, J. (1990d). An exploratory study of borderline personality disorder in women with eating disorders and psychoactive substance dependent patients. *Journal of Personality Disorders*, **4**, 372−80.

Derksen, J. (1991). Treatment of borderline outpatients. In: W. van den Brink & R. Giel (Eds), *Borderline personality disorder: diagnosis, etiology and treatment*. Amsterdam: The Royal Academy of Arts and Sciences, 89−92.

Derksen, J. (1992a). Ethiologie, prevalentie en diagnostiek van persoonlijkheidsstoornissen bij ouderen. In: Sektie Ouderenzorg, NIP, *Persoonlijkheidsproblematiek bij ouderen: diagnostiek en behandeling*. Nijmegen: NIP, 1−24.

Derksen, J. (1992b). Persoonlijkheidsstoornissen. In: H. Buijssen (Ed.), *Psychologische hulpverlening aan ouderen*. Nijkerk: Intro, 89 120.

Derksen, J., Cohen, L. & de Ruiter, C. (1993). The Comprehensive System in the Netherlands. *Rorschachiana XVIII, Yearbook of the International Rorschach Society*, **18**, 126−38.

Derksen, J. & Donker, F. (Eds) (1990). *De borderline-patiënt, diagnostiek, behandeling en onderzoek*. Amersfoort: Acco.

Derksen, J. & Hendriks, G. (1991). Psychoactive substance dependence and borderline personality disorder. In: G. Schippers, S. Lammers & C. Schaap (Eds), *Contribution to the Psychology of Addiction*. Lisse: Swets & Zeitlinger.

Derksen, J., Hummelen, J. & Bouwens, J. (1988). Structurele diagnostiek en het structurele interview. *Tijdschrift voor Psychiatrie*, **30**, 445–59.

Derksen, J., Hummelen, J. & Bouwens, J. (1989). Tussenbeoordelaars betrouwbaarheid van het structurele interview. *Tijdschrift voor Psychiatrie*, **31**, 662–74.

Derksen, J. & Klein Herenbrink, A. (1991). Psychische stoornissen in Japan. *NRC Handelsblad, Wetenschap en Onderwijs*. 3 januari, 1–2.

Derksen, J. & van de Loo, E. (1986). Over de verhouding tussen psyche en soma in de psychosomatiek. In: K. van de Loo, J. Derksen, E. van de Loo & I. Goldman (Eds), *Psychosomatiek, theoretische en klinische bijdragen*. Baarn: Ambo, 124–32.

Derksen, J. & van der Mast, R. (Eds) (1993). *Psychoanalytische psychotherapy en persoonlijkheidsstoornissen*. Amersfoort: Academische Uitgeverij Amersfoort.

Derksen, J. & de Mey, H. (1993). *U.S. and Dutch norms for the MMPI-2: a comparison*. Paper presented at the 28th Annual Symposium on Recent Developments in the Use of the MMPI. St. Petersburg Beach, Florida.

Derksen, J., de Mey, H., Sloore, H. & Hellenbosch, G. (1993). *MMPI-2. Handleiding bij afname, scoring en interpretatie*. Nijmegen: Pen Tests Publisher.

von der Dunk, H. (1992). *Sprekend over identiteit en geschiedenis*. Amsterdam: Prometheus.

Ellis, A. (1962). *Reason and Emotion in Psychotherapy*. New Jersey: Lyle Stuart.

Epstein, L. (1979). Countertransference with borderline patients. In: L. Epstein & A. Feinen (Eds) *Countertransference*. New York: Jason Aronson, 375–405.

Erdberg, P. (1993). The U.S. Rorschach scene: integration and elaboration. *Rorschachiana XVIII, Yearbook of the International Rorschach Society*, **18**, 139–51.

Erikson, E. (1971). *Identiteit, jeugd en crisis*. Utrecht: Het Spectrum.

Exner, J. (1986). *The Rorschach: A Comprehensive System, Volume I*. New York: John Wiley & Sons.

Eysenck, H. (1947). *Dimensions of Personality*. New York: Praeger.

Eysenck, H. (1957). *The Dynamics of Anxiety and Hysteria*. New York: Praeger.

Eysenck, H. (1987). The definition of personality disorders and the criteria appropriate for their description. *Journal of Personality Disorders*, **1**, 211–19.

Fiester, S. (1991). Self-defeating personality disorder: a review of data and recommendations for DSM-IV. *Journal of Personality Disorders*, **5**, 194–209.

Freeman, A. (1988). Cognitive therapy of personality disorders: general treatment considerations. In: C. Perris, I. Blackburg & H. Perris (Eds) *Cognitive Psychotherapy: Theory and Practice*. New York: Springer Verlag, 223–52.

Freud, A. (1954). The widening scope of indications for psychoanalysis: discussion. *Journal of the American Psychoanalytic Association*, **2**, 607–20.

Freud, S. (1905). Drei Abhandlungen zur Sexualtheorie. *Studienausgabe, Band V*. Frankfurt am Main: Fischer Verlag (1972).

Freud, S. (1908). Charakter und Analerotik. *Studienausgabe, Band VII*. Frankfurt am Main: Fischer Verlag (1973).

Freud, S. (1913). Die Disposition zur Zwangsneurose. *Studienausgabe, Band VII*. Frankfurt am Main: Fischer Verlag (1973).

Freud, S. (1915). Triebe und Triebschicksale. *Studienausgabe, Band III*. Frankfurt am Main: Fischer Verlag (1975).

Freud, S. (1916). Einige Charaktertypen aus der Psychoanalytischen Arbeit. *Studienausgabe, Band X*. Frankfurt am Main: Fischer Verlag (1969).

Freud, S. (1917). Vorlesungen sur Einfuhrung in die Psychoanalyse. *Studienausgabe, Band I*. Frankfurt am Main: Fischer Verlag (1969).

Freud, S. (1923). Das Ich und das Es. *Studienausgabe, Band III*. Frankfurt am Main: Fischer Verlag (1975).

Freud, S. (1931). Uber libidinöse Typen. *Studienausgabe, Band V*. Frankfurt am Main: Fischer Verlag (1972).

Freud, S. (1933). Angst und Triebleben. *Studienausgabe, Band I*. Frankfurt am Main: Fischer Verlag (1969).

Frosch, J. (1983). *The Psychotic Process*. New York: International Universities Press.

Gabbard, G. (1990). *Psychodynamic Psychiatry in Clinical Practice*. Washington, DC: American Psychiatric Press, Inc.

Graham, J. (1990). *MMPI-2 Assessing Personality and Psychopathology*. New York: Oxford University Press.

Green, C. (1987). Instrument review: Diagnostic Interview for Borderline Patients. *Journal of Personality Disorders*, **1**, 115–18.

Greenberg, J. (1991). *Oedipus and Beyond. A Clinical Theory*. Cambridge: Harvard University Press.

Greenberg, J. & Mitchell, S. (1983). *Object Relations in Psychoanalytic Theory*. Cambridge: Harvard University Press.

Groth-Marnat, G. (1990). *Handbook of Psychological Assessment*. New York: Wiley.

Grotstein, J., Solomon, M. & Lang, J. (Eds) (1987). *The Borderline Patient, Volumes I & II*. Hillsdale: The Analytic Press.

Gunderson, J. (1982). *Diagnostic Interview for Borderline Patients, Second Edition*. Roerig-Pfitzer.

Gunderson, J. & Kolb, J. (1976). *The Diagnostic Interview for Borderlines (DIB)*. Paper read before the 129th Annual Meeting of the American Psychiatric Association, Miami.

Gunderson, J., Kolb, J. & Austin, Y. (1981). The Diagnostic Interview for Borderline Patients. *American Journal of Psychiatry*, **138**, 896−903.

Gunderson, J., Links, P. & Reich, J. (1991). Competing models of personality disorders. *Journal of Personality Disorders*, **5**, 60−8.

Gunderson, J., Ronningstam, E. & Smith, L. (1991). Narcissistic personality disorder: a review of data on DSM-III-R descriptions. *Journal of Personality Disorders*, **5**, 167−77.

Gunderson, J., Zanarini, M. & Kisiel, C. (1991). Borderline personality disorder: a review of data on DSM-III-R descriptions. *Journal of Personality Disorders*, **5**, 340−52.

Gunderson, J., Frank, A., Ronningstam, E., Wachter, S., Lynch, V. & Wolf, P. (1989). Early discontinuance of borderline patients from psychotherapy. *The Journal of Nervous and Mental Disease*, **177**, 38−42.

Hartmann, H., Kris, E. & Lowenstein, R. (1946). Comments on the formation of psychic structure. *Psychoanalytic Study of the Child*, **2**, 11−38.

Hathaway, S. & McKinley, J. (1943). *The Minnesota Multiphasic Personality Schedule*. Minneapolis, MN: University of Minnesota Press.

Herman, J., Perry, J. & van der Kolk, W. (1989). Childhood trauma in borderline personality disorder. *American Journal of Psychiatry*, **146**, 490−5.

Heymans, G. (1929). *Inleiding in de speciale psychologie*. Haarlem: Bohn (V.U.B.).

Hirschfeld, R. (1993). Personality disorder: definition and diagnosis. *Journal of Personality Disorders*, Supplement, 9−17.

Hirschfeld, R., Shea, M. & Weise, R. (1991). Dependent personality disorder: perspectives for DSM-IV. *Journal of Personality Disorders*, **5**, 135−49.

Hoffmann, S. (1979). *Charakter und Neurose*. Frankfurt am Main: Suhrkamp Verlag.

Hogan, R. (1986). *Hogan Personality Inventory Manual*. Minneapolis, MN: National Computer Systems.

Horner, A. (1990). *The Primacy of Structure*. New Jersey: Jason Aronson Inc.

Horowitz, H., Marmer, Ch., Krupnick, N., Kaltreider, N. & Wallerstein,

R. (1984). *Personality Style and Brief Psychotherapy*. New York: Basic Books.

Hyler, S., Rieder, R., Williams, J., Spitzer, R., Hendler, J. & Lyons, M. (1988). The Personality Diagnostic Questionnaire: Development and preliminary results. *Journal of Personality Disorders*, **2**, 229–37.

Jong, A. (1987). *Intake voor psychotherapie*. Meppel: Boom.

Kalus, O., Bernstein, D. & Siever. L. (1993). Schizoid personality disorder: a review of current status and implications for DSM-IV. *Journal of Personality Disorders*, **7**, 43–52.

Kelly, G. (1955). *The Psychology of Personal Constructs*. Norton: New York.

Kernberg, O. (1967). Borderline personality organization. *Journal of the American Psychoanalytic Association*, **15**, 641–85.

Kernberg, O. (1975). *Borderline Conditions and Pathological Narcissism*. New York: Jason Aronson.

Kernberg, O. (1976). *Object Relations Theory and Clinical Psychoanalysis*. New York: Jason Aronson.

Kernberg, O. (1981). Structural interviewing. *Psychiatric Clinics of North America*, **4**, 169–95.

Kernberg, O. (1984). *Severe Personality Disorders: Psychotherapeutic Strategies*. New Haven: Yale University Press.

Kernberg, O., Selzer, M., Koenigsberg, H., Carr, A. & Appelbaum, A. (1989). *Psychodynamic Psychotherapy of Borderline Patients*. New York: Basic Books.

Kets de Vries, M. & Perzow, S. (1991). *Handbook of Character Studies: Psychoanalytic Explorations*. Madison: International Universities Press.

Kiesler, D. (1986). The 1982 interpersonal circle: an analysis of DSM-III personality disorders. In T. Millon & G. Klerman (Eds), *Contemporary Directions in Psychopathology, Toward the DSM-IV*. New York: The Guilford Press, 571–97.

Kilzieh, N. & Cloninger, R. (1993). Psychophysiological antecedents of personality. *Journal of Personality Disorders*, Supplement, 100–17.

Klein, D. (1977). Psychopharmacological treatment and delineation of borderline disorders. In P. Hartocollis (Ed.), *Borderline Personality Disorders: the Concept, the Syndrome, the Patient*. New York: International Universities Press, 365–83.

Klein, M. (1993). Issues in the assessment of personality disorders. *Journal of Personality Disorders*, Supplement, 18–33.

Klerman, G. (1986). Historical perspectives on contemporary schools of psychopathology. In T. Millon & G. Klerman (Eds), *Contemporary Directions in Psychopathology, Toward the DSM-IV*. New York: The Guilford Press, 3–28.

Knight, R. (1953). Borderline states. *Bulletin of the Menninger Clinic*, **17**, 1–12.

Kohut, H. (1971). *The Analysis of the Self*. London: The Hogarth Press.

Kolb, J. & Gunderson, J. (1980). Diagnosing borderline patients with a semi-structured interview. *Archives of General Psychiatry*, **37**, 37–41.

König, H. (1988). Von der vaterlosen zur mutterlosen Gesellschaft und darueber hinaus. *Luzifer-Amor*, **1**, 55–87.

Kouwer, B. (1977). *Persoon en existentie*. Groningen: Wolters-Noordhoff.

Kroes, R. (1992). *De leegte van Amerika*. Amsterdam: Prometheus.

Kuhn, T. (1972). *The Structure of Scientific Revolutions*, Second Edition. Chicago: The University of Chicago Press.

Lasch, C. (1979). *The Culture of Narcissism: American Life in An Age of Diminishing Expectations*. New York: Brunner/Mazel.

Leary, T. (1957). *Interpersonal Diagnosis of Personality*. New York: Ronald Press.

Liebowitz, M. (1979.) Is borderline a distinct entity? *Schizophrenic Bulletin*, **5**, 23–8.

Linehan, M. (1987). Dialectical behavior therapy for borderline personality disorder. *Bulletin of the Menninger Clinics*, **51**, 261–76.

Linehan, M. & Heard, H. (1992). Dialectical behavior therapy for borderline personality disorder. In: J. Clarkin, E. Marziali & H. Munroe-Blum (Eds), *Borderline Personality Disorder, Clinical and Empirical Perspectives*. New York: The Guilford Press, 248–67.

Linehan, M., Hubert, A., Suarez, A., Douglas, A. & Heard, H. (1991). Cognitive-behavioral treatment of chronically parasuicidal borderline patients. *Archives of General Psychiatry*, **48**, 1060–4.

Loranger, A. (1992). Are current self-report and interview measures adequate for epidemiological studies of personality disorders? *Journal of Personality Disorders*, **6**, 313–25.

Loranger, A., Hirschfeld, R., Sartorius, N. & Regier, D. (1991). The WHO/ADAMHA international pilot study of personality disorders: background and purpose. *Journal of Personality Disorders*, **5**, 296–306.

Lynn, S. & Garske, J. (1988). *Compendium psychotherapie. Deel I*. Rotterdam: Ad. Donker.

Mahler, M. (1971). A study of the separation–individuation process and its possible application to borderline phenomena in the psycho-analytic situation. *Psychoanalytic Study of the Child*, **26**, 403–24.

Mahler, M., Pine, F. & Bergman, A. (1975). *The Psychological Birth of the Human Infant: Symbiosis and Individuation*. New York: Basic Books.

Malan, D. (1979). *Individual Psychotherapy and the Science of Psychodynamics*. London: Butterworth.

Markus, H. & Kitayama, S. (1991). Culture and the self: implications for cognition, emotion and motivation. *Psychological Review*, **98**, 2, 224–53.

Masterson, J., Tolpin, M. & Sifneos, P. (1991). *Comparing Psychoanalytic Psychotherapies*. New York: Brunner/Mazel.

McCrae, R. & Costa, P. (1990). *Personality in Adulthood*. New York: Guilford Press.

McGlashan, Th. (1983). The borderline syndrome: I. Testing three diagnostic systems for borderline. *Archives of General Psychiatry*, **40**, 1311−18.

McGlashan, Th. (1986). The Chestnut Lodge follow-up study. *Archives of General Psychiatry*, **41**, 20−30.

McGuffin, P. & Thapar, A. (1992). The genetics of personality disorder. *British Journal of Psychiatry*, **160**, 12−23.

Meyer, R. (1989). *The Clinician's Handbook. The Psychopathology of Adulthood and Adolescence*. Boston: Allyn and Bacon.

Millon, T. (1981). *Disorders of Personality: DSM-III, Axis II*. New York: Wiley.

Millon, T. (1986). A theoretical derivation of pathological personalities. In T. Millon & G. Klerman (Eds), *Contemporary Directions in Psychopathology: Toward the DSM-IV*. New York: The Guilford Press, 639−69.

Millon, T. (1987a). On the genesis and prevalence of the borderline personality disorder: a social learning thesis. *Journal of Personality Disorders*, **1**, 354−72.

Millon, T. (1987b). *Millon Clinical Multiaxial Inventory-II Manual*. Minneapolis, MN: National Computer Systems.

Millon, T. (1990). *Toward a New Personology*. New York: John Wiley & Sons.

Millon, T. (1991). Avoidant personality disorder: a brief review of issues and data. *Journal of Personality Disorders*, **5**, 353−62.

Millon, T. (1994). *Millon Clinical Multiaxial Inventory-III*. Minneapolis, MN: National Computer Systems.

Millon, T. & Everly, G. (1985). *Personality and its Disorders*. New York: John Wiley & Sons.

Millon, T. & Frances, A. (1987). Editorial. *Journal of Personality Disorders*, **1**, i−iii.

Millon, T. & Klerman, G. (Eds) (1986). *Contemporary Directions in Psychopathology, Toward the DSM-IV*. New York: The Guilford Press.

Moore, B. & Fine. B. (1990). *Psychoanalytic Terms & Concepts*. New Haven: The American Psychoanalytic Association and Yale University Press.

Morey, L. (1988). Personality disorders under DSM-III and DSM-III-R: an examination of convergence, coverage, and internal consistency. *American Journal of Psychiatry*, **145**, 573−7.

Morey, L., Waugh, M. & Blashfield, R. (1985). MMPI scales for DSM-III Personality Disorders: their derivation and correlates. *Journal of Personality Assessment*, **49**, 245–51.

Morey, L., Blashfield, R., Webb, W. & Jewell, J. (1988). MMPI scales for DSM-III-Personality Disorders: a preliminary validation study. *Journal of Clinical Psychology*, **44**, 47–50.

Perris, C., Blackburn, I. & Perris, H. (1988). *Cognitive Psychotherapy, Theory and Practice*. Berlin: Springer-Verlag.

Perry, J.C. (1990). Challenges in validating personality disorders: beyond description. *Journal of Personality Disorders*, **4**, 273–89.

Perry, J.C. (1993). Longitudinal studies of personality disorders. *Journal of Personality Disorders*, Supplement, 63–85.

van Peursen, C. (1984). *De opbouw van de wetenschap*. Meppel: Boom.

Pfohl, B. (1991). Histrionic personality disorder: a review of available data and recommendations for DSM-IV. *Journal of Personality Disorders*, **5**, 150–66.

Pfohl, B. & Blum, N. (1991). Obsessive-compulsive personality disorder: a review of available data and recommendations for DSM-IV. *Journal of Personality Disorders*, **5**, 363–75.

Pfohl, B., Stangl, D. & Zimmerman, M. (1982). *Structured Interview for DSM-III Personality Disorders (SIDP)*. Iowa City: University of Iowa Hospitals and Clinics.

Phillips, K., Hirschfeld, R., Shea, M. & Gunderson, J. (1993). Depressive personality disorder: perspectives for DSM-IV. *Journal of Personality Disorders*, **7**, 30–42.

Pierloot, R. & Thiel, J. (1986). *Psychoanalytische therapieën*. Deventer: Van Loghum Slaterus.

Raczek, S. (1992). Childhood abuse and personality disorders. *Journal of Personality Disorders*, **6**, 109–16.

Rapaport, D. & Gill, M. (1959). The point of view and assumptions of metapsychology. *International Journal of Psycho-Analysis*, **40**, 153–49.

Ree, H. (1992). School. *NRC Handelsblad*, 21 januari, 12.

Regier, D. (1993). Introduction to special supplement on personality disorders. *Journal of Personality Disorders*, Supplement, 4–8.

Reich, J. (1987). Instruments measuring DSM-III and DSM-III-R personality disorders. *Journal of Personality Disorders*, **1**, 220–40.

Reich, W. (1928). Uber Charakteranalyse. *Internationale Zeitschrift für Psychoanalyse*, **14**, 180–98.

Reiche, R. (1991). Haben fruhe Storungen zogenommen? *Psyche*, **14**, 1045–66.

Renneberg, B., Goldstein, A., Philips, D. & Chambless, D. (1990). Intensive behavioral group treatment of avoidant personality disorder. *Behavior Therapy*, **21**, 363–77.

Riesman, D. (1950). *The Lonely Crowd: A Study of the Changing American Character*. New Haven: Yale University Press.

Rosenthal, D. & Kety, S. (Eds) (1968). *Transmission of Schizophrenia*. Oxford: Pergamon Press.

Rümcke, H. (1954). *Psychiatrie I Inleiding*. Amsterdam: Scheltema & Holkema.

Ryle, G. (1949). *The Concept of Mind*. London: Hutchinson.

Sampson, E. (1988). The debate on individualism. *American Psychologist*, **43**, 1, 15–22.

Shea, M. (1993). Psychosocial treatment of personality disorders. *Journal of Personality Disorders*, Supplement, 167–80.

Siever, L. (1991). Psychobiologic substrates of borderline personality disorder and their pathogenetic relevance. In: W. van den Brink & R. Giel (Eds), *Borderline Personality Disorder: Diagnosis, Etiology and Treatment*. Amsterdam: Koninklijke Akademie van Wetenschappen, 49–51.

Siever, L., Bernstein, D. & Silverman, J. (1991). Schizotypal personality disorder: a review of its current status. *Journal of Personality Disorders*, **5**, 178–93.

Siever, L., Trestman, R. & Silverman, J. (1992). Validation of personality disorder assessment by biologic and family studies. *Journal of Personality Disorders*, **6**, 301–12.

Skodol, A., Rosnick, L., Kellman, D., Oldham, J. & Hyler, S. (1988). *The validity of structured assessments of axis-II*. Paper presented at the 141st annual meeting of the American Psychiatric Association, Montreal, Canada.

Snijder, S., Pitts, W. & Gustin, Q. (1983). Absence of borderline personality disorder in later years. *American Journal of Psychiatry*, **140**, 271–2.

Spence, J. (1985). Achievement American style: the rewards and costs of individualism. *American Psychologist*, **40**, 1285–95.

Spitzer, R. & Williams, J. (1986). *Structured Clinical Interview for DSM-III-R Personality Disorders*. New York: Biometrics Research Department, New York State Psychiatric Institute.

Stein, D., Hollander, E. & Skodol, A. (1993). Anxiety disorders and personality disorders: a review. *Journal of Personality Disorders*, **7**, 87–104.

Stern, A. (1938). Psychoanalytic investigation of and therapy in the borderline group of neuroses. *Psychoanalytic Quarterly*, **7**, 467–89.

Stone, L. (1954). The widening scope of indications for psychoanalysis. *Journal of the American Psychoanalytic Association*, **2**, 567–94.

Stone, M. (Ed.) (1986). *Essential Papers on Borderline Disorders*. New York: Oxford University Press.

Stone, M. (1993). Long-term outcome in personality disorders. *British Journal of Psychiatry*, **162**, 299–313.

Stravynski, A., Lesage, A., Marcouiller, M. & Elie, R. (1989). A test of the therapeutic mechanism in social skills training with avoidant personality disorder. *Journal of Nervous and Mental Disease*, **177**, 739–44.

Sullivan, H. (1953). *The Interpersonal Theory in Psychiatry*. New York: Norton.

Tellegen, A., Lykken, D., Bouchard, T., Wilcox, K., Segal, N. & Rich. S. (1988). Personality similarity in twins reared apart and together. *Journal of Personality and Social Psychology*, **54**, 1031–9.

Thiel, J. (1986). Psychotherapie op analytische grondslag. In: R. Pierloot & J. Thiel (Eds), *Psychoanalytische therapieën*. Deventer: Van Loghum Slaterus, 72–93.

Trapnell, P. & Wiggins, J. (1990). Extension of the Interpersonal Adjective Scales to include the Big Five dimensions of personality. *Journal of Personality and Social Psychology*, **59**, 781–90.

Turner, R. (1987). The effects of personality disorder diagnosis on the outcome of social anxiety symptom reduction. *Journal of Personality Disorders*, **1**, 136–43.

Turner, R. (1989). Case study evaluation of a bio-cognitive behavioural approach for the treatment of borderline personality disorders. *Behavior Therapy*, **20**, 477–89.

Turner, S. & Turkat, I. (1988). Behavior therapy and the personality disorders. *Journal of Personality Disorders*, **2**, 342–9.

Turkat, I. (1990) *The Personality Disorders. A Psychological Approach to Clinical Management*. New York: Pergamon Press.

Tyrer, P. (1990). Personality disorder and social functioning. In: D. Peck & C. Shapiro (Eds), *Measuring Human Problems: A Practical Guide*. Chichester: John Wiley & Sons, 119–42.

Vaillant, G. (1987). A developmental view of old and new perspectives of personality disorders. *Journal of Personality Disorders*, **1**, 146–56.

Wallerstein, R. (1986). *Forty-two Lives in Treatment*. New York: The Guilford Press.

Weissman, M. (1993). The epidemiology of personality disorders: a 1990 update. *Journal of Personality Disorders*, Supplement, 44–62.

Widiger, T. (1991). Personality disorder dimensional models proposed for DSM-IV. *Journal of Personality Disorders*, **5**, 386–98.

Widiger, T. & Corbitt, E. (1993). Antisocial personality disorder: proposals for DSM-IV. *Journal of Personality Disorders*, **7**, 63–77.

Widiger, T., Frances, A., Warner, L. & Bluhm, C. (1986). Diagnostic criteria for the borderline and the schizotypal personality disorders. *Journal of Abnormal Psychology*, **95**, 43–51.

World Health Organisation (1992). *The ICD-10 Classification of Mental and Behavioural Disorders: Clinical Descriptions and Diagnostic Guidelines.* Geneva: World Health Organisation.

Zanarini, M., Gunderson, J. & Frankenburg, F. (1989). The revised diagnostic interview for borderlines: discriminating BPD from other Axis II disorders. *Journal of Personality Disorders*, **3**, 10–18.

Zanarini, M., Frankenburg, F., Chauncey, D. & Gunderson, J. (1987). The Diagnostic Interview for Personality Disorders (DIPD): Interrater and testretest reliability. *Comprehensive Psychiatry*, **28**, 467–80.

Zanarini, M., Gunderson, J., Marino, M., Schwartz, E. & Frankenburg, F. (1989). Childhood experiences of borderline patients. *Comprehensive Psychiatry*, **30**, 18–25.

Zetzel, E. (1968). The so-called good hysteric. *International Journal of Psycho-Analysis*, **49**, 256–60.

Zuckerman, M. (1991). *Psychobiology of Personality*. Cambridge: Cambridge University Press.

INDEX

Index compiled by Caroline Sheard

Wiley Titles of Related Interest

COGNITIVE BEHAVIOUR THERAPY FOR PSYCHOSIS
Theory and Practice
David Fowler, Philippa Garety *and* Liz Kuipers

A practical guide that highlights some of the difficulties encountered in working with psychotic patients and suggests ways of overcoming them.

0-471-93980-3 200pp 1995 Hardback
0-471-95618-X 200pp 1995 Paperback

PSYCHOLOGICAL MANAGEMENT OF SCHIZOPHRENIA
Edited by Max Birchwood *and* Nicholas Tarrier

Offers a practical guide for mental health professionals who want to develop and enhance their skills in new treatment approaches.

0-471-95056-4 176pp 1994 Paperback

A THEORY OF PERSONALITY DEVELOPMENT
Luciano L 'Abate, *with* Charles H. Bryson

Defines a theory of personality and personality development from a family interaction perspective. This theory sees normality and deviance as corollaries and extensions of one another.

0-471-30303-8 314pp 1994 Hardback

SYMPTOMS OF SCHIZOPHRENIA
Edited by Charles G. Costello

Approaches the psychopathology of schizophrenia from the perspective of symptoms rather than the more common view of disordered systems. Chapters cover symptoms such as thinking disorders, hallucinations, delusions, and social withdrawal.

0-471-54875-8 320pp 1993 Hardback